Other Kaplan titles related to English:

Inside the TOEFL iBT

Learn English through Classic Literature:
The Short Stories of Mark Twain

Test Prep and Admissions

TOEFL® iBT

with CD-ROM

Simon & Schuster

NEW YORK · LONDON · SYDNEY · TORONTO

Kaplan Publishing
Published by SIMON & SCHUSTER
Rockefeller Center
1230 Avenue of the Americas
New York, NY 10020

Editorial Director: Jennifer Farthing

Project Editor: Tonya Lobato

Production Manager: Michael Shevlin

Content Manager: Patrick Kennedy

Interior Design and Page Layout: Dave Chipps and Jan Gladish

Cover Design: Mark Weaver

Manufactured in the United States of America.
Published simultaneously in Canada.

10 9 8 7 6 5 4 3

September 2005

ISBN-13: 978-0-7432-6589-8
ISBN-10:   0-7432-6589-0

For information regarding special discounts for bulk purchases, please contact: Simon &
Schuster Special Sales at 1-800-456-6798 or business@simonandschuster.com.

KAPLAN ENGLISH PROGRAMS

Executive Editor
Roger Frantz
Senior Project Manager
Kaplan English Programs

Developmental Editor
Liz Henly
Senior Project Manager
Kaplan English Programs

Authors
Emily Hudon, Reading
Ian Clayton, Writing
Kurt Weissgerber, Listening
Priscilla Allen, Speaking

Contributing Editors
Tom Brown
Academic Manager
Seattle Kaplan Center

Deborah Crusan, Ph.D.
Associate Professor of TESOL/Applied Linguistics
Wright State University

Emily Pierre
Academic Manager
Boston Kaplan Center

Content Editor
Sandy Gade

Production Editor
Stephen O'Connell

Executive Director of Curriculum
Kathy Charlton

Contents

Introduction 1

Chapter 1, Lesson Set 1, Theme: History 17

Lesson 1—Reading: Introduction to the Reading Passage 17

Lesson 1—Writing: The Descriptive Essay 34

Lesson 1—Listening: Taking Notes 45

Lesson 1—Speaking: Content and Function Words 53

Chapter 1 Audio Transcripts 59

Chapter 2, Lesson Set 2, Theme: Science 63

Lesson 2—Reading: Details and Transitions 63

Lesson 2—Writing: Responding to a Reading Passage and Lecture 82

Lesson 2—Listening: Implication and Inference, Context and Tone 98

Lesson 2—Speaking: Paraphrasing and Expressing an Opinion 111

Chapter 2 Audio Transcripts 119

Chapter 3, Lesson Set 3, Theme: Education 127

Lesson 3—Reading: Transitions, Coherence, and Cohesive Devices 127

Lesson 3—Writing: The Persuasive Essay 147

Lesson 3—Listening: Turns 158

Lesson 3—Speaking: Informal vs. Formal 167

Chapter 3 Audio Transcripts 176

Chapter 4, Lesson Set 4, Theme: Business and Economics 181

Lesson 4—Reading: More About Transitions 181

Lesson 4—Writing: Compare and Contrast Essays 197

Lesson 4—Listening: Note-Taking Practice 214

Lesson 4—Speaking: Note-Taking from Conversations 224

Chapter 4 Audio Transcripts 231

Chapter 5, Lesson Set 5, Theme: Social Science 239

Lesson 5—Reading: The Main Idea, and Transitions and Rhetorical Function Revisited 239

Lesson 5—Writing: Another Look at Persuasive Essays 258

Lesson 5—Listening: Note-Taking and Key Words 268

Lesson 5—Speaking: Defining and Describing 279

Chapter 5 Audio Transcripts 291

Chapter 6, Lesson Set 6, Theme: Arts and Literature 299

    Lesson 6—Reading: The Importance of Details 299

    Lesson 6—Writing: More Practice with Descriptive Essays 316

    Lesson 6—Listening: Details 324

    Lesson 6—Speaking: Expressing an Opinion 339

    Chapter 6 Audio Transcripts 350

Chapter 7, Lesson Set 7, Theme: Technology 357

    Lesson 7—Reading: Context Clues, Antonyms, and Cohesive Devices 357

    Lesson 7—Writing: More Practice with Compare and Contrast Essays 378

    Lesson 7—Listening: Note-Taking, Main Idea, and Combined Skills 388

    Lesson 7—Speaking: Announcements and Notices 408

    Chapter 7 Audio Transcripts 420

Chapter 8, Lesson Set 8, Theme: Sports and Entertainment 427

    Lesson 8—Reading: Synonyms, Inference, and Cause and Effect 427

    Lesson 8—Writing: More Practice with the Response Essay 444

    Lesson 8—Listening: Taking Notes on a Conversation 454

    Lesson 8—Speaking: Paraphrasing and Summarizing 465

    Chapter 8 Audio Transcripts 473

Introduction

THE DESIGN OF THIS BOOK

This book contains an Introduction in which you will learn about TOEFL iBT, and eight chapters in which you will learn and practice the skills and strategies that will help you to succeed on test day. Begin using this book by thoroughly reading this Introduction, where you will learn some general information about TOEFL iBT and details about the different sections of the test. Then work through the chapters.

Each chapter has four lessons: Reading, Writing, Listening, and Speaking. As you will learn on the following pages, this is *not* the order of the sections on the TOEFL. The lessons are organized instead to move you from a receptive skill to its expressive counterpart. In each chapter, we will begin by working on your reading skills. In order to develop your reading skills, you will be studying how passages are written. That is, you will be studying someone else's writing, which will serve as a model for you as you enter the Writing lesson. Similarly, we will then work on your listening skills, and in order to develop your listening skills, you will be studying how conversations and lectures are delivered. That is, you will be studying someone else's speaking, which will serve as a model for you as you enter the Speaking lesson. From time to time within any lesson, there will be integrated skills activities in which you will read and listen then write or speak.

You will notice that the passages and activities in the eight chapters are thematically organized. The theme of Chapter 1 is history, the theme of Chapter 2 is hard sciences, Chapter 3 is education, Chapter 4 is business and economics, followed by social sciences, arts and literature, technology, and sports and entertainment. These themes represent the broad range of themes that TOEFL passages address, and they are also meant to provide variety and interest to your learning experience.

All the question types that you will encounter on TOEFL iBT are covered in Chapters 1–4. Chapters 5–8 repeat coverage of the same question types using different passages and activities. In this way, you will develop a foundational understanding in the first half of the book, then hone your skills and understanding in the second half of the book.

Every lesson in every chapter includes a limited number of examples of the question types covered in the lesson. You should know what question types to expect on the test, and how to look for distracter answer choices in the multiple-choice questions. This book will teach you those things. However, you will notice that chapters focus much more on explanations and activities designed to develop your skills and strategies for TOEFL iBT. The reason for this focus is the unique nature of TOEFL iBT. To succeed on this test, you must be able to read, listen, speak, and write proficiently in English.

When you are ready to practice the skills and strategies you learn from this book, use the four full-length practice tests on **CD-ROM#1,** which accompanies this book. And remember to refer to the tutorials on the CD-ROM to review some of the information in this introduction and to learn about the functionality, special features, and passage and question presentation on the test.

To practice your listening skills, use **CD-ROM #2,** which is also included with this book. It contains audio files for sample lectures, conversations, and sample responses found throughout the lessons. Transcripts of audio files are found at the end of each chapter.

TEST OVERVIEW

TOEFL iBT: A Communicative Academic English Language Skills Test

The Test of English as a Foreign Language (TOEFL) is a standardized test designed to measure the ability to understand and to use English as it is used in a North American academic setting, such as a university. Standardized tests are widely used in the United States for college and graduate school admissions and professional licensing. The TOEFL is produced and administered by the Educational Testing Service (ETS), a private, not-for-profit company based in Princeton, New Jersey.

Before 1998, the TOEFL was based on a model of language testing known as discrete-point testing. A discrete-point language test measures one isolated aspect of language knowledge and makes projections from this measurement about language proficiency. For example, on earlier versions of the test, a test taker's performance on questions that tested the meaning of vocabulary words was considered to be predictive of the test taker's reading comprehension skills. A test taker's performance on questions that tested the rules of English sentence structure was considered to be predictive of the test taker's writing abilities. Over time, some people questioned how well discrete-point language testing actually predicted test taker abilities, though. Some test takers might perform well on the sentence structure questions and yet not be able to write a solid, coherent essay in English. Some test takers might perform well on the test generally and yet not be able to speak English well. ETS decided to change the TOEFL.

The TOEFL computer-based test (CBT), which was launched in 1998, maintained some discrete-point testing, but it included direct skill testing as well. A test taker's reading comprehension skills were measured on the TOEFL CBT not only by his or her knowledge of the meaning of vocabulary words, but by the ability to infer the meaning of a word from the context of a reading passage, identify the main idea of the passage, make inferences about the author's meaning, and so on—all reading skills that any good reader must use. A test taker's writing skills were measured on the TOEFL CBT not only by his or her knowledge of the rules of English sentence structure, but by the ability to apply those rules, as well as rules of discourse organization, vocabulary usage, and so on, in writing an actual essay.

The TOEFL Internet-based test (iBT), launched in 2005, includes no discrete-point testing. TOEFL iBT is a direct measure of the test taker's communicative abilities in all four basic skills—reading, listening, speaking, and writing. This change has made some test takers nervous, particularly those who have learned *about* English but have not had much opportunity to *use* English to communicate. Perhaps you are among this group! Whether you are nervous about taking TOEFL iBT or not, this book will help you prepare for the TOEFL by familiarizing you with the test and by helping you focus on the specific skills and strategies you will need to succeed on the test. For all test takers, it is important to keep in mind that recent changes to the TOEFL are ultimately to your benefit. It is possible that you may now need to work a bit harder to get ready for TOEFL iBT, but you will then be better prepared for the TOEFL *and* better prepared for your ultimate goal—academic study in an English-speaking environment.

TOEFL iBT Highlights

1. TOEFL iBT measures receptive and expressive skills equally. Half the total score on the test is based on reading and listening abilities—on how well you receive and understand English. Half the total score is based on speaking and writing abilities—on how well you express yourself using English. This book will help you develop your receptive and your expressive skills for the test.

2. TOEFL iBT measures integrated skills. In the Speaking and Writing sections of the test, there are several questions in which you must read and/or listen, then speak or write based on what you read and heard. This book will show you examples of the integrated skills questions and teach you how to prepare for them.

3. TOEFL iBT contains no Structure section. As already mentioned, TOEFL iBT includes no discrete-point testing. Your knowledge of the grammar of English is measured within the skills sections of the test. For example, you must correctly apply rules of English grammar when speaking on the test.

4. TOEFL iBT uses more authentic language in the reading and listening passages. For example, in the Listening section, speakers in a conversation may interrupt each other, just as two people naturally do when engaged in conversation. All the reading and listening passages in this book are modeled on the TOEFL iBT passages, so you will learn what to expect on the actual test.

5. TOEFL iBT allows note-taking. You can, and in fact should, take notes in every section of the test. This book will help you develop your note-taking skills.

TOEFL iBT Sections

TOEFL iBT has four sections:

Section	Total Time	Tasks
Reading	60 minutes	Read 3 passages
		Answer 12 to 14 questions on each passage
Listening	45 minutes	Listen to 2 conversations
		Answer 5 questions on each conversation
		Listen to 4 short lectures, 2 of which include student comments
		Answer 6 questions on each lecture
Speaking	20 minutes	Speak based on familiar experience (2 independent tasks)
		Speak based on a reading and/or a listening passage (4 integrated tasks)
Writing	50 minutes	Write an essay based on a reading and a listening passage (1 integrated task)
		Write an essay based on a prompt only (1 independent task)

The times listed do not include the time needed to read and listen to section directions. The times listed for the Listening and Speaking sections are close approximations. There is a 10-minute break after the Listening section.

TOEFL iBT Scores

Each of the four sections of TOEFL iBT is scored on a scale of 0 to 30. The four section scores are then added together for a total test score of 0 to 120.

In addition to the section scores and total score, you will receive score descriptors as part of your result. These descriptors are brief explanations of what the numeric scores mean in terms of language skills and proficiency.

Most of the questions in the Reading and Listening sections are four-option multiple-choice. As you will learn in this book, several questions in these two sections are other variations of multiple-choice. Your raw scores—the total number of questions you answer correctly in these two sections—are converted into scaled scores of 0 to 30. The speaking samples you provide in the Speaking section and the two essays that you write in the Writing section are all rated by human raters after you have completed your test. The scores that these human raters assign to your speaking samples and essays are then also converted into scaled scores of 0 to 30.

TEST SECTIONS

Reading

Section Functionality and Special Features

Reading is the first section of TOEFL iBT. In the Reading section, reading passages appear on the right side of the divided computer screen, and questions appear on the left side. Because passages are long, it is necessary to scroll down to read an entire passage.

The first question for a passage appears with the passage. In the Reading section, you can move forward through questions by clicking the **Next** button at the top of the screen, and move back to previous questions by clicking the **Back** button at the top of the screen.

The TOEFL iBT Reading section includes a review function. Clicking the **Review** button at the top of the screen takes you to a Review screen where you can see all the questions in the section and their status—answered, not answered, not yet seen.

The Reading section also has a glossary feature. A word in blue in a passage indicates that a definition is available for the word. Clicking on the word brings up this definition.

A **Help** button in all sections takes you to a list of topics for which helpful explanations are available.

Use CD-ROM #1 to get a better understanding of how the passages and questions appear on the screen in the Reading section of the test and of how the special features work.

Reading Passages

The Reading section of the TOEFL measures the ability to read, understand, and analyze short passages similar in topic and style to those that North American college and university students encounter in their courses. The section contains 3 reading passages and 12 to 14 questions on each passage.

Each passage is roughly 675 to 725 words in length. Passages generally follow the typical American English organizational structure—a one-paragraph introduction, which includes a thesis statement, body paragraphs that develop the most important points as expressed in the thesis statement, and a one-paragraph conclusion that summarizes. Some passages may vary from this structure, such as by containing an introduction that spreads over more than one paragraph.

Reading Questions

There are 13 different types of TOEFL iBT Reading section questions. They can be divided into three general categories, according to what each is testing: (1) understanding of language use, (2) basic comprehension, and (3) the ability to read to learn.

Language use questions test understanding of how language is used to express meanings and of how to determine these meanings while reading. For example, one type of language use question tests understanding of the meaning of a word. Basic comprehension questions test understanding of details presented in a passage, general understanding of the main idea of a passage, and the ability to make inferences based on information in a passage. Reading-to-learn questions test the ability to analyze and synthesize information while reading; in other words, they test the ability to learn while reading. For example, one of these questions tests the ability to summarize the most important points of a reading passage.

Following is an overview of the question types you will find in the Reading section of TOEFL iBT. The number of each type per test is an approximation. The number on the actual test that you take may vary.

Language Use: These questions generally fall at the beginning of the set for a passage. Language-use questions constitute about half of the total Reading section questions.	
Inferring word meaning from context	7 to 9 per test
Locating a referent	3 per test
Defining a key term	1 or 2 per test
Understanding rhetorical function	3 or 4 per test
Paraphrasing	2 or 3 per test
Understanding coherence	3 per test
Basic Comprehension: These questions constitute roughly a third of the total Reading section questions.	
Understanding details	8 to 10 per test
Drawing an inference	3 or 4 per test
Identifying the main idea	1 per test
Reading to Learn: These questions generally fall at the end of the set for a passage. There are about 5 total reading-to-learn questions in the Reading section.	
Inferring the author's opinion or attitude	1 per test
Understanding details as they relate to the main idea (multiple choice)	1 per test
Understanding details as they relate to the main idea (schematic table)	1 per test
Summarizing the most important points	2 per test

All the language use questions refer to a word, sentence, or paragraph in the reading passage. Whenever a question refers to a particular word or sentence in the passage, the word or sentence is highlighted. You do not need to search for it. Detail questions on TOEFL iBT identify the particular paragraph in which the answer can be found, so you do not need to scan the passage in order to find the location of an answer to a detail question.

All Reading section questions are four-option multiple-choice, with the exception of coherence questions, details-related-to-the-main-idea schematic table questions, and most-important-points questions. These last two question types are also different from the others because they are each worth more than one point. A note appears with these questions telling you their point value.

Use CD-ROM #1 to get a better understanding of how the questions appear on the screen in the Reading section of the test.

Listening

Section Functionality and Special Features

Beginning in the Listening section and continuing through to the Writing section, you wear headphones that have a special microphone for speaking. Once you have your headphones on, you have the opportunity to set the volume before proceeding. After the section begins, a **Volume** button at the top of the screen can be used to change the volume at any time.

You use **OK** and **Next** buttons at the top of the screen to move through the Listening section. On choosing an answer for a question, you must click **Next** then **OK** to proceed to the next question. The **OK** button serves to confirm each answer choice, as it is not possible to return to any question in the Listening section.

While conversations and lectures play, photos of people in academic settings appear on the screen. These photos are sometimes helpful in providing context to the conversation or lecture. For example, the photo for a conversation between a student and a librarian may show two people in a library with one of them—the librarian—seated behind a reference desk. The photos do **not** offer any information that is directly relevant to answering the questions.

After a conversation or lecture has finished, questions appear on the screen one at a time. Each question is spoken by a narrator as it appears on the screen, though answer choices are not. A few Listening section question types require listening again to an excerpt from the conversation or lecture. In these cases, a photo appears on the screen as the excerpt plays.

A **Help** button in all sections takes you to a list of topics for which helpful explanations are available.

Use CD-ROM #2 to get a better understanding of how the conversations and lectures play.

Listening Passages

The Listening section of the TOEFL measures the ability to understand English as it is spoken in North American academic settings. The section contains:

- 2 conversations between two people, each followed by 5 questions
- 2 lectures with student comments and questions, each followed by 6 questions
- 2 straight lectures, each followed by 6 questions

The conversations are generally between a student and a professor or other university staff member, such as a librarian, counselor, administrative assistant in a university office, and so on. The conversations are often of a problem/resolution type, where the student needs assistance from the other person and must explain his or her needs in an attempt to obtain the desired assistance, and the other person attempts to assist the student. The conversations average two and a half minutes or more.

The lectures are on a range of topics, covering anything from American history, art, and business to hard science topics such as chemistry and geography to social science topics such as psychology and sociology. The lectures do not assume specialized knowledge, nor do they assume extensive knowledge of United States culture, government, history, etc. Lectures average four to five minutes.

Markers of authentic speech—such as pauses, trailing off, interruptions, hesitations, false starts (e.g., "I'm not . . . I don't really know the answer to that question"), and colloquial language (e.g., "The scientists were kind of surprised by the results")—are evident in both the conversations and lectures.

Listening Questions

There are 7 different question types on the TOEFL iBT Listening section. You can expect to find most or all of these question types on the lectures, but only 3 or 4 of them on the conversations. Like the Reading section questions, Listening section questions can be divided into three general categories, according to what each is testing: (1) understanding of language use, (2) basic comprehension, and (3) the ability to listen to learn.

Following is an overview of the question types you will find in the Listening section of the TOEFL. The number of each type per test is an approximation. The number on the actual test that you take may vary.

Language Use	
Understanding a speaker's implication	3 to 5 per test
Understanding an idiomatic expression in context	1 or 2 per test
Understanding rhetorical function	5 or 6 per test
Basic Comprehension	
Identifying the main idea (lectures only)	4 per test
Understanding details	12 to 14 per test
Drawing an inference	3 to 5 per test
Listening to Learn	
Summarizing the most important points (lectures only)	2 per test

For most of the language use questions, you will hear an excerpt—that is, a repeated portion—from the conversation or lecture which contains a word, expression, or comment that is the focus of the question. You should listen carefully to these excerpts, and you should also think back to the broader context of the conversation or lecture as you hear the excerpt.

All Listening section questions are four-option multiple-choice, with the exception of most-important-points questions. This question type comes in two formats, both of which present five options. In the first format, you must choose the three correct answers from the five choices. In the second format, you must click *yes* or *no* for each of the five options. In addition, one or two of the detail questions on lectures may ask you to choose two correct answers out of four options.

Use CD-ROM #1 to get a better understanding of how the questions appear on the screen in the Listening section of the test.

Speaking

Section Functionality and Special Features

The first thing you must do in the Speaking section is to adjust the microphone on your headset. This adjustment is done automatically as you respond to an easy question that appears on the screen.

There are six tasks in the Speaking section. In each case, you listen to and read both the directions and the task. Two of the tasks include reading passages and a conversation or lecture, and two others include a conversation or a lecture only. For each task, you speak for 45 or 60 seconds.

The timing throughout this section is pre-set. That is, unlike in the Reading and Listening sections, you do not choose when you have finished one question and are ready to move to the next. Instead, you have a given amount of time to listen to the task, prepare your response, and respond before the next task begins.

While conversations and lectures that are part of tasks play, photos of people in academic settings appear on the screen. These photos provide minimal context to the conversation or lecture. They do **not** offer any information that is directly relevant to answering the questions.

A **Help** button in all sections takes you to a list of topics for which helpful explanations are available.

Use CD-ROM #1 to get a better understanding of how the reading passages, conversations, lectures, and questions appear on the screen and play in the Speaking section of the test, as well as of how the special features work.

Speaking Tasks

The Speaking section contains six tasks on a range of topics. Tasks 1 and 2 are independent speaking tasks—you respond to a short prompt by speaking about a familiar topic. You are scored on your ability to speak clearly and coherently. Tasks 3 through 6 are integrated skills tasks—you read and/or listen first, then speak about what you have read and heard. You may take notes while you read and listen, and use your notes to help prepare your responses. You are scored on your ability to speak clearly and coherently, as well as your ability to accurately synthesize and summarize the information you've read and heard.

Following is an overview of the six tasks in the Speaking section of the TOEFL.

	Time	Task
1	15 seconds to prepare 45 seconds to speak	Speak about a familiar topic.
2	15 seconds to prepare 45 seconds to speak	Express and support an opinion based on a familiar experience.
3	30 seconds to prepare 60 seconds to speak	Read an announcement (of 100 words or less) about a university life topic, listen to a conversation (about one minute in length) on the same topic, then respond to a question by summarizing what you have read and heard.
4	30 seconds to prepare 60 seconds to speak	Read an academic passage (of 100 to 125 words), listen to a lecture (about one and a half minutes in length) on the same topic, then respond to a question by summarizing what you have read and heard and by expressing and supporting an opinion on the topic.
5	20 seconds to prepare 60 seconds to speak	Listen to a conversation (about one and a half to two minutes in length) between two students discussing some type of problem and two positions or solutions, then respond to a question by summarizing what you have heard and by expressing and supporting an opinion on the topic.
6	20 seconds to prepare 60 seconds to speak	Listen to a lecture (about one and a half to two minutes in length) on an academic topic, then respond to a question by summarizing and expressing information based on what you have heard.

Writing

Section Functionality and Special Features

There are two tasks in the Writing section. The first involves listening to a lecture, so you keep your headphones on until you begin writing your essay for the first task.

Hand writing an essay is no longer an option on TOEFL iBT. You must type both your essays. If you do not know how to type well, you should take typing lessons before taking the test.

While a lecture that is part of the first task plays, a photo of a professor appears on the screen. This photo provides minimal context to the lecture. It does **not** offer any information that is directly relevant to the essay that you must write.

You have the ability to cut, copy, and paste as you type your essays.

A **Help** button in all sections takes you to a list of topics for which helpful explanations are available.

Use CD-ROM #1 to get a better understanding of how the reading passage, lecture, and questions appear on the screen and play in the Writing section of the test, as well as of how the special features work.

Writing Tasks

The Writing section contains two tasks. Task 1 is an integrated skills task—you read and listen first, then you write an essay based on what you have read and heard. You may take notes while you read and listen, and use your notes to help prepare your essay. You are scored on how well you select and correctly present information from the lecture as it relates to information in the reading passage, as well as on how well you write generally. Task 2 is an independent writing task—you write an essay on a familiar topic based on a short prompt. You are scored on how well you address the topic, as well as how well you organize the essay and use vocabulary and grammar.

Following is an overview of the two tasks in the Writing section of the TOEFL.

	Time	Task
1	3 minutes to read 2 minutes to listen 20 minutes to write	Read an academic passage (of 250 to 275 words), listen to a lecture (up to two minutes in length) on the same topic, then respond to a question by summarizing what you have read and heard
2	30 minutes to write	Write about a familiar topic

INSTALLING CD-ROMS

System Requirements

Windows™
Win 98 SE, NT 4.0 SP6, ME, 2000, XP
Pentium® 266 MHz or higher
60 MB hard disk space
64 MB RAM
800 x 600, 16-bit high color monitor
SoundBlaster-compatible sound card, mouse, speaker, microphone
4x CD-ROM or faster
Printer (optional)
Note: an Internet connection is required for the Web features of the program.

Macintosh®
Mac OS 8.6, 9.1, 9.2.2, 10.1.3, 10.1.5, 10.2.4, 10.2.8, 10.3, 10.3.7, 10.3.8
PowerPC® G3, G4, or faster
120 MB hard disk space
64 MB RAM
800 x 600, 24-bit color depth
Sound output device, sound input device, mouse
Printer (optional)
Note: an Internet connection is required for the Web features of the program.

Installing and Launching the Software (CD-ROM #1)

Windows™
This CDROM has the *AutoPlay* feature enabled. Insert the CDROM and wait a few seconds for the installation to begin. Click on the **Install Program** button and then follow the on-screen instructions. If the CDROM does not start automatically:

1. Click on the **Start** button on your *Windows Taskbar* and then click on **Run**.
2. Type in **"d:\setup.EXE"** where **"d"** is the letter of your CDROM drive (ex. If your drive letter is **"e"** then you would type in **"e:\setup.EXE"**) into the Open box and click on **OK**.
3. Follow the on-screen instructions.
4. Once installation is complete, double-click on the *TOEFL* icon on your desktop to start the program.

Macintosh®
Once you have inserted the CDROM into the drive, wait for the CDROM icon to appear on your desktop and then double-click on it.

Double-click on the file called *"Install TOEFL"* and follow the on-screen instructions. You may need to restart your computer. To launch the program, double-click the *TOEFL* icon in the *TOEFL* folder.

USING THE APPLICATION—MAJOR SECTIONS OF THE SOFTWARE

At the main menu ("home") screen, you will have several options:

Tutorials—familiarize yourself with the different types of questions and strategies for answering these questions

Test Center—take up to four full-length practice TOEFL exams

My Test Scores—review your results on practice tests you've taken

More Information—learn more about the English language programs provided by Kaplan and about the TOEFL iBT

kaptest.com—go to the Kaplan English Programs area of our website to learn more about the exam

About the Audio Files (CD-ROM #2)

Every time you must listen to an audio passage within a lesson, you will see this headphone icon.

The information next to this icon will indicate which audio file you should listen to. Remember that the transcripts for all audio files are labelled and found at the end of each chapter.

Audio files are found on CD-ROM #2, and you will simply insert the CD-ROM into your computer to access them.

Double click on the file referenced in your book. The files are called out in each chapter as you will need to access them. Complete transcripts are found at the end of each chapter.

Please note that you must use a computer, not a portable stereo.

Audio files are labelled as follows.

01. 1L, Note-Taking Practice
02. 1S, Task 1
03. 1S, Task 6 Lecture
04. 1S, Task 6 Prompt
05. 1S, Task 6 Sample Response
06. 2R, Note-Taking Practice
07. 2W, Essay Practice
08. 2W, Essay Prompt
09. 2L, Practice 1
10. 2L, Practice 2
11. 2L, Practice 3a
12. 2l. Practice 3b
13. 2L, Practice 4
14. 2L, Practice 5a
15. 2L, Practice 5b
16. 2L, Practice 5c
17. 2L, Outlining Practice
18. 2S, Task 2
19. 2S, Task 2 Sample Response
20. 2S, Task 5
21. 2S, Task 5 Prompt
22. 2S, Task 5 Sample Response
23. 3L, Outlining Practice
24. 3S, (In)formal Practice
25. 3S, Task 3 Narrator
26. 3S, Task 3 Discussion
27. 3S, Task 3 Prompt
28. 3, Task 3 Sample Response
29. 3S, Synth/Summary Narrator
30. 3S, Synth/Summ Conversation
31. 3S, Synth/Summary Prompt
32. 3S, Synth/Summary Response
33. 4R, Summary Source Practice
34. 4W, Essay Practice
35. 4W, Essay Prompt
36. 4L, Note-Taking Practice
37. 4L, Conversation

38. 4S, Task 4 Narrator
39. 4S, Task 4 Lecture
40. 4S, Task 4 Prompt
41. 4S, Task 4 Sample Response
42. 4S, More Practice Narrator
43. 4S, More Practice Lecture
44. 4S, More Practice Prompt
45. 4S, More Practice Response
46. 5L, Note-Taking Practice
47. 5L, Outlining Practice
48. 5S, Practice Sample One
49. 5S, Practice Sample Two
50. 5S, Task 1 Prompt 1
51. 5S, Task 1 Sample Response 1
52. 5S, Task 1 Prompt 2
53. 5S, Task 1 Sample Response 2
54. 5S, Task 6 Lecture 1
55. 5S, Task 6 Prompt 1
56. 5S, Task 6 Sample Response 1
57. 5S, Task 6 Lecture 2
58. 5S, Task 6 Prompt 2
59. 5S, Task 6 Sample Response 2
60. 6R, Note-Taking Practice
61. 6L, Details Practice
62. 6L, Note-Taking Practice
63. 6S, Task 2 Sample Opinion
64. 6S, Task 2 Prompt
65. 6S, Task 2 Sample Response
66. 6S, Task 5 Conversation 1
67. 6S, Task 5 Prompt 1
68. 6S, Task 5 Sample Response 1
69. 6S, Task 5 Conversation 2
70. 6S, Task 5 Prompt 2
71. 6S, Task 5 Sample Response 2
72. 7L, Note-Taking Practice
73. 7L, Main Idea Practice
74. 7L, Combined Skill Practice

75. 7S, Task 3 Narrator 1
76. 7S, Task 3 Conversation 1
77. 7S, Task 3 Prompt 1
78. 7S, Task 3 Sample Response 1
79. 7S, Task 3 Narrator 2
80. 7S, Task 3 Conversation 2
81. 7S, Task 3 Prompt 2
82. 7S, Task 3 Sample Response 2
83. 8W, Note-Taking Practice
84. 8W, Essay Practice

85. 8W, Essay Prompt
86. 8L, Note-Taking Practice
87. 8L, Question Type 3
88. 8S, Task 4 Lecture 1
89. 8S, Task 4 Prompt 1
90. 8S, Task 4 Sample Response 1
91. 8S, Task 4 Narrator
92. 8S, Task 4 Lecture 2
93. 8S, Task 4 Prompt 2
94. 8S, Task 4 Sample Response 2

Chapter 1: **Lesson Set 1**
Theme—History

This chapter covers the first lessons of reading, writing, listening, and speaking skills and strategies you will need to do your best on the TOEFL. Make sure to complete all the practice exercises and sample questions so that you can get the most out of this chapter.

LESSON 1—READING: INTRODUCTION TO THE READING PASSAGE

In this first lesson, we will cover some reading skills and strategies that will help you succeed on test day. You will also learn about some of the different question types found on the Reading section of the TOEFL. If you want to proceed with more reading strategies when you finish this lesson, turn to Lesson 2—Reading: Details and Transitions in Chapter 2.

The Introduction of a Reading Passage

Before we review some reading strategies, let's learn a little more about the passages you will find in the Reading section of the TOEFL. TOEFL reading passages follow the typical organizational structure of academic English: there is an introduction, body paragraphs, and a conclusion.

Let's start with the beginning of any passage, the introduction. The introduction provides some important general information about a passage. Here are some things you should consider as you read an introduction.

- The first sentence in the introductory paragraph often establishes the topic of the reading; that is, it tells what the reading is generally about. As you read the introduction, you should ask yourself, "What is the topic of this passage?"

- Another question you should ask yourself as you read the introduction is, "Are the remaining sentences in the introduction more general or more specific than the first sentence?" Sentences that are more specific serve to more clearly define the topic.

- The last sentence in the introduction is often a thesis statement. A thesis statement introduces the main idea that the reading passage will develop. Ask yourself, "What is the thesis of this passage?"

If you ask yourself these questions as you begin reading, you will be able to learn about the topic and thesis of the passage, and you may also learn something about the organization and the function of the passage.

The Body Paragraphs of a Reading Passage

The introduction is followed by body paragraphs. These present and develop the most important points of the passage. Here are some things you should consider as you read body paragraphs.

- The first sentence of each body paragraph is often a topic sentence; that is, it presents the topic of the paragraph. As you read each body paragraph, you should ask yourself, "What is the topic of this paragraph?"
- The remainder of each body paragraph presents key details that support the topic. Ask yourself, "What are the most important points expressed in this paragraph?"

If you ask yourself these questions as you read, you will be able to learn about the most important points in the passage, as well as the organization and the function of the passage.

The Conclusion of a Reading Passage

The conclusion is usually the final paragraph of a reading passage. Occasionally, a conclusion is not a full paragraph, but the final sentence or two of the last body paragraph. The conclusion summarizes the most important points expressed in the passage. It does not present any new information.

Rhetorical Function

Another important feature of the passages you will be reading is their rhetorical function. The specific purpose of an academic writing is called its *rhetorical function*: this refers to how the author intends to persuade the reader that the content of the writing is sound and believable. Some of the ways that the author can convince the reader include:

- defining
- describing
- exemplifying
- explaining

It is important that you understand what rhetorical function is because the TOEFL Reading section includes 3–4 questions on this topic.

Now that you know the basics, it's time to cover some reading strategies.

Skimming

Skimming is a reading process in which you read quickly to identify important points and don't focus on specific details. Skimming a passage is a fast and effective way to determine its main idea, most important points, organization, and what type of text it is. There are a few key purposes for skimming:

- Identifying the thesis statement and topic sentences of the passage
- Recognizing the basic organization of the passage
- Noting repeated key words in the passage

Because the TOEFL is a timed test, you won't be able to read through every passage thoroughly, so skimming is critical. Use the Skimming Practice to improve this important skill.

Skimming Practice

Skim this passage on the Underground Railroad and answer the questions that follow.

The Underground Railroad

The Underground Railroad was one of the most fascinating and gripping phenomena to emerge from the brutal period of American slavery. In fact, it was neither underground nor any kind of railroad, but an intricate, loosely organized, and highly secretive network of people dedicated to helping black slaves escape from bondage in the southern states to freedom in the northern United States, Canada, Mexico, and the Caribbean. Because few of its members dared to keep records of their activities, much of the Railroad's history has been transmitted orally, or lost. Nevertheless, it is possible to reconstruct a vivid picture of the people involved and the great challenges they faced.

Established as early as the late 16th century, when the first captive laborers were brought to the New World from Africa, the Railroad consisted of an informal arrangement of "stationmasters"—people who provided food and refuge, their "stations"—the houses, shops, or barns where they provided shelter, and "conductors"—those who guided escaped slaves along the difficult routes to safety. All kinds of people worked on the Railroad, including preachers, politicians, farmers, storekeepers, former slaves, and even Native Americans. Most had no knowledge that they worked as part of an organization that reached all across the United States—but they were united by their hatred of the institution of slavery and their desire to help those struggling to escape.

Perhaps the most famous of Railroad workers was Harriet Tubman. Born a slave in Maryland, Tubman escaped through the Railroad at the age of 25, and eventually became a conductor herself. Over a ten-year period, she made nearly 20 trips back into the South to lead to safety many members of her family, and dozens of others besides, perhaps as many as 300 in all.

The conditions faced by runaways were severe. Often forced to travel at night, they would navigate by the North Star. Rivers, swamps, and forests lay in their way. They could carry little food, and depended on stationmasters and conductors to keep them from starvation. Sometimes the lucky ones could travel by wagon, ship, or horse, but most had to go on foot. If they were unable to actually leave the southern states, they might have no choice but to take up residence deep in swamps or in mountainous areas, separated from their families and isolated from the world, or to join communities of Native Americans.

The risks faced by fugitives were formidable. Recapture was unthinkable. Escapees would endure terrible punishments, including mutilation or amputation of limbs, harder labor even than before was virtually guaranteed, or sale "down the river"—deeper into the South and even farther from freedom. After the Fugitive Slave Law was passed in 1850, a new class of professional slave-hunters arose, paid handsomely to catch runaway slaves and return them to their owners; they could even pursue their quarry into the free northern regions. Young men were the most successful in traveling the Railroad, though sometimes women and children would also manage to escape. Strength and speed were critical. Slaves would occasionally employ disguises, trying to pass themselves as messengers on errands, or even, in the case of the lighter-skinned slaves, as whites. Holidays and weekends were the best times to escape, or any other circumstance that permitted a head start on the authorities.

Activity on the Railroad reached a peak in the last few decades before the outbreak of the American Civil War in 1861. The great political tension created by the institution of slavery was already tearing the country apart. Whites in the South generally felt that slavery was an indispensable part of their culture. Their economy certainly depended on it, and moreover, they resented being dictated to from the North and from Washington. Those in the North, on the other hand, could only see the brutality in slavery, and the hypocrisy it meant in a country claiming to be founded on the principle of freedom and equality for all mankind. Though terribly destructive, the Civil War ultimately settled the question, and with the ratification of the 13th amendment to the U.S. Constitution on December 18, 1865, it became law that "neither slavery nor involuntary servitude . . . shall exist in the United States."

1. How is the passage organized: by time, process, or category? What clues from the text helped you determine your answer?

   _____

   _____

2. Make a list of words that are frequently repeated throughout the text.

   _____

   _____

   _____

   _____

3. Which of the following best expresses the main idea of the passage? Circle your answer.

   (A) Slaves in the South faced difficult lives.

   (B) The Underground Railroad was a successful escape route for slaves.

   (C) The people and problems associated with the Underground Railroad can be described in detail.

   (D) The Underground Railroad was fascinating due to the time period in which it was developed.

4. According to the passage, the people who ran the Underground Railroad were

   (A) organized too informally to operate successfully

   (B) from different backgrounds, but had a similar goal

   (C) only expected to provide food or shelter to escaped slaves

   (D) descendants of the first captive laborers brought to the New World from Africa

5. Skim the passage one more time and choose one of the text types that you think best describes it. Circle your answer. Explain your choice.

   (A) Descriptive

   (B) Compare/contrast

   (C) Persuasive

   (D) Narrative

Explanation:

_____

_____

_____

Answers

1. The passage is organized by time. Specific dates are mentioned throughout the passage and transition words like *early* and *ultimately* are used.

2. Repeated words include: slaves, slavery, escape, railroad, freedom, conductor, safety, northern, southern

3. (B) The Underground Railroad was a successful escape route for slaves.

4. (B) from different backgrounds, but had a similar goal

5. (A) Descriptive. Explanation: The passage begins by explaining what the Underground Railroad was, and the rest of the passage provides details about the Underground Railroad and its history.

Note-Taking

Taking notes as you read is the best way to keep track of the information you process as you skim. There are many different ways to take notes. Each way can be used with different types of texts or for different parts of a text. One way that can be useful when taking notes from a descriptive text, such as "The Underground Railroad," is the *clustering* method. In this method you note down one main idea in a center circle, then add supporting points around it. Here is an example.

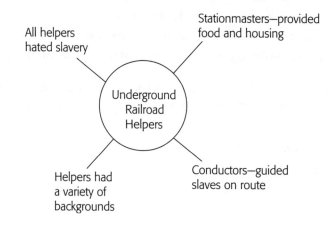

If you find clustering unfamiliar, try the following practice questions to improve your skills.

Note-Taking Practice

Use the following cluster charts to help you take notes on paragraphs 4 and 5.

Paragraph 4

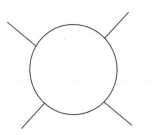

Paragraph 5

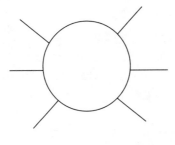

Answers

Answers will vary, but here is one example from each paragraph.

Paragraph 4

Traveled at night.
Navigated by N. Star through
rivers swamps & forests

Only a lucky few were able
to use horses, wagons,
ships: most on foot

Escapees couldn't carry much
food—Stat. masters & conductors
provided

If couldn't make north, some
hid in swamps or mountains, or
joined N. Amer.

Paragraph 5

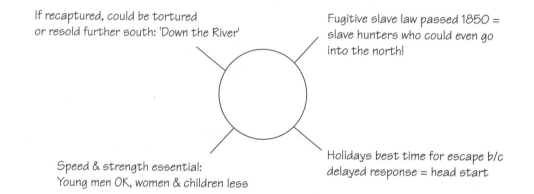

If recaptured, could be tortured
or resold further south: 'Down the River'

Fugitive slave law passed 1850 =
slave hunters who could even go
into the north!

Speed & strength essential:
Young men OK, women & children less

Holidays best time for escape b/c
delayed response = head start

Summarizing

The ability to summarize is essential for success on the TOEFL. Note-taking is a step in summarizing, whether you are reading a long text in the Reading section, listening to a lecture or a conversation in the Listening section, or reading or listening to shorter passages in the Speaking and Writing sections. Summarizing is also required in your responses to several of the tasks in the Speaking and Writing sections.

To summarize any type of reading passage you need to understand two important things:

- What is the main idea?
- Which supporting details are the most important?

Summarizing is a critical skill, so take the time to practice it now.

Summarizing Practice

Read the following short passage and take notes in the space provided. Make sure to note important details. Next, use your notes to answer the questions about the passage.

Announcement from the History Department

Due to a recent increased interest in the period of the Civil War, the History Department is pleased to offer a new course beginning spring quarter. This is an advanced level class that will focus on lesser-known aspects of the war. Topics to be covered may include the Roanoke Island Freedmen's Colony and rebel blockade runners. This class will be open only to history majors in their third or fourth year and will meet twice a week. For more information about the content and schedule of this course, please contact Professor Hudson in Office 332.

Notes

1. What is the main idea of the passage?

    _____

    _____

2. Which details from the passage are most important?

    _____

    _____

Using your notes and your answers to these questions, write a short summary of the passage in the space below. Include the main idea and important details, making sure to paraphrase—not copy or repeat word for word—points from the passage.

Answers

Answers will vary.

1. A new course about the Civil War period in the U.S. will be offered by the History Department.

2. The new course will be an advanced level class covering lesser-known facts. It will be offered twice a week to history majors in their third or fourth years. Contact Professor Hudson in Office 332.

Sample Summary

The History Department is offering a new course this spring to third and fourth-year history majors. The course will cover lesser known facts about the Civil War, and will meet twice a week. For more information, contact Professor Hudson in Office 332.

Understanding TOEFL question types is important for knowing how and where you can apply these strategies. Keep reading to learn more.

Question Types

There are several question types on the Reading section of the TOEFL. Three are:
- Identifying the Main Idea
- Summarizing the Most Important Points
- Understanding Rhetorical Function

It is important to understand what each of these question types is testing, as well as how they are presented.

Question Type 1—Identifying the Main Idea

There are 3 passages in the Reading section of the TOEFL, one of which is followed by 1 *main idea* question.

As you have learned, skimming is a process that can help you identify the main idea and most important points in a passage, and taking notes can help you organize this information.

Here is the passage that you already skimmed for the main idea.

The Underground Railroad

The Underground Railroad was one of the most fascinating and gripping phenomena to emerge from the brutal period of American slavery. In fact, it was neither underground nor any kind of railroad, but an intricate, loosely organized, and highly secretive network of people dedicated to helping black slaves escape from bondage in the southern states to freedom in the northern United States, Canada, Mexico, and the Caribbean. Because few of its members dared to keep records of their activities, much of the Railroad's history has been transmitted orally, or lost. Nevertheless, it is possible to reconstruct a vivid picture of the people involved and the great challenges they faced.

Established as early as the late 16th century, when the first captive laborers were brought to the New World from Africa, the Railroad consisted of an informal arrangement of "stationmasters"—people who provided food and refuge, their "stations"—the houses, shops, or barns where they provided shelter, and "conductors"—those who guided escaped slaves along the difficult routes to safety. All kinds of people worked on the Railroad, including preachers, politicians, farmers, storekeepers, former slaves, and even Native Americans. Most had no knowledge that they worked as part of an organization that reached all across the United States—but they were united by their hatred of the institution of slavery and their desire to help those struggling to escape.

Perhaps the most famous of Railroad workers was Harriet Tubman. Born a slave in Maryland, Tubman escaped through the Railroad at the age of 25, and eventually became a conductor herself. Over a ten-year period, she made nearly 20 trips back into the South to lead to safety many members of her family, and dozens of others besides, perhaps as many as 300 in all.

The conditions faced by runaways were severe. Often forced to travel at night, they would navigate by the North Star. Rivers, swamps, and forests lay in their way. They could carry little food, and depended on stationmasters and conductors to keep them from starvation. Sometimes the lucky ones could travel by wagon, ship, or horse, but most had to go on foot. If they were unable to actually leave the southern states, they might have no choice but to take up residence deep in swamps or in mountainous areas, separated from their families and isolated from the world, or to join communities of Native Americans.

The risks faced by fugitives were formidable. Recapture was unthinkable. Escapees would endure terrible punishments, including mutilation or amputation of limbs, harder labor even than before was virtually guaranteed, or sale "down the river"—deeper into the South and even farther from freedom. After the Fugitive Slave Law was passed in 1850, a new class of professional slave-hunters arose, paid handsomely to catch runaway slaves and return them to their owners; they could even pursue their quarry into the free northern regions.

KAPLAN

Test Prep and Admissions

Young men were the most successful in traveling the Railroad, though sometimes women and children would also manage to escape. Strength and speed were critical. Slaves would occasionally employ disguises, trying to pass themselves as messengers on errands, or even, in the case of the lighter-skinned slaves, as whites. Holidays and weekends were the best times to escape, or any other circumstance that permitted a head start on the authorities.

Activity on the Railroad reached a peak in the last few decades before the outbreak of the American Civil War in 1861. The great political tension created by the institution of slavery was already tearing the country apart. Whites in the South generally felt that slavery was an indispensable part of their culture. Their economy certainly depended on it, and moreover, they resented being dictated to from the North and from Washington. Those in the North, on the other hand, could only see the brutality in slavery, and the hypocrisy it meant in a country claiming to be founded on the principle of freedom and equality for all mankind. Though terribly destructive, the Civil War ultimately settled the question, and with the ratification of the 13th amendment to the U.S. Constitution on December 18, 1865, it became law that "neither slavery nor involuntary servitude . . . shall exist in the United States."

Main idea questions on the TOEFL do not ask, "What is the main idea of this passage?" Instead, part of the main idea is presented in the question, and part is presented in an answer choice. A TOEFL main idea question on the Underground Railroad passage might look like this:

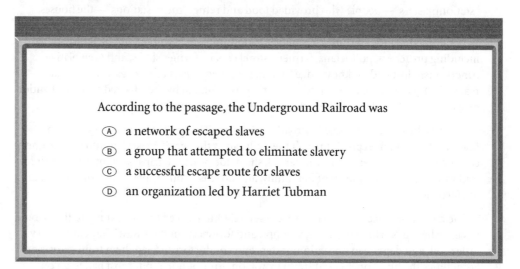

According to the passage, the Underground Railroad was

(A) a network of escaped slaves
(B) a group that attempted to eliminate slavery
(C) a successful escape route for slaves
(D) an organization led by Harriet Tubman

Based on your reading of the Underground Railroad passage, which answer choice is correct?

Look at the incorrect answer choices and think about why they are wrong. When a test maker creates a multiple-choice question, the incorrect answer choices are generally written so as to appear to be correct to some test takers. If the incorrect answer choices were all obviously wrong, every test taker would get most or all questions correct, and the test would not effectively measure anything. Incorrect answer choices are designed to distract test takers from the correct answer, and for this reason they are called *distracters*.

The distracters in *main idea* questions do not correctly express the main idea when joined to the information in the question. The Underground Railroad was in fact a network—it is labeled as such in the passage—and a few of the people in that network were escaped slaves, but most were not, so the Underground Railroad could not be called a network of escaped slaves. Choice (A) is a distracter. The people who made up the Underground Railroad may have hated slavery, but their main purpose was not to eliminate it. Choice (B) is also a distracter. Harriet Tubman is mentioned as a very important member of the Underground Railroad; however, there is no indication that she was its leader. Choice (D) is also a distracter. The Underground Railroad was in fact a successful escape route for slaves, so choice (C) is correct.

Question Type 2—Summarizing the Most Important Points

There are 3 passages in the Reading section of the TOEFL, two of which are each followed by 1 *most-important-points* question.

Two of the passages in the Reading section of the TOEFL are each followed by a question that requires you to summarize the most important points in the passage by choosing three sentences from a list of six. In order to answer this type of question correctly, you will need to skim and take notes, as well as use your summarizing skills to quickly determine the important points of the passage. You will also need to avoid distracters, answers that may seem right at first but are not.

The types of distracters for this type of question include:
- Answer choices which express ideas that are not mentioned in the passage
- Answer choices which express ideas that are only minor points in the passage

Look at the introductory sentence in bold that follows. Imagine that it is the first sentence of a brief summary of the passage you read on the Underground Railroad. Skim the passage again and refer to your notes, then complete the summary by selecting the THREE answer choices that express the most important ideas in the passage.

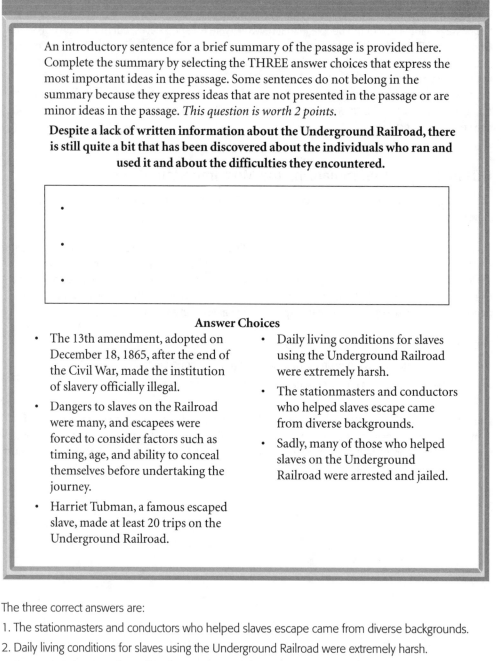

An introductory sentence for a brief summary of the passage is provided here. Complete the summary by selecting the THREE answer choices that express the most important ideas in the passage. Some sentences do not belong in the summary because they express ideas that are not presented in the passage or are minor ideas in the passage. *This question is worth 2 points.*

Despite a lack of written information about the Underground Railroad, there is still quite a bit that has been discovered about the individuals who ran and used it and about the difficulties they encountered.

-
-
-

Answer Choices

- The 13th amendment, adopted on December 18, 1865, after the end of the Civil War, made the institution of slavery officially illegal.

- Dangers to slaves on the Railroad were many, and escapees were forced to consider factors such as timing, age, and ability to conceal themselves before undertaking the journey.

- Harriet Tubman, a famous escaped slave, made at least 20 trips on the Underground Railroad.

- Daily living conditions for slaves using the Underground Railroad were extremely harsh.

- The stationmasters and conductors who helped slaves escape came from diverse backgrounds.

- Sadly, many of those who helped slaves on the Underground Railroad were arrested and jailed.

The three correct answers are:

1. The stationmasters and conductors who helped slaves escape came from diverse backgrounds.

2. Daily living conditions for slaves using the Underground Railroad were extremely harsh.

3. Dangers to slaves on the Railroad were many, and escapees were forced to consider factors such as timing, age, and ability to conceal themselves before undertaking the journey.

Question Type 3—Understanding Rhetorical Function

Each of the 3 passages in the Reading section of the TOEFL is followed by 1 or 2 *rhetorical function* questions, for a total of 3–6 *rhetorical function* questions in the Reading section.

Another type of question in the Reading section of the TOEFL asks about rhetorical function. As previously mentioned, rhetorical functions such as defining, describing, exemplifying, and explaining are often used by writers to support their main ideas.

Rhetorical Function Practice

In order to answer this type of question correctly, you will need to be able to recognize various rhetorical functions. Go through the chart that follows and match the rhetorical function on the left with a phrase that describes a way to achieve this function on the right.

A. Defining	1. Use of vocabulary such as *for example, for instance, perhaps the most,* and *notably*
B. Describing	2. Use of appositives, a noun phrase that directly follows a noun and gives another way to refer to that noun. For example: The book, *Gone with the Wind*, is an American classic.
C. Exemplifying	(*Gone with the Wind* is an appositive in the previous sentence.)
D. Explaining	3. Use of vocabulary such as *because, for this reason,* and *this is why*
	4. Use of adjectives or lists of nouns to show details about size, shape, or to appeal to the senses

Answers

A. 2

B. 4

C. 1

D. 3

Rhetorical Function Question Forms

Two forms of rhetorical function questions can be found on the Reading section of the TOEFL. The first form presents the rhetorical device and asks its function. Look at the example of this first form here, then answer the question.

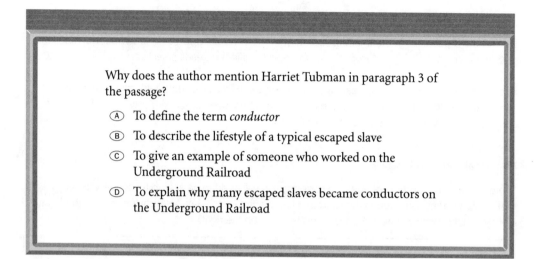

Why does the author mention Harriet Tubman in paragraph 3 of the passage?

   (A) To define the term *conductor*

   (B) To describe the lifestyle of a typical escaped slave

   (C) To give an example of someone who worked on the Underground Railroad

   (D) To explain why many escaped slaves became conductors on the Underground Railroad

Paragraph 2 of the passage describes the types of workers on the Underground Railroad and explains the variety of backgrounds from which they came. Paragraph 3 discusses Harriet Tubman as a way of exemplifying the information presented in paragraph 2. Choice (C) is correct. Although Harriet Tubman was a conductor, that term is defined within the second paragraph. Paragraph 3, then, does not serve the function of defining the term, so choice (A) is a distracter. Paragraph 3 does not really describe Tubman's lifestyle, so choice (B) is also a distracter. Choice (D) is likewise a distracter.

The second form of this question type presents the rhetorical function and asks how it is achieved. Look at the example of the second form, then answer the question.

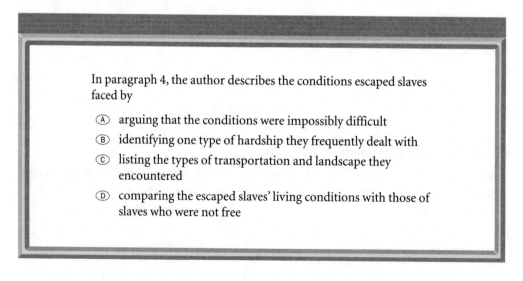

In paragraph 4, the author describes the conditions escaped slaves faced by

   (A) arguing that the conditions were impossibly difficult

   (B) identifying one type of hardship they frequently dealt with

   (C) listing the types of transportation and landscape they encountered

   (D) comparing the escaped slaves' living conditions with those of slaves who were not free

Paragraph 4 lists the ways that escaped slaves traveled and the landscapes they encountered in their travels, so choice (C) correctly answers how the rhetorical function in question is achieved.

To answer questions about rhetorical function correctly, you will also need to avoid distracters. Distracters for this type of question include:

- Answer choices which use words from the passage in a way unrelated to the question
- Answer choices which are untrue based on the information in the passage
- Answer choices which express ideas that are not mentioned in the passage
- Answer choices which cite an unrelated rhetorical function or device

Answer the following question based on the text. Then, determine which types of distracter has been used for each incorrect answer choice.

> In paragraph 6 of the passage, why does the author mention the differences in opinion about slavery?
>
> Ⓐ To explain how growing hostility between two parts of America led to war
>
> Ⓑ To describe the general atmosphere during the Civil War
>
> Ⓒ To compare the economy of the North with the economy of the South
>
> Ⓓ To give an example of a result of the great political tension that was tearing the country apart

Types of distracters:

_____

_____

_____

_____

In the final paragraph of the passage, the author explains how the differences in opinion about slavery, which had led to the creation of the Underground Railroad, eventually grew into hostility that resulted in the American Civil War, choice (A). The author is not describing the general atmosphere during the war, so choice (B) presents an unrelated rhetorical function. The author mentions the economy of the South in paragraph 6, but not to compare it to the economy of the North. Choice (D) uses words drawn directly from the second sentence of paragraph 6, but not in a way that answers the question.

Now that you have reviewed some reading strategies, let's move on to some writing strategies.

LESSON 1—WRITING: THE DESCRIPTIVE ESSAY

In this first writing lesson, we will cover some skills and strategies that will help lead to success on test day. You will learn about preparing to write an essay, as well as one type of essay found on the TOEFL. If you want to proceed with more writing strategies when you finish this lesson, turn to Lesson 2— Writing: Responding to a Reading Passage and Lecture in Chapter 2.

The Descriptive Essay

There are 2 tasks in the Writing section of the TOEFL.

In the first writing section, you must read a passage, listen to a lecture, then write an essay about what you have read and listened to. In the second, you must write an essay based only on a short prompt that asks you to describe or explain something or to express and support your opinion on an issue. In this lesson we will focus on the second type.

For this essay, you do not need any specialized knowledge. The prompt is based on topics that will be familiar to all test takers. You are given 30 minutes to plan, write, and revise this essay. Typically, an effective essay will contain a minimum of 300 words. Essays will be judged on the following:

- the quality of the writing, including idea development and organization
- the quality and accuracy of the language used to express these ideas

When you begin either writing task on the TOEFL, always read the prompt carefully to make sure that you know exactly which essay type you are being asked to write.

Recognizing Descriptive Essay Prompts

You might be wondering what a descriptive essay requires. The most important function of a descriptive essay is to provide information. The second function is to explain that information so that the reader can best understand it. A descriptive essay is not intended to argue a point or defend an opinion.

What does the prompt for a descriptive essay look like? Look at the following examples:

> What do you consider the distinctive qualities of a good student to be?

> Identify and describe the most interesting geographical feature of your country.

> In your opinion, what has been the most memorable event of the last ten years? Describe the event, supporting your answer with specific details.

The active verbs in these prompts include *consider*, *identify*, and *describe*. All of them are asking you to provide an explanation and details about a particular topic in order to help the reader to understand it better. That is the function of a descriptive essay.

Planning a Descriptive Essay

Good planning is essential to successful essay writing. Even experienced writers make careful plans before beginning to write.

There are several steps to planning an essay. All of them should be followed closely; following them will help you write your essay more easily. Following is a list of steps you should use to help you write a better essay. It is important to remember that the steps of the writing process do not necessarily have to be in this order, nor does one step need to be completed before another step is started.

1. Read the prompt (or the assignment) very carefully to make sure you understand what it is asking you to do.

2. Consider the topic thoroughly.

3. Brainstorm ideas about the topic.

4. Evaluate your ideas, and select those that will best help you respond to the prompt or assignment.

5. Organize your ideas in the order you wish to present them. (This is sometimes called outlining.)

6. Identify and list details, examples, and other supporting information you can use with each of the ideas in your list.

7. Write your introduction.

8. Write your body paragraphs.

9. Write your conclusion.

10. Revise, edit, proofread.

Note that at any point you can go back to an earlier step if you need to.

Let's explore some of these steps in greater detail.

Brainstorming

Brainstorming is a process that you use to generate ideas about a topic before you actually begin writing. If you have lots of ideas down on paper, you can think about each of them, how they best fit together, and which ones you actually want to use in your writing. With practice, you will learn how to use brainstorming quickly and efficiently to prepare to write an essay answer for the TOEFL.

There are several techniques for brainstorming. They are sometimes referred to as *listing, clustering,* and *freewriting.*

Listing

Listing is a good technique for getting lots of ideas on paper quickly. You simply note down every idea related to the topic that comes into your head. It isn't necessary to stop and consider each one—the main thing is just to get lots of ideas written down.

Here's a list a writer has generated in response to the prompt, "What are the most important impacts of automobiles on society?"

expense

smog

traffic accidents

can be beautiful

fun to drive

time spent commuting

noise

economic importance

convenience

At this point, you may decide to divide the list into positive and negative impacts. Another possibility is to select only those effects that are most clearly social, and not personal, that is, the importance of automobiles in the national economy, the pollution they cause, and the harm done by the many accidents that happen every year. Alternatively, you could select only those with which you have personal experience in the blank space below. It's up to you to rank, organize, or rearrange your list.

Clustering

One method of brainstorming is called *clustering*. Clustering is much like listing, except that it allows you to begin organizing your ideas as you think of them. You begin with just a few central ideas, and then link each new idea as you think appropriate. For example:

Negative: noise, smog, commuting, expense

Positive: convenience, economic importance, fun, artistic merit

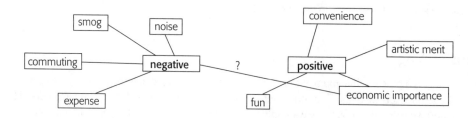

Freewriting

Another brainstorming technique is called freewriting, and it works just the way it sounds. You put pen to paper and start writing about the topic, noting down whatever thought comes into your head, until enough good ideas take shape to write the essay. There are two important things to remember about freewriting. First, don't worry about grammar and spelling. Those can be taken care of later. Second, don't stop writing until you're finished. It's important to let your thoughts keep flowing. Here's an example:

Impacts of automobiles on society, well, there are lots, there's the cost of ownership, fuel, insurance, and so on, there's traffic accidents, noise from engines, noise from alarms beeping, all the time you have to spend in your car if you commute to work—but I'm only thinking of negative things—let's see, they're sure convenient, and they can be fun to drive, and some them are really quite beautiful, and can be collector's items, and building them sure provides a lot of jobs for people. But smog's a real downside . . .

From this, you can draw lots of ideas for an essay. Freewriting also offers the advantage of allowing you to begin to experiment with expressing your ideas in phrases and sentences.

Now that you have learned three different kinds of brainstorming, it's time to practice them.

Brainstorming Practice

Choose one of the following topics, and brainstorm ideas about that topic using listing, clustering, or freewriting in the space below. If you have time, try again with a new topic.

Vegetarianism

Studying in the USA

A favorite sport

A hobby

Career plans

An influential teacher

A favorite author

A special memory

Answers

Answers will vary, but these are samples based on the topic of a favorite sport.
Listing:

fun

great exercise

simple equipment

good way to spend time with friends

cheap

can play indoors or outdoors

teaches teamwork and discipline

better use of time than watching TV

Clustering:

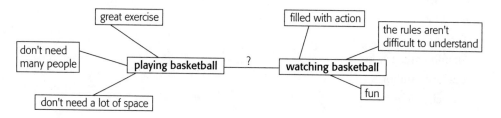

Freewriting:

My favorite sport is basketball; it's a great sport because you can play alone or with ten people. And you don't need a lot of space either, like baseball or football or soccer. You just need a ball and a hoop. And the rules are really simple—anyone can play. And it's great exercise. The action doesn't stop. You are running up and down and back and forth the entire time. And even watching basketball is fun. It's not violent like football or boring like baseball.

Outlining

Once you have generated enough good ideas for writing your essay, the next step is to organize them and to provide supporting details. A good way to plan your essay is to prepare an outline. An outline is a chart that shows exactly how the essay is to be organized, giving you a kind of blueprint to use as you write. This way you won't wander away from your topic, get distracted, or forget what you were going to say next.

In an outline, each subsection is listed in order using Roman numerals, and supporting ideas will be listed under each subsection using the alphabet.

Here is an outline for an essay about the impact of automobiles. If this were an outline for a 30-minute TOEFL essay, each Roman numeral would represent one paragraph of writing.

I. Introduction

II. Social

    A. Economic importance

    B. Traffic accidents

    C. Air pollution

III. Personal

    A. Time spent commuting

    B. Convenience

    C. Hobby

        1. Recreational driving

        2. Collecting

IV. Conclusion

An even more detailed outline could possibly be prepared, including all the supporting information and examples the author intends to use. It's not necessary to use so much detail, however—an outline like this one that uses just the main ideas and the supporting details can be very helpful on its own. Nor is it necessary to use all the numbers and letters exactly the way they are used here—just make sure that you can understand what the outline is telling you.

Finally, don't imagine that just because you've drawn an outline, you have to follow it exactly. As you write, you may change your mind about how to organize the essay. That's not a problem—just adjust the outline to reflect your changes.

Outlining Practice

Now that you have some idea about how to prepare an outline, use the brainstormed material from the Brainstorming Practice to create an outline of your own in the space below.

Answer

Answers will vary, but following is an example outline based on the impact of automobiles.

I. Introduction

II. Cultural

    A. History of Automobiles

        1. Steam cars

        2. Gas cars

    B. Henry Ford's Assembly Line

        1. Cheap cars for all

        2. The beginning of the love affair with the car

    C. Americans and Their Cars

        1. Route 66—Americans hit the road

        2. Living and Driving to work

III. Economic

    A. Cars and Trucks go to Work

    B. The Impact of Cars on Other Transportation Industries

IV. Environmental

    A. Why Cars Pollute

    B. Hybrids and Other Alternatives

    C. Cars and Urban Sprawl

V. Conclusion

Now that you have studied and practiced planning an essay, you are ready to work on writing your essay.

Writing the Introduction to a Descriptive Essay

Like any essay, a descriptive essay should be composed of several identifiable parts, each with its own specific function. These parts usually include an introduction, a body, and a conclusion. First, we will focus on the introductory paragraph.

You may recall some information about introductions from the reading lesson. Remember, an introduction must accomplish several tasks. First, it should introduce the topic of the essay. Ideally, this can be achieved in an interesting manner that catches and holds the reader's attention, which is a rhetorical device called a *hook*. Second, an introduction must provide some context for the discussion, including any information the reader may need to understand the essay as whole.

Third, an introductory paragraph to a descriptive essay should provide the reader with a good idea of the topics that will be addressed in the essay, and the order in which they will appear. This function is called *forecasting*, and it is accomplished in a *thesis statement*. Let's review these in greater detail.

The Hook

A hook can take several forms. It might be a fascinating fact, a provocative, emotionally charged statement, a novel interpretation of an accepted fact, or even a few sentences that briefly relate an event exemplifying or introducing the essay's topic. Whatever its form, the hook's principle function is to attract the reader's attention and make him or her want to read further.

Background Information

Having grabbed the reader's attention, the introductory paragraph can then provide any necessary background information. Some of this may have already been provided in the hook. It is important to provide enough information here to introduce the topic, but not so much that the introduction becomes a part of the discussion itself. You may need to answer some of these questions:

- Why is this topic important?
- What background information should the reader have before reading further?
- What has motivated me to address this topic?

Definitions are often helpful in introductions, especially when you suspect that readers may initially misunderstand the topic. It may also be desirable to identify for your reader what sources you used to find the information you used in the essay.

The Thesis Statement

The last sentence or two of the introduction to an essay is usually used to tell the reader what to expect from the essay, or to forecast. You can think of it as a kind of table of contents for the essay: a list of topics, and the order in which they occur. For shorter essays, you can simply list the topic of each paragraph of your discussion. Or, if your essay is divided into more general subsections, you can refer to the main idea of each of the subsections.

Writing the Body Paragraphs

When you have finished your introduction and have written your thesis statement, the next step is to write *body paragraphs*. A body paragraph has two main parts.

The Topic Sentence

The first part, the *topic sentence*, introduces the main idea that the paragraph will discuss. It also provides supporting details, which explain the topic. Usually, a topic sentence is a general comment about the idea that paragraph will discuss. Sometimes you can include a closing sentence, or a transition to the next paragraph, though these are not always necessary. Can you see how a body paragraph looks a lot like a mini-essay?

Supporting Details

Supporting details can also take a variety of forms. Typically, these can be descriptions, explanations, definitions, examples, or a mixture of the four. In all cases, the supporting information should include specific discussion of the idea introduced in the topic sentence and should be carefully chosen to help the reader understand the topic. A paragraph should never include information that is not directly related to its topic.

When describing an aspect of your topic, try to use words that are carefully chosen to carry the most information in the least space. Efficiency is important in academic writing. Remember that it is your goal to help your readers understand, not to overwhelm them with unimportant details.

The same is true of explanations. If your topic requires a reference to complex processes, mechanisms, or systems, supply only enough information to help your reader understand how this fits into the topic as a whole and no more. Too much information can quickly become exhausting for the reader, and writing it all down takes up your valuable time.

Definitions are most useful when you suspect that the reader may be unfamiliar with a particular term or label that is a key part of your essay. The definition supplied when the term is first mentioned prevents confusion.

Examples are the most important kind of supporting detail you can provide. Beginning writers often fail to use them enough. A well-chosen example can turn a weak argument into a strong one, help to convince a skeptical reader, and add a measure of interest and color to an otherwise dull discussion.

Using the skills and strategies you have learned in this lesson, complete the following Descriptive Essay Practice.

Descriptive Essay Practice

Following is an example of the second task in the Writing section of the TOEFL. Once you have written your essay, spend at least 15 minutes evaluating it according to the principles outlined in this lesson.

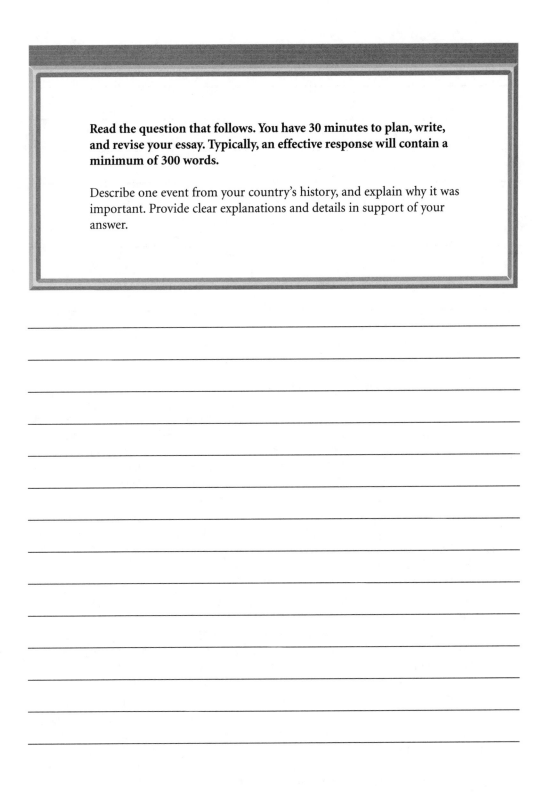

> **Read the question that follows. You have 30 minutes to plan, write, and revise your essay. Typically, an effective response will contain a minimum of 300 words.**
>
> Describe one event from your country's history, and explain why it was important. Provide clear explanations and details in support of your answer.

_____

_____

_____

_____

_____

_____

_____

_____

_____

Answer

Answers will vary, but here is one example of an essay.

Launched in July 1969, Apollo 11 was the culmination of more than 8 years of planning and innovation. In a speech to the United States Congress in May 1961, President John F. Kennedy described the new Apollo space program, a plan to send an American to the Moon by the end of the decade. The Soviet Union had just launched Yuri Gagarin, the first human being to travel into space, earlier in 1961, so President Kennedy was eager to demonstrate the technological abilities of the United States to the world.

The National Aeronautic and Space Administration, or NASA for short, immediately began building probes to orbit and even land on the surface of the moon. These robots gathered essential information about space travel and the geography of the moon's surface, which helped NASA scientists plan for the trip to the moon. These probes photographed potential landing sites and gathered other information for more than 5 years before.

At the same time that probes were investigating the moon, NASA was working hard to learn as much as it could about how to put people into space. The first American astronaut, Alan Shepard, reached space soon after President Kennedy's speech in 1961. Following that mission, NASA began intensive research programs called Mercury and Gemini to discover the possibilities and limitations of space travel for humans. These people who worked on these programs were responsible for the design, invention, and testing of all of the separate components that would go into the Apollo program.

Finally, on July 21, 1969, astronaut Neil Armstrong stepped off of the ladder of the moon lander Eagle and made the first human footprints on another heavenly body. In all, six of the Apollo missions landed on the moon, each performing experiments and bringing back samples for research. Since the last mission in 1972, this technological feat has yet to be repeated, although Japan, China and even the United States are considering a return to the moon.

This first lesson on the Writing section of the TOEFL and the skills and strategies you need to do your best is a good foundation for the rest of your studies. For now, let's move on to the Listening section.

LESSON 1—LISTENING: TAKING NOTES

In this first listening lesson, we will cover some skills and strategies that will help lead to success on test day. You will also learn about some of the different question types found on the Listening section of the TOEFL. If you want to proceed with more listening strategies when you finish this lesson, turn to Lesson 2—Listening: Implication and Inference, Context and Tone in Chapter 2.

Taking Notes

As you listen to lectures on the TOEFL, you should take notes, trying to:

- Write down key words, names, numbers, dates, or anything else you think is important
- Listen for strong general statements by the speaker, because they may be topic sentences or concluding sentences for paragraphs

The notes that you take as you are listening will help you answer questions such as:

- What is the main idea of the lecture?
- What is the purpose of this lecture: to inform, to persuade, to evaluate, to recommend?
- What are the important details in this lecture?

Note-Taking Practice

Listen to a lecture from a history class. As you listen, take notes on important details and on what you think are the topic and concluding sentences for different sections of the lecture. You will find a transcript of this audio passage (01.1L, Note-Taking Practice) at the end of the chapter.

 01.1L, Note-Taking Practice

Notes

Topic sentences:

_____

_____

_____

_____

_____

Concluding sentences:

_____

_____

_____

_____

_____

Answer

Answers will vary, but here are some examples.

Topic sentences:

The war we're going to talk about today had nowhere near the impact of that war, but it did produce one of the most celebrated expressions of patriotic fervor in our entire history: our national anthem.

The War of 1812 was the most strongly opposed war in America's history.

Well, the British wanted to prevent American goods from reaching France.

After their success in Washington, the British confidently turned on Baltimore.

At the time of that attack, Francis Scott Key was on board a British ship

It seemed impossible that American resistance could withstand such a pounding.

That sense of relief inspired our national anthem. Francis Scott Key wrote "The Star-Spangled Banner" right then and there, on the back of a letter he pulled from his pocket!

Concluding sentences:

Internationally, America gained prestige as a foe to be reckoned with.

The long-term legacy of the war of 1812 is, of course, our national anthem.

"The Star-Spangled Banner" was immediately popular and soon became a fixture in political campaigns and Fourth of July celebrations.

Outlining

If you just completed the writing lesson, you are probably familiar with outlining. Remember, an outline is a skeletal structure of a text. It contains the main and supporting ideas in the order they are presented, but does not necessarily include any specific details. Usually, an outline does not contain full sentences. Each subsection is listed in order using Roman numerals, and supporting ideas will be listed under each subsection using letters or numerals

Creating an outline as you listen to a conversation or lecture on the TOEFL will provide you with a more structured set of notes that you can then use to answer questions. Here is an example of the beginning of an outline based on the lecture you just heard:

I. War that produced American national anthem

II. War of 1812 strongly opposed

   A. Key for negotiations, not war

   B. Others fed up with British interference in American transatlantic trade

   C. War finally declared

Referring back to the notes you took on the "Star-Spangled Banner" lecture, as well as the lecture itself, complete the outline for the lecture.

Outlining is important, but to do your best on the TOEFL Listening section it's critical to understand the types of questions you will have to answer. Keep reading to learn more.

Question Types

There are several different question types on the Listening section of the TOEFL. This lesson will cover two of these question types:

- Understanding Rhetorical Function
- Understanding an Idiomatic Expression in Context

Question Type 1—Understanding Rhetorical Function

There are 2 conversations and 4 lectures in the Listening section of the TOEFL. Each lecture is followed by 1 or 2 *rhetorical function* questions, for a total of 5 or 6 *rhetorical function* questions in the Listening section.

One type of question that you will find on lectures—but generally **not** on conversations—in the Listening section of the TOEFL asks about rhetorical function. This type of question asks about the speaker's intent—for example, is the speaker defining, describing, exemplifying, explaining, or doing something else. In order to answer this type of question correctly, you will need to be able to recognize the rhetorical devices used to achieve various rhetorical functions, as well as other context and intonation cues.

Rhetorical Function Question Forms

There are four different forms of the rhetorical function question type in the Listening section. Two forms are the same as those in the Reading section—there is simply a question and four answer choices. In the first form, the question presents a rhetorical device and asks its function. In the other form, the question asks what a speaker does to achieve a given rhetorical function.

Following is an example of the second form. Notice that the function is presented in the question, and you must determine how it is achieved. Remember that the question and the four answer choices in listening questions appear on the computer screen, but only the question is spoken by the narrator.

> How does the professor support his statement that "America was the underdog" in the war?
>
> (A) With an anecdote about Key's negotiation for a prisoner's release
>
> (B) With Key's letter describing what he saw from the enemy's battleship all night
>
> (C) With testimony from a presumed expert
>
> (D) With an explanation of Britain's interference with American trade

Choice (C) is correct. In the lecture, the professor follows his statement about America being the underdog with a quote from a person named David Hickey about how the American army was poorly prepared for war. Choice (B) describes what Key witnessed from the British ship that he found so devastating. Choices (A) and (D) are also unrelated to this particular topic sentence, even though the idea of interference or being a prisoner seem to be key words that fit with "underdog" or "hostilities."

In the third form of a rhetorical function question in the Listening section, you will hear an excerpt from the lecture, then the question will present a rhetorical device and ask its function.

Following is the transcript of a rhetorical function question, including an excerpt from the lecture on "The Star-Spangled Banner." On the actual test, you will only hear the excerpt—you will not be able to read it. Remember also that the question and the four answer choices in listening questions appear on the computer screen, but only the question is spoken by the narrator.

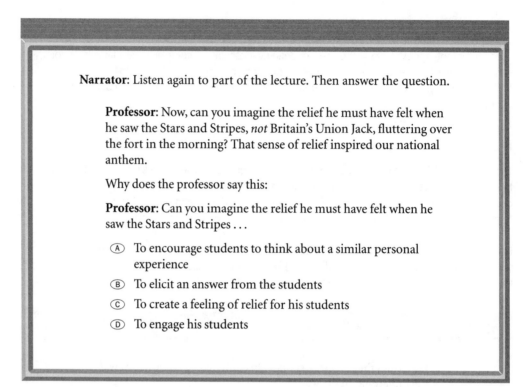

Narrator: Listen again to part of the lecture. Then answer the question.

Professor: Now, can you imagine the relief he must have felt when he saw the Stars and Stripes, *not* Britain's Union Jack, fluttering over the fort in the morning? That sense of relief inspired our national anthem.

Why does the professor say this:

Professor: Can you imagine the relief he must have felt when he saw the Stars and Stripes . . .

(A) To encourage students to think about a similar personal experience

(B) To elicit an answer from the students

(C) To create a feeling of relief for his students

(D) To engage his students

The professor's question in this excerpt does not seek an answer. It is merely a hook that speakers use to attract interest and signal the announcement of an impressive, surprising, or shocking statement. Choice (A) tries to distract you with a more literal and specific definition of *imagine*. However, if taken as a literal question, it would lead the lecture off topic. Choice (B) tries to distract you by inferring that the professor is looking for an answer, as is normally the case for a question. Choice (C) tries to distract you by including one of the professor's words, *relief*, in the answer. Choice (D) best expresses the rhetorical function of the speaker's words in this case.

The fourth form of a rhetorical function question in the Listening section also presents a short excerpt from the lecture, and asks what the rhetorical function of the entire excerpt is.

Following is the transcript of another rhetorical function question. Remember that you will not see the transcript on the test.

> Why does the professor say this:
>
> **Professor:** As soon as hostilities began, it was clear that America was the underdog. David Hickey says, "The American army was understaffed, poorly equipped and led by incompetent officers." The British? Well, they had the most powerful navy on Earth.
>
> (A) To elaborate an important point
>
> (B) To present another person's viewpoint
>
> (C) To show a contrast with something said earlier
>
> (D) To elicit an answer from the students

The disparity between the American and the British forces is an important point in the lecture, and in this quote, the professor introduces and elaborates this point. Therefore, (A) is correct.

Question Type 2—Understanding an Idiomatic Expression in Context

There are 1 or 2 *idiomatic expression* questions on the lectures in the Listening section of the TOEFL.

Idiomatic expressions are words or phrases in which the literal meaning of each word does not necessarily help you understand the meaning of the words together. Look at the following examples:

- John really looks blue today.
- John is looking a bit green.

Neither sentence is saying that John's skin is blue- or green-colored. Which sentence means that John looks sad? Which means that John looks sick?

You will probably encounter one question, sometimes two, on the lectures—but generally **not** on the conversations—in the Listening section of the TOEFL that tests your understanding of an idiomatic expression in context. You can often guess at the meaning of an idiomatic expression by looking at the parts of the sentence that you do understand.

Following are the transcripts of two idiomatic expression questions. Read the examples and choose your answers. Remember that you will not see the narrator's introduction or the transcript of the excerpt on the test.

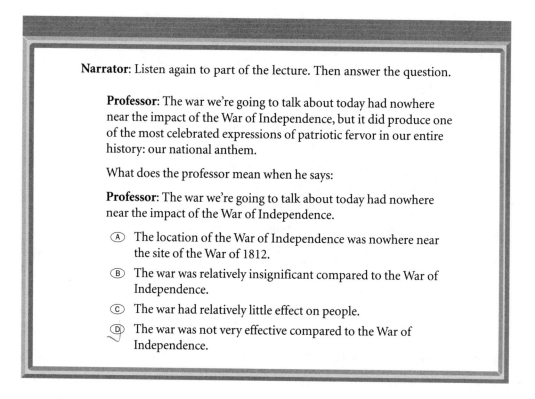

Narrator: Listen again to part of the lecture. Then answer the question.

Professor: The war we're going to talk about today had nowhere near the impact of the War of Independence, but it did produce one of the most celebrated expressions of patriotic fervor in our entire history: our national anthem.

What does the professor mean when he says:

Professor: The war we're going to talk about today had nowhere near the impact of the War of Independence.

- (A) The location of the War of Independence was nowhere near the site of the War of 1812.
- (B) The war was relatively insignificant compared to the War of Independence.
- (C) The war had relatively little effect on people.
- (D) The war was not very effective compared to the War of Independence.

Choice (B) is the correct answer. Choice (A) tries to distract you by playing off the literal meaning of *nowhere* as a place that doesn't exist. Choice (C) is too vague. In choice (D), the word *effective* has a positive connotation for producing good results. The lecture is not emphasizing what the war achieved compared to the War of Independence. Choice (B) provides the correct answer, explaining that the war the professor is about to discuss is not as historically significant in terms of lives lost, freedom gained, and its impact on the future.

> **Narrator**: Listen again to part of the lecture. Then answer the question.
>
> **Professor**: The British? Well, they had the most powerful navy on Earth. On the evening of August 24, 1814, British troops landed in Washington. They torched the Capitol, the Treasury, and the President's house. At that moment, even the most, uh, hawkish members of government may have been regretting their decision.
>
> What does the professor mean when he says this?
>
> **Professor**: They torched the Capitol, the Treasury, and the President's house.
>
> (A) The British burned buildings.
> (B) The British occupied Washington.
> (C) The British killed several people.
> (D) The British captured the President.

The correct answer is (A). The word *torch* is used idiomatically by the professor, meaning "to burn," in this case some buildings. Can you see how the three distracter answer choices might appear as potentially correct if you didn't know the idiomatic use of *torch*?

When you're ready, move on to the next lesson, Speaking: Content and Function Words.

LESSON 1—SPEAKING: CONTENT AND FUNCTION WORDS

In this first speaking lesson, we will cover some skills and strategies that will help lead to success on test day. You will also learn about the different tasks found on the Speaking section of the TOEFL. If you want to proceed with more speaking strategies when you finish this lesson, turn to Lesson 2— Speaking: Paraphrasing and Expressing an Opinion in Chapter 2.

Two of the speaking tasks that are covered in this lesson include:
- Describing Something from Your Own Experience
- Summarizing a Lecture

First, here is a review of content and function words.

Content and Function Words

Whether a word in a sentence is stressed or unstressed in spoken English depends on several factors. One factor is the importance of the meaning of a word to the phrase or sentence in which it appears. Which words or phrases do you think are the most important for the meaning of the following sentence?

America was the underdog in the War of 1812.

The words that carry more meaning are in **bold** in the sentence that follows. The other words contribute less to the overall meaning of the sentence, though they convey grammatical meaning.

America was the **underdog** in the **War** of **1812**.

The words that carry the meaning of a sentence are called *content words*. Content words are often nouns, adjectives, verbs, and adverbs. The words that convey grammatical meaning are called *function words*. Articles, conjunctions, and prepositions are often function words. A tendency in spoken English is to stress many of the content words. The function words generally remain unstressed, but this depends on the context and message being conveyed.

Content and Function Words Practice

Look at a silly poem about the TOEFL. Underline the words that are most important to the meaning of the sentences and circle the words that convey grammatical meaning. Then read the poem aloud, stressing the content words.

The TOEFL, the TOEFL, it's such a hard test!

The TOEFL, the TOEFL, how can we do our best?

There's nothing we can do but practice, practice.

There's nothing we can do but practice without rest.

Answer

The <u>TOEFL</u>, the <u>TOEFL</u>, it's (such) a <u>hard test</u>!

The <u>TOEFL</u>, the <u>TOEFL</u>, <u>how</u> can <u>we</u> do our <u>best</u>?

There's <u>nothing</u> <u>we</u> can do (but) <u>practice</u>, <u>practice</u>.

There's <u>nothing</u> <u>we</u> can do (but) <u>practice</u> (without rest).

Task 1—Describing Something from Your Own Experience

There are 6 tasks in the Speaking section of the TOEFL. The first requires a 45-second speech sample based on personal experience.

The first question of the Speaking section asks you to talk about something from your personal experience. You will be asked to describe or explain something about yourself, your family, your country, or some similar topic.

In the following TOEFL question, you will be asked to describe your country's national anthem or national flag. Before you start thinking about your own national flag or national anthem, think of and write down questions you would like to ask someone else about their flag or anthem. Don't just think about what the flag looks like. You could also ask about its history, what it represents, and how it is used today.

_____

_____

_____

_____

_____

_____

Brainstorm everything you know about your national flag or your national anthem.

Organize your ideas, and plan how to introduce each idea using appropriate rhetorical devices and linking words.

Now practice the following TOEFL question. If you have a study partner who can listen to your response, ask to work with him or her. Remember that you will not see the narrator's introduction to the question on the test, and you will both hear and read the question. Listen to this introduction and question. You will find a transcript of this audio passage (02.1S, Task 1) at the end of the chapter.

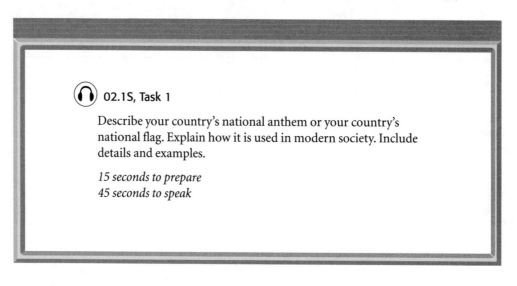

02.1S, Task 1

Describe your country's national anthem or your country's national flag. Explain how it is used in modern society. Include details and examples.

15 seconds to prepare
45 seconds to speak

Notes

Evaluate yourself using the following criteria:

Criteria	Comments	Action to Improve
Clarity and pronunciation		
Organization		
Details and examples		
Grammar and vocabulary		

Task 6—Summarizing a Lecture

There are 6 tasks in the Speaking section of the TOEFL. The sixth requires a 60-second summary of an academic lecture.

The sixth question on the Speaking section of the TOEFL asks you to summarize information from a short lecture. You will listen to a short lecture. As you listen, you should take notes on the main idea and important points. Then you will present a summary of the lecture.

When taking notes:
- Identify what kind of lecture it is: descriptive, cause and effect, informative, narrative, etc.
- Identify key parts by listening for stressed words and phrases
- Note key pieces of information such as names, dates, and places
- Identify how the lecture is organized, what the main points are, and what are examples

When summarizing:
- Present the main idea of the lecture
- Paraphrase some of the examples and details

Practice the following TOEFL question. If you have a study partner who can listen to your response, ask to work with him or her. Listen to the short lecture. As you listen, take notes, and then summarize the main points using the strategies previously mentioned. Remember that you will not see the introduction nor the transcript of the passage on the test. You will find transcripts of these audio passages at the end of the chapter.

 03.1S, Task 6 Lecture

Notes

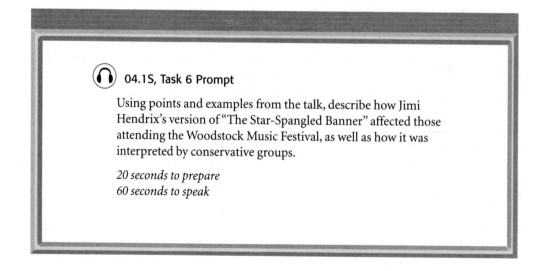

04.1S, Task 6 Prompt

Using points and examples from the talk, describe how Jimi Hendrix's version of "The Star-Spangled Banner" affected those attending the Woodstock Music Festival, as well as how it was interpreted by conservative groups.

20 seconds to prepare
60 seconds to speak

Evaluate yourself using the following criteria:

Criteria	Comments	Action to Improve
Clarity and pronunciation		
Organization		
Details and examples		
Grammar and vocabulary		

Now listen to the sample response. How is it different from yours? How is it similar? You will find a transcript of this audio passage (05.1S, Task 6 Sample Response) at the end of the chapter.

🎧 **05.1S, Task 6 Sample Response**

Congratulations! You've finished your first reading, writing, listening, and speaking lessons. When you are ready, turn to Chapter 2 to learn more skills and strategies for mastering the TOEFL.

CHAPTER 1 AUDIO TRANSCRIPTS

01. Lesson 1—Listening, Note-Taking Practice

Narrator: Listen to a professor in a history class.

Professor: Let's continue our discussion of early American history, moving on uh…from the War of Independence. The war we're going to talk about today had nowhere near the impact of that war, but it did produce one of the most celebrated expressions of patriotic fervor in our entire history: our national anthem.

With the possible exception of George W. Bush's Iraq war of 2003, the War of 1812 was the most strongly opposed war in America's history. In fact, Francis Scott Key, who ended up composing "The Star-Spangled Banner," was among those who originally advocated negotiations rather than war. On the other hand, many people were fed up with Britain's outrageous interference with American transatlantic trade. You remember, um, that Britain and France were battling for global domination? Well, the British wanted to prevent American goods from reaching France. Eventually the hawks won out and war was declared.

As soon as hostilities began, it was clear that America was the underdog. David Hickey says, [pause] "The American army was understaffed, poorly equipped and led by incompetent officers." The British? Well, they had the most powerful navy on Earth. On the evening of August 24, 1814, British troops landed in Washington. They torched the Capitol, the Treasury, and the President's house. At that moment, even the most, uh, hawkish members of government may have been regretting their decision.

After their success in Washington, the British confidently turned on Baltimore. At the time of that attack, Francis Scott Key was on board a British ship. He had been detained there after negotiating the release of an American doctor, William Beanes. Although Key had uh…persuaded the British commander to release the doctor, they could not return to land right away. They had to remain on the British ship for the duration of the battle.

The bombardment of the fort in Baltimore was devastating. Key wrote in a letter: …um…"It seemed as though mother earth had opened and was vomiting shot and shell in a sheet of fire and brimstone." Sounds horrific, doesn't it? He couldn't see much of what was going on although he watched all night from the British ship where he was being held. He saw the…"red glare" of Britain's gunpowder-propelled rockets. He was alarmed by the sounds of British "bombs bursting in air." It seemed impossible that American resistance could withstand such a pounding. Now, can you imagine the relief he must have felt when he saw the Stars and Stripes, not Britain's Union Jack, fluttering over the fort in the morning? That sense of relief inspired our national anthem. Francis Scott Key wrote "The Star-Spangled Banner" right then and there, on the back of a letter he pulled from his pocket!

Britain conceded. Key and his companions, including Dr. Beanes were released. The next day, Key's poem was printed for public distribution and set to the music of an English drinking song. By the end of the week, "The Star-Spangled Banner" was in newspapers across the nation.

So, what did America actually get out of this war? Well, not much, um, if you look at it only in terms of territorial gain. However, there were beneficial consequences. Internationally, America gained prestige as a foe to be reckoned with. At home, the defense of Baltimore gave an enormous boost to national self-esteem. You might say that people felt more uh…"American" and were able to set aside some of the political rivalries that had divided the young nation since its founding. Unfortunately, this unified spirit didn't last long. As you'll see…next week we'll discuss the build up to the Civil War.

The long-term legacy of the war of 1812 is, of course, our national anthem. As I mentioned, "The Star-Spangled Banner" was immediately popular and soon became a fixture in political campaigns and Fourth of July celebrations. But…it wasn't officially proclaimed the national anthem until 1931. Just like the war that inspired it, the choice was controversial. A lot of people felt the words were too complex and the tune too difficult. And . . .uh others protested that a song about military glory and "bombs bursting in air" was inappropriate. That debate still goes on, but I don't imagine "The Star-Spangled Banner" will concede its place of honor in sports stadiums all over this "land of the free"!

02. Lesson 1—Speaking, Task 1

Narrator: In this question, you will be asked to talk about a familiar topic. After you hear the question, you will have 15 seconds to prepare your response and 45 seconds to speak.

Describe your country's national anthem or your country's national flag. Explain how it is used in modern society. Include details and examples.

03. Lesson 1—Speaking, Task 6 Lecture

Narrator: In this question, you will listen to a short lecture about an unusual performance of "The Star-Spangled Banner." You will then answer a question that asks you to summarize the lecture. After you hear the question, you will have 20 seconds to prepare your response and 60 seconds to speak.

Professor: The genesis of the Woodstock Music Festival was indicative of the controversies that riddled the '60s. The small town in New York State where it was initially supposed to be held wouldn't even allow the event to take place there. Instead, the festival was moved to a nearby farm and to everyone's surprise over 400,000 people turned up in August 1969.

Most of those folks were present on the last Monday when Jimi Hendrix took the early morning stage. The set included his bombastic arrangement of "The Star-Spangled Banner," which he performed with an abandon that is still talked about today. His sonically explosive rendition illustrated the song with the sound effects of a modern war. It brought the words to life instrumentally through interludes and rambling annotations that were pure Hendrix. The younger generation, in thrall to this type of musical experience, accepted it for its storytelling power. At its most basic level it brought the Viet Nam war home with pictures painted in sound. In its most elevated passages Jimi's "Star-Spangled Banner" evoked feelings of unity among the assembled members of the peace movement.

Later on the media erupted. For many on the more conservative end of the social spectrum, this performance typified everything that was *bad* about the hippie generation. Worst of all, they felt, Hendrix had shown disrespect for a national symbol. Many institutions instigated regulations and guidelines specifying how the national anthem *should* be played. But for the folks that were there, it was an inspiration that led to many alternative renditions of the song. Many artists refer to it in later works. I quote Joni Mitchell:

By the time we got to Woodstock
We were half a million strong
And everywhere was song and celebration
And I dreamed I saw the bombers
Riding shotgun in the sky
And they were turning into butterflies
Above our nation.

04. Lesson 1—Speaking, Task 6 Prompt

Using points and examples from the talk, describe how Jimi Hendrix's version of "The Star-Spangled Banner" affected those attending the Woodstock Music Festival, as well as how it was interpreted by conservative groups.

05. Lesson 1—Speaking, Task 6 Sample Response

The speaker describes a performance by Jimi Hendrix at the Woodstock Music Festival. The Woodstock festival was a controversial musical event that took place in New York State in 1969. Hendrix played the Star Spangled Banner in a new and different way. He made it sound like war, with the sound of bombs. He used his instruments to create sound stories and pictures. The people who were there liked it very much, because it was very powerful. Some people were inspired and wrote poems and songs about it, others experimented with new ways of singing the anthem. On the other hand, more traditional people were shocked. Some places made new rules about how to the play the national anthem.

Chapter 2: **Lesson Set 2**
Theme—Science

Chapter 2 covers the second lessons of reading, writing, listening, and speaking skills and strategies you will need to score high on the TOEFL. Make sure to complete all the practice exercises and sample questions so that you can get the most out of this chapter.

LESSON 2—READING DETAILS AND TRANSITIONS

In this second lesson, we will cover more reading skills and strategies that will help lead to success on test day. You will have the opportunity to review the strategies you learned in Lesson 1 as well as to learn about other question types found on the Reading section of the TOEFL. If you want to proceed with more reading strategies when you finish this lesson, turn to Lesson 3—Reading: Transitions, Coherence, and Cohesive Devices in Chapter 3.

Details in a Reading Passage

The first paragraph or first few sentences of a news report is called the *lead*. The lead generally answers all or most of the main questions a reporter must answer:

- who
- what
- when
- where
- why
- how

Just think of how difficult it would be to understand a news story if these six questions weren't answered. That's because the answers to all six of these questions provide important details that together express the main idea of a news story. In this way, the lead to a news report is a concentration of the most important details in a passage, and it is an excellent example of how details combine to express the main idea.

Although none of the reading passages on the TOEFL is a news report, you will have to understand details in TOEFL reading passages—essentially, answers to the previous six questions—and how those details combine to express the main idea of the passage. The following reading practice will show you how details are presented in a news report and how details combine to express the main idea.

Details Practice

Read the following passage. Then answer the questions that follow.

Organically Grown

Doubtless you've seen the signs and labels in your local grocery stores by now.

"Organically grown" fruits and vegetables are no longer relegated to seasonal farmer's markets and naturalist co-ops. They've finally hit the big time—claiming ever-larger sections of the produce departments in major supermarket chains across America. But have you ever wondered what that "organically grown" sticker actually means?

It may come as a surprise to you that, among other things, it means bugs. Predatory insects have been used in agriculture for at least 1,700 years, beginning with the Chinese, who used yellow citrus ants to control caterpillars and other pests in their orange groves. This technique did not cross the ocean to the United States until 1915, after several researchers were sent to Asia to find a remedy for a serious pest influx in the Florida orchards. But as large-scale corporate farms slowly began to take over from family-owned homesteads, intensive chemical programs eliminated the need for such "archaic" techniques.

Today, organic farming has brought the bugs back. From the cutest to the creepiest, crawliest versions, several types of beneficial bugs are returning to their former place of honor in farmers' arsenals against more troublesome insects.

Ladybugs are both the most widespread and the prettiest agricultural aids of the six-legged kind. Typically red with black dots, the majority of people can recognize a ladybug at a glance. While many harbor a general fear of insects, this fear rarely extends to the diminutive ladybug. It is hard then to reconcile their dainty reputation with the reality of their voracious predatory instincts.

Throughout its short life, one lone ladybug is capable of consuming more than 5,000 aphids. Any plant that is being attacked by aphids will benefit from the presence of ladybugs, but vegetable, grain, strawberry, and tree crops are most frequently targeted by organic farmers for help from these beetles.

Grayish-brown in color with pincer-like jaws that jut out from its head, a lacewing larva is certainly less attractive than a ladybug, but no less helpful. Lacewing larvae can eat 100 or more pest bugs per day. Favorite meals are small caterpillars and aphids. Adult lacewings can also be predaceous, but as they primarily feed on pollen or fruit nectar, they are not as effective as their progeny in the control of pests.

Ichneumoid wasps, made famous by the late evolutionary biologist Stephen Jay Gould in his essay *Nonmoral Nature*, a nightmarish description of these insects' grotesque feeding rites, are nevertheless considered beneficial bugs. Not only do adults prey on caterpillars and other soft-bodied insects that can destroy crops, but their babies, after hatching from eggs deposited in or on the bodies of live victims, slowly eat numerous pests as well.

But why not simply use a chemical pesticide to rid farms of unwanted guests? Besides the obvious and documented health risks to humans that many pesticides engender, chemical solutions to agricultural pest problems seem to cause more problems in the long run. "Bad" bugs become resistant to the pesticides while "good" bugs are killed off. This upsets the natural balance of the insect world and eventually leads to an increase in pests in the chemically treated area.

Unfortunately, the use of insects in pest control has its downsides as well. Substantial knowledge about the life cycles and feeding habits of both prey and predator is essential in order to successfully contain pest populations. Owners of corporate farms make a thus far uncontested point in arguing that without their surrounding lands, pests now controlled by chemical means would multiply and invade the small pockets of organic farms which, for the time being anyway, can hold their own against the "reduced" quantity of pests.

And of course, the control of pests in organic farming cannot be accomplished by beneficial insects alone. Rotating crops to interrupt pest reproduction cycles, planting companion crops that discourage pests, and employing row covers that protect crops during pest migration periods, are a few other ways of defeating harmful critters.

No matter the limitations of beneficial bugs to organic farming, one thing is certain: with more than a million different species on Earth, bugs whether of the pest or predatory sort, are here to stay. Judging by the contents of the grocery cart in front of me, organic farming will not go out of fashion anytime soon either.

Now look at the following sentences from the passage.

Doubtless you've seen the signs and labels in your local grocery stores by now.

"Organically grown" fruits and vegetables are no longer relegated to seasonal farmer's markets and naturalist co-ops. They've finally hit the big time—claiming ever-larger sections of the produce departments in major supermarket chains across America. But have you ever wondered what that "organically grown" sticker actually means?

It may come as a surprise to you that, among other things, it means bugs.

Which of the following questions can be answered by the information presented in the lead?

Who?

What?

When?

Where?

Why?

How?

Look at the entire passage again and find details to answer the previous questions more completely. Then fill out the chart that follows. An example has been done for you.

Who?	What?	When?	Where?	Why?	How?
	Use Ladybugs				

Answers

Who?	What?	When?	Where?	Why?	How?
Organic farmers	Use Ladybugs (and other insects)	Sometime after 1915	in the United States	Protect vegetable, grain strawberry, and tree crops	By consuming more than 5,000 aphids during lifespan

Transitions

Transitional words and phrases help you move from one idea to the next. This is important in a news report, since journalists must convey many ideas in a short passage. It is also important in academic passages, such as those on the TOEFL, which present a good deal of information in a short space.

One way to transition effectively is to repeat or to use synonyms for the key words or phrases. For example, in the sentences from the previous text, the journalist uses the synonym *insects* to transition from the word *bugs* in the previous sentence.

> It may come as a surprise to you that, among other things, it means bugs.

> Predatory insects have been used in agriculture for at least 1,700 years, beginning with the Chinese, who used yellow citrus ants to control caterpillars and other pests in their orange groves.

Transitions Practice

Look again at the passage "Organically Grown," and then answer the following questions.

1. Which words are repeated in order to transition from one paragraph to the next?

   _____

   _____

2. Which synonyms are used in order to transition from one paragraph to the next?

_____

_____

Answers

Answers will vary.

1. organic
   bug
   farming
   ladybug

2. insect, pest
   crops, fruit
   pest control, pesticide

Skimming

Remember from the first reading lesson that skimming a passage is the best way to determine its main idea and important points, as well as what type of text it is. To skim a passage, pass your eyes quickly over the text (maybe in as few as 15–20 seconds), not really reading, but trying to notice the important parts. In this way, you get a general overview of the passage. In Lesson 1—Reading: Introduction to the Reading Passage you also learned that when you skim you should try to:

- Identify the thesis statement and topic sentences
- Recognize the basic organization
- Note repeated key words

Keep this in mind as you complete the following practice questions.

Skimming Practice

Skim the following passage to answer the questions.

Simple Machines

Have you ever used a bottle opener? Raised a flag to the top of a pole? Ridden a bicycle up a hill? If so, you have made use of an important category of human tools: simple machines. All simple machines have two common features: first, they must be structurally basic—it must be impossible to remove any component from the machine without destroying it—and second, they all do work by changing the direction, magnitude, or travel of a moving force. This force is called the effort, or input, and the work the machine accomplishes is called its load. Though simple machines vary in size and form, all of them can be placed into one of three categories: levers, inclined planes, or pulleys.

The lever is the simple machine we see most often in our daily lives. It consists of a body of rigid material along which effort is transferred to the load. During its operation, one end of the lever may move, or its two ends may move in opposite directions. In either case, there will be a point somewhere along the length of the lever that is motionless. This point is called the fulcrum. Moving the fulcrum closer to the load increases the lever's mechanical advantage; moving the fulcrum closer to the effort decreases this advantage. Imagine using a bottle opener. The opener's tip is the fulcrum. The load—the edge of the bottle cap—is between the fulcrum and the effort (the user's hand). As the user pushes the opener upward, pulling the bottle cap with it, the lever transfers the effort to the bottle cap. If the user's hand rises by five centimeters, and the cap rises by one centimeter, then the magnitude of force applied at the load will be five times the original effort.

A good example of an inclined plane, the second most common simple machine, is a hilly road. If the road is very steep, climbing the hill on a bicycle is hard work; if the grade (or steepness) of the hill is reduced, the climb will be easier. If a hill ascends at a 45-degree angle, then a bicyclist who wants to gain 100 meters in altitude must travel 200 meters along the incline, twice the actual vertical distance, but the climb requires half the effort per meter. Thus, there is an inverse relationship between the effort required to raise a load using an inclined plane and the distance along the plane that must be traveled to raise the load the desired height.

Pulleys are more rare than either levers or inclined planes but are important simple machines nonetheless. A simple pulley consists of a grooved wheel and a rope passing over it, and serves only to change the direction of force. For example, to lift the flag to the top of the flagpole, the rope is passed over the pulley at the top of the pole and one end is attached to the flag. Then, when downward effort is applied to the other end of the rope, the flag is pulled upward. Each pulley can be mounted in a block with other pulleys, with the rope traveling back and forth between them. If one block is fixed and another is free and supporting the load, there results a mechanical advantage, or change in the magnitude of force. This change is a multiple of the total number of pulleys used. Thus, lifting a load of three tons with three pulleys requires the same initial effort as lifting one ton with one pulley; however, the point on the rope receiving the initial effort will need to travel three times as far.

The basic function of the simple machines is to convert energy into work. At the heart of the function of these machines is motion, which is the source of input to the machine and is modified into the output. Levers, inclined planes, and pulleys can all be used to a mechanical advantage but all exhibit a trade-off: the total amount of energy expended to do a task is always the same no matter how it is done, but the simple machine permits the energy expenditure to be distributed over a greater distance or time. This basic aspect of the simple machine is why they are critical elements of everyday tasks. To unlatch a door or remove a bottle cap without the simple machine would be anything but simple.

1. How does the passage seem to be organized—by time, process, or category?

   _____

2. Make a list of words that are frequently repeated throughout the text.

   _____

Next, using the information gathered from skimming, answer the following questions. Circle the correct answer.

3. Which of the following best expresses the main idea of the passage?

    (A) Simple machines serve many important purposes.

    (B) Levers, inclined planes, and pulleys are a few types of simple machines.

    (C) All simple machines have the same basic features, but can be further divided into one of three types.

    (D) The three types of simple machines all require motion that can be converted into output, but not without a trade-off.

4. According to the passage, an inclined plane

    (A) is the same as a hilly road

    (B) must always be placed at a 45 degree angle

    (C) requires more work per meter if the grade is reduced

    (D) reduces distance but increases effort as it becomes steeper

5. Skim the passage one more time and choose one of the text types that you think best describes it. **Explain your choice.**

    (A) Descriptive

    (B) Compare/contrast

    (C) Explanation of a process

    (D) Definition with examples

Explanation:

_____

_____

_____

Answers

1. The passage is organized by category: Lever, inclined plane, and pulley

2. simple, machines, force, effort, load, lever, inclined plane, pulley

3. (B) Levers, inclined planes, and pulleys are a few types of simple machines.

4. (D) reduces distance but increases effort as it becomes steeper

5. (D) Definition with examples Explanation: The passage defines simple machines and provides three examples.

Outlining

Remember from Lesson 1—Writing: The Descriptive Essay that when outlining you must first determine the main ideas and supporting information, then organize them in a logical manner. In this way, an outline clearly shows the relationship between the main idea, most important points, and supporting details. Here is an example of an outline of the first paragraph of the text on simple machines:

I. Definition of simple machines

    A. All simple machines have two features

        1. Structurally basic—can't remove any part

        2. Do work by change in direction, magnitude, or travel of a moving force

    B. Relevant vocabulary

        1. Moving force = Effort

        2. Work machine does = Load

    C. Three types

        1. Lever (bottle opener)

        2. Inclined plane (riding bike up hill)

        3. Pulley (raising flag)

Outlining Practice

Use the following outline chart to help you take notes on paragraph 2 of the passage on pulleys.

II.

    A.

        1.

        2. Two ways a lever can move

           a)

           b)

    B.

        1. It is a motionless point

        2. Moving it closer to load increases mechanical advantage

        3.

    C. Bottle opener example

        1.

        2.

        3.

Answers

II. Levers = most common type of simple machine

    A. Function

        1. Definition: a body of rigid material that transfers effort to load

        2. Two ways a lever can move

            a) one end moves

            b) two ends move in opposite directions

    B. Fulcrum

        1. It is a motionless point

        2. Moving it closer to load increases mechanical advantage

        3. Moving the fulcrum closer to effort decreases mechanical advantage

    C. Bottle opener example

        1. Tip = fulcrum

        2. Load = edge of bottle cap

        3. Upward movement = lever magnifies and transfers effort to bottle cap

Identifying Examples

Several transitional words or phrases can be used to give an example in writing. Some of these phrases are:

for example

for instance

in other words

in particular

namely

specifically

such as

thus

to illustrate

Different types of examples can be used to illustrate a point in writing. Some of these types include:

- statistics or equations
- detail that represents the idea
- anecdote, description, or situation that explains the idea

KAPLAN
Test Prep and Admissions

Identifying Examples Practice

Look at the following sentences from the text "Simple Machines." What types of examples are they? The first has been done for you as an example.

1. A good example of an inclined plane, the second most common simple machine, is a hilly road.

Type of example: Detail that represents the idea

2. If the road is very steep, climbing the hill on a bicycle is hard work; if the grade (or steepness) of the hill is reduced, the climb will be easier.

Type of example: _____

3. For example, to lift the flag to the top of the flagpole, the rope is passed over the pulley at the top of the pole and one end is attached to the flag. Then, when downward effort is applied to the other end of the rope, the flag is pulled upward.

Type of example: _____

4. Imagine using a bottle opener. The opener's tip is the fulcrum. The load—the edge of the bottle cap—is between the fulcrum and the effort (the user's hand).

Type of example: _____

5. Thus, lifting a load of three tons with three pulleys requires the same initial effort as lifting one ton with one pulley; however, the point on the rope receiving the initial effort will need to travel three times as far.

Type of example: _____

6. If one block is fixed and another is free and supporting the load, there results a mechanical advantage, or change in the magnitude of force.

Type of example: _____

Answers

1. A good example of an inclined plane, the second most common simple machine, is a hilly road.

Type of example: Detail that represents the idea

2. Type of example: Situation that explains the idea

3. Type of example: Description that explains the idea

4. Type of example: Description that explains the idea

5. Type of example: Statistics or equations

6. Type of example: Situation that explains the idea

Understanding the question types is important for knowing how and where you can apply your strategies. Keep reading to learn more.

Question Types

There are several question types on the Reading section of the TOEFL. In Lesson 1 we covered:

- Identifying the Main Idea
- Summarizing the Most Important Points
- Understanding Rhetorical Function

This lesson will cover three more types:

- Understanding Details
- Understanding Details as They Relate to the Main Idea (Multiple-Choice)
- Understanding Details as They Relate to the Main Idea (Schematic Table)

It is important to understand what each of these question types is testing, as well as how the types are presented. To learn more, keep reading.

Question Type 4—Understanding Details

There are 3 passages in the Reading section of the TOEFL, each of which is followed by 2–5 *detail* questions.

One type of question on the TOEFL requires you to answer questions about details found in a reading passage. In order to answer this type of question correctly, you will need to use several of the strategies you have been practicing:

- Skimming the passage for main ideas and important points
- Taking effective notes that summarize the main ideas and important points

Here is the passage on simple machines again, which you will use to answer the questions in this section.

Simple Machines

Have you ever used a bottle opener? Raised a flag to the top of a pole? Ridden a bicycle up a hill? If so, you have made use of an important category of human tools: simple machines. All simple machines have two common features: first, they must be structurally basic—it must be impossible to remove any component from the machine without destroying it—and second, they all do work by changing the direction, magnitude, or travel of a moving force. This force is called the effort, or input, and the work the machine accomplishes is called its load. Though simple machines vary in size and form, all of them can be placed into one of three categories: levers, inclined planes, or pulleys.

The lever is the simple machine we see most often in our daily lives. It consists of a body of rigid material along which effort is transferred to the load. During its operation, one end of the lever may move, or its two ends may move in opposite directions. In either case, there will be a point somewhere along the length of the lever that is motionless. This point is called the fulcrum. Moving the fulcrum closer to the load increases the lever's mechanical advantage; moving the fulcrum closer to the effort decreases this advantage. Imagine using a bottle opener. The opener's tip is the fulcrum. The load—the edge of the bottle cap—is between the fulcrum and the effort (the user's hand). As the user pushes the opener upward, pulling the bottle cap with it, the lever transfers the effort to the bottle cap. If the user's hand rises by five centimeters, and the cap rises by one centimeter, then the magnitude of force applied at the load will be five times the original effort.

A good example of an inclined plane, the second most common simple machine, is a hilly road. If the road is very steep, climbing the hill on a bicycle is hard work; if the grade (or steepness) of the hill is reduced, the climb will be easier. If a hill ascends at a 45-degree angle, then a bicyclist who wants to gain 100 meters in altitude must travel 200 meters along the incline, twice the actual vertical distance, but the climb requires half the effort per meter. Thus, there is an inverse relationship between the effort required to raise a load using an inclined plane and the distance along the plane that must be traveled to raise the load the desired height.

Pulleys are more rare than either levers or inclined planes but are important simple machines nonetheless. A simple pulley consists of a grooved wheel and a rope passing over it, and serves only to change the direction of force. For example, to lift the flag to the top of the flagpole, the rope is passed over the pulley at the top of the pole and one end is attached to the flag. Then, when downward effort is applied to the other end of the rope, the flag is pulled upward. Each pulley can be mounted in a block with other pulleys, with the rope traveling back and forth between them. If one block is fixed and another is free and supporting the load, there results a mechanical advantage, or change in the magnitude of force. This change is a multiple of the total number of pulleys used. Thus, lifting a load of three tons with three pulleys requires the same initial effort as lifting one ton with one pulley; however, the point on the rope receiving the initial effort will need to travel three times as far.

The basic function of the simple machines is to convert energy into work. At the heart of the function of these machines is motion, which is the source of input to the machine and is modified into the output. Levers, inclined planes, and pulleys can all be used to a mechanical advantage but all exhibit a trade-off: the total amount of energy expended to do a task is always the same no matter how it is done, but the simple machine permits the energy expenditure to be distributed over a greater distance or time. This basic aspect of the simple machine is why they are critical elements of everyday tasks. To unlatch a door or remove a bottle cap without the simple machine would be anything but simple.

On the TOEFL, you will need to be able to identify the key words in a question and answer choices, and skim the passage for those same words or their synonyms. For example, the question here has key words that have been underlined.

According to the passage, <u>to raise</u> a <u>flag</u> to the top of a <u>flagpole</u>...

From your skimming and outlining, you might already remember that *flag* and *flagpole* are words that are used frequently in the middle of paragraph 4. If not, you can skim the passage quickly to find them. By skimming, you can also find a synonym for the key phrase *to raise*; it is *to lift*, which can be found in paragraph 4.

Now look at the question and two answer choices, and answer the questions that follow.

According to the passage, to raise a flag to the top of a flagpole

Ⓐ an upward effort must be applied to the end of the rope which is not attached to the flag

Ⓑ one end of a rope must be fastened to the flag while the rope slides over the pulley at the highest point of the pole

1. What are the key words in the answer choices?

_____

_____

2. Which of the key words in the answer choices are repeated in paragraph 4?

_____

_____

3. Which of the key words in the answer choices have synonyms in paragraph 4?

_____

_____

4. Based on your answers to the previous questions, is (A) or (B) a better answer choice?

_____

_____

Answers

1. effort, applied, rope, not attached, flag, rope, fastened, flag. slides over, pulley, highest point, pole

2. upward, effort, rope, flag, applied, over,

3. effort, force

4. (A) is a better choice, because it talks about force being applied, while (B) only mentions that the rope must be fastened.

Using the skill of skimming and looking back at the notes you have taken on paragraphs 2, 3, and 4, answer the questions that follow.

All of the following are mentioned in paragraph 2 as characteristics of a fulcrum EXCEPT

- (A) it is a motionless point
- (B) it is located between the load and the effort
- (C) it augments a lever's mechanical advantage the closer it is to the load
- (D) it creates a decreased mechanical advantage as it approaches the effort

The correct answer is (B) because, according to the reading, the fulcrum is located on one side of the load and the effort is located on the other side. Therefore, the correct order is fulcrum-load-effort, not load-fulcrum-effort. Choice (A) is not correct because this is actually a fact mentioned about the fulcrum in the reading, whereas, the question asks for something that is not a characteristic of the fulcrum. Choices (C) and (D) are both incorrect for the same reason as choice (A): they are mentioned as characteristics of the fulcrum.

In deciding on the correct choice for *detail* questions, be aware of distracters that:
- Use key words, phrases, or information from the passage in a way unrelated to the question
- Use key words or phrases from the passage but are untrue
- Express ideas that are not mentioned in the passage

Now read and answer the following *detail* questions.

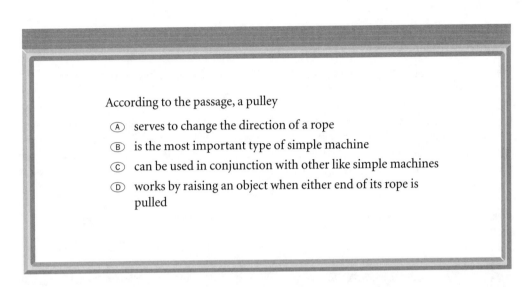

According to the passage, a pulley

(A) serves to change the direction of a rope

(B) is the most important type of simple machine

(C) can be used in conjunction with other like simple machines

(D) works by raising an object when either end of its rope is pulled

Choice (C) is correct because the passage mentions examples of two or three pulleys being used in conjunction. Choice (A) is incorrect because it uses key words from the passage but not correctly. A pulley serves only to change the direction of force, not of a rope. Choice (B) uses words or phrases from the passage but it is an untrue statement. The passage states that pulleys are important simple machines, not that they are the most important simple machines. Choice (D) also uses key words, but is an untrue statement; only one end of the rope can be pulled in a pulley.

What makes simple machines a crucial part of daily work?

(A) They can be used to a mechanical advantage but with a trade-off.

(B) They convert energy into work that humans cannot do by themselves.

(C) They are found in every home and work place, so are easy to find and utilize.

(D) They allow the amount of energy expended to be spread over a longer time or distance.

The correct answer is (D). Look at the distracter answer choices and determine how they are written to distract you.

Question Type 5—Understanding Details as They Relate to the Main Idea (Multiple-Choice)

There are 3 passages in the Reading section of the TOEFL, one of which is followed by 1 *details-related-to-the-main-idea* question in multiple-choice format.

There are two questions in the Reading section of the TOEFL that test your understanding of how details relate to the main idea of the passage. One of these questions is in four-option multiple-choice format, and the other, which is covered later in this lesson, is in schematic table format. Both questions will appear on the same reading passage. To answer the multiple-choice format question, you must understand the main idea of the passage as well as how key details develop the main idea.

Looking back at the notes you have taken on the passage "Simple Machines," answer the following question.

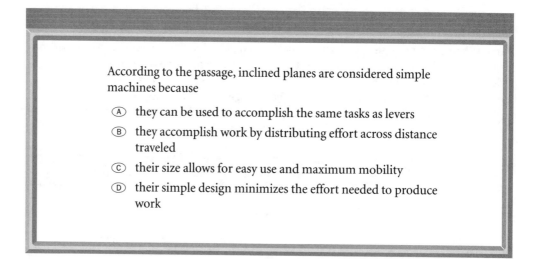

According to the passage, inclined planes are considered simple machines because

   Ⓐ they can be used to accomplish the same tasks as levers

   Ⓑ they accomplish work by distributing effort across distance traveled

   Ⓒ their size allows for easy use and maximum mobility

   Ⓓ their simple design minimizes the effort needed to produce work

The passage discusses simple machines as tools that have a simple structure and can convert energy into work. Various details describe the three types of simple machines and thereby develop this main idea of the passage. In the case of inclined planes, the passage explains that they convert energy into work by distributing effort across the distance one travels on the plane, so choice (B) is correct. Even if levers and inclined planes could be used for the same tasks, this would not be sufficient reason to classify inclined planes as simple machines. Choice (A) is incorrect. Choice (C) is designed to distract you by implying that simple machines are fairly small in size. However, the passage notes that simple machines are not limited in size. Choice (D) is designed to distract you by referring to simple design, which is a requirement of simple machines, though nothing in the passage states that there is a relationship between the simple design of simple machines and minimization of effort needed.

Question Type 6—Understanding Details as They Relate to the Main Idea (Schematic Table)

There are 3 passages in the Reading section of the TOEFL, one of which is followed by 1 *details-related-to-the-main-idea* question in schematic table format.

The schematic table format of a details-related-to-the-main-idea question asks you to select several appropriate phrases from a list and match them to the category to which they relate. To answer this question, you must understand how particular supporting details presented in the passage develop two or three important points in the passage. As with regular *detail* questions, in order to answer this type of question correctly, you will need to skim while using your notes to quickly find the answers in the passage.

Look at the answer choices in the following chart, and then do the following:

1. Without looking at the text and based only on your memory from skimming the passage, write down in which paragraph you think each of the answer choices might be mentioned.

_____

_____

2. Identify the key words in each answer choice.

_____

_____

Now, using the skill of skimming, select the appropriate phrases from the answer choices. Match them to the type of small machine to which they relate. TWO of the answer choices will NOT be used. ***This question is worth 4 points.***

Answer Choices	Levers
Are objects made of inelastic material	
Consist of a rope and a wheel	
Generate an inverse relationship between the effort required to raise a load and the distance which must be traveled to raise the load the desired height	
Benefit from increased mechanical advantage depending on the position of a fulcrum	**Pulleys**
Can be used to raise or lower a flag	
May have one or both ends moving when being used	
Require the same effort no matter how many are used and how large the load	
Are capable of displacing the effort from the user to the load as the user pushes upward	
Create a mechanical advantage when one is mounted in a fixed block and another is mounted in a free block that supports the load	

Here are the answer explanations.

The following answer choices belong in the box under the heading Levers:

Are objects made of inelastic material

Benefit from increased mechanical advantage depending on the position of a fulcrum

Are capable of displacing the effort from the user to the load as the user pushes upward

The following answer choices belong in the box under the heading Pulleys:

Consist of a rope and a wheel

Can be used to raise and lower a flag

Create a mechanical advantage when one is mounted in a fixed block and another is mounted in a free block that supports the load

Require the same effort no matter how many are used and how large the load

The answer choice

Generate an inverse relationship between the effort required to raise a load and the distance that must be traveled to raise the load the desired height

is incorrect because it includes information from the passage in a way unrelated to the question. This information is about inclined planes, not pulleys or levers.

The answer choice

May have one or both ends moving when being used

is incorrect because it uses key phrases from the passage, but it is untrue. In this case, one end moves, but the other must remain fixed.

Distracters

Now review distracters in *details-related-to-the-main-idea* questions. Two kinds of distracters to be aware of are distracters which:

- Use key words, phrases, or information from the passage in a way unrelated to the question
- Use key words or phrases from the passage but are untrue

Distracter Practice

Read the four following incorrect answers for the *details-related-to-the-main-idea* question about levers and pulleys and write which type of distracter is used.

Are the second most common simple machines

_____

When used as a bottle opener, the opener's handle is the fulcrum

_____

Will result in a change in the magnitude of force when the load is freed

_____

Make work easier by decreasing the steepness of a grade

_____

Answers

Are the second most common simple machines: Uses key words or phrases from the passage but is untrue

When used as a bottle opener, the opener's handle is the fulcrum: Uses key words or phrases from the passage but is untrue

Will result in a change in the magnitude of force when the load is freed: Uses key words, phrases, or information from the passage in a way unrelated to the question

Make work easier by decreasing the steepness of a grade: Uses key words, phrases, or information from the passage in a way unrelated to the question

Now that you have reviewed some reading strategies, let's move on to some writing strategies.

LESSON 2—WRITING: RESPONDING TO A READING PASSAGE AND LECTURE

In this second lesson, we will cover more writing skills and strategies that will help lead to success on test day. You will have the opportunity to review the strategies you learned in Lesson 1 as well as to learn more about the Writing section of the TOEFL. If you want to proceed with more writing strategies when you finish this lesson, turn to Lesson 3—Writing: The Persuasive Essay in Chapter 3.

Writing an Essay in Response to a Reading Passage and a Lecture

When you take the TOEFL, you will write an essay in which you use information you have learned from both reading and listening sources. First you will have three minutes to read a passage on an academic topic. You may take notes while you read. Then you will listen to and take notes on a lecture about the same topic. Information in the lecture will conflict somewhat with the information in the reading passage; that is, a different perspective on the topic will be presented.

You will have 20 minutes to write this essay. You may use the notes you took to help you write your essay. An effective essay will be 150–225 words long.

Make sure to read the prompt carefully to determine exactly what it is asking you to do. In your response, be prepared to do the following:

- Summarize information provided in the reading passage and the lecture
- Define a specific term or idea
- Provide examples from the reading passage and lecture

Planning a Definition Essay

While this first essay in the Writing section of the TOEFL cannot be categorized as a traditional essay type, it may have characteristics of a definition essay. The reading passage and the lecture essentially define the topic in different ways, and you must synthesize and summarize those definitions. You will not be asked to express your opinion. This lesson focuses on writing a definition essay, so that you can learn and then apply the relevant skills to writing the first essay on the TOEFL.

Before you begin writing a definition essay, you should always take a little time to plan. There are two things you should include in your planning:

- the message and information you wish to communicate in the essay
- a strategy for organizing that information

Here is a list of steps to follow to help you plan your essay and a description of each step.

1. Identify the message or purpose of your essay.

The most important aspect of any essay you write is its purpose. This purpose must be communicated clearly to the reader. The best place to do this is in the introduction, and the most common device for doing so is called the *thesis statement*. Usually, the thesis statement is the last sentence of the introductory paragraph.

Remember the discussion of the thesis statement in Lesson—Writing: The Descriptive Essay? If not, here's a brief review of thesis statements.

A thesis statement can do two important things. First, the thesis statement can identify the writer's purpose in writing the essay: the message, lesson, or principal idea the writer wishes to communicate. Second, the thesis statement can give a clear indication of the organization of the essay by listing each of the topics to be discussed in the body of the essay, and doing so in the same order that the reader will actually encounter them. This is called *forecasting* and is an important courtesy to your reader; a detailed thesis statement is like a map to the essay.

2. Identify two or three aspects of the main topic, as expressed in the reading passage and the lecture, that you will discuss in your essay.

Each of them should be a subtopic of the essay's main idea. Once you know what they are, formulate each into a sentence. These will be your topic sentences, and will introduce each of your body paragraphs.

3. Make a list of information that you can use to detail, exemplify, or support each of your topic sentences. You should have at least two or three pieces of information for each topic sentence.

For the first task in the TOEFL Writing section, this information should come from what you have read and heard.

4. Draw an outline of the essay you are going to write. Preparing an outline ahead of time will give you a clear mental picture of your essay, allowing you to visualize each step you will follow as you write. Your outline does not need to be thoroughly detailed, but it should, at minimum, refer to the thesis, body topics, and supporting information you identified in steps 1 through 3.

KAPLAN
Test Prep and Admissions

Here is a model outline for a definition essay with supporting examples. (Of course, you do not need to have exactly three body paragraphs, with exactly two details per paragraph. This is a basic structure.)

I. Introductory paragraph

   A. Background information

   B. Thesis statement

II. First body paragraph

   A. First supporting detail

   B. Second supporting detail

III. Second body paragraph

   A. First supporting detail

   B. Second supporting detail

IV. Third body paragraph

   A. First supporting detail

   B. Second supporting detail

V. Conclusion

Note-Taking

Taking notes from reading and listening passages requires identifying the information which is critical to understanding the central ideas expressed, and distinguishing this information from less critical material. Here is a list of strategies to help you do this more effectively.

1. **Pay careful attention to the introduction of the reading passage and the lecture.** The introduction will usually tell you the writer or speaker's purpose. It is essential for your summary to reflect that purpose.

2. **The last sentence of the introduction is usually the thesis statement.** The thesis statement can do two things. First, it may indicate the feeling or opinion the author has about the topic, and so helps you identify the purpose. But, it may also list the key points that will be addressed. You can note these down; they will help you know what to look for or listen for later.

3. **Use the topic sentences.** Topic sentences are another way of identifying key points and will also tell you when the writer or speaker is leaving one topic and moving to a new one. Your notes should reflect each of these topics.

4. **Pay attention to examples.** Examples are carefully chosen to illustrate the topic and will help not only you, but also the readers of your summary to understand the points being discussed. If each example illustrates a contrast or difference, it will be useful to note each one down. However, if there are several examples illustrating a single subtopic, it is not necessary to note all of them. Choose the most important one or the one that is easiest for you to understand.

5. **Numbers, dates, and statistics are carefully chosen for their importance and relevance.** They are also relatively easy to hear and quick to note down. Pay attention to them.

Note-Taking Practice

Now you will have an opportunity to practice note-taking, using a sample reading passage and a short lecture similar to those you will find on the TOEFL, although there is no conflict between the information in the two.

Read the following passage carefully and take notes on what you read. Try to employ the note-taking strategies previously discussed.

Wetlands

Wetlands are an important and highly varied type of ecosystem. They can take many forms, including marshes, swamps, and peat lands. Though wetlands can be found nearly anywhere, they favor low-lying areas near the edges of rivers, lakes, and oceans. They can occur at nearly any latitude, from tropical or equatorial regions such as the Amazon to subarctic regions like Canada's Hudson Bay area. However, all wetlands have three features in common: surface water, hydric soils, and specialized plant life.

All wetlands depend on the prolonged presence of surface water, from a river flooding during rainy seasons, as along North America's Mississippi River, or from the daily inflow of tidewater such as Long Island Sound. Sometimes wetlands form where high groundwater saturates surface soils, as in the peat bogs of central Alaska and northern Europe.

The second important component of wetland ecology is hydric soils, characterized by water saturation and the absence of oxygen. One subtype of hydric soil consists mostly of silt and clay with little organic material, which is washed away by forceful water circulation, as near riverbanks. But where there is little water circulation, organic material may accumulate, decomposing very slowly in the absence of oxygen, and forming layers of dark, spongy soil called peat.

Third, wetlands are home to hydrophytes, plants specially adapted to the wetlands environment. Hydrophytes range from the cattails found in many temperate marshes, to the giant cypress trees found in the Gulf Coast states, to the tropical mangroves growing along the Southeast Asian coastline and elsewhere. These hydrophytes in turn offer food and protection to many animal species, from ducks, geese, and other waterfowl, to crustaceans like shrimp and crabs, numerous fish species, and many kinds of frogs and other amphibians.

Humans also depend on wetlands, not merely for food derived from their great biological diversity, but also on the ability of wetlands to control flooding by absorbing excess rainfall, and to store and filter water for drinking and other household uses. Wetlands are truly a natural treasure.

Notes

Now that you have practiced taking notes from a written passage, you will apply the same principles to taking notes from a short lecture. You will find a transcript of this audio passage (06.2R, Note-Taking Practice) at the end of the chapter.

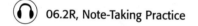 06.2R, Note-Taking Practice

Notes

Answers

From Reading passage:

I. Wetlands

  A. Types

    1. often low-lying near river/lake/ocean

    2. any latitude—Amazon to Canada

  B. Features

    1. surface water

    2. hydric soils

    3. specialized plant life

II. Relation to Water

  A. must have prolonged surface water

    1. from river flood

    2. tidal

    3. high groundwater (peat bogs in Alaska/Europe)

III. Hydric soils

  A. Definition

    1. Water saturated

    2. Absence of oxygen

  B. Types

    1. (subtype: if forceful water circulation silt and clay with little organic material—like near riverbanks)

    2. if little water circulation, organic material accumulates, decomposes in low oxygen and then forms peat

IV. Hydropytes

  A. Definition

    1. plants adapted to wetlands

      a. Cattails

      b. Cypress

      c. Tropical Mangroves

  B. Environmental function

    1. Support animal species: waterfowl, crustaceans, fish, amphibians

    2. Support humans

      a. food from biodiversity

      b. controls flooding by absorbing rain

      c. stores and filters water

From Listening passage:

I. Florida Everglades

   A. Details

      1. 13,000 km square

      2. Elevation: 2.5 meters

      3. Lakes, tidal inlets, small streams (even in dry seasons)

      4. Average rainfall 130mm (or higher)

II. Plant life

   A. Gulf Coast

      1. Cypress

   B. Seashore

      1. Mangrove Thickets

   C. Elsewhere

      1. Oak, palm, or pine trees

      2. Sawgrass

   D. Vegetation contributes to peat formation

III. Animal life

   A. Mammals: deer, mink, Florida panther

   B. Birds: red-winged blackbirds, ibises, wood storks

   C. Other: snails, frogs, crayfish

   D. Human impact

      1. diverted water from Everglades

      2. drained marshes

      3. pollution

   E. Increasing awareness of importance

      1. need for flood control

      2. source of drinking water

      3. ecological value

Summarizing

You have hopefully already read about summarizing in Lesson 2—Reading: Details and Transitions. To review, summarizing allows you to employ another person's ideas and information in order to focus and strengthen your own writing. Professional writers and researchers make frequent use of their summarizing skills. On the TOEFL, you will use summaries to demonstrate your ability to take information from written and spoken passages and to apply that information to a specific task. Here are several suggestions to guide you as you create a summary.

1. A summary should always be briefer than the original essay or talk. A five-paragraph essay, such as the "Wetlands" passage, should require no more than a paragraph to summarize. If your summary is more than about a quarter of the length of the original, look at your summary carefully to see if there is nonessential material you can remove.

2. A summary should consist almost entirely of the main points of the original. There should be a minimum of examples and specific details.

3. A summary should be written in your own words, rather than the words of the original writer or speaker. In other words, it should be *paraphrased*.

Paraphrasing

When you are using another person's ideas or information in your own essay, it is important to express them using your own words (paraphrasing), rather than simply writing things down exactly the way the writer did. There are several reasons for this. First, paraphrasing gives you an opportunity to practice and display your own English abilities. It allows you to make the work your own. Second, when you paraphrase, you are making certain that you really do understand what you've learned—by paraphrasing the material, you are helping yourself understand it better. Finally, paraphrasing allows you to avoid the ethical issues created by borrowing another person's words directly, which is called *plagiarism*. Plagiarism is strictly discouraged in the academic and professional worlds, unless the borrowed phrasing is placed within quotation marks and its source is clearly identified.

There are several ways to approach paraphrasing. A good strategy is to find synonyms for the original terms. For example, instead of using the word *saturate* from the "Wetlands" passage, you could write *soak*. Instead of *severely impacted*, (from the Everglades short talk), you could write *badly affected*. Paraphrasing is a good way to expand your vocabulary.

Another strategy is to alter the sentence structure of the original. This works well in conjunction with your newly found synonyms. For example, the sentence, "Unfortunately, the animal life we see in the Everglades now is much reduced from even a century ago," could be reflected in your notes this way: "There are fewer animals in the Everglades now than previously."

Now that you have learned strategies for summarizing and paraphrasing, you can put them into practice.

Summarizing and Paraphrasing Practice

Using the notes you took earlier, write a summary of either the "Wetlands" reading passage or the Everglades short talk (06.2R, Note-Taking Practice). When you are finished, review the sample response that follows this practice to evaluate your summary.

Answer

Answers will vary. Here is one sample summary.

> With its wide range of plant and animal life, the Everglades is more than just a swamp. In the past, people have taken advantage of the amazing variety of animal and plant life that lives there. People have also drained wetlands and diverted water in order to build. More recently, however, it has been determined that if the Everglades is kept healthy, it will continue to provide food, drinking water, and protection from flooding. Now increasing awareness of the real value of Everglades is growing, and people are beginning to work to restore it.

Writing the Body of a Definition Essay

Now it's time to review some of the strategies and skills that will help you write an effective essay on test day.

Remember from Lesson 1—Writing: The Descriptive Essay that body paragraphs are where all the actual discussion takes place in a definition essay. It is in these paragraphs that you are able to explain your ideas and provide all the information the reader needs to understand the ideas being discussed. Body paragraphs can contain a variety of different kinds of information, from statistics to dates, to short narratives. In a definition essay, examples and explanations are most commonly found.

All body paragraphs should have certain features in common. These common features are a *topic sentence*, and *supporting details*. With a little practice, you can learn to use these two parts of a paragraph to write strong, effective definition essays.

The Topic Sentence

Each body paragraph must have a topic sentence. Usually, this will be the first sentence of the paragraph and will specify the exact topic to be discussed. Ideally, each of these topics will have been mentioned in the introduction, in the same order in which they occur in the essay body. That will help the reader to navigate through the essay, by knowing exactly when and where you will be discussing each topic. The better the reader can understand the structure of the essay, the easier it will be for him or her to understand the content of the essay. In a definition essay, perhaps even more than any other kind of essay, this is critically important. Topic sentences help you to achieve this goal.

Let's look at the following model essay about simple machines. (You may recognize this from Lesson 2—Reading: Details and Transitions.) First, read the introduction carefully, paying particular attention to the last sentence. This is the thesis statement of the essay. It refers to three different topics: levers, inclined planes, and pulleys.

Next, read the first sentence of each of the body paragraphs. These are the topic sentences. Each topic sentence introduces the topic to be discussed in that paragraph, but provides only general information about it. Note that the three topics occur in the essay body in exactly the same order in which they are listed in the introductory paragraph.

Simple Machines

Have you ever used a bottle opener? Raised a flag to the top of a pole? Ridden a bicycle up a hill? If so, you have made use of an important category of human tools: simple machines. All simple machines have two common features: first, they must be structurally basic—it must be impossible to remove any component from the machine without destroying it—and second, they all do work by changing the direction, magnitude, or travel of a moving force. This force is called the effort, or input, and the work the machine accomplishes is called its load. Though simple machines vary in size and form, all of them can be placed into one of three categories: levers, inclined planes, or pulleys.

The lever is the simple machine we see most often in our daily lives. A lever consists of a body of rigid material along which effort is transferred to the load. During its operation, one end of the lever may move, or its two ends may move in opposite directions. In either case, there will be a point somewhere along the length of the lever that is motionless. This point is called the fulcrum. Moving the fulcrum closer to the load increases the lever's mechanical advantage; moving the fulcrum closer to the effort decreases this advantage. Imagine using a bottle opener. The opener's tip is the fulcrum. The load—the edge of the bottle cap—is between the fulcrum and the effort (the user's hand). As the user pushes the opener upward, pulling the bottle cap with it, the lever transfers the effort to the bottle cap. If the user's hand rises by five centimeters, and the cap rises by one centimeter, then the magnitude of force applied at the load will be five times the original effort.

A good example of an inclined plane, the second most common simple machine, is a hilly road. If the road is very steep, climbing the hill on a bicycle is hard work; if the grade (or steepness) of the hill is reduced, the climb will be easier. If a hill ascends at a 45-degree angle, then a bicyclist who wants to gain 100 meters in altitude must travel 200 meters along the incline, twice the actual vertical distance, but the climb requires half the effort per meter. Thus, there is an inverse relationship between the effort required to raise a load using an inclined plane and the distance along the plane that must be traveled to raise the load the desired height.

Pulleys are more rare than either levers or inclined planes but are important simple machines nonetheless. A simple pulley consists of a grooved wheel and a rope passing over it, and serves only to change the direction of force. For example, to lift a flag to the top of a flagpole, the rope is passed over the pulley at the top of the pole and one end is attached to the flag. Then, when downward effort is applied to the other end of the rope, the flag is pulled upward. Each pulley can be mounted in a block with other pulleys, with the rope traveling back and forth between them. If one block is fixed and another is free and supporting the load, there results a mechanical advantage, or change in the magnitude of force. This change is a multiple of the total number of pulleys used. Thus, lifting a load of three tons with three pulleys requires the same initial effort as lifting one ton with one pulley; however, the point on the rope receiving the initial effort will need to travel three times as far.

The basic function of the simple machines is to convert energy into work. At the heart of the function of these machines is motion, which is the source of input to the machine and is modified into the output. Levers, inclined planes, and pulleys can all be used to a mechanical advantage but all exhibit a trade-off: the total amount of energy expended to do a task is always the same no matter how it is done, but the simple machine permits the energy expenditure to be distributed over a greater distance or time. This basic aspect of the simple machine is why they are critical elements of everyday tasks. To unlatch a door or remove a bottle cap without the simple machine would be anything but simple.

Supporting Details

Because supporting details are so important, let's take some time to review them again.

After the topic sentence, each paragraph should include a number of supporting details. These details can take various forms: statistics, names and dates, short quotations, explanations, or examples. In a definition essay, the example is the most common kind of supporting information; explanatory sentences are also common.

Now, read each paragraph of the essay about simple machines from beginning to end. Notice that after each topic sentence, there are a number of supporting sentences that provide more detailed information about the topic. Each paragraph contains at least one example and a number of additional sentences that explain how the example illustrates the topic of the paragraph.

Let's look more closely at body paragraph number 2 (the third paragraph in the essay). The topic sentence tells us the topic of the paragraph: inclined planes. It also suggests how the author intends to explain that topic: by showing how hilly roads are examples of inclined planes. The second sentence places the reader into a situation that most people have probably experienced: climbing a steep hill on a bicycle. We also know from experience that a steeper hill is harder to climb than a less steep one. Only after providing this familiar example does the writer attempt to explain the topic in terms of abstract mathematics or science, which are often harder to understand than real life examples for many people. Thus, each sentence in this paragraph works to support the preceding ones.

Carefully chosen examples are always a strong addition to the discussion in any essay. A good example will be familiar to the reader or illustrate a process, principle, or idea with which he or she is already acquainted. Then, when the reader is trying to understand the writer's explanation, the example will permit the reader to relate the topic to his or her own experience, making the topic much more easily understood.

Now we can draw a model of a body paragraph. It should look something like this:

Topic sentence
↑
Supporting detail
↑
Supporting detail
↑
Supporting detail

Here's a rule to help you practice writing body paragraphs. A body paragraph should consist of at least four sentences, including the topic sentence. Fewer sentences suggest that the paragraph is insufficiently developed and needs to contain more information. If you find that you have only two or three sentences about your paragraph topic and are not sure what else to say, consider whether this topic should be included in the essay at all, or whether it is appropriate to connect it to another paragraph elsewhere in the essay. On the other hand, you may simply need to do more research or brainstorming on the underdeveloped topic.

The Conclusion

One part of the essay that often receives too little attention is the conclusion. In a timed writing situation, this is understandable since you may have very little time to devote to writing a good conclusion. However, the conclusion is the second most important part of the essay, after the introduction. The conclusion is the last impression the reader has of you—and of course, that should be a good impression. But conclusions don't have to be difficult or time-consuming if you keep a couple of basic rules in mind.

Rule 1: Conclusions do not need to be long. In fact, they shouldn't be. All of your information has already been presented in the body of the essay. Don't introduce new information in the conclusion.

Rule 2: The conclusion has a very clear task, which is to remind the reader what was important about the discussion, and what lesson or message should be taken from the essay. This should be done in a fresh way. Simply summarizing the discussion or repeating the thesis can be helpful, but neither makes a good conclusion all by itself.

Let's look at the model essay about simple machines one more time.

The conclusion of the essay is one of the two shortest paragraphs in the essay. No new information is included in this paragraph. Instead, the conclusion reviews the characteristics common to all simple machines and summarizes the principles that underlie their operation. Finally, the conclusion closes by reminding the reader why simple machines are an important part of our everyday lives.

In the following Essay Practice, try to remember these two rules, and you may find the task of writing the concluding paragraph of your essay to be much easier than you expected.

Essay Practice

Now you will read a passage, listen to part of a lecture, and write a response. This activity is similar to the first of two writing tasks that will be on the TOEFL. You will find a transcript of this audio passage (07.2W, Essay Practice) at the end of the chapter.

> You will have three minutes to read the following passage. You may take notes. After reading the passage, you will hear a short lecture on a related topic. Again, you may take notes while you listen.

Russian Autocracy

Huge, insular, and conservative, Russia was not easy to govern centrally. Regardless, a history of Russian monarchy is a history of autocratic government. Regarded by their peasant population as representatives of God's will on Earth, few *tsars* (the Russian word for emperor) were willing to tolerate any bounds on their power, and they went to great lengths to eliminate rivals and expand the "divine right" they enjoyed. Two tsars in particular are examples of the exercise and expansion of imperial power: Ivan IV, "the Terrible" (1533–1584), and Peter II, "the Great" (1682–1725).

Though Ivan IV held the reverence of his people, the people also lived in perpetual fear of their paranoid and unpredictable tsar. Having come to the throne as a young boy, Ivan distrusted the aristocracy because of the feuding and murderous intrigue he witnessed during his youth. He created a political police force six thousand strong that patrolled the country, terrorized and assassinated nobles that Ivan particularly suspected, and confiscated their property. In this way, Ivan virtually eliminated the Russian nobility as a challenge to imperial power.

Though less cruel and suspicious than Ivan, Peter II was no less influential over Russian society and civic life. An enormously energetic and visionary man, Peter introduced a new merit-based system of administration responsible only to himself, marginalizing the aristocrats previously controlling this aspect of government. In a successful effort to modernize his country, Peter thoroughly revolutionized and Europeanized conservative Russian society. Finally, to eliminate a last barrier to his plan for Russia's future, Peter rendered the previously autonomous Russian Church subordinate to imperial authority.

Notes

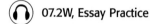 07.2W, Essay Practice

Notes

Directions: You have 20 minutes to plan and write your response. Your response will be judged on the basis of the quality of your writing and on how well your response presents the points in the lecture and their relationship to the reading passage. Typically, an effective response will be 150–225 words.

 08.2W, Essay Prompt

Summarizing the information provided in the passage and the lecture, describe the important features of the Russian imperial government.

_____

_____

_____

_____

_____

_____

Answer

Essays will vary, but compare your essay to the sample essay here.

> Despite its long history of supposedly autocratic regimes, the history of Russia also includes a tradition of democratic participation in government. Surprisingly, it was two of the strongest, most famous tsars who contributed directly to this tradition.
>
> Ivan IV was a very powerful ruler, and the Russian people lived in fear of his huge political police force, which he used to remove threats to his authority. Not every part of his government was dictatorial. Ivan also created the "zemsky sobor", which was a group of men who were not from the peasant class. He used the group as advisors when making decisions about foreign and domestic affairs.
>
> Peter the Great also contributed to Russian democracy when he took control of the Russia administrative system away from nobility and made it entirely merit-based. He was not nearly the despot that Ivan was, but during his reign he did force Russian society to Europeanize and brought the Russian church under his direct control.
>
> Later, in 1859, two more elected bodies were created. One was a rural council, and the other was urban. Both groups were responsible for making decisions about commerce, education, and infrastructure. These councils still worked under the leadership of the tsars, but they were key factors in the modernization of the Russian countryside.
>
> Although the balance of power in medieval Russia always leaned toward the tsars and their administrations, the people were not entirely unrepresented in the governments.

When you're ready, move on to the next lesson, Listening: Implication and Inference, Context and Tone.

LESSON 2—LISTENING: IMPLICATION AND INFERENCE, CONTEXT AND TONE

In this second lesson, we will cover more listening skills and strategies that will help lead to success on test day. You will have the opportunity to review the strategies you learned in Lesson 1 as well as to learn about other question types found on the Listening section of the TOEFL. If you want to proceed with more listening strategies when you finish this lesson, turn to Lesson 3—Listening: Turns in Chapter 3.

Implication and Inference

Something that is implied is not directly stated. An implication is the meaning of a statement that is not obvious in the literal meaning of the words. If you have been studying for a test with a fellow student for many hours and you want to stop, you might say, "I'm tired." Literally, you are stating that you are feeling a lack of energy, but you may also be implying that you want to stop studying.

Inference is the act of drawing a conclusion based on evidence. If you imply in saying "I'm tired" that you want to stop studying, your fellow student must infer your meaning. Sometimes it is necessary to consider more than just one statement from a speaker in order to draw an inference.

Context and Tone

Context refers to information presented before and after a statement or the setting in which a statement is uttered. Context is important in determining the meaning of a speaker's implication and in drawing inferences based on several pieces of information. In saying "I'm tired" to a fellow student with whom you've been studying, the context is the fact that you have been studying for several hours. This fact helps your fellow student infer that you may want to stop studying.

Tone refers to the way in which a statement is uttered. Tone is also important in determining the meaning of a speaker's implication. If you say "I'm tired" with a tone of finality, this tone helps your fellow student understand that you want to stop studying.

Implication and Inference Practice

Listen to the following short dialogues and answer the questions that follow. You will find transcripts of these audio passages at the end of the chapter.

 09.2L, Practice 1

1. What is the man suggesting?

_____

_____

_____

 10.2L, Practice 2

2. What does the woman mean?

_____

_____

_____

 11.2L, Practice 3a

3a. What does the man mean?

_____

_____

_____

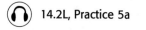 **12.2L, Practice 3b**

3b. What does the woman imply?

_____

_____

_____

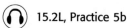 **13.2L, Practice 4**

4. What does the man mean?

_____

_____

_____

14.2L, Practice 5a

5a. Where are the speakers?

_____

_____

_____

15.2L, Practice 5b

5b. What had the man assumed about the woman?

_____

_____

_____

🎧 16.2L, Practice 5c

What does the man suggest about her problem?

_____

_____

_____

Answers

Answers will vary, but here are some sample answers.

1. That they should talk now

2. She might be able to give him a ride.

3. He is very tired.

   She is tired but not ready to give up.

4. Tony has not done any work.

5. They are at a dentist's office.

   He assumed that she had eaten too much candy.

   He suggests that her problem is caused by chewing on ice cubes.

Rhetorical and Interrogative Questions

Context and tone are also important in understanding the two general types of questions: *rhetorical* and *interrogative*. An interrogative question is a question used to gather information. When someone asks an interrogative question, he or she wants an answer. Rhetoric is the art of speaking or writing to persuade. A rhetorical question is one designed to influence the listener. There is no answer expected when a rhetorical question is asked.

Context and tone are usually required to distinguish the difference between an interrogative and rhetorical question. For example, the question "How old are you?" can be either rhetorical or interrogative given the circumstances. Two children getting to know each other often want to find out each other's age. Under these circumstances, the child asking "How old are you?" is asking an interrogative question. Most likely, she would stress the word *old* when asking the question. Now, let's say that a college student is misbehaving in class. Because of that student's childish behavior the professor might ask the same question, but with an emphasis on the word *how* or *are*. This gives the question a tone of sarcasm. The professor doesn't really want to know the student's age. The professor is trying to discourage the student's bad behavior by embarrassing him and implying that he is acting like a child.

Other purposes of rhetorical questions are:

To express an opinion

"Why is he so stupid?" in response to a pedestrian carelessly crossing the street in front of your car.

To express a feeling

"Why me?" in response to the third bad thing that has happened to you that day.

To give a command

"Would you stop talking?" as a teacher's response to students in class.

Outlining

You should be very familiar with outlines by now, but here is a brief review.

An outline is a skeletal structure of a text. It contains the main and supporting ideas in the order they are presented, but does not necessarily include any specific details. Usually, an outline does not contain full sentences.

Outlining Practice

Listen to the following discussion and take notes. Listen for speaker implications and use of questions. Then follow the instructions. You will find a transcript of this audio passage (17.2L, Outlining Practice) at the end of the chapter.

 17.2L, Outlining Practice

Notes

Here is an example of the beginning of an outline based on the discussion you just heard:

I. Best method for cougar study

II. Background on controversy

    A. Conservationists vs. developers

    B. Animal rights

    C. Human casualties/fatalities

III. Different methods

Using the notes that you wrote, write an outline of the lecture in the space provided here.

Answer

I. Why need a study?

  A. Controversial topic

    1. Conservationists want to protect

    2. Development wants to build in habitat

    3. Hunters think cougars kill too many deer

    4. Cougar-human conflict (kill and eat people)

II. How to study

  A. Challenges

    1. Solitary animals

    2. Little information is known (limited range, feeding, and behavior information)

  B. Possible Methods

    1. Sniffer-dogs to track feces

      a. can ID individual animals

      b. map roaming pattern

      c. familial data

      d. Diet information

  C. GPS (Radio) collars

    1. Capture, collar, and then track for detailed info

    2. Downside: Very expensive, no guarantee of good sample

III. Conclusion—Best option?

  A. Using dogs is least intervention

  B. Many biologists advocate low intervention

Understanding the question types is important for knowing how and where you can apply your strategies. Keep reading to learn more.

Question Types

There are several different question types on the Listening section of the TOEFL. Lesson 1 covered the following types:

- Understanding Rhetorical Function
- Understanding an Idiomatic Expression in Context

This lesson will cover two more question types:

- Drawing an Inference
- Understanding a Speaker's Implication

Question Type 3—Drawing an Inference

There are 2 conversations and 4 lectures in the Listening section of the TOEFL. Each conversation is generally followed by 1 *inference* question, and each lecture is followed by 0 or 1 *inference* question.

Inference questions ask you to draw conclusions about specific details in the passage or to make comparisons between details. In order to answer these types of inference questions, you should:

- Listen carefully to the details of the lecture or conversation
- Try to understand unfamiliar words from context
- Listen for conditionals, intonation, and suggestions made by the speakers while the conversation is happening so that you can anticipate certain inference questions
- Use your knowledge about the situation to guess what sort of conclusion might be logical

The following are examples of inference questions:

What probably happened to _____?

What will _____ probably do next?

What can be inferred about _____?

Now answer the following questions. Remember that on the actual test, you will only hear the excerpt—you will not be able to read it. If you want to get the most out of this listening practice do NOT simply read the excerpt. You might have a native speaker read the excerpt aloud to you, or have him or her record a reading of the excerpt on audiocassette. Remember also that the question and the four answer choices in listening questions appear on the computer screen, but only the question is spoken by the narrator.

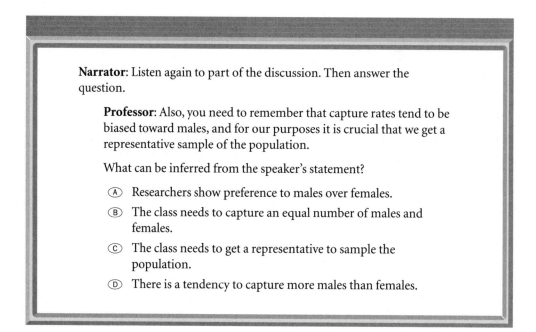

Narrator: Listen again to part of the discussion. Then answer the question.

> **Professor**: Also, you need to remember that capture rates tend to be biased toward males, and for our purposes it is crucial that we get a representative sample of the population.

What can be inferred from the speaker's statement?

- Ⓐ Researchers show preference to males over females.
- Ⓑ The class needs to capture an equal number of males and females.
- Ⓒ The class needs to get a representative to sample the population.
- Ⓓ There is a tendency to capture more males than females.

Choice (A) is a distracter that appeals to the popular definition of *bias* as preference. Choice (B) is incorrect because the speaker is not giving any specific instructions. Choice (C) is playing with the word *representative* as a noun, instead of a modifying noun, and the word *sample*, as a verb instead of a noun. Choice (D) is correct because the phrase, *biased toward males*, implies a higher number of males are captured.

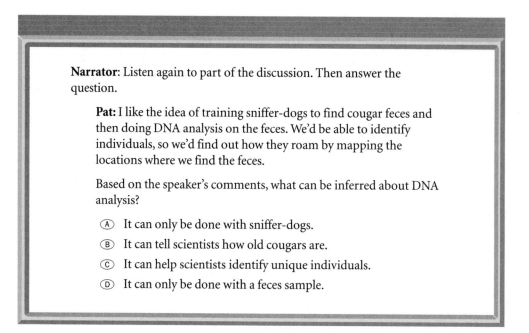

Narrator: Listen again to part of the discussion. Then answer the question.

> **Pat:** I like the idea of training sniffer-dogs to find cougar feces and then doing DNA analysis on the feces. We'd be able to identify individuals, so we'd find out how they roam by mapping the locations where we find the feces.

Based on the speaker's comments, what can be inferred about DNA analysis?

- Ⓐ It can only be done with sniffer-dogs.
- Ⓑ It can tell scientists how old cougars are.
- Ⓒ It can help scientists identify unique individuals.
- Ⓓ It can only be done with a feces sample.

Choice (A) is incorrect because dogs find the feces, but do not do the DNA analysis. (B) is incorrect because there is mention of age as part of the DNA analysis. Choice (D) is incorrect because there is no evidence to support this statement. Choice (C) is correct because the speaker explicitly mentions the identification of individuals through DNA analysis, and in the next sentence talks about finding family links between individuals.

The next two questions require you to draw an inference based on your understanding of the entire lecture.

What will the students probably do next?

   Ⓐ Learn another method for tracking cougars

   Ⓑ Start a research project on the cougars

   Ⓒ Debate the pros and cons of cougar conservation

   Ⓓ Learn more about using GPS technology to track cougars

Answering this question successfully requires an understanding of the entire lecture. At one point in the lecture the professor asks, "What do you guys think of the available research options," which implies that all of the options have already been discussed. So, choice (A) would not be a good inference. Choice (C) started to happen in the beginning of the conversation and the professor changed the topic back to research options. From this it's logical to assume that the teacher wants to focus on research options. Choice (D) is an example of a research option that was not well received by the professor. It's logical to assume that the reason they're talking about research options is to help them decide on one for their actual research; therefore, choice (B) is the correct inference since, logically, deciding on a method to carry out a task generally comes before doing it.

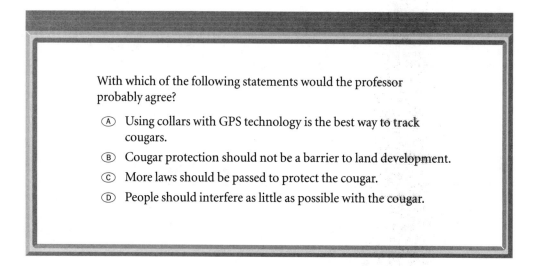

With which of the following statements would the professor probably agree?

- (A) Using collars with GPS technology is the best way to track cougars.
- (B) Cougar protection should not be a barrier to land development.
- (C) More laws should be passed to protect the cougar.
- (D) People should interfere as little as possible with the cougar.

This question tests your ability to make an inference based on several pieces of information within the entire lecture. Choice (A) is incorrect because, toward the end of the lecture, the professor talks negatively about using GPS collars. Choices (B) and (C) are statements that a development lobby and conservationist lobby, respectively, would probably agree with based on the student's comments. However, the professor is careful not to give his own opinion when he says, . . .*but I don't want to go into that debate just now.* Choice (D) is the correct answer. The professor implies this in his closing statement, *It sounds like several of you are leaning toward the approach that requires the least intervention. That pleases me. . .*

Question Type 4—Understanding a Speaker's Implication

There are 2 conversations and 4 lectures in the Listening section of the TOEFL. Each conversation is followed by 1 or 2 *speaker's implication* questions, and each lecture is followed by 0 or 1 *speaker's implication* question.

The answer choices for speaker's implication questions will contain situations that will further confuse you because they were not discussed or did not occur. You will also see synonyms (two words with a similar meaning), homophones (two words that sound the same but have different meanings), or other words repeated in the answer choices that are either out of context or not stated in the conversation.

The following are examples of implication questions:

What does the man probably mean?

What does the man suggest/imply?

What does the woman want to know?

What does the man say about _____?

What does the woman advise the man to do?

Why does _____ say _____?

What does _____ mean by _____?

Narrator: Listen again to part of the discussion. Then answer the question.

Professor: Then there are the hunters, who hate cougars because they think, um, they think the cougars kill too many of "their" deer.

What does the speaker imply about the hunters?

   (A) The hunters hate all animals that kill deer.

   (B) The hunters like other animals besides the cougar that kill deer.

   (C) The hunters are arrogant in their claim over the deer.

   (D) The hunters are angry because cougars kill deer they own.

Choice (A) is not an implication the speaker could make in this context. Even if you consider other animals, it's possible they don't kill as much as the cougar. In choice (B) we don't know from the context whether other animals are known for killing as many deer as the cougar. Choice (C) is correct, with the key being the emphasis placed on the word *their,* as if only the hunters, in their view, hold a claim over the deer population. Choice (D) tries to distract with the literal idea of ownership communicated by the word *their,* which you might have chosen had you not identified the sarcasm in the speaker's voice.

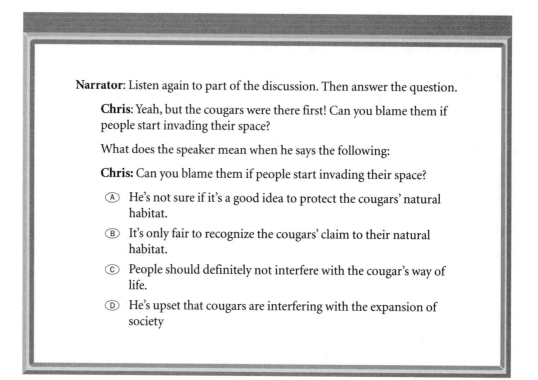

Narrator: Listen again to part of the discussion. Then answer the question.

Chris: Yeah, but the cougars were there first! Can you blame them if people start invading their space?

What does the speaker mean when he says the following:

Chris: Can you blame them if people start invading their space?

(A) He's not sure if it's a good idea to protect the cougars' natural habitat.

(B) It's only fair to recognize the cougars' claim to their natural habitat.

(C) People should definitely not interfere with the cougar's way of life.

(D) He's upset that cougars are interfering with the expansion of society

Choice (A) is testing whether you can identify the difference between a rhetorical question and a standard interrogative. Choice (C) would be taking an inference too far. You would have to get more information before you arrived at this conclusion. Choice (D) is the opposite of what he's implying. Choice (B) is the correct answer. The speaker is making a concession on behalf of people and challenging others on the justice of people's actions. This is evident in the speaker's combative tone.

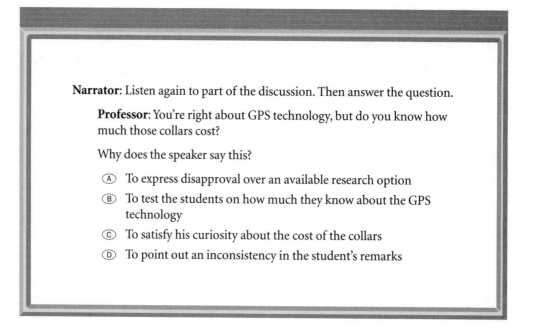

Narrator: Listen again to part of the discussion. Then answer the question.

Professor: You're right about GPS technology, but do you know how much those collars cost?

Why does the speaker say this?

(A) To express disapproval over an available research option

(B) To test the students on how much they know about the GPS technology

(C) To satisfy his curiosity about the cost of the collars

(D) To point out an inconsistency in the student's remarks

In choice (D), if the student had an inconsistency the speaker would indicate this with different wording. Choices (B) and (C) are both distracters that look attractive as answers to a standard interrogative. However, this is a rhetorical question, and the speaker's tone is skeptical. Choice (A) is the correct answer because the tone of the speaker's rhetorical question communicates skepticism about or disapproval of the student's answer.

When you're ready, move on to the next lesson, Speaking: Paraphrasing and Expressing an Opinion

LESSON 2—SPEAKING: PARAPHRASING AND EXPRESSING AN OPINION

In this second lesson, we will cover more speaking skills and strategies that will help lead to success on test day. You will have the opportunity to review the strategies you learned in Lesson 1 as well as to learn about other tasks on the Speaking section of the TOEFL. If you want to proceed with more speaking strategies when you finish this lesson, turn to Lesson 3—Speaking: Informal vs. Formal in Chapter 3.

Remember that in Lesson 1 we covered two speaking tasks:
- Describing Something from Your Own Experience
- Summarizing a Lecture

This lesson covers two more speaking tasks:
- Expressing and Supporting an Opinion Based on Personal Experience
- Summarizing a Conversation and Expressing an Opinion

Before we review these tasks, let's review an important skill you should already be familiar with: paraphrasing.

Paraphrasing

In the TOEFL, you will listen to presentations. You will then be asked to summarize the information in the presentation (that is, give a short version that includes the main ideas and some supporting ideas, but no specific details, examples, etc.) Earlier in this chapter, in Lesson 2—Writing: Responding to a Reading Passage and Lecture you learned that summarizing often requires the skill of *paraphrasing*— that is, expressing someone else's ideas using your own words. In order to paraphrase, it is helpful to know synonyms. Synonyms are words that are similar in meaning.

Paraphrasing Practice

Think of synonyms for the phrases that follow. If you can't think of any, look up key words in a monolingual dictionary. Write your synonyms here. The first one has been done for you as an example.

1. we strongly recommend

our strong suggestion is, we firmly suggest
_____

2. go ahead with something

_____

3. isn't worth anything

_____

4. make it beautiful

_____

5. there is no doubt

_____

6. surrounding towns

_____

7. attract wealthy people

_____

8. local golfers

_____

9. enjoy the amenities

_____

10. healthy pastime

_____

Answers

Answers will vary. Here are some sample responses.

1. we strongly recommend

our strong suggestion is, we firmly suggest

2. go ahead with something

begin, move forward, start

3. isn't worth anything

valueless, insignificant, of no value

4. make it beautiful

decorate, beautify, touch up

5. there is no doubt

without question, for sure, surely

6. surrounding towns

nearby towns, neighboring towns, adjacent towns

7. attract wealthy people

appeal to the rich, draw the affluent

8. local golfers

sportsmen, club members

9. enjoy the amenities

take advantage of the services

10. healthy pastime

vigorous hobby, beneficial diversion, fit leisure activity

Understanding the speaking tasks is critical for knowing how and where you can apply your strategies. Keep reading to learn more.

Task 2—Expressing and Supporting an Opinion Based on Personal Experience

There are 6 tasks in the Speaking section of the TOEFL. The second type requires a 45-second speech sample in which you give and support an opinion based on your personal experience.

You will both listen to and hear a speaking prompt. You will then have 15 seconds to prepare a spoken response of 45 seconds to this prompt. Remember that you will not see the narrator's introduction to the question on the test.

Here is a list of phrases that can be used to state an opinion.

Stating an Opinion

I believe…
I agree with the idea of …ing
I don't think …
I think…
I agree that it is important to …
I disagree with the idea of…
I feel…
I support the idea of …ing
If you ask me …
Some people might say … …, but I think …

When you respond to the sample question that follows, be sure to state and support your opinion.

Practice the following sample TOEFL questions. Remember that you will not see the narrator's introduction to the question on the test. If you have a study partner, or someone that can listen to your response, ask to work with him or her. You will find a transcript of this audio passage (18.2S, Task 2) at the end of the chapter.

18.2S, Task 2

Some people think that wildlife does not belong outside of its natural habitat. They do not think that zoos should exist. Others believe that zoos serve an educational purpose that is more important than the rights of the wild animals. Which side of this argument do you support and why? Include details and examples in your explanation.

15 seconds to prepare
45 seconds to speak

Notes

Evaluate yourself using the following criteria:

Criteria	Comments	Action to Improve
Clarity and pronunciation		
Organization		
Details and examples		
Grammar and vocabulary		

Now listen to the sample response. How is it different from yours? How is it similar? You will find a transcript of this audio passage (19. Lesson 2—Speaking, Task 2 Sample Response) at the end of the chapter.

🎧 **19.2S, Task 2 Sample Response**

Task 5—Summarizing a Conversation and Expressing an Opinion

There are 6 tasks in the Speaking section of the TOEFL. The fifth requires that you summarize a conversation in which two people are discussing a problem then give your opinion on a solution.

In the fifth task in the Speaking section, you will listen to a conversation between two people. The two people generally discuss a topic related to life at a university. The topic is framed as a problem, and at least two solutions or attitudes to the problem are presented during the conversation.

As you listen to the conversation, remember that you will have to do the following in your response to the fifth Speaking section task:

- Identify the topic the speakers are discussing
- Summarize the two (or more) solutions or opinions that the speakers express, making sure to paraphrase what the speakers say
- Present your own opinion on the topic
- Justify your opinion or say why you have that opinion

Now practice the following TOEFL question. Remember that you will not see the narrator's introduction to the question on the test. If you have a study partner, or someone that can listen to your response, ask to work with him or her. You will find a transcript of this audio passage (20.2S, Task 5) at the end of the chapter.

 **20.2S, Task 5**

Notes

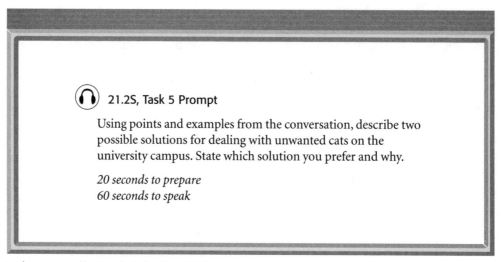

21.2S, Task 5 Prompt

Using points and examples from the conversation, describe two possible solutions for dealing with unwanted cats on the university campus. State which solution you prefer and why.

20 seconds to prepare
60 seconds to speak

Evaluate yourself using the following criteria:

Criteria	Comments	Action to Improve
Clarity and pronunciation		
Organization		
Details and examples		
Grammar and vocabulary		

Now listen to the sample response. How is it different from yours? How is it similar? You will find a transcript of this audio passage (22.2S, Task 5 Sample Response) at the end of the chapter.

 22.2S, Task 5 Sample Response

Great job! You have finished your second reading, writing, listening, and speaking lessons. When you are ready, turn to Chapter 3 to learn more skills and strategies for mastering the TOEFL.

CHAPTER 2 AUDIO TRANSCRIPTS

06. Lesson 2—Reading, Note-Taking Practice

Narrator: Listen to a professor in a biology class.

Professor: If you've ever visited the Florida Everglades, you know that they form a beautiful and unique wetlands ecosystem. Covering 13,000 square kilometers of the Florida Peninsula, the whole region averages an elevation of only 2.5 meters above sea level and is criss-crossed with lakes, tidal inlets, and small streams even during dry seasons. The average rainfall in the Everglades is 130 millimeters annually, but during a bad hurricane season, that number can be much higher.

The Everglades is home to a great variety of plant life. Some regions are dominated by cypresses, massive trees well adapted to wetlands regions of the Gulf Coast. Near the seashore, we can find mangrove thickets, and elsewhere we might find oaks, palms, or pine trees. Much of the Everglades is covered by thick, impenetrable sawgrass. This heavy growth of vegetation contributes to the formation of Everglades peat, a hydric soil of low oxygen content composed principally of accumulated organic material.

Unfortunately, the animal life we see in the Everglades now is much reduced from even a century ago. Nevertheless, there are still many mammals like deer, mink, and the endangered Florida panther; birds such as red-winged blackbirds, ibises, and wood storks; and smaller creatures like snails, frogs, and crayfish.

The Everglades has been severely impacted by the large neighboring human population, who in turn are discovering that a healthy Everglades can only benefit them. People have diverted water from the Everglades, and drained much of the marsh for building. Pollution is a threat to plant and animal life. But increasing human awareness of the role of the Everglades in flood control and as a source of drinking water, as well as of its ecological value, has led to efforts to restore the Everglades. So we can be optimistic that this unique wetland will remain vibrant and healthy for generations to come.

07. Lesson 2—Writing, Essay Practice

Narrator: Now, listen to part of a lecture on the topic you have just read about.

Professor: Though it's certainly true that imperial Russia was an autocratic society and, uh, that both Ivan the Terrible and Peter the Great contributed to the power of the autocracy, it should also be remembered that even in Russia there were institutions that were in some ways democratic and that the tsars recognized the need for deliberative bodies to advise them.

Ivan himself introduced the "zemsky sobor," a council of advisors drawn from all classes of society except the, uh, peasantry. While at first this body had little influence, in later years it would often be called to consider questions of imperial succession, treaties, and other foreign and domestic matters.

Two more representative bodies were introduced in 1859. The "zemstvo," or rural council, was elected by, uh, male members of all classes in the area, and was empowered to make decisions concerning regional commerce, education, and infrastructure. Its urban counterpart was the "duma," with similar administrative authority. Both systems were instrumental in bringing a measure of literacy and modernization to the medieval Russian countryside. However, neither body could in any way be considered a challenge to the central power of the tsar.

08. Lesson 2—Writing, Essay Prompt

Summarizing the information provided in the passage and the lecture, describe the important features of the Russian imperial government.

09. Lesson 2—Listening, Practice 1

Woman: We haven't seen each other for so long. When are we ever going to catch up on old times?

Man: Well…there's no time like the present.

Narrator: Number 1

1. What is the man suggesting?

10. Lesson 2—Listening, Practice 2

Man: I know you have a lot of studying to do, but do you think that some time today you might be able to drive me to the library?

Woman: It's not out of the question.

Narrator: Number 2

2. What does the woman mean?

11. Lesson 2—Listening, Practice 3a

Man: Aren't you tired of working on this chemistry project? I can't even keep my eyes open anymore!

Woman: Yeah, I'm pretty drained. But we're so close to being finished I'd hate to give up now.

Narrator: Number 3

3. What does the man mean?

12. Lesson 2—Listening, Practice 3b

What does the woman imply?

13. Lesson 2—Listening, Practice 4

Woman: Why are you so angry with Tony?

Man: He's supposed to be working on our group report and he hasn't lifted a finger.

Narrator: Number 4

4. What does the man mean?

14. Lesson 2—Listening, Practice 5a

Woman: I always hate coming here.

Man: Well, maybe if you didn't eat so much candy, you wouldn't have to come here as often.

Woman: I don't have a cavity. I have a chipped tooth.

Man: Well, you *do* have a bad habit of chewing on ice cubes.

Narrator: Number 5

5. Where are the speakers?

15. Lesson 2—Listening, Practice 5b

What had the man assumed about the woman?

16. Lesson 2—Listening, Practice 5c

What does the man suggest about her problem?

17. Lesson 2—Listening, Outlining Practice

Narrator: Listen to a professor and a group of students discussing research methods for studying cougars.

Professor: Well, here we are again. Today I want to talk about the most appropriate method to use for our cougar study. Before we look at the various options, let's just make sure everyone is familiar with the background to this discussion. Why do we need a cougar study?…yes?

Joe: Um…well, cougars are a pretty hot topic for lots of people, and managing cougars is really controversial. On the one hand are the conservationists who want to protect the whole ecosystem including this large predator. On the other hand is the development lobby that sees the wilderness as a potentially lucrative building site. Then there are the hunters, who hate cougars because they think, um, they think the cougars kill too many of "their" deer. Oh, and at the opposite end of that spectrum are the animal rights people who don't believe in hunting or killing anything. The entire debate is overshadowed by concern about cougar-human conflict. There have been several instances over the past few years of cougars attacking, and um, sometimes even killing and eating humans.

Chris: Yeah, but the cougars were there first! Can you blame them if people start invading their space?

Pat: That's ridiculous! People should be able to live in their homes without fear of getting eaten up by a dangerous predator! We need to kill them, especially if they hang around areas where humans live or play.

Professor: All right, everyone, those are all interesting points, but I don't want to go into that debate just now. All we're going to do today is try to decide what methods would be best for studying cougars. Joe mentioned that cougar management is a delicate issue. One of the reasons it is so controversial is that we know very little about these cats. Because of their solitary nature, their stealth, and their perfect adaptation to their habitat, they have always been elusive research subjects. As biologists, we rarely get a chance to observe them in the wild to find out about their ecology. We don't know how far they range, what or how much they eat, how they interact with each other, how young adults establish new home-ranges, how they relate to other predators like bears and wolves… We also don't know much about how they respond to anthropogenic influences. I mean, um, impact from the presence of humans. Our ignorance means we don't know how to manage them. We don't know how much land…in what areas we need to set aside for healthy cougar populations to survive; we don't know how deer hunting affects their prey base; we don't know how a cougar hunt might affect their population. Lots of questions. What do you guys think of the available research options?

Pat: I like the idea of training sniffer-dogs to find cougar feces and then doing DNA analysis on the feces. We'd be able to identify individuals, so we'd find out how they roam by mapping the locations where we find the feces. Um, we could also identify familial relationships between individuals, which would tell us about intra-species interaction. Oh, yeah…of course we'd also be able to tell what the cats have been eating by analyzing whatever hairs and bones we find in the feces.

Joe: What about GPS collars? You know, the kind of radio-collars that use satellites, like the thing you can get in cars nowadays to tell you where you are. I propose we capture and place GPS collars on as many cats as we can. That technology is so advanced now we'd get extremely detailed location data.

Professor: You're right about GPS technology, but do you know how much those collars cost? I don't think our project budget will allow us to buy enough to get the data we need. Also, you need to remember that capture rates tend to be biased toward males and for our purposes it is crucial that we get a representative sample of the population.

Chris: I support Pat's suggestion of using dogs to locate feces and then doing food studies and DNA analysis. That way, we wouldn't need to lay hands on the cats at all. There's always a risk when you capture an animal in the wild and we don't want to damage these creatures if we can help it.

Professor: Well…it sounds like several of you are leaning toward the approach that requires the least intervention. That pleases me, because your suggestions are in line with what many biologists are currently advocating in the literature.

18. Lesson 2—Speaking, Task 2

Narrator: In this question, you will be asked to state and support your opinion about an issue. After you hear the question, you will have 15 seconds to prepare your response and 45 seconds to speak.

Some people think that wildlife does not belong outside of its natural habitat. They do not think that zoos should exist. Others believe that zoos serve an educational purpose that is more important than the rights of the wild animals. Which side of this argument do you support and why? Include details and examples in your explanation.

19. Lesson 2—Speaking, Task 2 Sample Response

Ok, so zoos. Do they serve a useful purpose? Well, in my opinion they do. I think zoos are important for a couple of different reasons. For one thing, they can really inspire people to care about the natural world. Um…when someone makes a personal connection with an animal at the zoo, it can have a profound effect. That person might become interested in the fate of that animal in the wild. That's the really important role for zoos. Education, I mean. Zoos can inform people about the real dangers of extinction that exists for so many species nowadays, like tigers and rhinos and oh, I don't know, snow leopards… And the other thing that zoos do that's really important is that they offer opportunities for breeding endangered species. I just read something about this. A few zoos in Europe had an endangered species of horses in their collections and they bred them. Recently they reintroduced the horses back into their native homeland in Mongolia. So basically, for educational and breeding purposes, I think zoos play a useful role.

20. Lesson 2—Speaking, Task 5

Narrator: In this question, you will listen to a conversation. You will then answer a question about it. After you hear the question, you will have 20 seconds to prepare your response and 60 seconds to speak.

Student A (man): Hi, Joan. What are you reading?

Student B (woman): Oh, just the daily campus newsletter.

Student A: Anything new and exciting happening today?

Student B: Well, I see the university has a plan to deal with the problem of, uh, stray cats on campus.

Student A: Oh? . . . I didn't know there was a problem.

Student B: Well, there are a lot of strays that seem to have, uh, made the campus their home recently. You haven't noticed them? They can make a bit of a mess . . . and, uh, apparently the university decided something needed to be done when many of the flowers that were planted around campus a couple weeks ago – did you notice the new flowers?

Student A: Sure, they add a lot of color to the campus.

Student B: Well, it seems the cats dug a bunch of them up.

Student A: So what's the school's solution?

Student B: The suggestion is to bring in a pest control company. They'd try to capture the cats and take them away.

Student A: Seems like that could work.

Student B: I guess . . . But, um, I don't know. I don't know if I like the idea.

Student A: Why not?

Student B: Well, for one thing, it's not clear to me what would happen to the cats.

Student A: That's a good question. The article doesn't say anything about that?

Student B: No . . . I guess I really don't believe that the cats are such a problem.

Student A: Hmm.

Student B: They don't bother me, and to tell you the truth, I've seen some students putting out food for them, feeding them. So I think there are students who, uh, like them around, you know. I've read that there's a type of, uh, some kind of chemical that can be sprayed that keeps animals away from plants. If that was used, the school wouldn't have to worry about the cats digging up the new flowers.

Student A: I suppose. But, uh, I'm not sure I like the idea of chemicals being sprayed around campus.

Student B: Hmm . . . there could be a natural repellent. That would be better than a chemical one, right? I think I'm going to do some research on this, and then maybe I'll, uh, take my idea to the university office that's responsible for dealing with the problem.

21. Lesson 2—Speaking, Task 5 Prompt

Using points and examples from the conversation, describe two possible solutions for dealing with unwanted cats on the university campus. State which solution you prefer and why.

22. Lesson 2—Speaking, Task 5 Sample Response

One of the students explains that the university they are attending has a lot of stray cats around, on the campus. She says that the cats make a mess sometimes. An example of this is that the university planted some new flowers, and the cats dug the flowers up, so they made a mess by doing that. One solution to the problem would be to have a company catch the cats and take them away from the campus. I think the student doesn't really like this solution. She thinks the cats can just stay on the campus, but the university can spray something around to keep the cats away from the plants. I like the idea of deterring cats from entering an area by giving them a negative experience, but I don't know if it would really work. Besides, the cats can make a mess in other ways on the campus, and I think a lot of students wouldn't like to have the cats around. So even if there are a few students who don't mind the cats, I think the university should try to get rid of them just to make the campus a cleaner environment for all the students.

Chapter 3: **Lesson Set 3**
Theme—Education

This chapter covers the next lessons of reading, writing, listening, and speaking skills and strategies you will need to do your best on the TOEFL. Make sure to complete all the practice exercises and sample questions so that you can get the most out of this chapter.

LESSON 3—READING: TRANSITIONS, COHERENCE, AND COHESIVE DEVICES

In this third lesson, we will cover more reading skills and strategies that will help lead to success on test day. You will have the opportunity to review some of the strategies you learned in previous lessons as well as to learn about other question types found on the Reading section of the TOEFL. If you want to proceed with more reading strategies when you finish this lesson, turn to Lesson 4—Reading: More About Transitions in Chapter 4.

Transitions and Coherence

A *transition* from one paragraph to the next involves changing the reader's focus from one idea to another. In addition to using transitional expressions (*next, then, in addition, in conclusion*, etc.), you can make a transition flow more smoothly for the reader by using other techniques, like the following:

- repetition of a word
- use of a synonym of a word
- use of pronouns
- use of determiners (*the, this, that, these, those, their*, etc.)
- definition, development, or contrast of a key word

This is done both within a paragraph and between paragraphs to make the text flow more smoothly.

Look at some examples within a paragraph from the text that follows:

> The year 1880 heralded the first wave of **immigrants** to **the United States**. These immigrants, mostly European, continued to pour into the country in ever increasing numbers until World War I began, and multiplied once more after the war concluded. As time passed, the number of immigrants declined slowly, but more significantly, their

countries of origin changed. Since 1965, the majority of <u>immigrants</u> have come from Asia or South America. Yet one point in common for many of <u>these immigrants</u>, no matter where <u>they</u> were born or when <u>they</u> arrived, has been the language barrier. Without English ability, job availability has typically been limited to manual labor. To combat this problem, many types of English programs have been established.

Cohesive Devices

There are many different ways to smoothly transition between sentences when writing. These transitional words and phrases are called *cohesive devices*. The following sentences include commonly used cohesive devices.

Pronouns

Today's teachers are faced with a stark choice. **They** must decide whether to teach in a way that helps students pass standardized exams or teach in way that actually helps students learn.

Demonstrative pronouns

Speaking a foreign language is an enormous asset in the modern world. **This** is why so many junior high and elementary schools are now offering language classes.

Demonstrative adjectives

The teachers had an idea for an impromptu fundraiser. **This idea** was to auction off the children's artwork.

Articles

Many children find there are too many distractions in **the** typical classroom to be able to focus on their studies. **The** distractions that tend to be universal are desire to socialize with classmates or to play with toys they have brought from home.

Transitional phrases

Peers and older siblings have a major influence on how schoolchildren behave. **For instance**, young children often repeat bad words they hear from their friends or brothers and sisters.

Repetition, synonym, or slight variation of a word

To foster **healthy relationships** between children in a classroom, teachers should provide time for games and fun activities. Having **healthy relationships** with their peers helps children gain confidence useful in other parts of their lives.

OR

Before choosing a public or a private school for their children, parents should take into account the **cost**. The **price** of a private school is usually much higher than that of a public school.

OR

Many people feel that money is a panacea for our **educational problems**. Unfortunately, the **problems in education** we now face are too extensive to be solved by money alone.

Understanding the question types is important for knowing how and where you can apply your strategies. Keep reading to learn more.

Question Types

There are several question types on the Reading section of the TOEFL. We have already reviewed six types in Lessons 1 and 2. These are:

- Identifying the Main Idea
- Summarizing the Most Important Points
- Understanding Rhetorical Function
- Understanding Details
- Understanding Details as They Relate to the Main Idea (Multiple-Choice)
- Understanding Details as They Relate to the Main Idea (Schematic Table)

In this lesson we will review four more types:

- Inferring Word Meaning from Context
- Defining a Key Term
- Locating a Referent
- Understanding Coherence

It is critical to understand what each of these question types are testing as well as how they are presented.

Question Type 7—Inferring Word Meaning from Context

There are 3 passages in the Reading section of the TOEFL. Each passage is followed by 2 or 3 *word-meaning* questions.

Having an extensive vocabulary is extremely important in order to be able to understand the meaning of a text or lecture, but sometimes the meaning of new words can be inferred (guessed) from the context. Some typical techniques for inferring the meaning of words are:

- Looking for examples
- Looking for contrasting words or ideas
- Identifying synonyms or an explanation in other parts of the passage

Read the following passage and then look at three examples taken from it.

Homeschooling

American parents today are faced with a stark choice. The country's public schools are becoming more crowded, more violent, and less effective in preparing children for employment or college. Private schools may be too expensive or unavailable. To ensure that their children receive an adequate education, an increasing number of parents are simply teaching their children at home. While homeschooling offers many benefits to both child and parent, its three most important advantages are its flexibility of curriculum, its adaptability to different learning styles and speeds, and its more positive, supportive social environment.

First, a curriculum designed around the interests of a particular child is an enormous asset in education. If, for example, the child is interested in dinosaurs, that subject could be used to teach scientific concepts from geology, biology, or even history. Moreover, in the home environment, there is plenty of room for spontaneous discussion, impromptu field trips, and other learning experiences that classroom logistics make difficult, expensive, or challenging. Homeschooling puts the child's natural curiosity to use, limited only by the imagination of the child and parent.

Furthermore, the home classroom adapts to individual learning styles. Children can move through the material at a rate which challenges them positively. In the conventional classroom, most lessons are aimed at the middle level of ability. Thus, some students are rushed along much faster than optimal, or faster than necessary for satisfactory results, while others yawn or find distractions because the pace is too slow. Nor can a teacher pay much attention to any single student in a classroom of thirty or discover how individual students learn best. But the parent at home, who knows the child better than any teacher, can readily make adjustments to content, teaching strategy, or pace, as the child requires.

The final important advantage of homeschooling lies in the socialization children are able to receive. Home-schooled children are less subject to the stresses and pressures experienced by conventional students who spend six, seven, or eight hours a day with their peers. They are less likely to become involved with gangs or drugs. On the other hand, home-schooled children spend much more time in the company of appropriate role models: parents, other adults, and older siblings. In this environment, they are better able to learn from actual life situations, and how to interact with people of all ages. In particular, homeschooling fosters healthy family relationships because both children and their parents are able to play larger and more complete roles in one another's lives.

Though there are important advantages to homeschooling, there are also certain disadvantages, which a parent considering this option should take into account. The first of these is simply a practical one. If both parents work out of the home, care must be found for young children while the parents are away. Indeed, working parents may be unable to find the time to provide schooling for their children at all, and hiring a tutor to fill that role is an expensive proposition. Second, parents may be attacked for choosing what many people feel is an antisocial or elitist option—for thinking that their children are better than anyone else's, for refusing to participate in an important social institution, or even for trying to destroy public schools by depriving them of students and funding. Third, not all parents will be comfortable in the role of teacher. They may not have the patience required, the basic knowledge of the material, nor the energy to encourage and motivate their children when necessary.

Homeschooling is not a panacea for the institutional deficiencies found in American public schools; these can only be addressed through a large-scale restructuring of public education policies nationwide. Nevertheless, homeschooling offers a number of significant advantages to parents and children. And it works. Home-schooled children, on average, place in the 87th percentile on standardized exams—the national average is the 50th percentile—and have been admitted to all major universities and military academies in the country. Clearly, homeschooling is a serious, positive alternative for motivated parents and their children.

Determine which inference techniques can be used to find the meanings of the words in bold in the following sentences, and then write a synonym or definition for each.

1. First, a **curriculum** designed around the interests of a particular child is an enormous asset in education. If, for example, the child is interested in dinosaurs, that subject could be used to teach scientific concepts from geology, biology, or even history.

   Inference technique:

   _____

   Synonym:

   _____

   Definition:

   _____

2. Thus, some students are rushed along much faster than optimal for them, while others yawn or find **distractions** because the pace is too slow.

   Inference technique:

   _____

   Synonym:

   _____

   Definition:

   _____

3. The country's public schools are becoming more crowded, more violent, and less effective in preparing children for employment or college. Private schools may be too expensive or unavailable.... Homeschooling is not a panacea for the institutional **deficiencies** found in American public schools; these can only be addressed through a large-scale restructuring of public education policies nationwide.

Inference technique:

_____

Synonym:

_____

Definition:

_____

Answers

1. Inference technique: identifying synonyms or and explanation in other parts of the passage
Synonym: set of courses
Definition: All of the subjects taught in a school situation

2. Thus, some students are rushed along much faster than optimal for them, while others yawn or find **distractions** because the pace is too slow.
Inference technique: looking for contrasting words or ideas
Synonym: diversion
Definition: things that take attention away from something else

3. The country's public schools are becoming more crowded, more violent, and less effective in preparing children for employment or college. Private schools may be too expensive or unavailable.... Homeschooling is not a panacea for the institutional **deficiencies** found in American public schools; these can only be addressed through a large-scale restructuring of public education policies nationwide.
Inference technique: looking for examples
Synonym: shortcomings
Definition: things or situations that do not meet set standards

Now, using the inference strategies you have just practiced, go back to the passage on homeschooling and answer the questions that follow.

The word **conventional** in the passage is closest in meaning to

- Ⓐ beneficial
- Ⓑ antiquated
- Ⓒ traditional
- Ⓓ intermediate

The sentence in which *conventional* appears and the sentences in the remainder of that paragraph present information that is in contrast with the ideas of homeschooling, which is not a conventional type of schooling. This context provides the clue that *conventional* is closest in meaning to *traditional*, so choice (C) is correct. Choice (A) is a distracter directed at a test taker who doesn't understand that the sentence in which *conventional* appears begins the contrast with homeschooling. Such a test taker might see a connection in meaning between the word *positively* in the passage and the word *beneficial* and choose this answer. In a similar way, choice (D) is a distracter directed at a test taker who sees a connection between the phrase *middle level of ability* and the word *intermediate*. The passage states that conventional teaching aims at the middle level of ability, but it should not be inferred from this that *conventional* means middle or intermediate. Finally, the meanings of both *antiquated* and *conventional* relate to past time period, but otherwise the meanings of the two words are not close, so choice (B) is also a distracter.

The word **proposition** in the passage is closest in meaning to

- Ⓐ bill
- Ⓑ plan
- Ⓒ education
- Ⓓ opportunity

In the context of the passage and sentence, the word *proposition* is closest in meaning to the word *plan*, which is choice (B). The topic of the paragraph where *proposition* appears is the disadvantages of homeschooling. One of those disadvantages is finding time to do the actual homeschooling, especially for working parents. The passage then talks about one way or choice or *proposition* to work around that problem: hiring a tutor. Choice (A) might be attractive to you if you see the word *expensive* and mistakenly think that *proposition* is a synonym for *cost*. Choice (C) is related to the overall topic, so it is attractive. Choice (D) would be an attractive distracter to you if you do not understand the topic of the passage, which is negative: the disadvantages of homeschooling. The word *opportunity* generally refers to positive chances and therefore does not fit the sentence where the tested word appears.

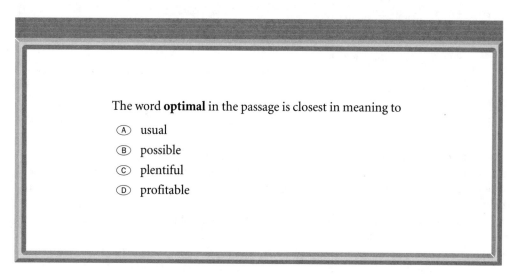

The word **optimal** in the passage is closest in meaning to

- (A) usual
- (B) possible
- (C) plentiful
- (D) profitable

The word that is closest in meaning to *optimal* as it is used in the passage is *profitable* (D). *Optimal* means the best or the most suitable, so it has a positive meaning. *Profitable* also is positive; it means causing a profit (making money) or causing a good result. One of the keys to understanding this term is in the sentence that precedes it: "In the conventional classroom, most lessons are aimed at the middle level of ability." This means that the students who are smarter or less smart than average are at a disadvantage. They will not receive the best results. Another key to understanding this term is in the explanatory phrase that follows it: "or faster than necessary for satisfactory results." The context provides clues that "faster than optimal" means "faster than is good," and (D) is the choice that is closest in meaning to *good*. None of the other answer choices can be called a synonym of *good,* so they are not as close in meaning to *optimal* as *profitable* is.

Question Type 8—Defining a Key Term

There are 3 passages in the Reading section of the TOEFL. Each passage is followed by 0 or 1 *term-definition* question.

The best way of guessing the meaning of a new word or phrase when it is a key term—that is to say, it is a term which is important to the main idea of the passage—is to identify its definition somewhere in the passage. A key term definition will often be presented in one of the four following ways:

Between commas

Homeschooling is not a panacea**, or a perfect solution,** for the institutional deficiencies found in American public schools.

Between dashes

Homeschooling is not a panacea**—not a perfect solution—**for the institutional deficiencies found in American public schools.

After the verbs "to be" or "to mean" or the phrase "defined as"

Homeschooling is not a panacea, **which means a perfect solution**, for the institutional deficiencies found in American public schools.

After phrases such as "in other words" or "in short"

Homeschooling is not a panacea for the institutional deficiencies found in American public schools. **In other words**, homeschooling is not the perfect solution.

Look at the three following sentences from the passage. Rewrite each sentence by adding a definition of the phrase in bold using one of these four ways for presenting definitions.

1. Moreover, in the home environment, there is plenty of room for spontaneous discussion, impromptu field trips, and other learning experiences that **classroom logistics** make difficult, expensive, or challenging.

    _____

    _____

2. On the other hand, home-schooled children spend much more time in the company of appropriate **role models**: parents, other adults, and older siblings.

    _____

    _____

3. Homeschooling is not a panacea for the institutional deficiencies found in American public schools; these can only be addressed through a **large-scale restructuring** of public education policies nationwide.

    _____

    _____

Answers

Answers will vary.

1. Moreover, in the home environment, there is plenty of room for spontaneous discussion, impromptu field trips, and other learning experiences that **classroom logistics** make difficult, expensive, or challenging. **In other words, a parent would not have to make travel arrangements for an entire class of children the way a teacher would.**

2. On the other hand, home-schooled children spend much more time in the company of appropriate **role models, meaning parents, other adults, and older siblings.**

3. Homeschooling is not a panacea for the institutional deficiencies found in American public schools; these can only be addressed through **a large-scale restructuring, or system-wide change,** of public education policies nationwide.

Using the contextual definition strategies you have just practiced, answer the questions that follow.

> Based on the information in paragraph 4, which of the following best explains the term **conventional students**?
>
> (A) Students who dislike homeschooling
>
> (B) Students in public or private schools
>
> (C) Students who experience less stress and pressure
>
> (D) Students whose parents want them to spend 6, 7, or 8 hours a day with their peers

The key to answering this question lies in understanding the term *peers*. The sentence tells us "conventional students spend six, seven, or eight hours a day with their peers." If you know that *peers* means people who are the same age, then the answer is clear: choice (B). This is because only children who are in regular schools, public or private, spend that many hours every day with other children. But even if you don't know the meaning of *peer*, understanding the overall topic of the paragraph will help lead to the correct choice. The topic of the paragraph is a comparison of how children who are homeschooled and children who aren't, are socialized. Children who aren't homeschooled are children who are spending six to eight hours a day with other children: children in public or private schools. There is no evidence to support choice (A); it is just repeating the term *homeschooling* from the passage. Choice (C) repeats information from the sentence and would be attractive to you if you do not look carefully back at the passage to see that it is homeschooled children who are subject to less stress and pressure, not the children in schools. Choice (D) is repeating information from the passage but there is no evidence to support it.

> Based on the information in paragraph 5, which of the following best explains the term **elitist option**?
>
> (A) A refusal to be kind to anyone else
>
> (B) A type of schooling now popular with many parents
>
> (C) A choice made because you think you are better than others
>
> (D) An important institution that teaches children socialization skills

This paragraph is talking about disadvantages of homeschooling. One stated disadvantage is that other people or parents might think that parents who homeschool are choosing an elitist option. The key to answering this term comes in the phrase that immediately follows the tested term. It tells you that this means that the parents think "their children are better than anyone else's," so choice (C) is the best answer. Choice (A) will be attractive to you if you see the word *antisocial* and know that it means not being social and mistakenly think *antisocial* and *elitist* have similar meanings. There is no evidence to support choice (B); it is simply repeating *schooling* and *parents*. Choice (D) is repeating *institution* and a form of the word *social*.

Question Type 9—Locating a Referent

There are 3 passages on the Reading section of the TOEFL. Each passage is generally followed by 1 *referent* question.

On the TOEFL, it will not only be necessary for you to determine the meaning of words in a passage, but also to locate *referents*, that is, another word or phrase used to refer to a word. All types of pronouns can be used to refer back to a word, phrase, or idea. Often, as you've already seen, these referents are used to create smooth transitions between sentences. Since there are usually many word, phrases, and ideas in a sentence, it can be difficult to locate which one the pronoun refers to. Some techniques that may help you include:

- Eliminating choices that do not correspond in number or gender
- Replacing the pronoun with the choices and check for meaning or logical words
- Looking for words or phrases that have similar grammatical functions

Look at the following sentence from the homeschooling passage.

> Homeschooling is not a panacea for the institutional deficiencies found in American public schools; **these** can only be addressed through a large-scale restructuring of public education policies nationwide.

The pronoun *these* is plural. Therefore, we can automatically eliminate the first two choices, *homeschooling* and *panacea,* which are singular nouns. *Schools* is a plural noun, but *schools* cannot be addressed. *Problems*, *people*, *an audience*, *deficiencies*, and *questions* are all words that can be found with the word *addressed*.

> Home-schooled children are less subject to the stresses and pressures experienced by conventional students who spend six, seven, or eight hours a day with their peers. **They** are less likely to become involved with gangs or drugs.

The pronoun *they* is plural. However, all of the answer choices are plural, so this does not help us eliminate any answer choices. The two remaining techniques can help us to identify the correct answer. First, the function of *they* in this sentence is as a subject. The correct answer, *homeschooled children*, is also the subject of its sentence. Second, *stresses and pressures* are not people. Thus, they cannot become involved in gangs or drugs. Also, because of the general meaning of the sentence, which is that home-schooled children have fewer stresses and pressures than conventional students, it is unlikely that *conventional students* or their *peers* are *less* likely to become involved in gangs or drugs.

Now, look at the sentences that follow and circle the word or phrase to which the underlined pronouns refer. When you are finished, explain how you determined your answers.

1. Though there are important advantages to homeschooling, there are also certain disadvantages, which a parent considering this option should take into account. The first of <u>these</u> is simply a practical one.

2. Second, parents may be attacked for choosing what many people feel is an antisocial or elitist option—for thinking that their children are better than anyone else's, for refusing to participate in an important social institution, or even for trying to destroy public schools by depriving <u>them</u> of students and funding.

_____

_____

_____

_____

_____

_____

Answers

1. Though there are important advantages to homeschooling, there are also certain disadvantages, which a parent considering this option should take into account. The first of <u>these</u> is simply a practical one.

The sentence begins with *Though*, which means that *advantages* are being contrasted with *disadvantages*. *These* is the subject of the sentence, and *disadvantages* is also the subject of its sentence. *These* is plural and cannot match *parent*, which is singular. *These* must refer to the other plural noun *disadvantages*.

2. Second, parents may be attacked for choosing what many people feel is an antisocial or elitist option—for thinking that their children are better than anyone else's, for refusing to participate in an important social institution, or even for trying to destroy public schools by depriving <u>them</u> of students and funding.

The prepositional phrase "by depriving them" directly follows the subject "schools." The word "them" is a noun that refers back the head noun "schools." Nouns that refer back to other nouns almost always refer back to the noun that is closest, and do not refer back to nouns beyond a sentence pause or break, such as that indicated by a comma. To double-check the answer, think about the meaning: ask yourself what would logically be deprived of students and funding. "Schools" is the only noun that makes sense.

Now look again at the passage on homeschooling and answer the questions that follow. Use the referents strategies you just learned.

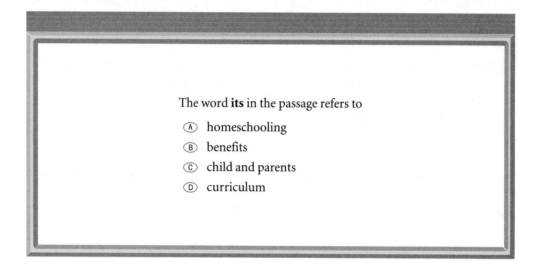

The possessive pronoun *its* is singular, therefore its referent must also be singular. Choice (B) is wrong because it is plural. Choice (C) is wrong because it refers to several people, and therefore is also plural. Choice (D) is singular, but it occurs in the sentence after the pronoun *it*. Generally, *it* is used to refer to a noun that has already been mentioned.

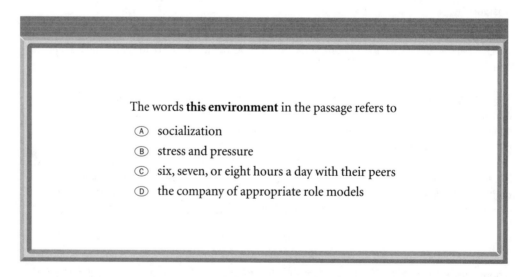

Choice (D) is correct. An *environment* is something that one can be *in*. The previous sentence stated that children are "in the company of appropriate role models." Choice (A) is incorrect because it is not an environment. Choice (B) is incorrect because it is not an environment; however, the phrase could describe an attribute or quality of an environment. But one is generally "under" stress and pressure, not "in." Choice (C) is incorrect because it does not describe an environment, rather, it describes a condition.

Question Type 10—Understanding Coherence

There are 3 passages on the Reading section of the TOEFL. Each passage is followed by 1 coherence question.

You have learned about cohesive devices such as pronouns, demonstrative adjectives, and transitional phrases. These devices are essential to questions on the TOEFL that require you to indicate where a sentence might best fit in the passage.

Review the homeschooling passage again.

Homeschooling

American parents today are faced with a stark choice. The country's public schools are becoming more crowded, more violent, and less effective in preparing children for employment or college. Private schools may be too expensive or unavailable. To ensure that their children receive an adequate education, an increasing number of parents are simply teaching their children at home. While homeschooling offers many benefits to both child and parent, its three most important advantages are its flexibility of curriculum, its adaptability to different learning styles and speeds, and its more positive, supportive social environment.

First, a curriculum designed around the interests of a particular child is an enormous asset in education. If, for example, the child is interested in dinosaurs, that subject could be used to teach scientific concepts from geology, biology, or even history. Moreover, in the home environment, there is plenty of room for spontaneous discussion, impromptu field trips, and other learning experiences that classroom logistics make difficult, expensive, or challenging. Homeschooling puts the child's natural curiosity to use, limited only by the imagination of the child and parent.

Furthermore, the home classroom adapts to individual learning styles. Children can move through the material at a rate which challenges them positively. In the conventional classroom, most lessons are aimed at the middle level of ability. Thus, some students are rushed along much faster than optimal, or faster than necessary for satisfactory results, while others yawn or find distractions because the pace is too slow. Nor can a teacher pay much attention to any single student in a classroom of thirty or discover how individual students learn best. But the parent at home, who knows the child better than any teacher, can readily make adjustments to content, teaching strategy, or pace, as the child requires.

The final important advantage of homeschooling lies in the socialization children are able to receive. Home-schooled children are less subject to the stresses and pressures experienced by conventional students who spend six, seven, or eight hours a day with their peers. They are less likely to become involved with gangs or drugs. On the other hand, home-schooled children spend much more time in the company of appropriate role models: parents, other adults, and older siblings. In this environment, they are better able to learn from actual life situations, and how to interact with people of all ages. In particular, homeschooling fosters healthy family relationships because both children and their parents are able to play larger and more complete roles in one another's lives.

Though there are important advantages to homeschooling, there are also certain disadvantages, which a parent considering this option should take into account. The first of these is simply a practical one. If both parents work out of the home, care must be found for young children while the parents are away. Indeed, working parents may be unable to find the time to provide schooling for their children at all, and hiring a tutor to fill that role is an expensive proposition. Second, parents may be attacked for choosing what many people feel is an antisocial or elitist option—for thinking that their children are better than anyone else's, for refusing to participate in an important social institution, or even for trying to destroy public schools by depriving them of students and funding. Third, not all parents will be comfortable in the role of teacher. They may not have the patience required, the basic knowledge of the material, nor the energy to encourage and motivate their children when necessary.

Homeschooling is not a panacea for the institutional deficiencies found in American public schools; these can only be addressed through a large-scale restructuring of public education policies nationwide. Nevertheless, homeschooling offers a number of significant advantages to parents and children. And it works. Home-schooled children, on average, place in the 87th percentile on standardized exams—the national average is the 50th percentile—and have been admitted to all major universities and military academies in the country. Clearly, homeschooling is a serious, positive alternative for motivated parents and their children.

Now look at the four sentences that follow and choose a place in the passage you think they might best fit. Explain your answers and list which cohesive devices helped you make your choice.

1. This type of program is aptly named "homeschooling."

    _____

    _____

    _____

    _____

    _____

    _____

2. If the child prefers music, songs could be adapted to teach the required content.

    _____

    _____

    _____

    _____

    _____

    _____

3. The typical American schoolteacher is hard-pressed enough just to get through the day's basic curriculum.

   _____

   _____

   _____

   _____

   _____

4. In fact, many parents of home-schooled children admit that they don't think homeschooling is the only choice for their children, simply the best option currently available.

   _____

   _____

   _____

   _____

   _____

Answers

1. This type of program is aptly named "homeschooling."

This sentence is simple and declarative. It needs to be connected to something in the passage that offers an explanation of what homeschooling is. As the topic of the passage is homeschooling, it is likely that this sentence belongs somewhere in the beginning of the passage, probably before the first time "homeschooling" is used in a sentence. The third sentence in the first paragraph offers an description of homeschooling, and the word first appears in the passage in the next sentence. The sentence *This type of program is aptly named homeschooling* should be placed between sentence three and sentence four of the first paragraph.

2. If the child prefers music, songs could be adapted to teach the required content.

The sentence to be inserted is an example of how the presentation of *required content* can be *adapted* to suit a child's preferences. Paragraph two talks about designing curriculum around the interests of a particular child. The second sentence is about adapting scientific concepts for a child who likes dinosaurs, and is grammatically similar to the sentence to be inserted. Therefore the sentence can be inserted between the second and third sentences of paragraph two.

3. The typical American schoolteacher is hard-pressed enough just to get through the day's basic curriculum.

This sentence describes a regular classroom teacher and curriculum, which contrast with the topic of the passage. The sentence likely belongs in a paragraph that compares the curriculum and teaching of homeschooling to that of public schooling in some way. The sentence says that a public school teacher finds it difficult just to complete the content they have to teach—which implies that they do not have time for other activities that a homeschool parent might. Paragraph three describes how a homeschool parent can adapt curriculum to a student, while public school teachers cannot pay attention to any single student. Sentence five states that a teacher cannot pay individual attention to any students, and the last sentence of the paragraph describes how a parent can adjust content to meet a child's needs. In order to complete the comparison, the sentence can be inserted before the last sentence of paragraph three.

4. In fact, many parents of home-schooled children admit that they don't think homeschooling is the only choice for their children, simply the best option currently available.

This sentence begins with *in fact*, so it must demonstrate something stated in the sentence before it. The sentence talks about how parents feel that homeschooling is *not* the *only choice*, so the sentences around it discuss parents' feelings and options to homeschooling. Paragraph six is the concluding paragraph, and it talks about how homeschooling is *not the panacea for institutional deficiencies*, meaning that it is not

Using the coherence strategies you have just practiced, answer the following TOEFL questions based once again on the homeschooling passage.

Homeschooling

American parents today are faced with a stark choice. The country's public schools are becoming more crowded, more violent, and less effective in preparing children for employment or college. Private schools may be too expensive or unavailable. To ensure that their children receive an adequate education, an increasing number of parents are simply teaching their children at home. While homeschooling offers many benefits to both child and parent, its three most important advantages are its flexibility of curriculum, its adaptability to different learning styles and speeds, and its more positive, supportive social environment.

First, a curriculum designed around the interests of a particular child is an enormous asset in education. If, for example, the child is interested in dinosaurs, that subject could be used to teach scientific concepts from geology, biology, or even history. Moreover, in the home environment, there is plenty of room for spontaneous discussion, impromptu field trips, and other learning experiences that classroom logistics make difficult, expensive, or challenging. Homeschooling puts the child's natural curiosity to use, limited only by the imagination of the child and parent.

Furthermore, the home classroom adapts to individual learning styles. Children can move through the material at a rate which challenges them positively. In the conventional classroom, most lessons are aimed at the middle level of ability. Thus, some students are rushed along much faster than optimal, or faster than necessary for satisfactory results, while others yawn or find distractions because the pace is too slow. Nor can a teacher pay much attention to any single student in a classroom of thirty or discover how individual students learn best. But the parent at home, who knows the child better than any teacher, can readily make adjustments to content, teaching strategy, or pace, as the child requires.

The final important advantage of homeschooling lies in the socialization children are able to receive. ☐ [A] Home-schooled children are less subject to the stresses and pressures experienced by conventional students who spend six, seven, or eight hours a day with their peers. ☐ [B] They are less likely to become involved with gangs or drugs. ☐ [C] On the other hand, home-schooled children spend much more time in the company of appropriate role models: parents, other adults, and older siblings. In this environment, they are better able to learn from actual life situations, and how to interact with people of all ages. ☐ [D] In particular, homeschooling fosters healthy family relationships because both children and their parents are able to play larger and more complete roles in one another's lives.

Though there are important advantages to homeschooling, there are also certain disadvantages, which a parent considering this option should take into account. The first of these is simply a practical one. If both parents work out of the home, care must be found for young children while the parents are away. Δ [A] Indeed, working parents may be unable to find the time to provide schooling for their children at all, and hiring a tutor to fill that role is an expensive proposition. Δ [B] Second, parents may be attacked for choosing what many people feel is an antisocial or elitist option—for thinking that their children are better than anyone else's, for refusing to participate in an important social institution, or even for trying to destroy public schools by depriving them of students and funding. Δ [C] Third, not all parents will be comfortable in the role of teacher. They may not have the patience required, the basic knowledge of the material, nor the energy to encourage and motivate their children when necessary. Δ [D]

Homeschooling is not a panacea for the institutional deficiencies found in American public schools; these can only be addressed through a large-scale restructuring of public education policies nationwide. Nevertheless, homeschooling offers a number of significant advantages to parents and children. And it works. Home-schooled children, on average, place in the 87th percentile on standardized exams—the national average is the 50th percentile—and have been admitted to all major universities and military academies in the country. Clearly, homeschooling is a serious, positive alternative for motivated parents and their children.

Look at the four squares ☐ that indicate where the following sentence could be added to the passage.

In contrast to the idea that many people have about homeschooled children, they do not actually suffer from less interaction with children their own age.

Where would the sentence best fit?

Ⓐ

Ⓑ

Ⓒ

Ⓓ

Choice (A) is incorrect. It is attractive because what follows does not deal with interacting with students. Choice (B) is incorrect. It is unattractive because the sentences before and after the insertion point do not deal with children suffering from less interaction with peers. Choice (C) is incorrect. It is not attractive, because it is contrasting a point ("On the other hand ..."), and the sentence to be added is also contrasting a point ("In contrast ..."). Choice (D) is correct. This is the best place because the previous sentence is addressing the topic of interacting with people. What follows lends support to the idea expressed in the sentence to be inserted.

Look at the four triangles Δ that indicate where the following sentence could be added to the passage.

Yet another disadvantage of homeschooling is simply the fact that children in this environment tend to be more sheltered, more shocked when they face people or problems from the "real world."

Where would the sentence best fit?

Ⓐ

Ⓑ

Ⓒ

Ⓓ

Notice the structure of the paragraph: It is making a series of points, which are cued with "Second, ..." and "Third, ...". When you see a serial structure like this, you can often eliminate choices. The sentence after (B) begins "Second, ..." and the sentence before (C) begins "Third, ..." Obviously, nothing can be inserted between these. Eliminate choice (C) immediately. If there's a "Second,..." there must be a "First, ..." or an equivalent expression somewhere. The sentence to be inserted begins "Yet another ..."

Does that mean "first"? No. Looking further back in the paragraph, we can see a reference to "The first of these is, ..." occurring before choice (A). Therefore, eliminate choice (A). Can "Yet another ..." be inserted between "The first of these is ..." and "Second, ..."? No. Eliminate choice (B). With (A), (B), and (C) eliminated, the correct choice must be (D). To check, review the logic of the series: "The first of these is, ...", "Second, ...", "Third, ...", "Yet another ...".

Now that you have reviewed some reading strategies, let's move on to some writing strategies.

LESSON 3—WRITING: THE PERSUASIVE ESSAY

In this lesson, we will cover more writing skills and strategies that will help lead to success on test day. You will have the opportunity to review some of the strategies you learned in previous lessons as well as to learn about other information regarding the Writing section of the TOEFL. If you want to proceed with more writing strategies when you finish this lesson, turn to Lesson 4—Writing: Compare and Contrast Essays in Chapter 4.

Recognizing Persuasive Essay Prompts

One of the essay types that may appear on the TOEFL is the persuasive essay. In a persuasive essay, you will be asked to choose a position on a particular issue and attempt to persuade your audience to agree with the position you've chosen. The structure of a persuasive essay is superficially similar to other essays you may write for the TOEFL; that is, a persuasive essay requires an introduction, body paragraphs, and a conclusion, just like other essays. The difference is that in a persuasive essay, you will not simply be reporting facts; instead, you will be using facts and other information that you have carefully chosen to support your opinion.

Generating Ideas for a Persuasive Essay

Once you have read the prompt carefully, and have established that you are being asked to write a persuasive essay, what comes next? What if you have never thought about this topic and have no opinion about it? What strategies can you use to overcome these obstacles and write a great essay? Keep reading to explore several strategies for generating ideas about a topic and formulating those ideas into a well-organized persuasive essay.

Choosing a Point of View

Before you can even start writing, you must decide which point of view you will support in your essay. Your best choice will probably be the position that is *easiest to defend*, not necessarily the one that you personally agree with. On the TOEFL, you have a limited amount of time, so it is important to make the most of what you have.

Before you decide which position to support, carefully consider both sides of the issue. Once you have done this, choosing a position may be a great deal easier. One strategy to help you is to make a list in which you make an inventory of all the ideas you have about the topic. What facts and arguments favor side A? What information and arguments, on the other hand, support side B? After you have completed the list, it will be much easier to see which position is the strongest and the easiest to support in your essay.

An alternative to listing is freewriting. Remember from Lesson 1—Writing: The Descriptive Essay that when freewriting, you write continuously for several minutes, noting down every idea or thought about the topic that comes into your mind. Again, when you have finished freewriting, the relative strengths of the possible positions on the topic should be clearer, and you will be able to choose the best one to support in your essay.

Choosing a Point of View Practice

Look at the following prompts. Choose the prompt that seems the most interesting to you.

> Many people feel that it is a responsibility of the national government to provide financial support for the arts. Do you agree that funding artistic expression is a governmental responsibility? Why or why not? Provide reasons and details in your response.

> It is a common theme in science fiction to describe human colonization of the moon. Do you think that such colonization is a worthwhile endeavor? Explain why or why not.

> In your opinion, is money the key to happiness? Provide examples and details to support your answer.

Now carefully consider all sides of the issue it discusses, and make a note of each idea, argument, or fact you can think of related to this issue. List them in the following chart:

Side A	Side B

Answers

Answers will vary, but here is one example based on the prompt of government funding of the arts.

Side A: *Government SHOULD*	**Side B:** *Government SHOULDN'T*
Many people with good ideas don't have enough money to make them happen	*Government is responsible for providing basic necessities for everyone who needs them*
Children need to be exposed to music, art and theater in order to have a quality education	*Schools don't have enough money to provide children with a good basic math, reading and writing skills*
Arts are an important part of what makes culture. Government should provide funding to things that advance culture	*Art is subjective. Government should not spend money on things that do not directly benefit a majority of its taxpayers*

Outlining a Persuasive Essay

Once you've brainstormed the topic, chosen your position, written your thesis statement, and decided which arguments to use to support your position, you're ready for the next step in preparing your essay: organizing it. Before you begin to actually write your essay, you should always have a clear idea how you will present your ideas. An excellent technique to help you with this is to prepare an outline.

Remember, it is not essential that the outline be extensively detailed. It should contain enough information to keep you on track, but not so much that you cut into the time you need for actually writing the essay.

Here is a model outline for a persuasive essay.

I. Introductory paragraph

    A. Hook: a device for capturing reader's attention

    B. Background information: to help reader understand topic

    C. Thesis statement: clear statement of your position

II. First supporting argument: strong reason supporting your position

    A. Topic sentence: general factual sentence introducing paragraph

    B. Facts, examples, arguments to support and prove argument

III. Second supporting argument (as in II)

    A. Topic sentence

    B. Facts, examples, arguments

IV. Third supporting argument (as in II and III)

    A. Topic sentence

    B. Facts, examples, arguments

V. Conclusion

    A. Reviews important points from the discussion

    B. Clearly states what lesson or message should be taken from the essay

Writing the Introduction to a Persuasive Essay

The introduction of a persuasive essay has a more important role than any other part of the essay. It should do four things.

- **First, a good introduction should attract the reader's attention as quickly as possible, ideally within its first sentence or two.** This is called a hook. (Remember this from Lesson 1—Writing: The Descriptive Essay?) A good hook can take many forms: an anecdote, a provocative rhetorical question (a question directed to the reader), an interesting fact, or a strong, clearly opinionated claim about the topic. Any of these strategies, if carefully applied, will make an effective hook.

- **Second, the introduction should provide useful background information about the topic that the essay discusses.** You must choose this information so as to cast the most favorable light on the point of view presented in the essay. If you intend to propose and support a position, you will want to present from the start the information or conditions that clearly demonstrate that a decision or course of action is necessary. (Later, in the body, you will demonstrate that the opinion or course of action *you* are recommending is the best one.) Moreover, it is helpful if you can provide enough background information to enable your reader to understand the topic.

- **Third, your introduction should make clear to the reader what feelings you have on the topic. Your opinion or recommendation must be clearly stated.** The best way to do this is with a thesis statement, a strongly worded statement of your position on the topic. Generally, this will be the last sentence of the introduction.

- **Finally, your introduction should include a reference to the main arguments you intend to mention in the essay to support your position, in which you list these arguments in the same order you will be presenting them in the body.** This forecasting will help your reader understand how your essay is organized and how your arguments will be constructed. Forecasting is either done within the thesis statement or in another sentence immediately following the thesis.

Here is a summary of what the introductory paragraph of a persuasive essay should include:

- a hook, to attract the reader's attention
- background information, to set the stage for your discussion
- a thesis statement, which clearly states your opinion or recommendation
- forecasting, a brief listing of all the main arguments your essay will discuss

Introduction Practice

Read the introduction to the model essay, "Homeschooling." After the essay, describe how this introduction does or does not accomplish the four essential tasks of a persuasive essay introduction.

Homeschooling (introduction)

American parents today are faced with a stark choice. The country's public schools are becoming more crowded, more violent, and less effective in preparing children for employment or college. Private schools may be too expensive or unavailable. To ensure that their children receive an adequate education, an increasing number of parents are simply teaching their children at home. While homeschooling offers many benefits to both child and parent, its three most important advantages are its flexibility of curriculum, its adaptability to different learning styles and speeds, and its more positive, supportive social environment.

Hook:

_____

_____

Background:

_____

_____

Thesis statement:

_____

_____

Forecasting:

_____

_____

Answers

Answers will vary slightly, but here are some examples.

Hook: Parents faced with a stark choice
Background: Public schools too crowded and less effective, private schools too expensive
Thesis statement: Homeschooling offers many benefits to child and parent
Forecasting: advantages are flexibility, adaptability, and supportive social environment

Writing Thesis Statements and Topic Sentences for a Persuasive Essay

The thesis statement of a persuasive essay is different from those you may write in some other essay types in one important way: it must be a firm statement of *opinion*, not simply a fact—it must reflect the judgment you have made about the topic, and must identify the point of view or recommendation you are putting forward for the reader's consideration. This opinion is what the rest of the essay will be devoted to defending.

Remember, when you are writing a persuasive essay on the TOEFL, choose the point of view that is *easiest* for you to defend with the information you have available. This might *not* be the position you personally favor. Without solid arguments to support your thesis, you have no persuasive essay. It is also important to remember that there is no *right* or *wrong* position on any TOEFL essay question. The test evaluators are only interested in how well you can present and defend your opinion, not which side you choose.

A good way to write your thesis statement is to read the original question or claim closely, and then carefully paraphrase it in a new sentence that also expresses the opinion you have about that question or claim. Remember, to paraphrase is to rewrite the original idea in your own words, without changing the meaning.

Let's consider an example. Suppose you are given the following prompt:

> Do you agree that schools should make daily exercise a part of their curriculum? Explain why or why not.

In response, you could write a thesis statement like one of the following:

- I feel strongly that regular exercise should be a component of any child's education for the following reasons: exercise reduces stress, prevents weight gain, and improves academic performance.
- Because habitual exercise reduces stress, prevents weight gain, and improves academic performance, such exercise should be made a part of any school's curriculum.

A carefully written thesis statement offers three benefits. First, and most importantly, such a thesis statement will help prevent you from accidentally wandering from the precise topic the prompt is asking you to address; straying from the topic could lead to a substantial reduction in the score you receive for your essay. Second, a good thesis statement will clearly tell the reader where you stand on the issue, and how you will defend that position in the body of the essay. Third, good paraphrasing will give you an opportunity to demonstrate your knowledge of English.

Writing Topic Sentences

Each body paragraph of your persuasive essay should begin with a sentence that clearly identifies the argument that paragraph will make in support of the essay's thesis: its topic sentence. You might remember the discussion of the topic sentence in Lesson 2—Writing: Responding to a Reading Passage and Lecture. If not, a brief review follows.

A topic sentence should work like a good umbrella: it should cover everything found underneath it. That is, the topic sentence should be general enough to include all the information you wish to include in that paragraph. By the same token, the paragraph should include no information that is outside the general topic introduced by the topic sentence.

Another important feature of a good topic sentence is the transition words or phrases that indicate the progression of ideas in your essay and the logical connections between them. There are several ways you can do this. Using words like *first*, *second*, or *finally* tells your reader that you are leaving one idea and going on to the next. Words like *moreover* and *furthermore* tell your reader that you are about to make another point that is connected to the previous topic. Phrases and words like *on the other hand*, *however*, and *by contrast* tell the reader that you are about to discuss an idea that contrasts with or opposes the previous idea.

Thesis Statement and Topic Sentence Practice

Read the body of the homeschooling essay. Pay close attention to the topic sentence of each paragraph, and answer the questions that follow.

Homeschooling (body)

First, a curriculum designed around the interests of a particular child is an enormous asset in education. If, for example, the child is interested in dinosaurs, that subject could be used to teach scientific concepts from geology, biology, or even history. Moreover, in the home environment, there is plenty of room for spontaneous discussion, impromptu field trips, and other learning experiences that classroom logistics make difficult, expensive, or challenging. Homeschooling puts the child's natural curiosity to use, limited only by the imagination of the child and parent.

Furthermore, the home classroom adapts to individual learning styles. Children can move through the material at a rate which challenges them positively. In the conventional classroom, most lessons are aimed at the middle level of ability. Thus, some students are dragged along much faster than optimal for them, while others yawn or find distractions. Nor can a teacher pay much attention to any single student in a classroom of thirty, or discover how individual students learn best. But the parent at home, who knows the child better than any teacher, can readily make adjustments to content, teaching strategy, or pace, as the child requires.

The final important advantage of homeschooling lies in the socialization children are able to receive. Home-schooled children are less subject to the stresses and pressures experienced by conventional students who spend six, seven, or eight hours a day with their peers. They are less likely to become involved with gangs or drugs. On the other hand, home-schooled children spend much more time in the company of appropriate role models: parents and other adults, and older siblings. In this environment, they are better able to learn from actual life situations, and how to interact with people of all ages.

KAPLAN
Test Prep and Admissions

In particular, homeschooling fosters healthy family relationships, because both children and their parents are able to play larger and more complete roles in one another's lives.

Though there are important advantages to homeschooling, there are also certain disadvantages, which a parent who is considering this option should take into account. The first of these is simply a practical one. If both parents work out of the home, care must be found for young children while the parents are away. Indeed, working parents may be unable to find the time to provide schooling for their children at all, and hiring a tutor to fill that role is an expensive proposition. Second, parents may be attacked for choosing what many people feel is an antisocial or elitist option—for thinking that their children are better than anyone else's, for refusing to participate in an important social institution, or even for trying to destroy public schools by depriving them of students and funding. Third, not all parents will be comfortable in the role of teacher. They may not have the patience required, the basic knowledge of the material, nor the energy to encourage and motivate their children when necessary.

Homeschooling is not a panacea for the institutional deficiencies found in American public schools; these can only be addressed through a large-scale restructuring of public education policies nationwide. Nevertheless, homeschooling offers a number of significant advantages to parents and children. And it works. Home-schooled children, on average, place in the 87th percentile on standardized exams—the national average is the 50th percentile—and have been admitted to all major universities and military academies in the country. Clearly, homeschooling is a serious, positive alternative for motivated parents and their children.

1. Is each topic sentence general enough to include all the ideas and information discussed in the paragraph?

   _____

   _____

2. What kind of transition words or phrases does each use?

   _____

   _____

3. Would you make any changes to these topic sentences?

   _____

   _____

Answers

1. Yes.

2. First, Furthermore, The final, Though, Nevertheless

3. *Answers will vary.*

The Body of a Persuasive Essay

Once you have brainstormed the topic and written your thesis statement, decide exactly what information you will include in the body of the essay to support and defend the thesis.

A good persuasive essay will have at least two well-developed body paragraphs. Three is better. Each paragraph will discuss a particular aspect of the topic, and contain both a general topic sentence and several sentences containing information and examples that support the topic sentence.

Earlier in this lesson we saw this sample thesis statement:

> Because habitual exercise reduces stress, prevents weight gain, and improves academic performance, such exercise should be made a part of any school's curriculum.

This sentence mentions three subtopics that can be used to argue in favor of the thesis: stress reduction, weight gain prevention, and improved academic performance. Each of these subtopics will be turned into the topic sentence of a body paragraph; each may also contain a transition word that shows where it belongs in the overall essay structure. Here are examples showing how this could be done:

1. First, habitual exercise is a great outlet for the stress that many students feel in the academic environment.

2. Moreover, regular exercise has been shown to be more effective than any diet in preventing excessive weight gain and all the illnesses associated with being overweight.

3. Most importantly, students who exercise regularly display superior academic performance.

When you are ready, use the skills and strategies you have learned in this lesson and complete the following Persuasive Essay Practice.

Persuasive Essay Practice

Following is an example of the second task in the Writing section of the TOEFL.

> Read the question that follows. You have 30 minutes to plan, write, and revise your essay. Typically, an effective response will contain a minimum of 300 words.
>
> > Your government is considering a new law that would limit the size of each class to 20 students. Supporters say this would allow teachers to offer more attention to each student and reduce the stress and alienation many students feel in bigger classes. Opponents suggest that smaller classes would be more expensive in the long run and lead to a reduction of resources for students. Which position would you support? Provide reasons and examples in your response.

_____

_____

_____

_____

_____

_____

_____

_____

_____

_____

_____

_____

_____

_____

_____

_____

_____

_____

Answer

Answers will vary, but here is one sample essay.

While the fact that education is growing more and more expensive cannot be denied, classroom size is an important issue that must be dealt with immediately. Students today face an overwhelming number of challenges as they work their way through schools. They must perform well on high-stakes tests in order to succeed, they have to learn to resist the constant temptations that distract them from their studies; and they need adult advice and mentorship to guide them as they make choices. If the number of students in a classroom were to be reduced to a reasonable number, there is no question that students would benefit in all of these areas.

Student performance on standardized tests is becoming a gateway to the opportunities that lie before a student when they complete their studies. The scores that students receive on tests like the SAT or ACT are important factors in determining the college or university that a student attends in the United States. Large class sizes force teachers to focus on discipline, which prevents them from spending time making sure that students have the facts and skills they need in order to perform well on these important tests.

Other challenges that students face are the constant temptations that surround them every day. Cell phones, music players, and even video games and DVD players are all being carried into classrooms. With the general noise and confusion in today's classrooms, it is easy to hide and even use them during class, which prevents the user, and often people around them, from getting the most out of the curriculum.

Finally, with so many students in classes, teachers no longer have enough time to work with each student individually. In a 50 minute class with an average sized class of 30 students, if a teacher spent 20 minutes teaching a particular lesson, he or she would have just one minute to spend per student. There is a lot for a young person to learn from working in a close relationship with someone who is older and more experiences, and that sort of relationship just isn't possible in today's classrooms.

Reducing class size is not only a matter of relieving pressure. It will enhance what a student learns, how they learn it, and even the person they learn it from.

When you are ready, move on to Listening: Turns.

LESSON 3—LISTENING: TURNS

In this third lesson, we will cover more listening skills and strategies that will help lead to success on test day. You will have the opportunity to review some of the strategies you learned in previous lessons as well as to learn about other question types found on the Listening section of the TOEFL. If you want to proceed with more listening strategies when you finish this lesson, turn to Lesson 4—Listening: Note-Taking Practice in Chapter 4.

Turns

In an essay, the main element of organization is the paragraph; in conversation it is called the *turn*. A turn is a statement or question and the response that follows. These go together to form a coherent unit—they relate to the same idea. As you see in the following conversation, a turn can be a question and direct response:

Sam: What time should I come over on Saturday?

Josh: About 7:00.

However, a turn can extend over several statements and responses, as you see in the following conversation:

Sam: What time should I come over on Saturday?

Josh: What time are you off work?

Sam: I finish around 6:30.

Josh: Do you have to go home and change after work?

Sam: Is this a formal dinner?

Josh: Of course not. Why don't you come by around 7:00? Oh, can you pick up a bottle of wine on your way?

In this example, the response to Sam's question about what time to arrive at Josh's is not answered directly. The actual response to this question comes after several statements and questions between Josh and Sam. You may also notice that Josh's response in the second conversation is not as direct as in the first. In the second conversation, he answers Sam's direct question with an indirect question: "Why don't you come by around 7:00?"

You can see that the structure of a conversation can be very complex. On the TOEFL, you will answer questions based on conversations that involve numerous turns, as well as on lectures that include student comments and questions in turns with what the professor is saying.

Outlining

By now you should be familiar with an outline. If not, recall that an outline is a skeletal structure of a text. It contains the main and supporting ideas in the order they are presented, but does not necessarily include any specific details.

Outlining Practice

Listen to the following lecture with student comments and questions and be sure to take notes. Then review an example of the beginning of an outline based on the lecture. You will find a transcript of this audio passage (23. Lesson 3—Listening, Outlining Practice) at the end of the chapter.

🎧 **23.3L, Outlining Practice**

Notes

I. Brain science—new revolutionary research on learning

II. Brain rules

   A. Exercise

   B. Sleep

   C. Stress

   D. . . .

Now using the notes that you wrote, write an outline of the rest of the discussion in the space that follows.

Answers

I. Brain science—new revolutionary research on learning

II. Brain rules

   A. Exercise

   B. Sleep

C. Stress

D. Hypothesizing and testing

E. Visual stimulation

F. Repetition

3 more after the break!

Understanding the question types is critical for knowing how and where you can apply your strategies. Keep reading to learn more.

Question Types

There are several different question types on the Listening section of the TOEFL. Lessons 1 and 2 covered the following types:

- Understanding Rhetorical Function
- Understanding an Idiomatic Expression in Context
- Drawing an Inference
- Understanding a Speaker's Implication

This lesson will cover three more question types:

- Identifying the Main Idea
- Summarizing the Most Important Points
- Understanding Details

Question Type 5—Identifying the Main Idea

There are 2 conversations and 4 lectures in the Listening section of the TOEFL. Each lecture is followed by 1 *main idea* question, for a total of 4 *main idea* questions in the Listening section.

Main idea questions ask you to consider the entire lecture. While listening to the lecture, you should do the following things in order to identify the main idea:

- Listen carefully to the short introductory statement at the beginning of each lecture for key information about the context or topic.
- Understand how the speaker feels about the ideas he or she is presenting.

Wrong answers relate to points in the lecture, but they do not summarize the lecture well. Distracters may either summarize one portion of the lecture but not the whole lecture, and thus are too narrow, or they may be too broad given the specific focus of the lecture.

Common stems for this kind of question are as follows:

- This talk is mainly about …
- The professor is mainly discussing …
- What is the main topic/idea of the lecture?

You may refer to your notes when answering all listening questions. In the listening questions, the question and the answer choices appear on the computer screen, but only the question is spoken by the narrator.

Here is a main idea question based on the "brain rules" discussion you heard earlier in this lesson. The lecture is reprinted here. You can also listen to (23.3L, Outlining Practice) again.

Narrator: Listen to a professor in an education program talking to a group of teacher trainees.

Professor: Today I'd like to outline some findings from research laboratories that might turn education on its head. We in the education world keep discovering uh, "silver bullets" that are going to solve all our problems. Ten years later we find a new one, and we say to ourselves "weren't we stupid?" and start all over again. Many of our experiments are not scientifically tested; we make assumptions and jump onto bandwagons without really knowing what we are doing. Our poor students, from pre-schoolers through Ph.D. candidates are the unfortunate guinea pigs for our sometimes, uh, disastrous experiments.

Now, I am personally hopeful that a more scientific approach to learning might finally be possible. After decades of fads, you might think this is just another fad that will go away in a decade. But this is based on science, the science of how we actually learn. I mean hard, observable, testable, provable science. I mean brain science. Neuroscientists are able to make scientifically defendable statements about what factors affect learning. If we could take that understanding, that hard science, into account in our…ah…yes…you have a question?

Student: Yeah, um, it seems kind of obvious that educators should teach according the how humans learn. Why hasn't anybody done this before?

Professor: Good question. The fact is that much of this is new. Brain research is in its infancy. Naturally scientists are reluctant to encourage educators to change methods and policies based on um. . .limited information. It is only recently that they've had enough data to be able to make conclusive statements about how we learn. The other thing is that the fields of neurobiology and education just haven't crossed paths before. But we are working on that.

So, what can the brain scientists tell us that would influence how we should be teaching? Well, they have identified nine "brain rules." The first two are associated with general lifestyle: sleep is important to the learning process, and exercise aids learning. You might think you already know this, but do you realize how important it is? Apparently, during sleep, we process all the, um, input that we have received during the day and store it in the appropriate place. If we don't sleep enough, the information never gets put away so the knowledge is never secure.

Exercise. Wow. The data is incredible. Sorry—that is the wrong word to use, this is science, it has all been tested, it is believable. But it really is remarkable to note the different levels of achievement on a standardized test between groups that did regular aerobic exercise and those that didn't. Why don't our schools and colleges have exercise bikes in every hallway? Why are physical education programs always the first to get cut when things are tight? Why do students preparing for an important exam give up their places on the basketball team? It's the most imp... yes? Question...

Student: Is this related to the stuff we read about stress?

Professor: Bingo! Another brain rule. Long-term chronic stress, uh, actually diminishes learning ability. There are biochemical reasons for this that I won't go into now, but you're right. Stress is bad, and there is nothing like exercise for reducing stress.

What's the next rule, oh yeah, I love this one. Humans are natural explorers. Apparently, from a very early age (about one hour old) we start making and testing hypotheses. A child playing peek-a-boo is testing the hypothesis that, uh, mommy will appear again after disappearing. When the hypothesis (that she will reappear) is confirmed, it feels good. It's the discovery that enables learning. It's not the instruction. We should be giving our students opportunities to discover, rather than just telling them stuff. Which brings me to another brain rule: we shouldn't be telling them stuff at all, or even having them read stuff. We are visual learners. Think about it, we can absorb, in very little time, incredible amounts of information about what something looks like when we have actually seen it. Compare that to reading or hearing a description...

Student: I can believe both of those rules. I love looking at stuff and figuring things out. But how about remembering it all?

Professor: Ah—another brain rule: repetition is important for memory. Apparently we need to see or hear or experience something many, many times before it is secure. It might take years. On that note, we'll take a break there and talk about the last three brain rules later.

What is the lecture mainly about?

 Ⓐ The ineffectiveness of current educational methods

 Ⓑ The promise of a new educational method based on science

 Ⓒ An overview of how the brain works

 Ⓓ How exercise and sleep affect the brain

Choice (A) is too narrow, and it is mentioned in the introduction to underscore the significance of brain science. Choice (C) may be a tempting answer because *brain* is a keyword in the lecture that is frequently repeated; however, this answer is too broad because it fails to place the brain within the context of learning only. Choice (D) presents only two examples of things that affect the brain's ability to learn well and is therefore too narrow in scope. Choice (B) correctly ties together both the learning and the science.

Question Type 6—Summarizing the Most Important Points

There are 2 conversations and 4 lectures in the Listening section of the TOEFL. Each lecture is followed by 0 or 1 *most-important-points* question, for a total of 2 *most-important-points* questions in the Listening section.

This type of TOEFL question asks you to identify the three most important points in the lecture, the points that combine to express the main idea. The incorrect options either provide points that don't support the main idea or points that are inaccurate. This question can be presented in two distinct formats:

- Choose three out of five options—the first question that follows
- Click on *yes* or *no* for each of five options—the second question that follows

As in all listening questions, the question and the answer choices appear on the screen, but only the question is spoken by the narrator.

> According to the lecture, which of the following would be the most effective ways to enable learning?
>
> Click on 3 answers.
>
> Ⓐ Listening to a lecture
> Ⓑ Experiencing the same thing many times
> Ⓒ Participating in a lecture
> Ⓓ Staying up late to study for an exam
> Ⓔ Playing games to test hypotheses

Choice (A) is not the best way to learn, according to the lecture, because humans learn better through exploration than they do through instruction. Choice (D) is clearly implied by the professor as something that is not desirable for optimal learning because he emphasizes the importance of getting enough sleep for processing new information. Choices (B), (C), and (E) are all correct. Choice (B) is a paraphrase of repetition, one of the brain rules. Choice (C) is more exploration-oriented than (A), which is instruction-oriented. Choice (E) is also correct because the professor uses an example of the game peek-a-boo to illustrate how it supports exploration-oriented learning.

> In the lecture, the professor talks about new research findings in the field of education. Indicate whether he mentions the following information about these findings.
>
> | **Click in the correct box for each phrase.** | | |
> |---|---|---|
> | | **Yes** | **No** |
> | (A) They are based on the science of how we learn. | | |
> | (B) They are "silver bullets" that will solve our problems. | | |
> | (C) They are a new fad that will last only a decade. | | |
> | (D) They may enable a more scientific approach to learning. | | |
> | (E) They are related to new information from another field. | | |

The professor explicitly states that the new approach is based on the science of learning in the second paragraph, so choice (A) is *yes*. The professor talks about silver bullets that will solve our problems, but he says that we later find out these silver bullets don't work (paragraph 1), so (B) is *no*. He mentions that there have been decades of fads in the field of education, but he then implies that the new findings are not based on fads because they are based on hard science (paragraph 2), so (C) is *no*. He says he is hopeful that the new findings will result in a more scientific approach to learning (paragraph 2), so (D) is *yes*. The professor talks about the relationship between neurobiology and the field of learning in paragraph 4 and again about brain science and learning in paragraph 5, so (E) is *yes*.

Question Type 7—Understanding Details

There are 2 conversations and 4 lectures in the Listening section of the TOEFL. Each conversation is followed by 2 or 3 *detail* questions, and each lecture is followed by 1 or 2 *detail* questions.

Detail questions will require you to recall specific information from the spoken text. The answer choices will contain three inaccurate statements and one right one.

To answer direct information questions, you should do the following as you take notes:

- Listen carefully to the conversation.
- Try to understand unfamiliar words from context.
- Pay special attention to numbers and proper nouns.

The most common stem for this type of question is:

According to ___, who,/what/ when/where/ why/how many/how much. . .?

You will be able to use your notes when you answer detail questions. Remember that on the listening questions, both the questions and the answer choices will appear on the screen, but only the question will be spoken.

Here is an example of a detail question.

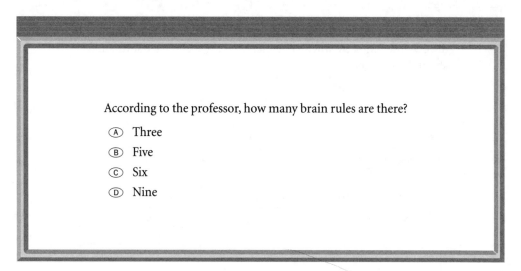

According to the professor, how many brain rules are there?
- (A) Three
- (B) Five
- (C) Six
- (D) Nine

Choice (A) is the number of brain rules NOT covered that the professor will discuss in the next class. Choice (B) is an arbitrary number that has no relation to the lecture. Choice (C) is the number of brain rules that the professor has discussed so far. Choice (D) is the correct answer—the total number of brain rules. The professor explicitly says there are nine brain rules, before they are discussed in detail.

On some detail questions you will be instructed to click on more than one correct answer, as shown here.

What does the professor say about brain science?

Click on 2 answers.
- (A) It is a trend that will disappear in a decade.
- (B) It is relatively new.
- (C) It is able to be tested and proved.
- (D) It is based on assumptions.

Choice (A) is incorrect because the professor implies that brain science is a growing, not diminishing, field. Choice (B) is correct because the professor states that "Brain research is in its infancy." Choice (C) is correct because the professor indicates that scientists are beginning to make conclusive statements about how we learn, thereby implying that brain science can be tested and proved. Choice (D) is incorrect because it refutes choice (C), which is established above as correct.

A variation of the *detail* question is one in which you are presented with three correct answers and one incorrect answer. You need to choose the answer that is wrong, or NOT true. These questions take the following format:

- Which of the following is/is NOT...?
- All of the following . . . EXCEPT...

All of the following are mentioned as "brain rules" EXCEPT

Click on 2 answers.

- Ⓐ Humans learn by testing hypotheses.
- Ⓑ Stress diminishes learning.
- Ⓒ It is able to be tested and proved.
- Ⓓ It is based on assumptions.

Choices (A) and (B) are mentioned in the lecture as brain rules that aid learning, so you should NOT choose these choices. Choices (C) and (D) are correct. They are phrases used to describe science in the lecture, but are not listed as "brain rules."

When you are ready, begin Lesson 3—Speaking: Informal vs. Informal.

LESSON 3—SPEAKING: INFORMAL VS. INFORMAL

In this third lesson, we will cover more speaking skills and strategies that will help lead to success on test day. You will have the opportunity to review some of the strategies you learned in previous lessons as well as to learn about other tasks found on the Speaking section of the TOEFL. If you want to proceed with more speaking strategies when you finish this lesson, turn to Lesson 4—Speaking: Note-Taking from Conversations in Chapter 4.

Remember that in Lessons 1 and 2 we covered the following speaking tasks:

- Describing Something from Your Own Experience
- Summarizing a Lecture
- Expressing and Supporting an Opinion Based on Personal Experience
- Summarizing a Conversation and Expressing an Opinion

This lesson covers one more speaking task:

- Synthesizing and Summarizing Information

Before we review this task, let's cover some other important skills and strategies.

Informal vs. Formal

In English, there are many ways of saying the same thing. A speaker or writer chooses particular words and expressions depending on his or her goal and who makes up his or her audience. For example, you probably wouldn't speak to a professor in the same way you would speak to your best friend. That is an example of the differences between formal and informal language.

Informal vs. Formal Practice

Listen to these two statements of opinion. Think about what language is formal and what language is informal. You will find a transcript of this audio passage (24.3S, (In)formal Practice) at the end of the chapter.

🎧 24.3S, (In)formal Practice

Now make a note of words and phrases from the statements that have the same meaning but different tone. Write them in the correct column. An example has been filled in for you.

Informal/Conversational	Formal	Either Informal or Formal
freak out	get very nervous	get very nervous

Answers

Informal/Conversational	Formal	Either Informal or Formal
freak out	get very nervous	get very nervous
bomb	do poorly	do poorly
really good at	quite skilled at	really good at
learn tricks	develop strategies	
ace	perform well	perform well
a clue	knowledge	
lucky	fortunate	lucky
cool	calm	
buddies	classmates	
flunk	fail to give correct answers	

Gliding

What is *gliding*? Gliding is one way that English speakers link particular words together. They tend to pronounce words in thought groups rather than individually. There are no pauses between these words.

Here is an example:

from an early age

If one word ends in a vowel sound *(early)* and the next word begins with a vowel sound *(age)*, how is it possible to link them without pausing? That's where gliding comes in. A kind of consonant called a glide is added between the two vowels when it is spoken: *from an early*[y]*age*

The consonant that is added is either a [y] sound or a [w] sound, depending on the last vowel sound of the first word. Don't worry about this detail now. Just think about where a glide may occur.

Gliding Practice

Look at the following sentences and draw a line connecting two words that would probably be pronounced with an added glide. The first one has been done for you as an example.

1. Those two are always talking about the effects of exercise!

2. Do you know why it's so important?

3. Apparently exercise aids learning.

4. It's only two in the afternoon.

5. I'll be in the library if you need me.

6. I'll probably go on Friday.

7. Maybe it's better to rely on hard science.

8. Scientists need to invest more time on the issue in the future.

9. Basically, I think this should be essential to instruction from now on.

10. Let's do it soon; we only have one more day to finish it.

Answers

1. Those two are always talking about the effects of exercise!

2. Do you know why it's so important?

3. Apparently exercise aids learning.

4. It's only two in the afternoon.

5. I'll be in the library if you need me.

6. I'll probably go on Friday.

7. Maybe it's better to rely on hard science.

8. Scientists need to invest more time on the issue in the future.

9. Basically, I think this should be essential to instruction from now on.

10. Let's do it soon; we only have one more day to finish it.

Task 3—Synthesizing and Summarizing Information

There are 6 tasks in the Speaking section of the TOEFL. The third requires you to read an announcement, listen to a conversation about the announcement, and answer a question that asks you to synthesize and summarize information from both the announcement you read and the conversation you heard. You have 30 seconds to prepare your response, and your response should be about 60 seconds in length.

When reading the notice and listening to the conversation you should:
- Identify the main points
- Identify the main speaker's opinion and the reasons he or she holds that opinion

Listen to the narrator's introduction. Remember that you will not see the narrator's introduction to the question on the test. If you have a study partner, or someone that can listen to your response, ask to work with him or her. You will find transcripts of the audio passages from this section at the end of the chapter.

🎧 25.3S, Task 3 Narrator

Announcement from the Examinations Committee

Yoga instruction will be available free of charge to all students who will take exams this semester. Qualified instructors, with special expertise in stress relief, will teach the classes. The service is being offered in response to requests from students and from the university mental health providers. Exam-related stress affects not only students and their exam results but is also a burden on the university's mental health care facilities. In order to encourage participation, yoga classes will be held in three locations at two different times of day. Check your departmental timetable for more details.

Notes

 **26.3S, Task 3 Discussion**

Notes

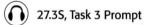 **27.3S, Task 3 Prompt**

The woman expresses her opinion of the announcement from the Examinations Committee. State her opinion and explain the reasons she gives for holding that opinion.

30 seconds to prepare
60 seconds to speak

Now evaluate yourself using the following criteria:

Criteria	Comments	Action to Improve
Clarity and pronunciation		
Organization		
Details and examples		
Grammar and vocabulary		

Now listen to the sample response. How was it different from yours? How was it similar? You will find a transcript of this audio passage (28.3, Task 3 Sample Response) at the end of the chapter.

🎧 **28.3, Task 3 Sample Response**

More Practice Synthesizing and Summarizing Information

This section will give you more practice on this particular TOEFL speaking task in *synthesizing and summarizing information*. To review, this task requires you to read a notice and listen to a short conversation about the information presented in the notice. You will be able to take notes both as you read and as you listen. You will have 30 seconds to prepare a 60-second response in which you summarize the speaker's opinion about the notice and give reasons why the speaker holds that opinion.

Pretend that you are taking the TOEFL as you go through this item. Listen to the audio passage. Remember that you will not see the narrator's introduction to the question on the test. If you have a study partner, or someone that can listen to your response, ask to work with him or her. You will find transcripts of these audio passages at the end of the chapter.

🎧 29.3S, Synth/Summary Narrator

Announcement from the Student Residence Manager

You will incur a slight increase in dorm fees due to changes in cafeteria services. Recipes were developed in collaboration with the School of Health Sciences to ensure that you receive a nutritional diet. Only organic ingredients are used. The use of animal fats and other unhealthy ingredients has been reduced. In addition, as part of our commitment to fair trade, the cafeteria is purchasing the majority of its goods through the college co-op at slightly higher prices than our previous supplier's. The increase is just under one percent. It will be reflected on your next fee statement.

Notes

🎧 **30.3S, Synth/Summ Conversation Notes**

🎧 **31.3S, Synth/Summary Prompt**

The man expresses his opinion of the announcement from the Student Residence Manager. State his opinion and the reasons he gives for holding that opinion.

30 seconds to prepare
60 seconds to speak

Now evaluate yourself using the following criteria:

Criteria	Comments	Action to Improve
Clarity and pronunciation		
Organization		
Details and examples		
Grammar and vocabulary		

Now listen to the sample response. How was it different from yours? How was it similar? You will find a transcript of this audio passage (32.3S, Synth/Summary Response) at the end of the chapter.

🎧 **32.3S, Synth/Summary Response**

Great work! You are now one chapter closer to completing this book. If you are ready, turn to Chapter 4 for more reading, writing, listening, and speaking lessons.

CHAPTER 3 AUDIO TRANSCRIPTS

23. Lesson 3—Listening, Outlining Practice

Narrator: Listen to a professor in an education program talking to a group of teacher trainees.

Professor: Today I'd like to outline some findings from research laboratories that might turn education on its head. We in the education world keep discovering uh, "silver bullets" that are going to solve all our problems. Ten years later we find a new one, and we say to ourselves "weren't we stupid?" and start all over again. Many of our experiments are not scientifically tested; we make assumptions and jump onto bandwagons without really knowing what we are doing. Our poor students, from pre-schoolers through Ph.D. candidates are the unfortunate guinea pigs for our sometimes, uh, disastrous experiments.

Now, I am personally hopeful that a more scientific approach to learning might finally be possible. After decades of fads, you might think this is just another fad that will go away in a decade. But this is based on science, the science of how we actually learn. I mean hard, observable, testable, provable science. I mean brain science. Neuroscientists are able to make scientifically defendable statements about what factors affect learning. If we could take that understanding, that hard science, into account in our…ah…yes…you have a question?

Student: Yeah, um, it seems kind of obvious that educators should teach according the how humans learn. Why hasn't anybody done this before?

Professor: Good question. The fact is that much of this is new. Brain research is in its infancy. Naturally scientists are reluctant to encourage educators to change methods and policies based on um…limited information. It is only recently that they've had enough data to be able to make conclusive statements about how we learn. The other thing is that the fields of neurobiology and education just haven't crossed paths before. But we are working on that.

So, what can the brain scientists tell us that would influence how we should be teaching? Well, they have identified nine "brain rules." The first two are associated with general lifestyle: sleep is important to the learning process, and exercise aids learning. You might think you already know this, but do you realize how important it is? Apparently, during sleep, we process all the, um, input that we have received during the day and store it in the appropriate place. If we don't sleep enough, the information never gets put away so the knowledge is never secure.

Exercise. Wow. The data is incredible. Sorry—that is the wrong word to use, this is science, it has all been tested, it is believable. But it really is remarkable to note the different levels of achievement on a standardized test between groups that did regular aerobic exercise and those that didn't. Why don't our schools and colleges have exercise bikes in every hallway? Why are physical education programs always the first to get cut when things are tight? Why do students preparing for an important exam give up their places on the basketball team? It's the most imp… yes? Question…

Student: Is this related to the stuff we read about stress?

Professor: Bingo! Another brain rule. Long-term chronic stress, uh, actually diminishes learning ability. There are biochemical reasons for this that I won't go into now, but you're right. Stress is bad, and there is nothing like exercise for reducing stress.

What's the next rule, oh yeah, I love this one. Humans are natural explorers. Apparently, from a very early age (about one hour old) we start making and testing hypotheses. A child playing peek-a-boo is testing the hypothesis that, uh, mommy will appear again after disappearing. When the hypothesis (that she will reappear) is confirmed, it feels good. It's the discovery that enables learning. It's not the instruction. We should be giving our students opportunities to discover, rather than just telling them stuff. Which brings me to another brain rule: we shouldn't be telling them stuff at all, or even having them read stuff. We are visual learners. Think about it, we can absorb, in very little time, incredible amounts of information about what something looks like when we have actually seen it. Compare that to reading or hearing a description…

Student: I can believe both of those rules. I love looking at stuff and figuring things out. But how about remembering it all?

Professor: Ah—another brain rule: repetition is important for memory. Apparently we need to see or hear or experience something many, many times before it is secure. It might take years. On that note, we'll take a break there and talk about the last three brain rules later.

24. Lesson 3—Speaking: Informal vs. Formal Practice

I think standardized tests are stupid. Some people just freak out when they have to take a test. People like that often bomb even if they are really good at whatever is being tested. It's not fair 'cause other people just learn tricks and manage to ace tests even though they don't really have a clue about the stuff. I guess I'm one of the lucky ones. I usually stay cool on test day, so I do pretty good. But loads of my buddies, who work much harder than me, they just lose it, and then they flunk really basic questions.

In my opinion there are serious flaws to standardized testing. Some people get very nervous in test situations. People like that often do poorly, despite being quite skilled at the subject. It may not be a fair test of ability. Other people develop strategies and perform well despite very limited knowledge of the subject. I consider myself to be among the fortunate few who remain calm on test day, so I generally do all right. However, several of my classmates, who work much harder than I do, sometimes panic. As a result, they fail to give correct answers on relatively simple questions.

25. Lesson 3—Speaking, Task 3 Narrator

Narrator: In this question, you will read a notice and listen to a conversation about the content of the notice. You will then answer a question. After you hear the question, you will have 30 seconds to prepare your response and 60 seconds to speak.

City University is planning to provide free yoga sessions to students who will be taking exams this semester. Read the announcement from the Examinations Committee about this. You have 45 seconds to read the announcement. Begin reading now.

26. Lesson 3—Speaking, Task 3 Discussion

Narrator: Now listen to two students as they discuss this announcement.

Male: Yoga? What are they thinking? Like anybody has time for sitting around on a mat pretending to be a flying swan!

Female: Actually, I think it's a great idea. I used to go to a yoga class, but I had to pay for it, and I couldn't afford to keep going. This is wonderful. It's free!

Male: You think it does any good?

Female: Oh sure. It really helps my stress. I get so worked up during exams, I stop eating properly…and sleep? Forget about it. But when I do yoga regularly, I just feel much better.

Male: Is it really worth the time? Wouldn't you be better off studying than learning how to "breathe like a tiger"?

Female: Don't be silly, it's not like that. You just practice really simple relaxation techniques. And yes it's worth the time. When you're not feeling so stressed, you can actually study much more efficiently 'cause you can concentrate better. Anyway, they're offering classes at different times, so it should be easy to fit it in.

Male: Well it sounds like you really think it's a good thing. Maybe I should try it.

Female: Right on—you've got nothing to lose! It's free. Remember?

27. Lesson 3—Speaking, Task 3 Prompt

The woman expresses her opinion of the announcement from the Examinations Committee. State her opinion and explain the reasons she gives for holding that opinion.

28. Lesson 3—Speaking, Task 3 Sample Response

The student is happy about the free yoga classes. She used to do yoga, but she can't, ah, she couldn't ah, um…she doesn't have enough money to pay for classes, so she is happy that these classes are free…um…she thinks yoga is very healthy. It's good for stress because it helps her to sleep well. Um…oh yeah, um, she also said it is good for studying because it…um…I mean, because doing yoga helps improve her concentration. And she thinks it is good that there will be classes at different times of day. The other student thought yoga is kind of a waste of time, but the one who likes yoga encourages her to try it. So anyway, basically, the student thinks yoga is good for health and for studying, and she is happy that the university is providing free classes at convenient times.

29. Lesson 3—Speaking, Synthesizing and Summarizing Narrator

Narrator: In this question, you will read a notice and listen to a conversation on the same topic. You will then answer a question about them. After you hear the question, you will have 30 seconds to prepare your response and 60 seconds to speak.

City University Student Residence is going to change its menu and increase fees. Read the announcement from the Student Residence Manager about this. You will have 45 seconds to read the announcement. Begin reading now.

30. Lesson 3—Speaking, Synthesizing and Summarizing Conversation

Narrator: Listen to two students as they discuss this announcement.

Student A: Wait a minute! They're upping dorm fees again? What's that all about?

Student B: Hey, don't worry about it. The increase in fees is tiny, less than ten dollars a month. Haven't you noticed how great the food has been recently?

Student A: I guess…but I kind of miss those greasy fries they used to have.

Student B: Are you kidding? Man, since they introduced this new menu with all the salads and soups and whole grain breads and everything, I've lost 5 pounds and I feel fantastic.

Student A: Well, yeah, you're right. It certainly is much healthier.

Student B: And you know what? It's actually working out cheaper too. I used to go out to eat quite a lot 'cause the cafeteria food was so gross. Now, I just pay my dorm fees and I hardly ever go out. I don't mind paying a little bit more.

Student A: True enough. And I have to say…I like the fact that they support the co-op. Anyway, I'm hungry. Let's see how the organic chicken noodle soup is today.

31. Lesson 3—Speaking, Synthesizing and Summarizing Prompt

The man expresses his opinion of the announcement from the Student Residence Manager. State his opinion and the reasons he gives for holding that opinion.

32. Lesson 3—Speaking, Synthesizing and Summarizing Sample Response

The man doesn't mind the increase in dorm fees. Um…the dorm fees are going to go up a little because they have improved the cafeteria food. But the man doesn't mind because he feels the food is really a lot better than it used to be. The food is healthier and it tastes good. I think he said it tastes good… um, not sure though. Anyway he didn't like the cafeteria food the way it was before, he said it was "gross." And he doesn't mind having to pay a little more because it works out cheaper for him in the long run because he rarely goes out to eat now. He likes eating the cafeteria food.

Chapter 4: **Lesson Set 4**
Theme—Business and Economics

Chapter 4 covers more reading, writing, listening, and speaking skills and strategies you will need to score high on the TOEFL. Make sure to complete all the practice exercises and sample questions so that you can get the most out of these lessons.

LESSON 4—READING: MORE ABOUT TRANSITIONS

In this lesson, we will cover more reading skills and strategies that will help lead to success on test day. You will have the opportunity to review some of the strategies you learned in previous lessons as well as to learn about other question types found on the Reading section of the TOEFL. If you want to proceed with more reading strategies when you finish this lesson, turn to Lesson 5—Reading: The Main Idea, and Transitions and Rhetorical Function Revisited in Chapter 5.

More about Transitions

Recall from Lesson 3—Reading: Transitions, Coherence, and Cohesive Devices that transitional words and phrases can help the reader identify which type of text an author has written. For example, words and phrases such as:

unlike, compared to, on the other hand, likewise, similarly

might point to a compare/contrast essay, while words and phrases such as:

offers a number of advantages, some benefits include, an additional reason is

might indicate a persuasive argumentative type of text.

Summarizing Two Sources

You have learned that both the ability to summarize and the ability to paraphrase from lectures, texts, and conversations are essential skills for students in an American university. In this part of the lesson, you will practice these skills again in order to synthesize, or combine, the information from a text and a lecture.

Summarizing Two Sources Practice

Read the following passage.

Market Regulation

It is rare for any type of market structure to run with absolute efficiency. If lack of efficiency is the result of too much power on the part of a few firms or even a single company, the government may use regulatory methods in hopes of preventing market failure. Regulatory methods first came into effect in 1887 when the Interstate Commerce Commission was established to control the prices, routes, and services of certain transportation firms, including bus lines and railroads. Over the next 90 or so years, commissions were formed to regulate telephone service, mail rates, and oil prices, to name a few. In fact, by the mid-1970s regulation affected almost one fourth of the U.S. economy. Though the current trend is to deregulate many industries, several arguments against this trend should be noted.

Economic regulation can benefit either the producer or the consumer. Because regulatory laws can only be created by politicians, producers and consumers must organize themselves to convince lawmakers that regulation in their favor is necessary. If a public interest group is powerful enough, regulatory laws that lead to a price decrease in an industry will be passed. Conversely, if industry leaders are more organized, the regulatory laws will lead to an increase in profit for companies. Regulation is therefore a positive example of the effectiveness of democracy. Moreover, the direct costs of regulation, that is, the costs of operating regulatory commissions, are quite negligible. Furthermore, recent deregulation in several industries seems to have led to low quality goods and service. The airline industry, with its new "cattle-car" philosophy, is one example.

Notes

Now listen to a lecture on the same topic. You will find a transcript of this audio passage (33.4R, Summary Source Practice) at the end of the chapter.

 33.4R, Summary Source Practice

Notes

Now write a short summary that includes combined information from both the passage and the lecture telling what you have learned about regulation and deregulation. Try using some of the following expressions as you write.

To show similarities:

similarly, likewise, also, as well, like, both

To show differences:

however, on the other hand, although, yet, whereas, unlike, in contrast

Answer

Answers will vary, but here is one sample summary.

Regulation is a method of ensuring that a company or small group of companies does not dominate a particular market or industry. Regulation laws are created by politicians, who can represent either the interests of the companies or the consumers. Regulation first came about in the United States in 1887 to deal with prices, routes, and services of transportation companies. Soon telephone services, mail delivery, and oil were all similarly regulated. By the 1970s, one quarter of the U.S. economy was affected by regulation, at a cost of $100 billion in 1975. In contrast, the costs of deregulation are not very high. Also, following deregulation, prices typically fall because of an increase in competition. When the airline industry was deregulated in 1978, the drop in prices was accompanied by a drop in the quality of service, though this may have been due to mergers and acquisitions.

Compare and Contrast

There are two basic ways of writing a compare and contrast text. One is called the *point-by-point format* and the other is called the *block format*. You will study these text types in detail in the writing lesson, but a quick way to recognize these two formats is to ask yourself the following questions about the body of the essay:

- Are the objects of comparison discussed in separate paragraphs?
- Does the body begin with a discussion of the features of one object and then move on to a comparison with the features of the second object in later paragraphs?

If so, the text is written in block format. If not, ask yourself the following questions:

- Are the two (or more) objects being compared discussed in the same paragraphs?
- Does the body begin with a discussion of how both objects compare in regards to one feature and then move on to compare the two objects on the basis of other features?

If so, the text is written in point-by-point format.

Compare and Contrast Practice

Now read the following text, "Two Economic Giants."

Two Economic Giants

The last two decades have witnessed an important shift in the global distribution of economic power. Since the middle of the twentieth century, the United States has been the paramount economic force in the Western Hemisphere, with a peerless industrial base and strong technology and service sectors. Yet the United States is by no means the world's only economic dynamo. In the last twenty years, and especially in the last ten, China has emerged as a powerhouse, eclipsing Japan in the Pacific as Asia's largest economy and rapidly overtaking the global lead of the United States. As a consequence, many economic parallels can now be added to existing geographic similarities between China and the United States. Despite these similarities, there remain a number of significant economic and demographic disparities between these two economic giants.

Both China and the United States are very large nations. At 9.5 million square kilometers, China is only slightly smaller than the United States, at 9.6 million. Both countries occupy a similar range of latitude, with an attendant diversity of climatic conditions, and have long coastlines and good ports. Like the United States, China is gifted with diverse natural resources, including metals and timber, and significant domestic energy sources, especially fossil fuels and hydropower.

Physical similarities are now joined by economic congruities. China's economic base is coming to rely on manufacturing and other industry. The country is quickly catching up with the United States in this area, with a $6.5 trillion gross domestic product (GDP), as compared to the American $11 trillion GDP. Like the U.S. government, China's government depends heavily on deficit spending: the U.S. public debt is currently at 60 percent of the American GDP, and China's has reached 30 percent of the Chinese GDP. However, annual inflation of consumer prices is below 3 percent in both countries.

Despite these similarities, a number of important differences must be noted, both in the two countries' economies and their demographic bases. China's economy, though rapidly industrializing, cannot be considered a free-market economy based on the U.S. model, since major segments of the Chinese economy are government-run enterprises sheltered from competition. Dependent on the mood of foreign consumers and investors, China's export-driven economy needs to develop a large and stable domestic market before it can achieve the diversity and resiliency of the U.S. economy. Not all of the differences between the two economies place China at a disadvantage, however. For example, China's 9 percent annual growth is triple that of the United States; the country enjoys a positive balance of payments, at +$40 billion, in contrast to the massive $540 billion U.S. trade deficit; and China's capital investment rate far exceeds that of the United States.

The huge and increasingly well-educated Chinese workforce, which at 750 million is five times the size of America's, can be given much of the credit for China's rapid growth. Foreign investment finds the abundance of inexpensive labor an important advantage over the expensive U.S. labor market; nevertheless, at least 10 percent of the urban Chinese population is unemployed, probably more in rural regions, whereas the U.S. unemployment rate hovers around 6 percent. A further consequence of China's large population is that, distributed among so many people, its $6.5 trillion gross domestic product is only $5,000 per capita, compared to $38,000 in the United States.

Persistent American fears of being overshadowed economically by China are not entirely unfounded; the Asian nation is indeed growing very rapidly. However, a developing energy shortage promises to slow that growth, and as Chinese labor costs rise, as they inevitably must, the country will become less attractive to foreign investment. By that time, however, China may well have acquired a healthy component of domestic capital, and its increasingly affluent population will in turn become a market for American exports. The next few years are likely to see the economic connection between China and the United States develop into a prosperous partnership.

First decide in which type of format it is written. Then make an outline of how you could reorganize the text in the other format.

Answers

The passage is written in point-by-point format. Here is a sample block format outline.

I. Intro: Shift in Global economics

II. The U.S.

    A. Geography

    B. Economy

    C. Population

III. China

    A. Geography

    B. Economy

    C. Population

IV. Conclusion

    A. Issues in the future

    B. Partnership

Understanding the question types is critical for knowing how and where to apply your strategies. Keep reading to learn more.

Question Types

There are several question types on the Reading section of the TOEFL. We have already reviewed ten types in the first three lessons. These are

- Identifying the Main Idea
- Summarizing the Most Important Points
- Understanding Rhetorical Function
- Understanding Details
- Understanding Details as They Relate to the Main Idea (Multiple-Choice)
- Understanding Details as They Relate to the Main Idea (Schematic Table)
- Inferring Word Meaning from Context
- Defining a Key Term
- Locating a Referent
- Understanding Coherence

In this lesson we will review three more types:

- Drawing an Inference
- Inferring the Author's Opinion or Attitude
- Paraphrasing

Question Type 11—Drawing an Inference

There are 3 passages in the Reading section of the TOEFL. Each passage is followed by 0 to 2 *inference* questions, for a total of 3 or 4 per test.

One particularly difficult reading skill to master is the skill of *drawing inferences*. A good inference is one which is supported by information in the text, but which is not directly stated. Look at the following sentences from the passage.

> The last two decades have witnessed an important shift in the global distribution of economic power. Since the middle of the twentieth century, the United States has been the paramount economic force in the Western Hemisphere, with a peerless industrial base and strong technology and service sectors.

Based on these sentences we can infer that:

> In 1850, the United States was not the paramount economic force in the Western Hemisphere.

This is a good inference because although the date 1850 is not directly stated in the text, it is a date before the middle of the twentieth century.

> The United States is not the only economic force in the Western Hemisphere today.

This is also a good inference because the first sentence tells us that there has been a shift in the global distribution of economic power.

In attempting to draw a good inference, it is important to pay attention to dates and numbers. Key words such as those in the following list can be equally useful when reading for what is implied.

- *not only/not exclusively*
- *many/most/much of*
- *some/several/a few*
- *may/can/could*
- *used to be/was/were*
- *at one time/previously*

As you answer the following questions, be aware of these key words and any others which will help you make good inferences.

To answer inference questions correctly, you will also need to avoid distracters. The types of distracters for this type of question include:

- Answer choices that include words from the passage but that are untrue.
- Answer choices that you think are true based on previous knowledge or intuition, but which are unsupported by information in the passage.

> Based on the information in paragraph 2, what can be inferred about the range of latitude in China and the United States?
>
> (A) The range is wider in China than in the United States.
> (B) Because the range is wide, both countries have good ports.
> (C) The wide range gives both countries a variety of types of weather.
> (D) The latitude in both countries covers zones from sub-arctic to tropical.

Choice (A) is not correct because it is untrue. The passage says that both countries have a similar range of latitude. Choice (B) is not correct because although it includes words from the passage, it is not supported by the passage. The passage does not say there is a cause-effect relationship between the range of latitude and the quality of ports. Choice (D) is incorrect because the passage does not support this information, whether or not it is true. Choice (C) is correct because the information is supported by the following statement:

> Both countries occupy a similar range of latitude, with an attendant diversity of climatic conditions...

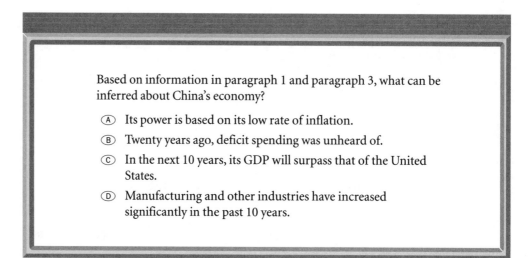

Based on information in paragraph 1 and paragraph 3, what can be inferred about China's economy?

(A) Its power is based on its low rate of inflation.

(B) Twenty years ago, deficit spending was unheard of.

(C) In the next 10 years, its GDP will surpass that of the United States.

(D) Manufacturing and other industries have increased significantly in the past 10 years.

Choice (A) is incorrect because it is not supported in either paragraph 1 or 3, regardless of whether it is true or not. Choice (B) is incorrect. Paragraph 3 includes similar words to the answer choice, but neither paragraph 1 or 3 gives any indication that this is true. Choice (C) is incorrect because there is nothing in either paragraph 1 or 3 that supports this information. Choice (D) is correct because it can be inferred that China's reliance on manufacturing and other industry is a recent phenomenon:

China's economic base is coming to rely on . . .

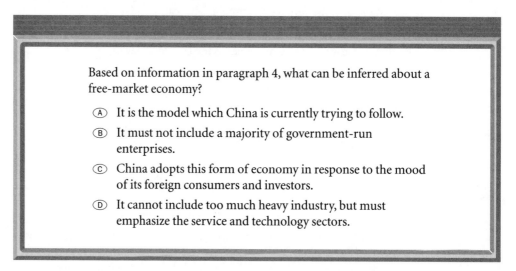

Based on information in paragraph 4, what can be inferred about a free-market economy?

(A) It is the model which China is currently trying to follow.

(B) It must not include a majority of government-run enterprises.

(C) China adopts this form of economy in response to the mood of its foreign consumers and investors.

(D) It cannot include too much heavy industry, but must emphasize the service and technology sectors.

Choice (A) is not correct because although it includes words from the passage, the answer is incorrect. Choice (B) is correct because one can infer that a free-market economy cannot include a majority of government-run enterprises from the statement:

. . .China's economy. . . cannot be considered be considered a free-market economy. . .since major segments of the Chinese economy are government-run enterprises. . .

Choice (C) is incorrect because the paragraph does not imply that China has adopted a free-market economy, so the answer choice is untrue. Choice (D) is incorrect because this answer is not supported by the paragraph.

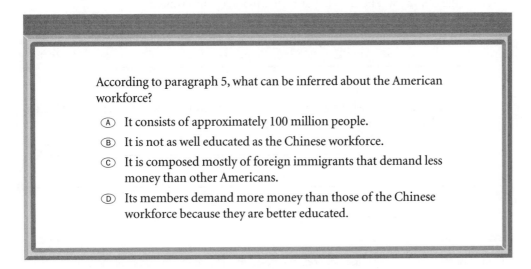

According to paragraph 5, what can be inferred about the American workforce?

- (A) It consists of approximately 100 million people.
- (B) It is not as well educated as the Chinese workforce.
- (C) It is composed mostly of foreign immigrants that demand less money than other Americans.
- (D) Its members demand more money than those of the Chinese workforce because they are better educated.

Choice (D) is the correct answer because the reader can infer that the American workforce is better educated from the reading.

Inference Practice

Now look at the following sentences and sets of sentences from the text. What can you infer from each?

1. Dependent on the mood of foreign consumers and investors, China's export-driven economy needs to develop a large and stable domestic market before it can achieve the diversity and resiliency of the U.S. economy.

   _____

   _____

2. For example, China's 9 percent annual growth is triple that of the United States; the country enjoys a positive balance of payments, at +$40 billion, in contrast to the massive $540 billion U.S. trade deficit; and China's capital investment rate far exceeds that of the United States.

   _____

   _____

3. Persistent American fears of being overshadowed economically by China are not entirely unfounded; the Asian nation is indeed growing very rapidly. However, a developing energy shortage promises to slow that growth, and as Chinese labor costs rise, as they inevitably must, the country will become less attractive to foreign investment.

_____

_____

4. The next few years are likely to see the economic connection between China and the United States develop into a prosperous partnership.

_____

_____

Answers

1. China's domestic economy is too dependent on exports to be as stable as that of the U.S.

2. China's overall economy is growing much faster than that of the U.S.

3. China's continued growth will depend on how it deals with growing energy and labor issues.

4. China and the U.S. will probably come to mutually beneficial economic agreements.

Question Type 12—Inferring the Author's Opinion or Attitude

There are 3 passages in the Reading section of the TOEFL. One passage is generally followed by 1 *author's opinion* question.

A specific inference you will have to draw on one passage in the Reading section is the author's opinion or attitude regarding the topic of the passage. The passages in the Reading section are expository, so the author's opinion is not explicitly stated and may not be obvious. However, as you skim a passage to identify the main idea, most important points, and organizational structure, you can watch for clues that indicate author's opinion or attitude. Ask yourself these questions:

- Which statements can be interpreted as positive and which can be interpreted as negative?
- Are there more positive statements or more negative statements?

Adjectives often give a statement a positive or negative tone. Look at the following sentence from the passage "Two Economic Giants."

> The huge and increasingly well-educated Chinese workforce (which at 750 million is five times the size of America's) can be given much of the credit for China's rapid growth.

In the context of a passage on economic power, the adjective *huge* and the adjective phrase *increasingly well-educated* can both be interpreted as a positive commentary on the Chinese workforce. And of course giving credit to the workforce for rapid growth is also a positive commentary. From this one sentence alone, then, we might infer that the author admires the Chinese workforce and feels positively about its contribution to China's economic growth.

Now look at the final sentence of the passage.

> The next few years are likely to see the economic connection between China and the United States develop into a prosperous partnership.

What can you infer about the author's opinion from this one sentence? What can be inferred about the author's belief about the future relationship between China and the U.S. from the adjective *prosperous* used with the noun *partnership*? What can be inferred from this about the author's opinion of China's economic growth?

To answer author's opinion questions correctly, you will also need to avoid distracters. The incorrect answer choices in an author's opinion question are generally plausible opinions on the given topic, but the passage does not provide sufficient evidence to conclude that the author holds these opinions.

Which of the following statements most accurately reflects the author's opinion about Chinese economic growth?

Ⓐ Both China and the U.S. will benefit from current changes in China's economy.

Ⓑ China will likely eclipse the U.S. as the predominant global economic power within two decades.

Ⓒ The U.S. should emulate some Chinese practices in order to stay competitive.

Ⓓ Chinese labor costs will soon compare to those in the U.S., hindering further growth.

Choice (A) is correct. Given the tone of the passage, it can be inferred that the author feels generally positive about China's economic growth and believes that both China and the U.S. will benefit from this growth. It is possible that the author of the passage holds the opinions in choices (B) and (C), but there is not sufficient evidence in the passage to infer this with certainty. Although the author mentions the fact that increasing labor costs in China will eventually slow economic growth, it cannot be inferred that the author believes labor costs will soon compare to—in other words, be relatively close to—those in the U.S., so choice (D) is also a distracter.

Question Type 13—Paraphrasing

There are 3 passages in the Reading section of the TOEFL. Each passage is followed by 0 or 1 *paraphrasing* question, for a total of 2 or 3 per test.

Throughout this book you will notice that you are often asked to rewrite sentences or paragraphs in your own words. Rewriting sentences using your own words, also called paraphrasing, is extremely important both in university work and for the TOEFL. Paraphrasing questions ask you to choose the answer which best expresses the meaning of a sentence in a reading passage. Incorrect answers either:

> change the meaning of the sentence

OR

> do not include all of the information in the sentence

Which of the sentences below is the best paraphrase of the following sentence?

In the last twenty years, and especially in the last ten, China has emerged as a powerhouse, eclipsing Japan in the Pacific as Asia's largest economy and rapidly overtaking the global lead of the United States.

Ⓐ Within the last two decades, China has come out as a strong country, surpassing both Japan and the United States in terms of economic power.

Ⓑ The Chinese economy has improved in recent years to the point that the country now presents a challenge to other countries in the region.

Ⓒ China has strengthened its economy so significantly in the past two decades that it has overshadowed Japan and become serious competition for America in the world market.

Ⓓ In the past 10 years alone, China has become the biggest economic power in Asia and is set to become the biggest in the world within the next few years.

Choice (A) is incorrect because it changes the meaning of the original sentence, which does *not* state that China has become a bigger economic power than the U.S. Choice (B) is incorrect because it is too vague and does not include all of the information in the original sentence—it refers only to "other countries in the region," whereas the original sentence also refers to the "global" economy. Choice (C) is the best choice because it uses synonyms effectively and has a change in word order without changing the meaning of the sentence. Choice (D) is incorrect because nothing in the original sentence implies that China will be the biggest global economic power in the near future.

Which of the sentences below is the best paraphrase of the following sentence?

Dependent on the mood of foreign consumers and investors, China's export-driven economy needs to develop a large and stable domestic market before it can achieve the diversity and resiliency of the U.S. economy.

(A) China's economy will not be as robust as the American economy until it attains a greater balance between its reliance on external sources and a steady internal consumer market.

(B) The next step that China must take if it is to achieve an economy that is as strong as that of the U.S. is to replace its export-driven focus with an import-driven focus.

(C) China is overly dependent on money that it makes outside its borders, and as a result its economy does not have the flexibility of the U.S. economy.

(D) The U.S. economy presents China with a good model for developing its internal market and thereby becoming less reliant on foreign sources.

Choice (A) is the correct answer. It uses synonyms effectively and has a change in word order without changing the meaning of the sentence. The sentence from the passage does not suggest that China replace its export-driven focus, only that it balance it, so (B) is incorrect. Choice (C) omits the important point that China must "develop a large and stable domestic market." Choice (D) is incorrect because it suggests that China look to the U.S. as a model, something not suggested in the original sentence.

Paraphrasing Practice

As you can see, paraphrasing effectively requires the use of synonyms and the ability to change word form and structure. Practice these techniques by paraphrasing the following sentences.

1. Yet the United States is by no means the world's only economic dynamo.

    _____

    _____

2. China's economic base is coming to rely on manufacturing and other industry.

    _____

    _____

3. Foreign investment finds the abundance of inexpensive labor an important advantage over the expensive U.S. labor market; nevertheless, at least 10 percent of the urban Chinese population is unemployed, probably more in rural regions, whereas the U.S. unemployment rate hovers around 6 percent.

    _____

    _____

4. Persistent American fears of being overshadowed economically by China are not entirely unfounded; the Asian nation is indeed growing very rapidly.

    _____

    _____

Answers

Answers will vary, but here are some sample paraphrased sentences.

1. But the United States is not the only global economic power.

2. Manufacturing and other industries are growing into the foundation of the Chinese economy.

3. Despite foreign investments attracted by low-cost labor, nearly ten percent of the urban Chinese population is unemployed, with an even higher percentage likely in rural areas, while the more costly U.S. labor market has an unemployment rate of around 6 percent.

4. It is not unreasonable that Americans are becoming concerned about the rapid economic growth of China.

When you are ready, move on to Lesson 4—Writing: Compare and Contrast Essays.

LESSON 4—WRITING: COMPARE AND CONTRAST ESSAYS

In this lesson, we will cover more writing skills and strategies that will help lead to success on test day. You will have the opportunity to learn more about the tasks required for the Writing section of the TOEFL. If you want to proceed with additional writing strategies when you finish this lesson, turn to Lesson 5—Writing: Another Look at Persuasive Essays in Chapter 5.

Lesson 4 covers two types of essays found on the TOEFL. These are:

- Compare/Contrast Essays
- Essays in Response to a Reading Passage and a Lecture

Keep reading to learn more.

Recognizing Compare/Contrast Essay Prompts

There are two tasks in the Writing section of the TOEFL. In the first, you must read a passage, listen to a lecture, and then write an essay about what you have read and listened to. In the second, you must write an essay based only on a short prompt that asks you to describe or explain something or to express an opinion on an issue. You do not need any specialized knowledge to write this second essay. The prompt is based on topics that will be familiar to all test takers. You are given 30 minutes to plan, write, and revise this essay. Typically, an effective essay will include a minimum of 300 words. Essays will be judged on the quality of the writing, including idea development, organization, and the quality and accuracy of the language used to express these ideas.

One of the essay types that you may need to write for this second Writing section task is the compare/contrast essay. In a compare/contrast essay, you will discuss the ways in which two topics are similar (comparing them), and the ways in which they differ (contrasting them). Sometimes this analysis will be the only requirement of the prompt. Most times, however, the prompt will be asking you to identify your own preference among the options offered and to use comparison and contrast to support that point of view.

How will you recognize a prompt that requires a compare/contrast essay in response? There are several ways. Let's consider them.

1. The prompt will often directly ask for comparison and contrast, using those words.

   Compare and contrast the benefits of learning from school versus learning from experience. Use specific examples and details in your response.

2. The prompt will usually suggest two or more different topics, and ask you to make observations about the features of all of them.

   Some people would much rather live in a large city than in a small town; other people find small towns to be preferable. Explain your own preference by describing the advantages and disadvantages of each.

3. The prompt may ask you to decide between two options, and explain your reasons for doing so. Comparative or superlative (-er or -est) forms of adjectives and adverbs in the prompt will indicate that a compare/contrast essay would be appropriate.

> Many people feel that history, literature, and other liberal arts are the most important topics to study in school. Others think that technical subjects like math, engineering, or physics are more useful. In your view, which of these viewpoints is stronger? Use specific examples and reasons in your answer.

Compare/Contrast Practice

Read the following prompts and circle those which require a compare/contrast essay in response. Then write what kind of essay is required for the others.

1. Some people suggest that businesses should be required to pay no income taxes. Do you agree with this view? Why or why not?

   _____

   _____

2. Many people like to spend lots of time with their friends. Others like to see their friends only once in a while. Which kind of person are you? Provide reasons and examples to support your answer.

   _____

   _____

3. Both fiction and nonfiction are important forms of literature. Which do you prefer to read? Explain your preference by describing the differences and similarities between the two.

   _____

   _____

Answers

1. This prompt requires an Agree/Disagree essay.

2. This prompt requires a Descriptive essay.

3. Both fiction and nonfiction are important forms of literature. Which do you prefer to read? Explain your preference by describing the differences and similarities between the two.

Creating a Thesis Statement for a Compare/Contrast Essay

Usually a compare/contrast essay prompt will require you to choose between the options or points of view it mentions. You will express that choice in your essay's introduction as a *thesis statement*, a clear statement of your opinion or point of view, which the rest of your essay will be devoted to supporting.

Writing Topic Sentences

Once you have a thesis statement, your next task is to create topic sentences to introduce each of your body paragraphs. Your topic sentences should be statements that identify the general topic you intend to address in each of your body paragraphs.

Let's use the following sample response to a prompt requiring you to compare and contrast the advantages of working for a large or small company:

Preference: large company

Small company advantages:
- friendlier
- easier to make an impression
- greater autonomy

Large company advantages:
- greater resources
- higher salary
- opportunities for posting in foreign countries
- better on resume

Because each topic—small companies and large companies—has a different set of points to discuss, the sample uses a block-format essay. Therefore, the first body paragraph will be about the advantages of smaller companies. The second body paragraph will be a discussion of the superior advantages of larger companies. So the following topic sentences are used to introduce each body paragraph:

I.   Small companies do seem to offer certain advantages.
II. Although small companies offer some advantages, they are outweighed by the advantages of working for a large multinational company.

Both of these sentences are general enough to include all the points needed in each of the body paragraphs. The second topic sentence has the added feature of reminding the reader of the writer's point of view: that larger companies are superior to smaller companies as places of employment. Notice also that the second topic sentence begins with the word *although*, a transition signal telling the reader that the following discussion will contrast with what went before.

Structuring a Compare/Contrast Essay

Compare/contrast essays can be written in one of two different patterns of organization. As an example, let's compare apples and oranges. Look at the two outlines that follow. Both are outlines for the body of an essay that compares and contrasts apples and oranges.

A	B
Paragraph 1: Apples a. color b. flavor c. varieties	Paragraph 1: Color of apples and oranges
	Paragraph 2: Flavor of apples and orange
Paragraph 2: Oranges a. color b. flavor c. varieties	Paragraph 3: Varieties of apples and oranges

Explain the differences in the organization of the two essays that would be written from these two outlines.

_____

_____

Now answer the following questions.

1. Which outline deals with apples in one paragraph and oranges in another?

   _____

2. Which outline discusses apples and oranges within the same paragraph?

   _____

3. What features of apples and oranges are mentioned in both outlines?

   _____

4. Which outline mentions all of the features in the same paragraph?

_____

5. Which outline mentions one feature per paragraph?

_____

Answers

The two patterns are called *block format*, illustrated by (A), and *point-by-point format*, illustrated by (B).

1. A. Block format
2. B. Point-by-point format
3. Colors, flavors and varieties
4. A. Block format
5. B. Point-by-point format

Block Format

In block organization, each of the two items being compared and contrasted occupies a separate section of the essay. For example, the writer of the model essay, "Two Economic Giants" in Lesson 4— Reading: More About Transitions might have chosen to present all the information about China in the first part of the essay, and in the second part of the essay, all the information about the United States. Each paragraph in the first section would only contain information about China. There would be a paragraph in which the writer presented all the information about China's geography, another about the Chinese population, and a third about features of China's economy.

In the second half of the essay, there would be another set of paragraphs on the same topics, but containing information about the United States instead of China.

Block format works best if you have more information about one of your topics than the other.

An outline of the block organization might look like this:

Block Format Outline

  I. Introduction

 II. Topic 1

    A. Point 1

    B. Point 2

    C. Point 3

    D. (Possible additional points)

III. Topic 2

    A. Point 1

    B. Point 2

    C. Point 3

    D. (Possible additional points)

IV. Conclusion

Point-by-Point Format

In this method of organization, each point of comparison or contrast occupies its own paragraph; within each paragraph, the author provides information about both topics as they relate to that point. For this reason, the point-by-point format works best if you have the same amount of information about each of your topics.

Here's an example outline for such an essay.

Point-by-Point Format Outline

  I. Introduction

 II. Point 1

    A. Topic 1

    B. Topic 2

III. Point 2

    A. Topic 1

    B. Topic 2

IV. Point 3

    A. Topic 1

    B. Topic 2

 V. Conclusion

Writing the Conclusion of a Compare/Contrast Essay

Unfortunately, conclusions are often the most neglected part of an essay, partly because they come last, and partly because writers are sometimes unsure exactly what to do when the time comes to write a conclusion. In this lesson, you will learn strategies for solving both of those problems.

Budgeting Your Time

In timed writing conditions, when you have to plan, write, and proofread an essay within a given time limit, it is important to leave time to write a good conclusion. With practice you will learn what system works best for you, but a good rule is that for a 30-minute essay, about 3–4 minutes are needed for each paragraph of your essay, including the conclusion. Here are some tips for writing an essay within a 30-minute time limit.

- 8–10 minutes for prewriting and planning
- 15 minutes for writing (4–5 paragraphs)
- 5 minutes for editing and proofreading

Once you have practiced budgeting your time carefully, all sections of your essay will improve, and you will be able to feel more comfortable and relaxed as you write.

What Is the Function of a Conclusion?

The English word *conclude* has two meanings. The first meaning is simply *to come to an end*. For example, we might say

The meeting concluded on time.

OR

The movie concluded with an explosive scene.

On the other hand, conclude may mean to come to a decision after considering the available evidence. For instance, a person might say

I have concluded that X is the best course of action.

OR

After long deliberation, the jury concluded that the defendant was guilty as charged.

It is this second meaning of *conclude* that you should be thinking of when it is time to write the conclusion to your essay. A concluding paragraph is not simply the place where your essay comes to an end. Instead, it is the part of the essay that identifies the solution, resolution, or decision that is the logical outcome of the discussion and information you have provided in the essay body.

Here are two rules to keep in mind as you write your conclusion.

1. The job of your conclusion is to identify or emphasize the lesson, message, or decision that the essay discussion logically leads the reader to. This lesson or message should agree with or confirm the thesis presented in the introduction. A brief summary of your main points from the body may help to lead your reader to that message.

2. Long conclusions are unnecessary. It is best to avoid introducing any new information or arguments in the conclusion—those belong in the body of the essay.

Conclusion Practice

Read the conclusion of the essay found in Lesson 4—Reading: More About Transitions once again.

> Persistent American fears of being overshadowed economically by China are not entirely unfounded; the Asian nation is indeed growing very rapidly. However, a developing energy shortage promises to slow that growth, and as Chinese labor costs rise, as they inevitably must, the country will become less attractive to foreign investment. By that time, however, China may well have acquired a healthy component of domestic capital, and its increasingly affluent population will in turn become a market for American exports. The next few years are likely to see the economic connection between China and the United States develop into a prosperous partnership.

Now answer the following questions.

1. How well does this conclusion demonstrate the two rules previously given? Is it long-winded?

2. Does it introduce new information?

3. Does it present a solution or resolution that follows from the essay's discussion?

4. Which of the two meanings of *conclude* is demonstrated by this concluding paragraph?

Answers

1. Not very well. It is a little long-winded.

2. Yes. There are developing energy and labor problems.

3. Yes. China and the U.S. will likely become economic partners.

4. *to come to a decision after considering the available evidence*

Now use the skills and strategies you have learned so far in this lesson and complete the following Compare/Contrast Essay Practice.

Compare/Contrast Essay Practice

Write an essay in which you compare and contrast the business culture of your own country and that of another country. Try to apply the strategies for budgeting time and for writing conclusions discussed in the lesson.

_____

_____

_____

_____

_____

_____

_____

_____

_____

_____

_____

_____

_____

_____

_____

_____

_____

Answer

Answers will vary, but here is one sample essay.

> The United States and Japan are very different countries culturally speaking, and the way business is conducted in each can be very confusing to visitors. Even social actions that one might think of as simple, such as greeting a new person, attending a meeting, or even socializing after work can be very different.
>
> For example, when two people meet for the first time in a business setting in the U.S., it is customary to shake hands, say, "Nice to meet you" and perhaps ask a very simple question like "How are you?" In Japan, the custom is very different. When two people meet for the first time, it is expected that both will bow to a specific depth, depending on the status of the other person, and both will exchange business cards by holding them out with two hands. Once someone has given out their business card, the receiver must then carefully put the card away in a pocket so as to show a proper level of respect to its owner.
>
> Business meetings are very different, too. In the U.S., when an important business meeting is held, it may be to gather the appropriate people together into a room in order to make a decision. In this case, everyone who is invited to the meeting is expected to participate, and more often than not, any person in the meeting is able to speak if they have a valuable and relevant contribution to the conversation. In Japan, a business meeting is more likely to be called when higher levels of management need to inform their staff of a decision that has been made. In these meetings, only senior members of the staff participate in any discussion that takes place.
>
> Last comes social activity after work. While in the United States it is not uncommon for groups of people to occasionally go out after work, it is for the most part a voluntary activity. On the other hand, in Japanese business culture, it is often expected that employees will go out quite often after work with their coworkers and perhaps even their superiors. This is sometimes seen as an important teambuilding exercise, and the highest ranking person in a group will often end up paying the largest portion of the bill as a courtesy to the rest of the employees.
>
> Despite all of these differences, business relations between Japan and the U.S. seem to be going strong. Every day people are flying across the Pacific Ocean in both directions. With a little studying and an open mind, they will be prepared to do business in a different culture.

When you are ready, proceed with the lesson by reviewing another essay type found on the Writing section of the TOEFL.

Writing an Essay in Response to a Reading Passage and a Lecture

There are 2 tasks in the Writing section of the TOEFL. The first is a 20-minute essay based on a reading passage and a lecture.

For the first essay in the TOEFL Writing section, you will have 3 minutes to read a passage about an academic topic. You may take notes as you read. Then you will listen to a lecture about the same topic and take notes while you listen. Information in the lecture will conflict somewhat with the information in the reading passage; that is, a different perspective on the topic will be presented.

After reading and listening, you will have 20 minutes to write a response to a question that asks you about the relationship between the reading and the lecture. The question will not ask you to express your opinion. You will be able to see the reading passage again when it is time for you to write, and you will be able to use the notes you took while reading and listening.

An effective response will be approximately 150–225 words long. It will be judged on the quality of your writing and on the completeness and accuracy of what you write.

Recall from Lesson 2—Writing: Responding to a Reading Passage and Lecture that we discussed the fact that the essay required for this task may have characteristics of a definition essay. The reading passage and the lecture essentially define the topic in different ways, and you must synthesize and summarize those definitions. Because the reading passage and the lecture present a contrast on the topic, it is possible that your essay will also include elements of a compare/contrast essay, which is why that essay type is covered in this lesson as well.

Make sure to read the prompt carefully to determine exactly what it is asking you to do. In your response, be prepared to do the following:

- Summarize information provided in the reading passage and the lecture
- Define a specific term or idea
- Provide examples from the reading passage and lecture

Note-Taking

It is to your advantage that you can take notes on this writing assignment. The basis of good note-taking skills is being able to identify key information that must be noted and organizing notes in such a way that they are of maximum use. Here is a list of strategies that will help you become a more effective note taker.

- **The introduction of both readings and lectures will generally tell you exactly what the writer or speaker's main purpose is.** If you understand the purpose of the passage or lecture, it will be much easier for you to identify essential information.
- **It is common for the introduction to forecast, that is, list the main arguments or topics that will be discussed in the text, especially in longer talks or texts.** If you can identify these topics, you can organize your notes around them.
- **Topic sentences will also tell you what the key points of the discussion or reading passage are.** You can use the topic sentences even if there is no forecasting in the introduction.

- **Pay careful attention to examples.** Note down those that seem clearest or most important. In shorter texts or talks, there may only be one or two. Make sure you make a note of them for later.
- **Listen carefully for statistics, dates, or other numbers.** They are almost always key information. Write them down.
- **Be organized.** List key ideas in order, leaving space next to each for related examples and information.
- **If your information is numerical, make certain you know what it means.** Does that "1492" mean years? Millimeters? Dollars? Population?

You will practice taking notes on a reading and short lecture similar to those on the TOEFL at the end of this lesson.

Summarizing

The 20-minute writing task on the TOEFL will often ask you to summarize the ideas or points of view expressed in the reading passage and short talk. You know by now that summarizing is a valuable tool, and an excellent way for you to strengthen your own writing and reading skills. Here are four points to remember about writing a good summary:

1. A summary should not be more than about 20–25% as long as the original material, and can be much shorter, as long as it satisfies the following point.

2. A summary will reflect the author or speaker's purpose, main ideas, and conclusion, as well as the most important information or examples that support them.

3. Use the notes you made while reading or listening as the basis of your summary.

4. As you summarize, you should paraphrase, or use your own words to express the ideas found in the original reading or talk.

You will practice summarizing the ideas of a reading and short lecture similar to those on the TOEFL at the end of this lesson.

Paraphrasing

Paraphrasing is important for several reasons. First, using your own words in academic and professional settings helps you to avoid problems with plagiarism (Remember the discussion of this topic in Lesson 2—Writing: Responding to a Reading Passage and Lecture), a serious ethical violation that arises from borrowing another's words without giving that author proper credit. Second, paraphrasing allows you to demonstrate your own knowledge of English, an important component of your score in the Writing section of the TOEFL.

Here are two main strategies for paraphrasing effectively:

- Use synonyms
- Rewrite sentences

Sometimes several sentences can be boiled down to a single sentence, helping you to summarize efficiently. Consider this paragraph:

> In today's global economy, the U.S. government is as likely to borrow from foreign lenders as from those at home. That kind of deficit spending results in a net financial loss, because the interest paid on the borrowed funds does not reenter the national economy, and ultimately can produce a negative economic impact.

This paragraph could be summarized this way:

> Interest paid to foreign lenders drains money from the domestic economy.

You will practice paraphrasing the ideas of a reading and short lecture similar to those on the TOEFL now.

Essay Practice

Now you will have an opportunity to practice taking notes, summarizing, paraphrasing, and writing a response to a prompt. Following is an example of the first task in the Writing section of the TOEFL. You will find transcripts of audio passages at the end of the chapter.

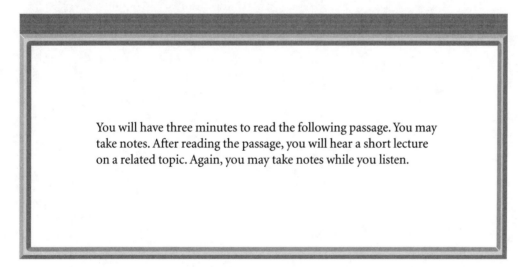

You will have three minutes to read the following passage. You may take notes. After reading the passage, you will hear a short lecture on a related topic. Again, you may take notes while you listen.

Deficit Spending: An Essential Tool

One of the most persistent debates in American politics today is the size of the federal budget deficit. Annual federal budget shortfalls in the United States regularly run in the hundreds of billions of dollars. At present, the U.S. government owes investors approximately seven and a half billion dollars, an admittedly very large number that critics of deficit spending regularly point to as a sign that fiscal disaster is just around the corner.

But these doomsayers are overlooking some important facts. Since at least the Great Depression of the 1930s, deficit spending has been a mainstay of American fiscal policy. John Maynard Keynes, perhaps the most influential economist of the twentieth century, recommended deficit spending as a means to help the United States escape from the economic quagmire that had trapped the country since the stock market crash of 1929. There were some very good reasons for this. When the government spends more money, this amounts to an increase in demand. Greater demand equals greater employment, and greater employment leads to more money in the pockets of people who will spend it, which in turn will create greater demand. So when the economy is running below capacity as in a recession or depression, deficit spending is an important way for the government to "prime the pump," or to get the economy running normally again.

Deficits are far from a sign of imminent economic disaster. Rather, such spending is no more than a symptom of the central government's efforts to keep the nation's economy healthy and stable.

Notes

🎧 **34.4W, Essay Practice**

Notes

Directions: You have 20 minutes to plan and write your response. Your response will be judged on the basis of the quality of your writing and on how well your response presents the points in the lecture and their relationship to the reading passage. Typically, an effective response will be 150 to 225 words.

🎧 **35.4W, Essay Prompt**

Compare and contrast the points of view expressed in the reading passage and the short talk. What are the similarities between the two? What are the differences? Which position is stronger? Use details and examples to support your answer.

_____

_____

_____

_____

_____

_____

_____

_____

_____

_____

_____

_____

_____

_____

_____

_____

_____

_____

_____

_____

_____

Answer

Answers will vary. Here is one sample essay.

> Deficit spending occurs when a government spends more money than it has, leaving it in debt to investors. According to the passage, the United States federal budget deficit is currently very high, at seven and a half billion dollars. The passage and lecture agree that deficit spending is an effective tool, but they clash over how willing a government should be to use deficit spending to make corrections to an underperforming economy.
>
> The author of the passage points out that the United States has been applying deficit spending since the 1930s, with beneficial results. The passage states that when a government spends money, it creates demand, which then creates jobs, so that more people have money to spend, which will lead to economic growth. This allows a government to have a level of control over the economy.
>
> The lecturer agrees that deficit spending can be used to jumpstart an economy, but makes the point that this is not a strategy that is appropriate for an economy that is already healthy. The professor points out that government spending in good economic times can increase demand to a point where it actually causes inflation of prices, as in the post-Vietnam's 1970s. This means that currency has less value, and can lead to high unemployment and high interest rates.
>
> I believe that the lecturer makes a stronger point about how carefully deficit spending must be applied. Increased government spending clearly has an effect on an economy that is experiencing depression, as with Keynes' policies in the 1930s. However, to me, a situation like that of the stagnant 1970s, when government overspent and caused inflation, which then decreased the wealth of its citizens, is not only bad planning, but it can be dangerous. I think that deficit spending, while a good tool in lean times, is not a policy that can be applied lightly.

Now that you have practiced both types of TOEFL Writing section essays, you are ready to begin Lesson 4—Listening: Note-Taking Practice.

LESSON 4—LISTENING: NOTE-TAKING PRACTICE

In this lesson, we will cover more listening skills and strategies that will help lead to success on test day. You will have the opportunity to review the strategies you learned in previous lessons as well as to learn about other question types found on the Listening section of the TOEFL. If you want to proceed with more listening strategies when you finish this lesson, turn to Lesson 5—Listening: Note-Taking and Key Words in Chapter 5.

Note-Taking

Remember that as you listen to the passages on the TOEFL, you should be taking notes. You must:

- Listen for strong statements by the speaker that indicate the speaker's opinion and attitude
- Write down key words, names, numbers, dates, or anything else you think is important

Note-Taking Practice

Listen to a conversation between a professor and a student. Take notes as you listen. You will find a transcript of this audio passage (36.4L, Note-Taking Practice) at the end of the chapter.

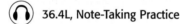 **36.4L, Note-Taking Practice**

Notes

Now use your notes to answer the following questions. You may need to listen to parts of the lecture a second time.

1. What is the professor's initial attitude toward Sean?

    _____

    _____

2. What can you infer about Sean's typical behavior as a student?

    _____

    _____

3. Why didn't the class discuss the handouts the day Sean was absent?

    _____

    _____

4. What does the professor suggest that Sean do?

    _____

    _____

5. What does Sean need to remember for Monday?

    _____

    _____

Answers

1. The professor is not pleased that Sean has been missing class.

2. Sean seems to miss class a lot, but is willing to try and catch up.

3. The professor decided to have the discussion after the class had seen a video.

4. The professor suggests that Sean watch the second half with the rest of the class tomorrow, then watch the first half over the weekend.

5. Sean needs to bring the video back to the professor on Monday.

Outlining

You know by now that an outline is a skeletal structure of a text. It contains the main and supporting ideas in the order they are presented, but does not necessarily include any specific details.

The outlining of a conversation is different from the outlining of a lecture, because it involves constant turn-taking between two people who have different viewpoints on the topic. One speaker can disagree with the other and introduce a new argument, or even change the subject entirely. As a result, the natural speech of a conversation doesn't have the same carefully planned transitions found in lectures for moving from one supporting point to another.

For a conversation you should try to identify the following elements:
- The two characters involved in the conversation
- The central character (the one who has a particular need)
- The central character's need
- The central character's conflict (who or what is preventing him/her from satisfying the need)
- The resolution of the conflict (how his/her need is satisfied)

Understanding the question types is critical for knowing how and where to apply your strategies. Keep reading to learn more.

Question Types

There are several different question types on the Listening section of the TOEFL. The previous lessons covered the following types:
- Understanding Rhetorical Function
- Understanding an Idiomatic Expression in Context
- Drawing an Inference
- Understanding a Speaker's Implication
- Identifying the Main Idea
- Summarizing the Most Important Ideas
- Understanding Details

This lesson will review two question types, focusing on how they apply to conversations:
- Drawing an Inference
- Understanding a Speaker's Implication

Question Type 3—Drawing an Inference

There are 2 conversations and 4 lectures in the Listening section of the TOEFL. Each conversation is generally followed by 1 *inference* question, and each lecture is followed by 0 or 1 *inference* question.

Remember that *inference* questions ask you to draw conclusions about specific details in what you hear or to make comparisons between details. In order to answer these types of questions, you should:

- Listen carefully to the details of the lecture or conversation
- Try to understand unfamiliar words from context
- Listen for conditionals, intonation, and suggestions made by the speakers while the conversation is happening so that you can anticipate certain inference questions
- Use your knowledge about the situation to guess what sort of conclusion might be logical

The following are examples of inference questions:

"What probably happened to _____?"

"What will _____ probably do next?"

"What can be inferred about _____?"

Now listen to a conversation between a professor and a student. Take notes as you listen. You will find a transcript of this audio passage (37.4L, Conversation) at the end of the chapter.

🎧 **37.4L, Conversation**

Notes

Following are several *inference* questions based on the conversation you heard between the professor and student about insider trading. Use your notes to answer the questions.

> With which of the following statements would the professor probably agree?
>
> (A) Danny needs to be careful about who he talks to about the problem.
> (B) Danny is engaged in insider trading with Mary Stewart.
> (C) Danny is embarrassed about something he did at work.
> (D) Danny is feeling sick about what's happening at work.

This question tests your ability to make an inference based on several pieces of information within the entire lecture. Choices (B) and (C) twist facts from the conversation into the wrong context. Danny is not engaged in insider trading; someone at work is. Danny is embarrassed about something that happened at work, but not something he did. Choice (D) also misrepresents concepts from the lecture; feeling sick is merely an excuse that he gave at work for not being there. Choice (A) is the correct answer. The professor is concerned and asks Danny whether he had talked to anybody else at work about this problem, and then goes on to say that he did the right thing by not doing so.

The next inference question contains an excerpt from the conversation. Remember that on the actual test, you will only hear the excerpt—you will not be able to read it. Remember also that the question and the four answer choices in listening questions appear on the computer screen, but only the question is spoken by the narrator.

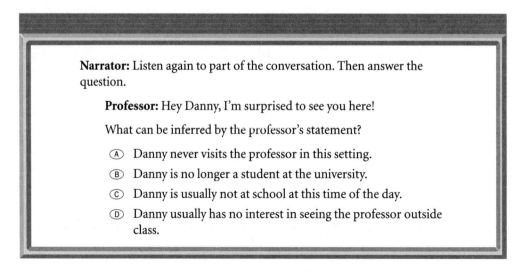

> **Narrator:** Listen again to part of the conversation. Then answer the question.
>
> **Professor:** Hey Danny, I'm surprised to see you here!
>
> What can be inferred by the professor's statement?
>
> (A) Danny never visits the professor in this setting.
> (B) Danny is no longer a student at the university.
> (C) Danny is usually not at school at this time of the day.
> (D) Danny usually has no interest in seeing the professor outside class.

This question tests your ability to make an inference based on a single statement. Choice (A) is incorrect because even though the professor is surprised to see Danny, to say that Danny *never* visits the professor is too extreme. Choice (B) is incorrect because from other details in the conversation, it is obvious that Danny is a current student. Choice (D) is another inference that is too extreme, especially considering the good relationship the professor and Danny seem to have with each other. Choice (C) is correct.

What will the student and professor probably do next?

(A) Review what Danny learned in his business ethics class.

(B) Blow the whistle on Danny's boss.

(C) Call Mary Stewart at IRU.

(D) Create a plan on how to deal with the problem.

Answering this question successfully requires an understanding of the entire lecture. Choice (A) is tempting because the professor uses these words the last time she speaks, but it is incorrect because it does not address the underlying reason for reviewing the basics. Choices (B) and (C) are also incorrect because it's too hard to predict at this time what action they will take. They probably won't know this until after they have a discussion about the problem and how to deal with it, which is why choice (D) is correct.

Narrator: Listen again to part of the conversation. Then answer the question.

Student: Do you mind if I close the door while we discuss this...

What can be inferred about the speaker?

(A) He's a shy and private person.

(B) He believes the information should be private.

(C) He thinks there's too much noise in the hall.

(D) He cannot hear what the professor is saying.

Choice (A) is incorrect considering the specific context. It is reasonable for any person, shy or outgoing, to be private about sensitive information. There are no clues in the conversation to suggest that choice (C) or (D) is correct. Therefore, choice (B) is the correct answer.

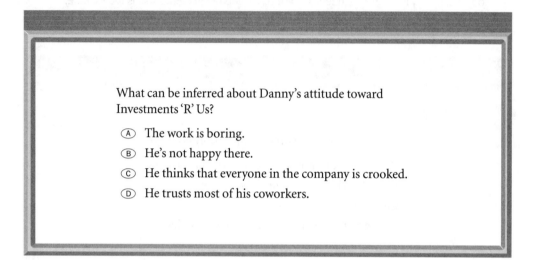

What can be inferred about Danny's attitude toward Investments 'R' Us?

Ⓐ The work is boring.

Ⓑ He's not happy there.

Ⓒ He thinks that everyone in the company is crooked.

Ⓓ He trusts most of his coworkers.

Choice (A) is incorrect because he never mentions or describes the content of his job. Choice (C) is incorrect because this inference is too broad, especially in light of the concession he makes about Mary Stewart's not being involved. Choice (D) is incorrect, because if Danny trusted any of his coworkers, he wouldn't be secretly discussing the problem with his professor. Choice (B) is a correct inference, because he's obviously upset about something that's happening at work.

Question Type 4—Understanding a Speaker's Implication

There are 2 conversations and 4 lectures in the Listening section of the TOEFL. Each conversation has 1 or 2 *speaker's implication* questions, and each lecture has 0 or 1 *speaker's implication* question.

Remember from your review of this question type in Lesson 2, Listening that something that is implied is not directly stated. An implication is the meaning of a statement that is not obvious in the literal meaning of the words.

The answer choices for implication questions will contain situations that will further confuse you because they were not discussed or did not occur. You will also see synonyms, homophones (words with different spellings but the same pronunciation, for example: *our*, *hour*), or other words repeated in the answer choices that are either out of context or not stated in the conversation.

The following are examples of implication questions:

- What does the man probably mean?
- What does the man suggest/imply?
- What does the woman want to know?
- What does the man say about _____?

- What does the woman advise the man to do?
- Why does _____ say _____?
- What does _____ mean by _____?

Following are some sample speaker's implication questions. Each question includes an excerpt from the conversation between the student and professor about insider trading. First, listen to the question, and then look at the transcript and answer the question. Remember that on the test, you will hear everything printed here, but you will not see the transcript of the excerpt from the conversation.

Narrator: Listen again to part of the conversation. Then answer the question.

> **Student:** Well, I just feel that one of my coworkers, at IRU…well, I can't really call him a coworker, I am just an intern…but anyway, I just think…um…I just think there's some not so good stuff going on.

What does the student mean when he ways this?

> **Student:** I just think there's some not so good stuff going on.

- (A) He's concerned about IRU's financial performance
- (B) He doesn't think he works with good people
- (C) Something illegal is happening
- (D) IRU does less than mediocre work

Choice (A) is incorrect. *Not-so-good* is a subtle way of saying *bad*. The most important goal of any company is to have good financial results, so this answer tries to trap you into equating good or bad with financial performance. Choice (D) is also playing with the idea of *not-so-good* as quality standard for the company's overall performance. Choice (B) is incorrect because he's not making a broad generalization that all of his coworkers are bad. He's merely saying that something bad is happening by an unnamed person or persons, which is why choice (C) is correct.

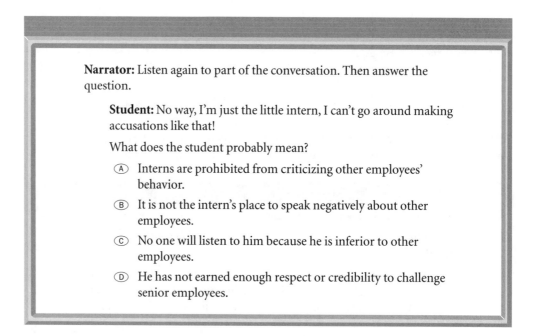

Narrator: Listen again to part of the conversation. Then answer the question.

    Student: No way, I'm just the little intern, I can't go around making accusations like that!

    What does the student probably mean?

      (A) Interns are prohibited from criticizing other employees' behavior.

      (B) It is not the intern's place to speak negatively about other employees.

      (C) No one will listen to him because he is inferior to other employees.

      (D) He has not earned enough respect or credibility to challenge senior employees.

Choice (A) is a literal translation of *can't*. Choices (B) and (C) are similar ideas that brand him into a specific roles, as if they were social standards or rules to be followed and enforced. Choice (D) is what Danny means and emphasizes with his word choices (*little intern*) and sarcastic tone (as *if* it were a rule).

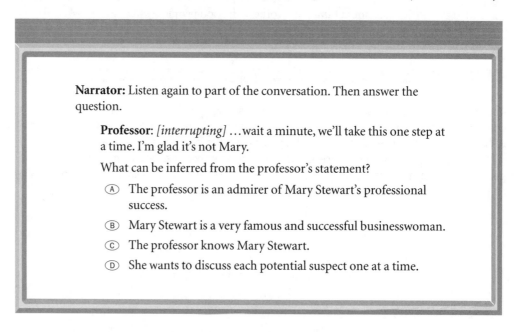

Narrator: Listen again to part of the conversation. Then answer the question.

    Professor: *[interrupting]* …wait a minute, we'll take this one step at a time. I'm glad it's not Mary.

    What can be inferred from the professor's statement?

      (A) The professor is an admirer of Mary Stewart's professional success.

      (B) Mary Stewart is a very famous and successful businesswoman.

      (C) The professor knows Mary Stewart.

      (D) She wants to discuss each potential suspect one at a time.

Choices (A) and (B) are incorrect because we usually don't refer to people we don't know by their first names. Choice (D) is incorrect because Danny already identified the account manager as the inside trader. This answer choice is trying to distract you with the professor's words *one step at a time*, which you might interpret as analyzing the people involved in insider trading one at a time.

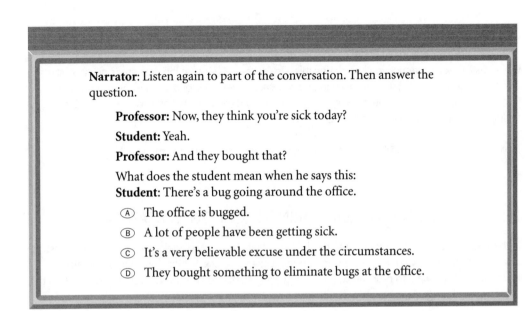

Narrator: Listen again to part of the conversation. Then answer the question.

> **Professor:** Now, they think you're sick today?
>
> **Student:** Yeah.
>
> **Professor:** And they bought that?
>
> What does the student mean when he says this:
> **Student:** There's a bug going around the office.
>
> Ⓐ The office is bugged.
>
> Ⓑ A lot of people have been getting sick.
>
> Ⓒ It's a very believable excuse under the circumstances.
>
> Ⓓ They bought something to eliminate bugs at the office.

Choice (A) means there is a surveillance device for recording peoples' conversations, which may be used to catch them in the act of planning criminal activity such as this; however, in this context it's not the correct definition. Choice (B) is what the man says directly but it doesn't capture the reason why he said it, which is important for understanding the main idea of their conversation. Choice (D), like (A), is a synonym distracter. This time *bugs* literally mean insects, which need to be killed. Choice (C) is the best answer because it establishes the relationship between being sick and his excuse for not being at work.

Narrator: Listen again to part of the conversation. Then answer the question.

> **Professor:** Why don't you start by telling me how you found out about it?
>
> What does the professor want to know?
>
> Ⓐ Why Danny is reluctant to speak about his boss' insider trading
>
> Ⓑ How Danny's boss is doing insider trading
>
> Ⓒ How Danny discovered that insider trading was going on
>
> Ⓓ Why the new account manager is doing insider trading.

With a different tone of voice, and in a different context, this question may mean, choice (A). But this is clearly not the rhetorical intent of the professor's question in this context. Choice (D), like (A), uses the *why* question word to tempt you into picking this answer choice, because the professor's question starts with this same word (*why*). Choice (B) is incorrect because the professor doesn't want to know how Danny's boss is doing the insider trading, rather how Danny discovered that his boss is doing insider trading, choice (C); choice (C) is the correct answer.

Now that you have reviewed some listening strategies, let's move on to some speaking strategies.

LESSON 4—SPEAKING: NOTE-TAKING FROM CONVERSATIONS

In this lesson, we will cover more speaking skills and strategies that will help lead to success on test day. This lesson will continue to review an important speaking task, Synthesizing and Summarizing Information. If you want to proceed with more speaking strategies when you finish this lesson, turn to Lesson 5—Speaking: Defining and Describing in Chapter 5.

Remember that in Lessons 1, 2, and 3 we covered the following speaking tasks:
- Describing Something from Your Own Experience
- Summarizing a Lecture
- Expressing and Supporting an Opinion Based on Personal Experience
- Summarizing a Conversation and Expressing an Opinion
- Synthesizing and Summarizing Information

Two separate tasks in the Speaking section require you to synthesize and summarize information, so this lesson also covers:
- Synthesizing and Summarizing Information

First, let's cover some other important speaking skills and strategies.

Note-Taking

Note-taking is a very important skill for the TOEFL, for academic success, and for life in general. We receive a lot of information every day, and we cannot remember all of it. Look at the following conversation:

Johnny: Can I get your phone number?

Polly: Sure. It's area code 5-0-1, then 7-double-2...

Johnny: Hang on... 5-0-1, 7-7-2... go on...

Polly: No, it's 7-2-2. Not 7-7-2.

Johnny: Oh sorry, 7 double 2… and then. . .

Polly: Then 5-0-8-9.

Johnny: Ok, let me read this back: 5-0-1, 7-2-2, 5-0-8-9.

Polly: You got it!

Note-Taking Practice

During this conversation, Johnny is taking notes. Answer the following questions.

1. What do you think he will have written down by the end of this conversation?

2. What is the key information?

3. Why does he need that information?

Answers

1. 501-722-5089

2. the numbers

3. so that he has an accurate phone number for Polly

You need to be able to identify and take notes on key information. Later you might use those notes to remind yourself of that information.

Speaking and Pronunciation: Unstressed Words and Syllables

English is a rhythmic language. Some words and syllables are stressed, while others are not. The stressed words and syllables are the beat of the language. Usually, the unstressed words and syllables are shorter in duration and less loud in volume. Sometimes they almost disappear. The vowels in unstressed words and syllables are often reduced to the sound [_] or [I].

Task 4—Synthesizing and Summarizing Information

There are 6 tasks in the Speaking section of the TOEFL. The fourth task asks you to read and listen to material on related topics. After reading and listening, you must give a 60-second response to a question about what you read and heard.

The fourth task in the Speaking section of the TOEFL is similar to the third task, in that you must read a passage, listen to someone speak on the same topic, and then synthesize and summarize what you have read and heard. However, the third task includes a short announcement followed by a conversation about the announcement, whereas the fourth task includes an academic text followed by a lecture on the academic topic.

As in the third task, you have 45 seconds to read the passage. You may take notes during the lecture. Then you have 30 seconds to prepare your response to a question that you will see and hear. You then have 60 seconds to respond. On the actual test, you will not see the narrator introduction to the question.

When reading the passage and listening to the talk you should:

- Identify the main points
- Make a note of key words and ideas
- Listen for examples and details that support the main ideas

Following is a sample TOEFL question. Listen to the narrator's introduction. Remember that you will not see the narrator's introduction to the question on the test. If you have a study partner, or someone that can listen to your response, ask to work with him or her. You will find a transcript of these audio passages at the end of the chapter.

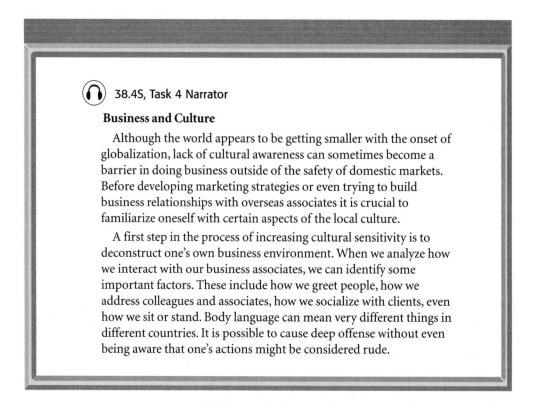

38.4S, Task 4 Narrator

Business and Culture

Although the world appears to be getting smaller with the onset of globalization, lack of cultural awareness can sometimes become a barrier in doing business outside of the safety of domestic markets. Before developing marketing strategies or even trying to build business relationships with overseas associates it is crucial to familiarize oneself with certain aspects of the local culture.

A first step in the process of increasing cultural sensitivity is to deconstruct one's own business environment. When we analyze how we interact with our business associates, we can identify some important factors. These include how we greet people, how we address colleagues and associates, how we socialize with clients, even how we sit or stand. Body language can mean very different things in different countries. It is possible to cause deep offense without even being aware that one's actions might be considered rude.

Notes

 39.4S, Task 4 Lecture

Notes

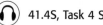 40.4S, Task 4 Prompt

The professor describes some social differences between India and America. Explain how these differences relate to doing business.

30 seconds to prepare
60 seconds to speak

Evaluate yourself using the following criteria:

Criteria	Comments	Action to Improve
Clarity and pronunciation		
Organization		
Details and examples		
Grammar and vocabulary		

Now listen to the sample response. How was it different from yours? How was it similar? You will find a transcript of this audio passage (41.4S, Task 4 Sample Response) at the end of the chapter.

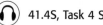 41.4S, Task 4 Sample Response

More Practice Synthesizing and Summarizing Information

Following is another sample synthesizing and summarizing TOEFL question. Remember that you will not see the narrator's introduction to the question on the test. If you have a study partner, or someone that can listen to your response, ask to work with him or her.

42.4S, More Practice Narrator

Real Estate: Is It a Bubble?

Owning real estate remains a popular and largely safe investment for many Americans. The home is, for most families, their greatest asset as well as the greatest debt they will ever hold. It is no wonder therefore, that people fear a bubble in the housing market. A bubble can be defined as a rapid increase in housing prices fuelled by unreasonable demand. When the bubble bursts, prices fall as dramatically as they went up.

If the current increased demand and higher prices turns out to be a bubble as opposed to a real increase in value, then a burst is inevitable. A sudden decline in housing prices nationally could precipitate an increase in unemployment and have a negative impact on GDP.

Notes

43.4S, More Practice Lecture

Notes

 44.4S, More Practice Prompt

The professor discusses some factors to show that homebuyers don't need to worry about a real estate bubble. Summarize her advice to potential buyers.

30 seconds to prepare
60 seconds to speak

Evaluate yourself using the following criteria:

Criteria	Comments	Action to Improve
Clarity and pronunciation		
Organization		
Details and examples		
Grammar and vocabulary		

Now listen to the sample response. How was it different from yours? How was it similar? You will find a transcript of this audio passage (45.4S, More Practice Response) at the end of the chapter.

🎧 **45.4S, More Practice Response**

Way to go! You're half way through Kaplan's *TOEFL iBT with CD-ROM*. But there's still more to learn and review. When you are ready, turn to Chapter 5 for more reading, writing, listening, and speaking strategies.

CHAPTER 4 AUDIO TRANSCRIPTS

33. Lesson 4—Reading, Summarizing Two Sources Practice

Professor: So those are some of the arguments against deregulation. Now let's take a look at the arguments in favor. Frankly speaking, it's...uh...much, *much* easier to find the advantages of deregulation. First...cost. Direct costs of regulation are not very high, but the indirect costs are phenomenal. All those public interest groups campaigning, not always getting what they want mind you, and industries throwing millions of dollars at politicians they hope will make regulatory laws in their favor. In 1975 the cost of regulation was said to be about $100 billion dollars! Deregulation does not incur such outrageous costs.

Next, prices typically fall after deregulation. This is because of an increase in competition. Remember I said that one aspect of regulation is entry into the industry? In other words, only a certain number of firms are allowed to operate in one industry. Well...isn't it obvious that if entry restrictions are abolished, competitor, and therefore competition, will increase? And equally obvious is that competition leads to drops in price...the consumer's dream.

Let's move on to an example...the airline industry is often cited as an example of deregulatory failure...but when we examine the effects of airline deregulation closely, we can see that the problem is not *really* deregulation. After the airlines were deregulated in 1978, prices initially dropped, but quality of service decreased dramatically, too. And then, prices started to edge up again without an accompanying improvement in level of service. But what was to blame for this was not deregulation but a series of mergers and acquisitions in the airline industry which was leading to a monopolistic environment. This is a very interesting example, so for tomorrow, I'd like you to research what has been happening in the airline industry most recently.

34. Lesson 4—Writing, Essay Practice

Narrator: Now, listen to part of a lecture on the topic you have just read about.

Professor: Let's talk about the issue of deficit spending. As you may know, defenders of the federal government's steadily increasing budget gaps are, uh, fond of claiming that such Keynesian spending is merely a tool to keep the national economy on an even course. They claim that greater government spending in times of economic hardship is an effective means of restoring stability and energy to the economy. Well, in part, they are correct: when private demand is insufficient to keep the economy running at capacity, deficits can provide stimulation to a stagnant fiscal environment. But if this policy is used carelessly, deficit spending can have a negative impact on the national economy.

In the first place, if the government runs deficits during a healthy economy, the government is, uh, competing with the private market for limited amounts of credit, which will drive up interest rates and reduce the amount of credit available to private investors, resulting in under-investment. If the economy's production capacity is already maximized, increased government demand will compete with private-sector demand, and price inflation will result. In fact, this is exactly what happened with the Kennedy tax-cuts of the early sixties: the tax cuts took effect during a time of economic health, encouraging inflation at the same time the rate of government spending went up because of the Vietnam war. The result, as some of you may remember, was the stagnant economy of the 1970s, characterized by high unemployment, high interest rates, and high inflation.

Second, in today's global economy, the U.S. government is as likely to borrow from foreign lenders as from those at home. That kind of deficit spending results in a net financial loss, because the interest paid on the borrowed funds does not reenter the national economy, and ultimately can produce a negative economic impact.

So, because it can easily damage the country's economy instead of helping it, deficit spending is a dangerous, double-edged tool that must be kept under control.

35. Lesson 4—Writing, Essay Prompt

Compare and contrast the points of view expressed in the reading passage and the short talk. What are the similarities between the two? What are the differences? Which position is stronger? Use details and examples to support your answer.

36. Lesson 4—Listening, Note-Taking Practice

Narrator: Listen to a conversation between a professor and a student.

Student: Excuse me, Professor Carter?

Professor: Oh, hi Sean. Did you get up a little late this morning?

Student: I'm sorry for missing your class again professor. But this time it's because I was a little under the weather.

Professor: Oh, I'm sorry to hear that. Are you feeling better now?

Student: Yeah, much better, thank you. Uhh…and I, I just came by to get any homework you might have passed out.

Professor: Did you do the reading assignment from yesterday?

Student: Which reading assignment?

Professor: Weren't you in class yesterday?

Student: Oh, you mean the handouts. Yes, I did.

Professor: Good. Because we're going to talk about it tomorrow.

Student: Oh, I thought you went over that today.

Professor: Well, at first, I was going to, but then I decided it would be better to hold that conversation off until after we finished the video. Remember we started talking about Enron toward the end of class yesterday? Well, we talked some more about that and accounting fraud in general, which led us to the Securities Act of 1933.

Student: What was that?

Professor: Well, I don't really have time to go into it now because I have another class, but we also watched a video in class on that topic which we're going to finish tomorrow…and…have a quiz on Monday. So, uh…….hmmm…..do you have a VCR at home?

Student: Yes, I do.

Professor: Well, I'll tell you what. I'll lend you the video as long as you get it back to me before class tomorrow, because we still have to watch the second half.

Student: Yeah. No problem. That, That'd be great. I'm sure I can get it back to you even sooner, like tomorrow morning.

Professor: Ok. Ummm…(changing his mind)…well…you know what? Why don't we do this? After class tomorrow…you will be in class tomorrow, right?

Student: Yes. I will.

Professor: Good. Let's do this then: Watch the second half tomorrow, and then I'll let you borrow the videotape over the weekend. That way you have two full days to watch it, and you won't have to worry about getting it back to me so soon. How does that sound?

Student: Sounds good to me.

Professor: All right. Good. Just remember to bring it to class with you on Monday.

Student: I will.

Professor: And also, don't forget you'll have a quiz over both the video and the reading assignment.

Student: I certainly won't forget that either.

Professor: Okay. Good. I'll see you in class tomorrow.

Student: Thank you very much professor.

37. Lesson 4—Listening, Conversation

Narrator: Now listen to part of a conversation between a student and a professor.

Student: Excuse me, Professor Stein?

Professor: Hey Danny, I'm surprised to see you here! How's life at Investments 'R' Us?

Student: Well, actually…um…I actually called in sick today because I wanted to come in to talk to you about something.

Professor: My goodness…ah…you've always been such a conscientious student I can't imagine you would do that lightly. Take a seat, what's troubling you?

Student: Oh, I don't know. This is probably going to seem really stupid. Um…

Professor: Danny, I know you are a good student and a serious MBA candidate, I am not going to think you're being stupid. What is the problem?

Student: Well, I just feel that one of my coworkers, at IRU...well, I can't really call him a coworker, I am just an intern...but anyway, I just think...um ...I just think there's some not so good stuff going on.

Professor: Danny...what are you talking about?

Student: Oh man...um...I think my boss is doing insider trading.

Professor: Yikes. Well, I can see why that would be an issue for you. Have you talked about it with anyone there?

Student: No way, I'm just the little intern, I can't go around making accusations like that!

Professor: Of course not. I just wondered if the subject had come up with any of your coworkers. But...no, no...you did absolutely the right thing by coming to talk with me about it first. So, ah...well...um ... *[shocked realization]* are you talking about Mary Stewart?

Student: *[swift reassurance]* No, no, no. I hardly have any interactions with Ms. Stewart. No, it's one of the new account managers. He was just hired last month. His name is...

Professor: *[interrupting]* ...wait a minute, we'll take this one step at a time. I'm glad it's not Mary. Now, they think you're sick today?

Student: Yeah.

Professor: And they bought that?

Student: There's a bug going around.

Professor: OK. Well, Danny, I've always thought you were a good student. Um, let's see how much you got out of your business ethics class.

Student: Well, you know...that is one of the main reasons I am here. After taking that class, I realized that this stuff is really important.

Professor: Good. Well, let's start at the beginning. Why don't you start by telling me how you found out about it?

Student: Do you mind if I close the door while we discuss this...

38. Lesson 4—Speaking, Task 4 Narrator

Narrator: In this question, you will read a short passage and listen to a talk about the same topic. After you hear the question, you will have 30 seconds to prepare your response and 60 seconds to speak.

Now read the passage about business and culture. You have 45 seconds to read the passage.

39. Lesson 4—Speaking, Task 4 Lecture

Narrator: Now listen to part of a lecture on this topic in a business class.

Professor: When it comes to doing business in India, it is important to bear in mind that the business environment tends to be much more time flexible than it is here in the US. Punctuality, especially in government offices, is simply not a very high priority. You may find yourself waiting for hours to meet someone even though you had fixed an appointment days in advance. To avoid frustration, it's a good idea to call ahead and make sure the person you need to see is actually there.

Greetings can be source of embarrassment, so be aware that Indian women prefer not to shake hands with men. By the same token, western women should not initiate a handshake with a man. Between men, on the other hand, a handshake is fine. The traditional greeting, which consists of hands pressed together like this, is always acceptable.

Talking of hands, avoid passing or receiving anything with your left hand. It is not polite. Also do not use a finger to point. Use your chin or your whole hand, held open.

If your associate is older than you are, make sure you find out the proper form of address. Indian elders are never addressed by their first name. If you happen to be older, do not be surprised if your associates are more comfortable addressing you with a title; don't insist on being called your first name, they may not be comfortable with such casual interaction.

40. Lesson 4—Speaking, Task 4 Prompt

The professor describes some social differences between India and America. Explain how these differences relate to doing business.

41. Lesson 4—Speaking, Task 4 Sample Response

Um…Cultural sensitivity is very important when doing business internationally. If you want to develop good relations with business associates it is important that you don't do anything to offend them. In India, for example, it is rude to point with a finger, instead you should point with your hand. In America, people use first names a lot, but in other countries that is not polite. In India, you should not call an older person by his given name, you should use a title, like Doctor or Ms. or Mr.

Ah…also, you shouldn't get angry about some differences… like timeliness for example. In America, people are always in a hurry and you mustn't be late, but in India people are more relaxed about being on time.

42. Lesson 4—Speaking, More Practice Narrator

Narrator: In this question, you will read a short passage and listen to a talk about the same topic. After you hear the question, you will have 30 seconds to prepare your response and 60 seconds to speak.

Now read the passage about real estate. You have 45 seconds to read the passage.

43. Lesson 4—Speaking, More Practice Lecture

Narrator: Listen to a professor addressing a group attending a seminar on buying a home.

Professor: Buying real estate—is it safe? If you buy and hold for the long term, I mean 15 plus years, you aren't likely to lose. Real estate values generally go up in the long run, whereas there is no such guarantee in the stock market—many of today's companies won't even be in business fifteen years from now!

If you buy and sell properties quickly, you need to pay close attention to the local situation. That is all that matters. If the local real estate market is "hot" you can sell fast, but you can't buy cheap. If the local market is weak, you can get great deals, but can you turn them around? You need to know where your market is going, but don't worry so much about a national real estate "bubble" bursting.

On the other hand, if you have negative cash flow and buy property with the expectation that values will increase soon, you're brave, possibly crazy! There is no guarantee that values will increase in 2–3 years. What if values decrease? What's your backup plan? Such activity is very risky, to say the least.

The bottom line is, real estate markets may go up, or they may go down. So what? Don't count on appreciation, buy below market value, and make sure you have a "plan B." Keep to these guidelines, and you'll see the "bubble theory" is full of hot air.

44. Lesson 4—Speaking, More Practice Prompt

The professor discusses some factors to show that homebuyers don't need to worry about a real estate bubble. Summarize her advice to potential buyers.

45. Lesson 4—Speaking, More Practice Sample Response

So, um…some people are worried that recent increases in house prices indicate that there is a bubble in the real estate market. In other words, people are nervous that the bubble will burst and that house prices will collapse and that the economy will go down the drain as a result. Um…the professor says that you don't need to worry about the bubble bursting if you buy a house and hold onto it for a long time—like 15 years or more. If you buy and sell fast, it all depends on the local market. And ahh…if you have negative cash flow, I don't know what that means, but anyway, if you have that, and you buy houses anyway, it's very risky. So basically, you should buy below market value if you can, and you should always have a plan B, um, you know…um, a backup plan. If you do that, you don't need to worry about the bubble theory.

Chapter 5: **Lesson Set 5**
Theme—Social Science

Chapter 5 reviews more reading, writing, listening, and speaking skills and strategies you will need to score high on the TOEFL. Make sure to complete all the practice exercises and sample questions so that you can get the most out of these lessons.

LESSON 5—READING: THE MAIN IDEA, AND TRANSITIONS AND RHETORICAL FUNCTION REVISITED

In this lesson, we will cover more reading skills and strategies that will help lead to success on test day. You will also have the opportunity to review some of the strategies you learned in previous lessons as well as to learn more about the question types found on the Reading section of the TOEFL. If you want to proceed with more reading strategies when you finish this lesson, turn to Lesson 6—Reading: The Importance of Details in Chapter 6.

Reading for Main Idea

Understanding and identifying the main idea of a passage or lecture is critical in life and on the TOEFL. It is important that you practice this important skill every time you read.

The passage that follows is a social sciences text, as you might read in an anthropology course. It is written in a fairly typical descriptive expository essay format. That is, it contains many descriptive statements and is written to teach about something. See if you can identify the main idea of the passage by completing the following practice.

Reading for Main Idea Practice

Read the passage. Take notes and answer the questions that follow.

Native American Social Structure

Most cultures in today's world have been organized around the power of men. They are patrilineal, meaning that children take their father's family name and sons inherit the wealth, patrilocal, meaning a wife typically leaves her family to live with her husband's relatives, and patriarchal, meaning the man has the most power or authority in the family and society in general. Because of this, it is difficult for many of us to imagine a society in which women are considered more important than men. Most modern societies are also organized by a class system, where the richest have the most power, or after a political ideal, such as democracy or socialism. It is thus equally hard to believe that a society could be patterned solely after a kinship structure in which family connections determine status. Yet a look at the daily lives of Native American tribes gives a clear picture of how the roles of both kinship and of women have influenced entire communities with decidedly positive effects.

For almost all Native Americans, social organization was determined by biological relationships. This meant that all tribe members had a precise knowledge of their family ties. Without this knowledge, it would have been impossible for them to assign authority. When most people think of Native American rulers, they tend to defer to their experience with old Western films, portraying the braided and befeathered chief smoking a peace pipe and offering slightly enigmatic pearls of wisdom to baffled white settlers. Chieftaincies were, in fact, the most common political structure in Native American culture, but leaders were often chosen by their descent line, an obvious result of kinship. In agricultural Native American societies, on the other hand, individual kinship groups maintained order among themselves without the help of any unifying chief. Kinship was of even greater importance in these societies since a person's role in the family was also his or her role in society. Although feuds between tribes were frequent in Native American culture, disagreements and bloodshed within a community were much more rare due to the fact that most members were related.

Another consequence of the close communal blood ties that Native Americans shared was the importance of childrearing. Native American tribes considered the raising of children a community task and developed effective ways of educating and disciplining a child. In many tribes, peer pressure moderated a child's behavior. Being mocked by friends, who were also siblings or cousins, made a child unlikely to continue an unacceptable act. If this was insufficient, the child was punished along with each member of his or her peer group. The shame of being the cause of other children's suffering deterred any future misbehavior. In hunting and gathering societies, grandparents were usually responsible for children. They acted both as disciplinarians and as teachers, passing on stories and cultural knowledge. Most interesting, however, was the practice of childrearing in matrilocal cultures such as the Iroquois. In this form of social structure a husband joined his wife's family, living rather as a foreigner in a new country. His biological children took his wife's name and inherited the wealth his wife's family had acquired. Even more surprising, it was his wife's brother who was expected to raise his children while he was required to train and discipline his sister's children. Recently, American psychologists and politicians have been citing the benefits of Native American kinship structure to children's mental health, urging parents to consider alternative methods for teaching responsibility and family values.

Women's position in Native American society merits description as well. The Iroquois are again a suitable example as they were not only matrilocal, but also matrilineal, and to some extent, matriarchal. Iroquois women owned all property, including land, housing, and tools. When a woman died, it was her daughter who inherited her wealth, not her son or husband. Moreover, it did not pay for a husband to anger his wife for it was her right to throw him out with only his meager belongings to console him; this action constituted a divorce, which the man had no authority to contest. Also in Iroquois society, despite ostensible rule by men, it was the women who nominated and impeached tribal leaders. They also wielded the power of veto and could counter any decision they deemed unnecessary or harmful. Finally, women were usually believed to be more spiritually powerful than men because of their ability to bear children.

In the largely Caucasian-ruled cultures of American and Western Europe especially, the question of whether women should be allowed more power has led to heated debates, fueling the feminist movement. At the same time, increasing social isolation, even isolation from close family members, has created great concern over future communal stability. Ironically, Native American cultures have been proving for thousands of years that women can and should be given many rights and that close communal bonds create balanced societies. It is surely worth a thought the next time a woman announces her intention to run for president or a neighbor attempts to discipline your child.

Notes

1. Describe the main idea of the text in your own words.

2. Briefly describe the ways in which Native American social structure was different from the social structure of most modern cultures.

3. What is the main idea of paragraph 2?

4. In paragraph 2, why does the author mention old Western films?

5. Fill in the following chart with brief descriptions. Part of the chart has been done as an example.

Aspect of Native American Social Structure	Description
Chieftaincy	
Individual Kinship Groups	no unifying chief, a person's role in the family was also his or her role in society
Peer Pressure in Childrearing	
Childrearing in Matrilocal Cultures	
	women owned all property, daughters inherited wealth, women could initiate divorce
Matriarchal Advantages	

6. Based on the information in paragraphs 3 and 4, what can you infer about Iroquois women?

Answers

1. While many world cultures are based on men and class standing, some Native American tribes have demonstrated that social structures based on women and ties of kinship can be quite successful.

2. The major differences were that societies were organized by family relationships, and that it was women, not men, who owned property, and passed their possessions from mother to daughter instead of from father to son.

3. Kinship was an essential part of the organization of almost all Native American societies.

4. What many people know about Native American society is based only on what has been portrayed in movies.

5.

Aspect of Native American Social Structure	Description
Chieftaincy	leadership often passed along family lines.
Individual Kinship Groups	no unifying chief, a person's role in the family was also his or her role in society
Peer Pressure in Childrearing	used to correct inappropriate behavior
Childrearing in Matrilocal Cultures	was considered to be a community task
Matriarchal Society	women owned all property, daughters inherited wealth, women could initiate divorce
Matriarchal Advantages	aids in teaching children responsibility and family values

6. Iroquois women had a lot more power and influence than women in Caucasian cultures did.

Transitions Revisited

Because the topic of transitions has appeared more than once in this book already, you should be familiar with them and understand their importance. Among other purposes, transitional words and phrases make a text coherent, enabling the reader to follow the development of ideas in a text. This in turn can be used to help identify the most important points and the main idea of a passage or paragraph.

One way to transition effectively is to use the word *this* either as a demonstrative pronoun or adjective. Look at the following example from the text about Native American social structures.

> For almost all Native Americans, <u>social organization was determined by biological relationships</u>. **This** meant that all tribe members had a precise knowledge of their family ties. Without this knowledge, it would have been impossible for them to assign authority.

The bolded *this* in the previous sentence is a demonstrative pronoun referring back to the underlined idea that precedes it.

> This meant that all tribe members had a precise **knowledge** of their family ties. Without **this knowledge**, it would have been impossible for them to assign authority.

Here the word *this* is a demonstrative adjective. It refers back to the word *knowledge* in the previous sentence, which is being repeated in order to transition smoothly.

Transitions Revisited Practice

Look again at the passage on Native American social structure and underline all examples of this you can find. Then:

- Determine whether they are being used as demonstrative pronouns or adjectives
- Identify to which word or idea they refer

Answers

The referent for each instance of *this* in the passage precedes it, and is highlighted in gray.

Native American Social Structure

Most cultures in today's world have been organized around the power of men. They are patrilineal, meaning that children take their father's family name and sons inherit the wealth, patrilocal, meaning a wife typically leaves her family to live with her husband's relatives, and patriarchal, meaning the man has the most power or authority in the family and society in general. Because of this [**demonstrative pronoun**], it is difficult for many of us to imagine a society in which women are considered more important than men. Most modern societies are also organized by a class system, where the richest have the most power, or after a political ideal, such as democracy or socialism. It is thus equally hard to believe that a society could be patterned solely after a kinship structure in which family connections determine status. Yet a look at the daily lives of Native American tribes gives a clear picture of how the roles of both kinship and of women have influenced entire communities with decidedly positive effects.

For almost all Native Americans, social organization was determined by biological relationships. This [**demonstrative pronoun**] meant that all tribe members had a precise knowledge of their family ties. Without this [**demonstrative adjective**] knowledge, it would have been impossible for them to assign authority. When most people think of Native American rulers, they tend to defer to their experience with old Western films, portraying the braided and befeathered chief smoking a peace pipe and offering slightly enigmatic pearls of wisdom to baffled white settlers. Chieftaincies were, in fact, the most common political structure in Native American culture, but leaders were often chosen by their descent line, an obvious result of kinship. In agricultural Native American societies, on the other hand, individual kinship groups maintained order among themselves without the help of any unifying chief. Kinship was of even greater importance in these societies since a person's role in the family was also his or her role in society. Although feuds between tribes were frequent in Native American culture, disagreements and bloodshed within a community were much more rare due to the fact that most members were related.

Another consequence of the close communal blood ties that Native Americans shared was the importance of childrearing. Native American tribes considered the raising of children a community task and developed effective ways of educating and disciplining a child. In many tribes, peer pressure moderated a child's behavior. Being mocked by friends, who were also siblings or cousins, made a child unlikely to continue an unacceptable act. If this [**demonstrative pronoun**] was insufficient, the child was punished along with each member of his or her peer group. The shame of being the cause of other children's suffering deterred any future misbehavior. In hunting and gathering societies, grandparents were usually responsible for children. They acted both as disciplinarians and as teachers, passing on stories and cultural knowledge. Most interesting, however, was the practice of childrearing in matrilocal cultures such as the Iroquois. In this [**demonstrative adjective**] form of social structure a husband joined his wife's family, living rather as a foreigner in a new country. His biological children took his wife's name and inherited the wealth his wife's family had acquired. Even more surprising, it was his wife's brother who was expected to raise his children while he was required to train and discipline his sister's children. Recently, American psychologists and politicians have been citing the benefits of Native American kinship structure to children's mental health, urging parents to consider alternative methods for teaching responsibility and family values.

Women's position in Native American society merits description as well. The Iroquois are again a suitable example as they were not only matrilocal, but also matrilineal, and to some extent, matriarchal. Iroquois women owned all property, including land, housing, and tools. When a woman died, it was her daughter who inherited her wealth, not her son or husband. Moreover, it did not pay for a husband to anger his wife for it was her right to throw him out with only his meager belongings to console him; this [**demonstrative adjective**] action constituted a divorce, which the man had no authority to contest. Also in Iroquois society, despite ostensible rule by men, it was the women who nominated and impeached tribal leaders. They also wielded the power of veto and could counter any decision they deemed unnecessary or harmful. Finally, women were usually believed to be more spiritually powerful than men because of their ability to bear children.

In the largely Caucasian-ruled cultures of American and Western Europe especially, the question of whether women should be allowed more power has led to heated debates, fueling the feminist movement. At the same time, increasing social isolation, even isolation from close family members, has created great concern over future communal stability. Ironically, Native American cultures have been proving for thousands of years that women can and should be given many rights and that close communal bonds create balanced societies. It is surely worth a thought the next time a woman announces her intention to run for president or a neighbor attempts to discipline your child.

Rhetorical Function Revisited

As already mentioned in Lesson 1—Reading: Introduction to the Reading Passage, authors write for many purposes and therefore use many different rhetorical functions as they write. *Defining, describing, exemplifying,* and *explaining* are some examples of rhetorical functions writers use.

Read the following passage.

The Electoral College

Among the democracies of the world, the United States is distinguished by the manner in which its people select the country's head of state. Neither a parliamentary system like that of the United Kingdom or Japan, nor a system of direct popular vote as in France or South Korea, the Electoral College used in the United States is complex, anachronistic, and a handicap to the democratic process. Some people argue that the elimination of the

College is necessary to bring the United States into the world of modern democracy, with an energetic, involved electorate and presidents who are in touch with the needs and wants of the citizens who vote for them.

The great complexity of the current system has the unfortunate consequence of blinding most citizens to its workings. In effect, the Electoral College makes the presidential election into a two-stage process. Each of the fifty states is allotted a number of electoral votes corresponding to the size of that state's Congressional delegation: two for each state's two Senators, and a variable number for each state's Representatives, for a total of about five hundred and fifty. As a result, states with small populations like Alaska and Vermont may have only three or four electors, while large states like California, Texas, or New York may have dozens. On election day, each state holds its own presidential vote, making the race into fifty little mini-elections. Within each state, a given presidential candidate will win or lose based on the popular vote, and the winner will be awarded all of that state's electors. The ultimate victor is the candidate who wins the largest number of electoral votes nationwide.

Why was such a complex and problematic system ever imposed in the first place? The answer lies in the origins of the American federal system. When the country was established, there was relatively little sense of national identity. People identified themselves as citizens of their states first, as Americans second. Each state functioned a lot like an independent country, and so it made sense to make decisions that affected the entire nation at the state level. Furthermore, even in its earliest days, the United States was a very large country, stretching over sixteen hundred kilometers of coastline. Communication and transportation systems between disparate parts of the country were extremely poor, and so running campaigns nationally, rather than on a state-by-state basis, would have been quite difficult. So the Electoral College was provided as a solution.

But neither of these factors is any longer the case. Americans have developed a very strong sense of national identity and demand to play a direct role in the selection of their leaders. Mass media and powerful party organizations make national political campaigns easy to conduct. But there are further problems with the Electoral College system. Because presidential candidates know that they only need electoral votes, not popular votes, they avoid campaigning in small states, or states where they know their opponents are likely to win, creating a gulf between themselves and a significant fraction of the electorate. Furthermore, many members of political minorities don't bother to vote at all, because they know that the candidate they support won't win in their state anyway. Both situations have the effect of reducing citizen representation, and form obstacles to a healthy democracy. The final problem with the electoral system is by far the largest one. Because of its "winner-take-all" nature, the Electoral College can actually elect a candidate who received fewer popular votes than the opposition, altogether thwarting the purpose of holding an election in the first place. This unfortunate circumstance has in fact come about several times in the nation's history, most recently in the 2000 election of George W. Bush.

Its original justifications outmoded, its operations inscrutable, and its effects at odds with the goals of a democracy, the Electoral College is an institution that some would like to abandon. In its place, the United States should adopt a modern system of electing the President, one that will promote, not discourage, the full participation of all citizens. Such a method will remind our presidential candidates that it is the peoples' voices that matter most.

The following sentence from the first paragraph shows the rhetorical function of *exemplifying*.

> Neither a parliamentary system like that of the United Kingdom or Japan, nor a system of direct popular vote as in France or South Korea, the Electoral College used in the United States is complex, anachronistic, and a handicap to the democratic process.

The examples of the United Kingdom, Japan, France, and South Korea are given to illustrate political systems that are different from that of the United States. The words *like* and *as* are indicators that an example will follow. The previous sentence also shows the rhetorical function of *describing*. Several adjectives, *complex* and *anachronistic*, are used to describe the Electoral College. Now look at another sentence from the text that shows the rhetorical function of *explaining*.

> Because presidential candidates know that they only need electoral votes, not popular votes, they avoid campaigning in small states, or states where they know their opponents are likely to win, creating a gulf between themselves and a significant fraction of the electorate.

The word *because* is an indicator that the function of this sentence is to explain.

Rhetorical functions are crucial to learn about, but understanding the question types is also important. Keep reading to learn more.

Question Types

There are 13 question types on the Reading section of the TOEFL, all of which we reviewed in the first four lessons. These are:

- Identifying the Main Idea
- Summarizing the Most Important Points
- Understanding Rhetorical Function
- Understanding Details
- Understanding Details as They Relate to the Main Idea (Multiple-Choice)
- Understanding Details as They Relate to the Main Idea (Schematic Table)
- Inferring Word Meaning from Context
- Defining a Key Term
- Locating a Referent
- Understanding Coherence
- Drawing an Inference
- Inferring the Author's Opinion or Attitude
- Paraphrasing

This lesson will review in greater detail the first three question types:

- Identifying the Main Idea
- Summarizing the Most Important Points
- Understanding Rhetorical Function

Question Type 1 Revisited—Identifying the Main Idea

One of the 13 types of questions on the Reading section of the TOEFL requires you to identify the main idea of a reading passage. Over 3 reading passages, there is one *main idea* question on the TOEFL.

A *main idea* question begins by presenting part of the main idea in the stem of the question, and the correct answer choice accurately completes the stem with information about the main idea of the text. To answer this type of question it is necessary to understand the meaning of a large portion of the reading. It is not possible to identify the main idea by simply looking at the thesis statement.

Skimming a passage is the best way to determine its main idea and important points, as well as what type of text it is. Remember that there are several key factors to skimming:

- Identifying the thesis statement and topic sentences of the passage
- Recognizing the basic organization of the passage
- Noting repeated key words in the passage

Look again at the passage on the Electoral College and underline words that are repeated frequently in the passage.

The Electoral College

Among the democracies of the world, the United States is distinguished by the manner in which its people select the country's head of state. Neither a parliamentary system like that of the United Kingdom or Japan, nor a system of direct popular vote as in France or South Korea, the Electoral College used in the United States is complex, anachronistic, and a handicap to the democratic process. Some people argue that the elimination of the College is necessary to bring the United States into the world of modern democracy, with an energetic, involved electorate and presidents who are in touch with the needs and wants of the citizens who vote for them.

The great complexity of the current system has the unfortunate consequence of blinding most citizens to its workings. In effect, the Electoral College makes the presidential election into a two-stage process. Each of the fifty states is allotted a number of electoral votes corresponding to the size of that state's Congressional delegation: two for each state's two Senators, and a variable number for each state's Representatives, for a total of about five hundred and fifty. As a result, states with small populations like Alaska and Vermont may have only three or four electors, while large states like California, Texas, or New York may have dozens. On election day, each state holds its own presidential vote, making the race into fifty little mini-elections. Within each state, a given presidential candidate will win or lose based on the popular vote, and the winner will be awarded all of that state's electors. The ultimate victor is the candidate who wins the largest number of electoral votes nationwide.

Why was such a complex and problematic system ever imposed in the first place? The answer lies in the origins of the American federal system. When the country was established, there was relatively little sense of national identity. People identified themselves as citizens of their states first, as Americans second. Each state functioned a lot like an independent country, and so it made sense to make decisions that affected the entire nation at the state level. Furthermore, even in its earliest days, the United States was a very large country, stretching over sixteen hundred kilometers of coastline. Communication and transportation systems between disparate parts of the country were extremely poor, and so running campaigns nationally, rather than on a state-by-state basis, would have been quite difficult. So the Electoral College was provided as a solution.

But neither of these factors is any longer the case. Americans have developed a very strong sense of national identity and demand to play a direct role in the selection of their leaders. Mass media and powerful party organizations make national political campaigns easy to conduct. But there are further problems with the Electoral College system. Because presidential candidates know that they only need electoral votes, not popular votes, they avoid campaigning in small states, or states where they know their opponents are likely to win, creating a gulf between themselves and a significant fraction of the electorate. Furthermore, many members of political minorities don't bother to vote at all, because they know that the candidate they support won't win in their state anyway. Both situations have the effect of reducing citizen representation, and form obstacles to a healthy democracy. The final problem with the electoral system is by far the largest one. Because of its "winner-take-all" nature, the Electoral College can actually elect a candidate who received fewer popular votes than the opposition, altogether thwarting the purpose of holding an election in the first place. This unfortunate circumstance has in fact come about several times in the nation's history, most recently in the 2000 election of George W. Bush.

Its original justifications outmoded, its operations inscrutable, and its effects at odds with the goals of a democracy, the Electoral College is an institution that some would like to abandon. In its place, the United States should adopt a modern system of electing the President, one that will promote, not discourage, the full participation of all citizens. Such a method will remind our presidential candidates that it is the peoples' voices that matter most.

Now answer the following questions.

1. What text type best describes this passage?

   (A) Descriptive expository

   (B) Classificatory expository

   (C) Compare/contrast

   (D) Problem-solution argumentative

2. Which of the following best describes the main idea of this passage?

   (A) The Electoral College system is not as good as the parliamentary system or the system of direct popular vote.

   (B) The process of electing a president in the United States is very complicated due to the existence of the Electoral College.

   (C) Because of the many problems it creates for America's democratic political system, the Electoral College should not continue as part of the election process.

   (D) The history of the Electoral College begins with the origins of the American federal system.

3. Which of the following details supports the main idea?

    (A) Each of the fifty states is allotted a number of electoral votes corresponding to the size of that state's Congressional delegation.

    (B) Even in its earliest days, the United States was a very large country, stretching over sixteen hundred kilometers of coastline.

    (C) Because of its "winner-take-all" nature, the Electoral College can actually elect a candidate who received fewer popular votes than the opposition.

    (D) Those who would cling to the Electoral College can be motivated by self-interest only, or by a misguided sense of tradition.

Answers

1. (D) Problem-solution argumentative

2. (C) Because of the many problems it creates for America's democratic political system, the Electoral College should not continue as part of the election process.

3. (C) Because of its "winner-take-all" nature, the Electoral College can actually elect a candidate who received fewer popular votes than the opposition.

Now review the following TOEFL questions.

According to the passage, the Electoral College is problematic because it

    (A) is not as effective as a parliamentary system or a system of popular vote

    (B) is a relatively new idea in the United States and is not yet well understood

    (C) involves a two-stage election process in which the winner of the election may not have won the majority of the popular vote

    (D) requires that the mass media and party organizations make political campaigns easy to follow

Choice (C) is correct. It best expresses the main idea of the passage which is that for the stated reasons, the Electoral College is problematic. Choice (A) is not correct because the passage mentioned the parliamentary system and system of popular vote as examples of systems that are different from the U.S. system. Choice (B) is incorrect because the Electoral College is an old idea in the United States. Paragraph 3 tells us that the Electoral College originated with the American federal system. Choice (D) is not correct because it is not accurate to say that the Electoral College does not require either the mass media or party organizations to do anything.

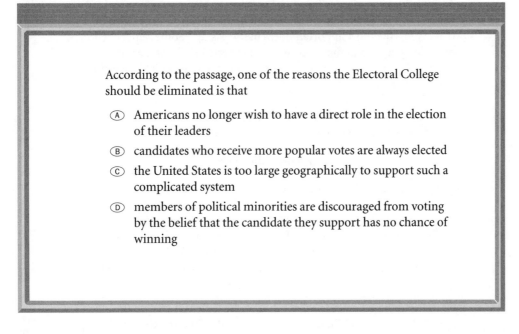

According to the passage, one of the reasons the Electoral College should be eliminated is that

(A) Americans no longer wish to have a direct role in the election of their leaders

(B) candidates who receive more popular votes are always elected

(C) the United States is too large geographically to support such a complicated system

(D) members of political minorities are discouraged from voting by the belief that the candidate they support has no chance of winning

Choice (D) is correct. It is a paraphrase of sentence 5 in paragraph 4.

Question Type 2 Revisited—Summarizing the Most Important Points

One of the 13 types of questions on the Reading section of the TOEFL requires you to summarize the most important points of the text. Over 3 reading passages, you should see 2 of these *most-important-points* questions. They will be at the end of the question section.

One type of question on the Reading section of the TOEFL requires you to summarize the most important points in a text by choosing three sentences from a list of six. In order to answer this type of question correctly, you will need to use your skimming skills to quickly determine the main points of the passage. Remember that note-taking will help you to keep the main points fresh in your mind. You will also need to avoid distracters, answers that may seem right at first, but are not. The types of distracters for this kind of question include answer choices that express:

- Ideas that are not mentioned in the passage
- Ideas that are only minor points in the passage

Now read and answer the following TOEFL question based on the passage about the Electoral College.

An introductory sentence for a brief summary of the passage is provided below. Complete the summary by selecting the THREE answer choices that express the most important ideas in the passage. Some sentences do not belong in the summary because they express ideas that are not presented in the passage or are minor ideas in the passage. This question is worth 2 points.

The Electoral College is a part of the American system for electing a president which should be abandoned.

Answer Choices	
The Electoral College came to be because of the way Americans traditionally identified themselves with their states and as a result of the size of the country.	Presently, there are several problems with the Electoral College system, the most important of which is the fact that a candidate who loses the popular vote can still be elected president.
Americans have begun to rally against the Electoral College system as their sense of national identity has grown.	Some people still cling to the idea of the Electoral College due to their traditional beliefs and values.
The current system for presidential elections is too complicated due to the added step of the Electoral College.	The United States is lucky to have a unique system for electing a president which distinguishes it from other democratic nations.

The following three statements are the answers to this question:

The Electoral College came to be because of the way Americans traditionally identified themselves with their states and as a result of the size of the country.

The current system for presidential elections is too complicated due to the added step of the Electoral College.

Presently, there are several problems with the Electoral College system, the most important of which is the fact that a candidate who loses the popular vote can still be elected president.

The second sentence in the left column is incorrect because it is not mentioned in the passage. Although the fourth paragraph of the text says that Americans have a stronger sense of national identity now than in the past, it does not say that they have begun to rally or protest against the Electoral College system. Since part of the sentence is untrue based on the information given in the text, it should not be included in the summary. The second sentence in the right column is also incorrect because it is not mentioned in the passage. The third sentence in the right column is incorrect because it is an opinion that is not presented in the passage.

Question Type 3 Revisited—Understanding Rhetorical Function

One of the 13 types of questions on the Reading section of the TOEFL requires you to understand rhetorical function. Over 3 reading passages, you should see 3 or 4 *rhetorical function* questions. They will generally be near the beginning of the question section.

As you saw earlier in this lesson, rhetorical functions such as defining, describing, exemplifying, and explaining are often used by writers to support their main ideas. Two different forms of rhetorical function questions can be found on the Reading section of the TOEFL. The first form presents the rhetorical device and asks its function. Look at the question and correct answer choice found here as an example.

Question:

> Why does the author mention the United Kingdom and Japan in paragraph 1 of the passage?

Answer:

To give examples of two countries with parliamentary systems

The second form of question presents the rhetorical function and asks how it is achieved. Look at the following question and correct answer choice as an example.

Question:

> In paragraph 4, how does the author explain why presidential candidates avoid campaigning in small states or states where they know their opponents are likely to win?

Answer:

By pointing out a problem with the Electoral College system

Now read and answer the following TOEFL questions.

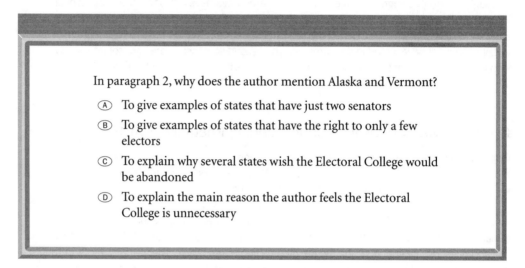

In paragraph 2, why does the author mention Alaska and Vermont?

(A) To give examples of states that have just two senators

(B) To give examples of states that have the right to only a few electors

(C) To explain why several states wish the Electoral College would be abandoned

(D) To explain the main reason the author feels the Electoral College is unnecessary

Choice (B) is correct because it identifies the rhetorical function of exemplifying. The word *like* in paragraph 2 is the clue that what follows is an example. Although choice (A) correctly identifies the rhetorical function of exemplifying, it is incorrect because it is untrue. All states have only two senators, not just Alaska and Vermont. Choice (C) is incorrect because this sentence is not explaining; it is exemplifying. Choice (D) is incorrect for the same reason as (C).

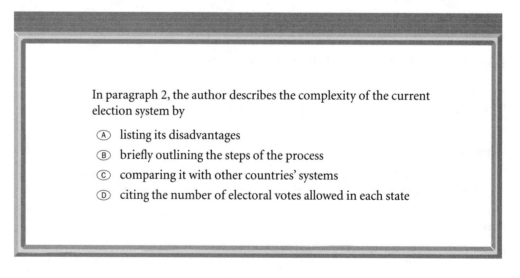

In paragraph 2, the author describes the complexity of the current election system by

(A) listing its disadvantages

(B) briefly outlining the steps of the process

(C) comparing it with other countries' systems

(D) citing the number of electoral votes allowed in each state

Choice (B) is correct because paragraph 2 is largely a description of the process of electing a president. Choice (A) is incorrect because the disadvantages are not discussed in paragraph 2. Choice (C) is incorrect because no comparisons with systems in other countries is made. Choice (D) is incorrect because this does not describe the complexity of the system; it is merely one detail of how the system works.

Eliminating Distracters in Questions about Rhetorical Function

To answer questions about rhetorical function correctly, you will also need to avoid distracters. As already mentioned in Lesson 1—Reading: Introduction to the Reading Passage, the types of distracters for this type of question include:

- Answer choices which use words from the passage in a way unrelated to the question
- Answer choices which are untrue based on the information in the passage
- Answer choices which express ideas that are not mentioned in the passage
- Answer choices which cite an unrelated rhetorical function or device

Answer the following question based on the text on the Electoral College, which is repeated here.

The Electoral College

Among the democracies of the world, the United States is distinguished by the manner in which its people select the country's head of state. Neither a parliamentary system like that of the United Kingdom or Japan, nor a system of direct popular vote as in France or South Korea, the Electoral College used in the United States is complex, anachronistic, and a handicap to the democratic process. Some people argue that the elimination of the College is necessary to bring the United States into the world of modern democracy, with an energetic, involved electorate and presidents who are in touch with the needs and wants of the citizens who vote for them.

The great complexity of the current system has the unfortunate consequence of blinding most citizens to its workings. In effect, the Electoral College makes the presidential election into a two-stage process. Each of the fifty states is allotted a number of electoral votes corresponding to the size of that state's Congressional delegation: two for each state's two Senators, and a variable number for each state's Representatives, for a total of about five hundred and fifty. As a result, states with small populations like Alaska and Vermont may have only three or four electors, while large states like California, Texas, or New York may have dozens. On election day, each state holds its own presidential vote, making the race into fifty little mini-elections. Within each state, a given presidential candidate will win or lose based on the popular vote, and the winner will be awarded all of that state's electors. The ultimate victor is the candidate who wins the largest number of electoral votes nationwide.

Why was such a complex and problematic system ever imposed in the first place? The answer lies in the origins of the American federal system. When the country was established, there was relatively little sense of national identity. People identified themselves as citizens of their states first, as Americans second. Each state functioned a lot like an independent country, and so it made sense to make decisions that affected the entire nation at the state level. Furthermore, even in its earliest days, the United States was a very large country, stretching over sixteen hundred kilometers of coastline. Communication and transportation systems between disparate parts of the country were extremely poor, and so running campaigns nationally, rather than on a state-by-state basis, would have been quite difficult. So the Electoral College was provided as a solution.

But neither of these factors is any longer the case. Americans have developed a very strong sense of national identity and demand to play a direct role in the selection of their leaders. Mass media and powerful party organizations make national political campaigns easy to conduct. But there are further problems with the Electoral College system. Because presidential candidates know that they only need electoral votes, not popular votes, they avoid campaigning in small states, or states where they know their opponents are likely to win, creating a gulf between themselves and a significant fraction of the electorate. Furthermore, many members of political minorities don't bother to vote at all, because they know that the candidate they support won't win in their state anyway. Both situations have the effect of reducing citizen representation, and form obstacles to a healthy democracy. The final problem with the electoral system is by far the largest one. Because of its "winner-take-all" nature, the Electoral College can actually elect a candidate who received fewer popular votes than the opposition, altogether thwarting the purpose of holding an election in the first place. This unfortunate circumstance has in fact come about several times in the nation's history, most recently in the 2000 election of George W. Bush.

Its original justifications outmoded, its operations inscrutable, and its effects at odds with the goals of a democracy, the Electoral College is an institution that some would like to abandon. In its place, the United States should adopt a modern system of electing the President, one that will promote, not discourage, the full participation of all citizens. Such a method will remind our presidential candidates that it is the peoples' voices that matter most.

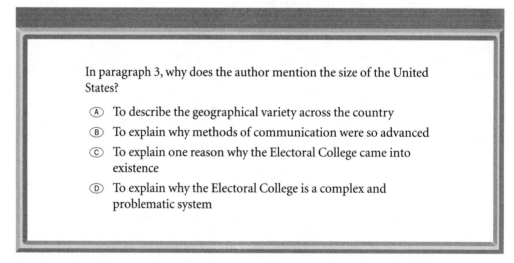

In paragraph 3, why does the author mention the size of the United States?

Ⓐ To describe the geographical variety across the country

Ⓑ To explain why methods of communication were so advanced

Ⓒ To explain one reason why the Electoral College came into existence

Ⓓ To explain why the Electoral College is a complex and problematic system

Choice (C) is the correct answer. It correctly describes the rhetorical function of explaining and is true based on the last sentence of paragraph 3. Choice (A) is incorrect because the rhetorical function used is not description. Choice (B) is incorrect because paragraph 3 tells us that methods of communication were not advanced at the time. Choice (D) is incorrect because it uses the words *complex* and *problematic* from the first sentence of paragraph 3 in a way unrelated to the question.

Now answer the following questions also based on the text.

> In paragraph 4, why does the author mention George W. Bush?
>
> Ⓐ To explain why one election was most important to U.S. history
>
> Ⓑ To give an example of the effect of reducing citizen representation
>
> Ⓒ To give an example of a president who received just as few popular votes as the opposition
>
> Ⓓ To give an example of a candidate who was elected solely due to the Electoral College

Choice (B) is correct.

> In paragraph 4, the author explains his opinion of the Electoral College by
>
> Ⓐ suggesting that the system be changed
>
> Ⓑ discouraging other countries from adopting it
>
> Ⓒ justifying its outmoded and inscrutable characteristics
>
> Ⓓ mentioning that a new tradition has already begun to spread across America

Choice (A) is correct.

When you are ready, move on to Lesson 5—Writing: Another Look at Persuasive Essays.

LESSON 5—WRITING: ANOTHER LOOK AT PERSUASIVE ESSAYS

In this lesson, we will cover more writing skills and strategies that will help lead to success on test day. You will have the opportunity to learn more about the tasks required for the Writing section of the TOEFL. If you want to proceed with additional writing strategies when you finish this lesson, turn to Lesson 6—Writing: More Practice with Descriptive Essays in Chapter 6.

Previous lessons have covered the following essay types:

- Descriptive Essays
- Definition Essays
- Persuasive Essays
- Compare/Contrast Essays
- Essays in Response to a Reading Passage and a Lecture

This lesson will continue to review persuasive essays.

Recognizing Persuasive Essay Prompts

There are two tasks in the Writing section of the TOEFL. In the first, you must read a passage, listen to a lecture, then write an essay about what you have read and heard. In the second, you must write an essay based only on a short prompt that asks you to describe or explain something or to express and support your opinion on an issue. You do not need any specialized knowledge to write this second essay. The prompt is based on topics that will be familiar to all test takers. You are given 30 minutes to plan, write, and revise this essay. Typically, an effective essay will contain a minimum of 300 words. Essays will be judged on the quality of the writing, including idea development, organization, and the quality and accuracy of the language used to express these ideas.

When you begin either writing task on the TOEFL, always read the prompt carefully to make sure that you know exactly which essay type you are being asked to write.

In persuasive essay questions, the prompt will provide two or three possible options, and ask you to decide between them, presenting the reasons for your decision. Alternatively, it will present you with a problem of some kind, and it will ask you to present the best solution to the problem.

As with any TOEFL writing task, it is important that you respond to the prompt with the appropriate essay type. In the Writing section, the test evaluators are not looking for a correct answer as on a multiple-choice question. Rather, they want to see that you provide an answer that is appropriate for the type of prompt you were given. For this reason, you should make sure that you can recognize the persuasive prompt when you encounter it on the TOEFL. In today's lesson, you will learn tips to help you recognize this type of prompt and write a strong and successful essay in response.

The following are tips for recognizing a persuasive prompt:

> A prompt of this kind may ask you to choose between two or more alternatives

OR

> The prompt may ask you whether you agree or disagree with a suggested view or course of action

OR

> The prompt may ask you to propose a solution to a problem mentioned in the prompt

AND

> A persuasive prompt will usually refer specifically to your opinion and ask you to support your opinion with specific reasons and examples.

Planning a Persuasive Essay

Before you begin writing your essay, it is always a good idea to have a clear plan about the direction you intend to follow as you write. An outline will help you evaluate your ideas, determine the best way to structure them, and organize your supporting details. An outline is also an excellent tool to keep you on track as you write.

Like other kinds of essays, a persuasive essay will usually follow a basic structure. The following outline demonstrates that structure. You can memorize this structure and easily use it for your own essays, simply adding your own thesis, topic sentences, and supporting details. Remember, three body paragraphs is merely a suggestion; you may have more. However, you should consider two to be the minimum. The introduction and conclusion, of course, are essential.

I. Introductory paragraph

   A. Hook: a device for capturing reader's attention

   B. Background information: to help reader understand topic

   C. Thesis statement: clear statement of your position

II. First supporting argument: strong reason supporting your position

   A. Topic sentence: general factual sentence introducing paragraph

   B. Facts, examples, arguments to support and prove position

III. Second supporting argument (as in II)

   A. Topic sentence

   B. Facts, examples, arguments

IV. Third supporting argument (as in II and III)

   A. Topic sentence

   B. Facts, examples, arguments

V. Conclusion

More Planning Strategies

One of the most important tasks for which we use writing is to convince other people to see things the way we do. Perhaps we are recommending a particular course of action, promoting a certain analysis of a problem, or seeking to persuade other people to agree with an opinion we hold. Persuasive writing is the most effective means for accomplishing any of those goals.

What does persuasive writing look like? In outline, a persuasive essay is very similar to any other essay: it has an introduction, a number of body paragraphs, and a conclusion. However, because the goal of a persuasive essay is to persuade the reader, the essay's writer must accomplish several tasks within the essay.

1. First, his or her opinion must be clearly expressed.

2. Second, the issue must be made plain to the reader in order to demonstrate that consideration is necessary.

3. Third, the author's strongest arguments for holding his or her opinion must be identified and supported.

4. Finally, the essay must consider any strong opposing arguments.

Introducing a Persuasive Essay

The introduction to any essay is its most important section. In a persuasive essay, this is especially true. A good introduction will help you convince your audience much more effectively; a bad one may prejudice your readers against your ideas before they have even considered them.

Your introduction should contain the following elements:

- **A hook to catch your reader's interest.** The hook can be an intriguing fact, a rhetorical question (intended to bring an issue to the reader's attention, often answered immediately by the writer as a way of leading the reader toward the writer's thesis), or a provocative statement of some kind. Usually, it will be the first sentence of the introduction.

- **Background of the problem or issue**, sufficient to allow your reader to understand the discussion that will follow in the essay body.

- **A statement of your thesis.** The thesis is your opinion or recommendation, the idea you are writing the essay to support. The thesis should be expressed clearly in a single sentence. Usually, the thesis statement will be the last sentence of the introduction.

- **Forecasting, or reference to the major points you will discuss in the essay.** Your introduction will list them in the same order in which they are found in the essay body. Forecasting will help your readers navigate your essay, by telling them what points to expect as they read. Forecasting can usually be found near the end of the introduction, sometimes as part of the thesis statement.

KAPLAN
Test Prep and Admissions

Introducing a Persuasive Essay Practice

Read the introduction to "The Electoral College." Be sure to answer the questions that follow.

The Electoral College

    Among the democracies of the world, the United States is distinguished by the manner in which its people select the country's head of state. Neither a parliamentary system like that of the United Kingdom or Japan, nor a system of direct popular vote as in France or South Korea, the Electoral College used in the United States is complex, anachronistic, and a handicap to the democratic process. Some people argue that the elimination of the College is necessary to bring the United States into the world of modern democracy, with an energetic, involved electorate and presidents who are in touch with the needs and wants of the citizens who vote for them.

1. What kind of hook does the writer use?

    _____

    _____

2. What do you learn about the problem or issue from the introduction?

    _____

    _____

3. Is there a thesis statement?

    _____

    _____

4. What is the viewpoint taken by the author?

    _____

    _____

5. Based on what you read in the essay's introduction, what topics do you expect to find discussed in the essay body? In what order?

    _____

    _____

Answers

Answers will vary.

1. Intriguing statement

2. That the electoral system used by the U.S. is out of date because it does not do a good job of connecting voters and presidents

3. Yes. *Neither a parliamentary system like that of the United Kingdom or Japan, nor a system of direct popular vote as in France or South Korea, the Electoral College used in the United States is complex, anachronistic, and a handicap to the democratic process.*

4. That the Electoral College needs to be replaced with a system that better represents voters

5. The history and function of the Electoral College, the advantages of other systems, and the disadvantages of the current system

Writing the Thesis of a Persuasive Essay

The most important single component of any persuasive essay is the thesis statement. The thesis statement is a single sentence that expresses the opinion or point of view that you intend to support in the essay. It is essential that your thesis be a statement of your opinion, a view that requires defense of some kind; without such a thesis, you will not have a persuasive essay. A good thesis statement makes your opinion, and thus the purpose of your essay, clear to your reader. It will also be much easier for you to write the essay once you have stated exactly what your position is. Usually your thesis statement will be the last sentence of your introduction.

When you are writing an essay in response to a prompt on the TOEFL, it is a good idea to refer specifically to the topic identified in the prompt. You should do this in your own words. A thesis written this way will show the test evaluator that you have read and understood the prompt and will also help to guide you as you plan and write your essay.

The following are tips for making sure that you have given your essay a good thesis statement:
- A good thesis statement will be your opinion, not a simple fact.
- A useful thesis will express a position that can be supported with strong arguments. If you have no arguments to support your position, rethink and rewrite your thesis.
- A thesis statement is not a restatement of the question asked by the prompt. It should, however, be a direct response to the question posed by the prompt.

Writing the Thesis of a Persuasive Essay Practice

Which of the following would make good thesis statements? Mark those with a T. Then, try to make the others into good thesis statements.

___ 1. Clean air is important for the health of the community.

_____

___ 2. Deserts are areas that receive little precipitation.

_____

___ 3. In my essay, I will describe the essential features of a successful business.

_____

___ 4. The light bulb was the most important invention of the nineteenth century.

_____

___ 5. Spending more money than you earn is a bad idea.

_____

___ 6. Ansel Adams was a powerful influence and inspiration for many of today's landscape
photographers.

_____

___ 7. Most paper used in offices today is not recycled.

_____

___ 8. The Ford Mustang is a far more beautiful car than the Chevrolet Corvette.

_____

___ 9. Vegetarianism is a much healthier dietary choice than eating meat.

_____

___ 10. Unless people act swiftly, global warming will become a serious and unsolvable problem.

_____

Answers

_T_ 1. Clean air is important for the health of the community.

___ 2. Desert precipitation ought to be monitored carefully.

___ 3. The essential features of a successful business are a clear mission, solid planning, and high quality execution.

_T_ 4. The light bulb was the most important invention of the nineteenth century.

_T_ 5. Spending more money than you earn is a bad idea.

___ 6. Ansel Adams was one of the most important influences and inspirations for many of today's landscape photographers.

___ 7. One of the first places waste reduction should be enforced is in offices, where most paper is not recycled.

_T_ 8. The Ford Mustang is a far more beautiful car than the Chevrolet Corvette.

_T_ 9. Vegetarianism is a much healthier dietary choice than eating meat.

_T_ 10. Unless people act swiftly, global warming will become a serious and unsolvable problem.

Writing the Body Paragraphs of a Persuasive Essay

A body paragraph generally has two parts: the topic sentence and supporting details.

The topic sentence identifies the controlling idea of the paragraph. Often it will contain few or no specific details about the topic. Usually it is the paragraph's first sentence.

Supporting details compose the rest of the paragraph, developing the general point introduced in the topic sentence. These details may include examples, statistics, logical arguments, or other details. The paragraph should not include information that does not support the paragraph's controlling idea as identified in the topic sentence.

Supporting details can be used to describe, to define, to argue, or to exemplify. In a persuasive essay, you may have to do any or all of these things. Description, definition, and argumentation are examples of rhetorical strategies. Remember, a rhetorical strategy is a technique writers use to communicate specific kinds of information and ideas to their readers. With practice, and using the following tips, you can learn how to use each of them effectively.

Description: A good description provides facts and other information to help your reader to understand your topic better. Your description may also serve the same function as the definition, to familiarize your reader with new ideas. Remember that more details are not necessarily better—provide only as much information as you think your audience will need to understand your topic. Well-chosen examples add strength to the descriptive paragraph.

Definition: You may need to define ideas or terms that are crucial to understanding your essay. A definition is a good idea whenever you suspect that your readers may be unfamiliar with the terms or ideas you are discussing. A good definition will include key features of the thing or idea defined that distinguish it from related or similar topics.

Argumentation: In a persuasive essay, it is not enough to simply define terms and describe ideas; you must also provide logical, factual, or moral reasons for holding your opinion. Strong, well-chosen, and well-expressed arguments will make your essay convincing. Weak, poorly chosen arguments will have the opposite effect. Don't try to list every argument you can think of; do try to include the strongest two, three, or perhaps four arguments. If you limit the number of arguments, you will make sure you have only strong ones, and you will also have more time to express or develop each of them well.

Examples: A well-chosen example will always add strength to any body paragraph. The best examples are those that describe unfamiliar ideas in ways that are already familiar to the reader.

Persuasive Essay Practice

Following is an example of the second task in the Writing section of the TOEFL.

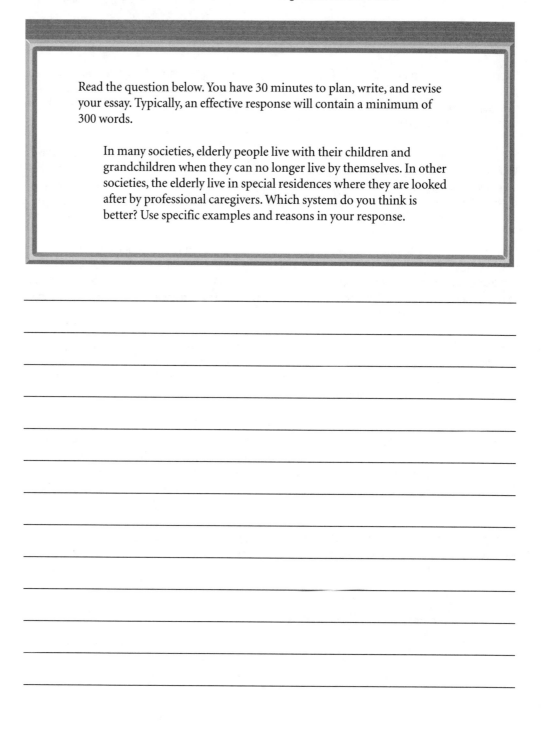

Read the question below. You have 30 minutes to plan, write, and revise your essay. Typically, an effective response will contain a minimum of 300 words.

In many societies, elderly people live with their children and grandchildren when they can no longer live by themselves. In other societies, the elderly live in special residences where they are looked after by professional caregivers. Which system do you think is better? Use specific examples and reasons in your response.

Answer

Answers will vary, but here is a sample essay.

> Attitudes toward the elderly are different from society to society. In societies which emphasize the importance of family, elderly people are considered the responsibility of the family, who take care of the their elderly relatives when they can no longer care for themselves. In societies which focus on independence and the family is not seen as a unifying force, the older family members live in retirement homes, apart and sometimes hundreds of miles away from their family. In my opinion, a system in which family members take care of their older members is much better for the family and its older members because of cost, the importance it places on elderly members of society, and for reasons relating to quality of life.
>
> The first advantage to having an elderly family member live with his or her family is an economic one. The cost of retirement homes is very high. Some families may not be able to afford the thousands of dollars that they cost every month. If an elderly family member can afford to pay for it themselves, that money will then not be passed on to other family members when that person dies. Although medical bills and other costs would still be incurred if an elderly family member lives with another relative, it's still a better financial solution for some families.
>
> Second, keeping family together is important. Societies which allow their older members to live separately from their families don't put a high value on the elderly. Those societies see getting old as a weakness and a bother. The elderly are a pivotal part of any family and should be treated with respect. Those people took care of other family members at one time in their lives, and so their children and grandchildren should take care of them when they need it. That's what being part of a family is all about.
>
> Third, quality of life needs to be taken into consideration. Why should an older grandmother or grandfather be alone in a retirement home when they could be living with family and helping care for younger members of the family if they are able? Grandmothers and grandfathers are increasingly helping with things like childcare in many homes. This is a benefit to the elderly, who get to spend time with their grandkids, and to the children themselves, who can learn from the experience of their elders. The lives of both generations can be enhanced in this way.
>
> To summarize, the elderly are a valuable part of society and deserve to be treated as such, not put in some home somewhere, forgotten about because people think they are a burden. The elderly should be able to live comfortable, productive lives surrounded by their loved ones for whom they once cared.

Now that you have practiced writing, you are ready to begin Lesson 5—Listening: Note-Taking and Key Words.

LESSON 5—LISTENING: NOTE-TAKING AND KEY WORDS

In this lesson, we will cover more listening skills and strategies that will help lead to success on test day. You will also have the opportunity to review some of the strategies you learned in previous lessons as well as to learn more about the question types found on the Listening section of the TOEFL.

If you want to proceed with more listening strategies when you finish this lesson, turn to Lesson 6—Listening: Details in Chapter 6.

Note-Taking and Key Words

Remember that as you listen to any lecture or conversation on the TOEFL, you should take notes. Always try to:

- Listen for strong general statements by the speaker, because they may be topic sentences or concluding sentences for paragraphs
- If there is more than one speaker, listen carefully to questions and answers that may serve as transitions to new supporting topics or prompts for restatement or clarification
- Write down key words

Remember, key words include:

- words that are repeated throughout the passage
- names
- numbers
- dates
- anything else you think is important

Note-Taking and Key Words Practice

Listen to a lecture on social anxiety disorder. Take notes as you listen, and answer the questions that follow. You will find a transcript of this audio passage (46.5L, Note-Taking Practice) at the end of the chapter.

🎧 **46.5L, Note-Taking Practice**

Notes

Use your notes to answer the following questions. You may need to listen to parts of the lecture a second time.

1. What is the talk mainly about?

   _____

   _____

2. Why does the professor talk about the man in the restaurant?

   _____

   _____

3. Pretend you're a psychiatrist or psychologist. What symptoms would you observe in a patient if you diagnosed him or her with social anxiety disorder?

   _____

   _____

4. What can happen to someone who suffers from the disorder, but never receives treatment?

   _____

   _____

5. How do you treat this disorder?

   _____

   _____

Answers

1. Social Anxiety Disorder

2. To provide an example of how someone who suffers from Social Anxiety Disorder might feel in public

3. Intense shyness; sweating, blushing, breathlessness, and confusion when in a social situation

4. They can develop other disorders like panic attacks, obsessive compulsive disorder, or depression. Lack of treatment could also lead to alcohol abuse, financial dependencies, and chronic unemployment.

5. Treatment differs from person to person. Cognitive therapy, visits to a psychiatrist, and role playing social situations can help with negative feelings, while selective serotonin reuptake inhibitors or beta blockers can be used to help with someone who requires medication.

Outlining

This book reviews the most important skills and strategies so that you can master them. Let's review outlining once more. An outline is a skeletal structure of a text. It contains the main and supporting ideas in the order they are presented, but does not necessarily include any specific details. Usually, an outline does not contain full sentences.

Outlining Practice

Listen to a lecture and take notes. You will use your notes to write an outline and answer some questions after you listen. You will find a transcript of this audio passage (47.5L, Outlining Practice) at the end of the chapter.

🎧 **47.5L, Outlining Practice**

Notes

Outline

Here is an example of the beginning of an outline based on the lecture you just heard:

I. Sociolinguistics

II. Feminine speech patterns

   A. More questions

   B. Softening devices

      1. tag questions

      2. hedges (i.e. kind of, sort of)

      3. indicators of opinion

Complete the outline on the lecture about speech patterns. First, review the notes you took. Using the notes, write an outline of the lecture in the space that follows.

Now use your notes to answer the following questions.

1. What is the talk mainly about?

2. What is the purpose of this lecture: to inform, to persuade, to evaluate, or to recommend?

3. Describe the difference between an assertive statement and a statement with softening devices.

4. What kinds of speech patterns or inflections are associated with "feminine speech"?

5. What is an honorific device?

KAPLAN
Test Prep and Admissions

Answers

Sample Outline

I. Sociolinguistics

II. Feminine speech patterns

    A. More questions

    B. Softening devices

        1. tag questions

        2. hedges (i.e. kind of, sort of)

        3. indicators of opinion

III. Current research

    A. Softer patterns may be more related to status than gender

    B. Status speech

IV. Observations

    A. 70 people divided—35 male/35 female

    B. Statements classified

        1. declarative with tag question

        2. declarative with rising inflection

        3. response to question that is phrased as question

        4. directly stated question that offers solution to a task problem

    C. Results—statistically no difference between the male/female groups

V. Conclusion

    A. Women with women speak similarly to men with men

    B. Need to further test with heterogeneous groups

        1. The talk is about the differences in the ways women speak when compared to men.

        2. To inform

        3. An assertive statement is a simple and direct declaration, while a statement with softening devices includes honorifics, tag questions, or other devices to make the speaker seem non-threatening.

        4. Tag questions, honorifics, and rising inflection

        5. Using a person's title or family name instead of using something less formal, like their first name.

Understanding the question types is important for knowing how and where you can apply your strategies. Keep reading to learn more.

Question Types

There are seven question types on the Listening section of the TOEFL, all of which we reviewed in the first four lessons. These are:

- Understanding Rhetorical Function
- Understanding an Idiomatic Expression in Context
- Drawing an Inference
- Understanding a Speaker's Implication
- Identifying the Main Idea
- Summarizing the Most Important Points
- Understanding Details

This lesson will review in greater detail the first two question types:

- Understanding Rhetorical Function
- Understanding an Idiomatic Expression in Context

Question Type 1 Revisited—Understanding Rhetorical Function

There are 2 conversations and 4 lectures in the Listening section of the TOEFL. Each lecture is followed by 1 or 2 *rhetorical function* questions, for a total of 5 or 6 *rhetorical function* questions in the Listening section.

One type of question that you will find on lectures—but generally **not** on conversations—in the Listening section of the TOEFL asks about rhetorical function. This type of question asks about the speaker's intent—for example, is the speaker defining, describing, exemplifying, explaining, or doing something else. In order to answer this type of question correctly, you will need to be able to recognize the rhetorical devices used to achieve various rhetorical functions, as well as other context and intonation cues.

Rhetorical Function Question Forms

There are four different forms of the rhetorical function question type in the Listening section. All are multiple-choice with four answer choices.

1. A question which presents a rhetorical device and asks its function.

    Why does the professor say X?

    To emphasize his point

    To illustrate his point

    etc.

2. A question which asks how a speaker achieves a given rhetorical function.

   How does the professor illustrate her point about X?

   By comparing X to Y

   By giving the dimensions of x

   etc.

3. An excerpt from a lecture followed by a question which presents a rhetorical device and asks its function.

   [short excerpt of a lecture previously heard is played]

   Why does the professor say this?

   [a specific sentence from the excerpt is repeated]

   To point out a flaw

   To repeat a point

   etc.

4. A question which asks the rhetorical function of an entire excerpt.

   Why does the professor say this?

   [short excerpt of a lecture previously heard is played]

   To define an important term

   To exemplify a key point

   etc.

Following is an example of rhetorical function question form 2: it asks specifically *how* the speaker achieves the desired function. You will not hear an excerpt for this question. Not only does it involve a much bigger part of the passage, but also it requires a broader understanding of the main idea. Use your notes from (47.5L, Outlining Practice) or listen to the passage again to help you answer this question.

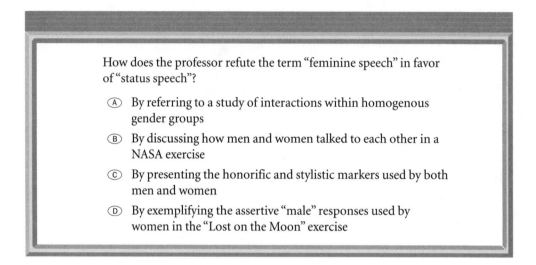

How does the professor refute the term "feminine speech" in favor of "status speech"?

- (A) By referring to a study of interactions within homogenous gender groups
- (B) By discussing how men and women talked to each other in a NASA exercise
- (C) By presenting the honorific and stylistic markers used by both men and women
- (D) By exemplifying the assertive "male" responses used by women in the "Lost on the Moon" exercise

Choice (A) is correct because the professor refers to the entire study to support the idea that it is not really feminine speech, but status speech. Choice (B) is incorrect because the exercise was performed by gender homogeneous groups; the groups were either all women or all men, but never mixed. Choice (C) is incorrect because it doesn't address either a gender gap or a status gap. Choice (D) fails to address why there is either a gender gap or a status gap.

Following is an example of rhetorical function question form 4. Remember that on the actual test, you will only hear the excerpt—you will not see it.

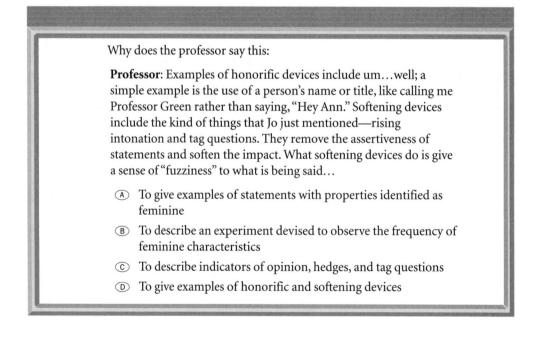

Why does the professor say this:

Professor: Examples of honorific devices include um…well; a simple example is the use of a person's name or title, like calling me Professor Green rather than saying, "Hey Ann." Softening devices include the kind of things that Jo just mentioned—rising intonation and tag questions. They remove the assertiveness of statements and soften the impact. What softening devices do is give a sense of "fuzziness" to what is being said…

- (A) To give examples of statements with properties identified as feminine
- (B) To describe an experiment devised to observe the frequency of feminine characteristics
- (C) To describe indicators of opinion, hedges, and tag questions
- (D) To give examples of honorific and softening devices

This question tests your ability to follow the development of a topic (honorific and softening devices) and the reasons and examples used to support it. Choice (D) is the correct answer.

Question Type 2 Revisited—Understanding an Idiomatic Expression in Context

There are 1 or 2 *idiomatic expression* questions on the lectures in the Listening section of the TOEFL.

These questions test your understanding of idiomatic expressions in context. You can often guess at the meaning of an idiomatic expression by looking at the parts of the sentence that you understand.

Idioms are words or phrases in which the literal meaning of each word or phrase does not necessarily help you understand the meaning of the words in a particular context. Look at the following two examples first mentioned in Lesson 1:

> John really looks blue today.

Do you know what *blue* means in this sentence? If you are not certain, but you know that John lost his job, can you infer its meaning?

> John really looks green.

Do you know what *green* means in this sentence? If you are not certain, but you know that John just got off the world's fastest roller coaster, and as soon as he got off he threw up, can you infer its meaning?

Neither sentence is saying that John's skin is blue- or green-colored. Which sentence means that John looks sad? Which means that John looks sick?

To help determine the meaning of idioms and vocabulary, you need to connect the unfamiliar words and expressions to the context of the lecture and the tone of the speaker.

Following are two *idiomatic expression* questions, both containing excerpts from the lecture. Remember that you will not see the narrator's introduction or the transcript of the excerpt on the test.

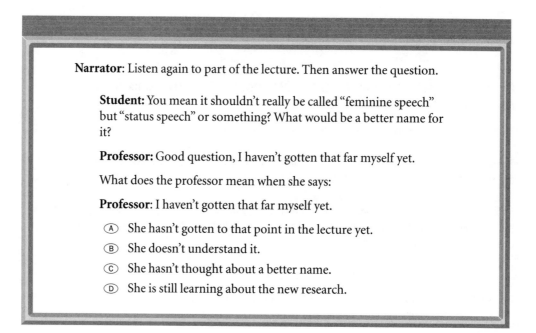

Narrator: Listen again to part of the lecture. Then answer the question.

Student: You mean it shouldn't really be called "feminine speech" but "status speech" or something? What would be a better name for it?

Professor: Good question, I haven't gotten that far myself yet.

What does the professor mean when she says:

Professor: I haven't gotten that far myself yet.

   (A) She hasn't gotten to that point in the lecture yet.
   (B) She doesn't understand it.
   (C) She hasn't thought about a better name.
   (D) She is still learning about the new research.

Choice (D) is correct because she hasn't "gotten far" enough, in terms of acquiring knowledge, to provide an appropriate name. The use of the adverb *yet* indicates that some idea or action is in process and is expected to be achieved in the future. Choice (A) is incorrect because of the word *myself*. This indicates that the professor doesn't understand it herself yet, so she can't have the information in her lecture. Choice (B) is incorrect because the idiom *haven't gotten that far* doesn't mean *don't understand*. The idiom for *don't understand* is *don't get it*. Choice (C) is incorrect because while she doesn't have a better name for it, it's not that she hasn't imagined a more clever name, but that she doesn't know enough about the reasons behind the speech to provide a name representative of these reasons.

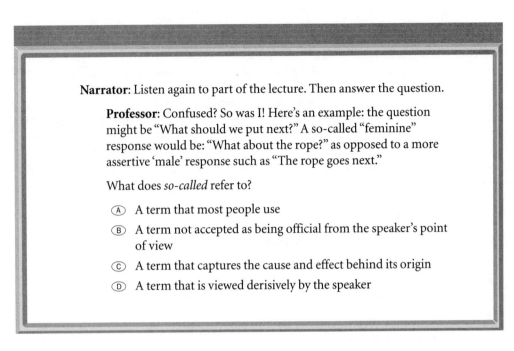

Narrator: Listen again to part of the lecture. Then answer the question.

Professor: Confused? So was I! Here's an example: the question might be "What should we put next?" A so-called "feminine" response would be: "What about the rope?" as opposed to a more assertive 'male' response such as "The rope goes next."

What does *so-called* refer to?

(A) A term that most people use

(B) A term not accepted as being official from the speaker's point of view

(C) A term that captures the cause and effect behind its origin

(D) A term that is viewed derisively by the speaker

Choice (B) is correct because the idiomatic meaning of *so-called* is "not accepted officially." When you are ready, move on to Lesson 5—Speaking: Defining and Describing.

LESSON 5—SPEAKING: DEFINING AND DESCRIBING

In this lesson, we will cover more speaking skills and strategies that will help lead to success on test day. You will have the opportunity to learn more about the tasks required for the Speaking section of the TOEFL. If you want to proceed with additional speaking strategies when you finish this lesson, turn to Lesson 6—Writing: More Practice with Descriptive Essays in Chapter 6.

Remember that in Lessons 1–4 we covered the following speaking tasks:

- Describing Something from Your Own Experience
- Summarizing a Lecture
- Expressing and Supporting an Opinion Based on Personal Experience
- Summarizing a Conversation and Expressing an Opinion
- Synthesizing and Summarizing Information

This lesson will review the following the Speaking section tasks in greater detail:

- Describing Something from Your Own Experience
- Summarizing a Lecture

Before we review these tasks, let's review some important skills you should already be familiar with: defining, describing, and exemplifying.

Defining, Describing, and Exemplifying

Speakers and writers in all languages use a variety of rhetorical devices to clarify to their audience what they are talking about. If a speaker is talking about an idea or concept that is new to the listener, he or she needs to **define** it. That means the speaker needs to say what it is: a thing, a feeling, an idea, a political system, a theory, a problem. If a speaker is describing an object, a place, a feeling, or an experience that the listener is not familiar with, he or she needs to **describe** it. That means the speaker needs to say what the thing is like: hot, cold, big, small, important, fun. The speaker might **compare** the thing to something that the listener does know about: "It's like a …"; "It's bigger than a …". **Metaphors** are a kind of "implied" comparison, without using the word *like*. For example: the eyes are windows to the soul. In all cases, the speaker might give **examples** of things that are familiar to the speaker.

Defining, Describing, and Exemplifying Practice

Listen to examples of people talking about difficult topics. For each speaker, make notes when you hear them use the respective rhetorical devices. You will find transcripts of these audio passages at the end of the chapter.

Sample one: Parliamentary Democracy

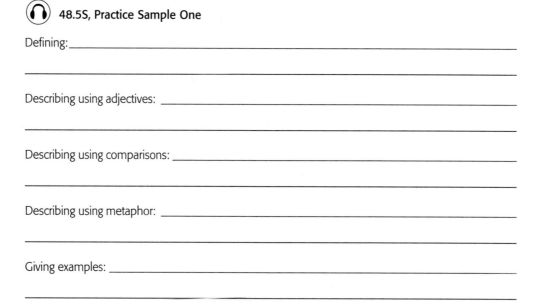 48.5S, Practice Sample One

Defining: _____

_____

Describing using adjectives: _____

_____

Describing using comparisons: _____

_____

Describing using metaphor: _____

_____

Giving examples: _____

_____

Sample two: Claustrophobia

 49.5S, Practice Sample Two

Defining: _____

_____

Describing using adjectives: _____

_____

Describing using comparisons: _____

_____

Describing using metaphor: _____

_____

Giving examples: _____

_____

Answers

Sample one: Parliamentary Democracy

Defining:

Parliamentary democracy is a democratic political system in which the party with the greatest number of representatives forms the government and its leader becomes prime minister.

All forms of democratic government are distinct from governments controlled by an absolute monarch or a minority class.

Describing using adjectives:

Parliamentary democracy originated in Britain in the seventeenth century and is the oldest form of democratic government widely in use today, for example in Australia, Canada, India and over thirty other countries.

Describing using comparisons:

On the surface, the predecessor of parliamentary democracy, i.e. direct democracy, may seem more democratic.

In a direct democracy, such as ancient Athens, all citizens participate in all decisions, whereas in a parliamentary democracy decisions are made by representatives on behalf of their electorate.

In reality, Athenian democracy was not as participatory as modern day parliamentary systems because the definition of "citizen" was very exclusive.

Describing using metaphor: *No examples used.*

Giving examples:

> Parliamentary democracy originated in Britain in the seventeenth century and is the oldest form of democratic government widely in use today, for example in Australia, Canada, India and over thirty other countries.

Sample two: Claustrophobia

Defining:

> The literal translation of the Greek roots of the word claustrophobia is "fear of closed spaces."
>
> A more accurate definition might be "fear of not being able to escape."
>
> Like many phobias, claustrophobia often results from some long forgotten childhood experience.
>
> Because it is a learned phobia, it can be unlearned

Describing using adjectives:

> As a result, claustrophobia can be a highly debilitating affliction.

Describing using comparisons: *No examples used.*

Describing using metaphor:

> Some sufferers say it feels as if the walls are closing in.

Giving examples:

> A person with claustrophobia may panic inside an enclosed space such as an elevator, airplane or crowded room.
>
> For people with claustrophobia, air travel can become impossible, car travel, difficult and even social situations can be so uncomfortable that they are avoided.
>
> One of my patients had an elder brother who used to smother him in a sleeping bag while they played wresting.

Task 1 Revisited—Describing Something from Your Own Experience

There are 6 tasks in the Speaking section of the TOEFL. The first requires a 45-second speech sample based on personal experience.

The first question on the TOEFL Speaking section asks you to talk about something from your personal experience. You will be asked to describe or explain something about yourself, your family, your country, or some similar topic.

If you are asked to talk about something personal, make sure that you describe it clearly. That means you need to *say what it is like*. You will probably use a variety of adjectives. You might also compare what you are describing with something that is likely to be familiar to everyone. Finally, you might give examples to further clarify what you are talking about.

If you are asked to talk about a specific thing, it is important that you define it. That means you need to *say what it is*: a thing, a feeling, an idea, a political system, a theory, a problem, or whatever it is. You might explain what it is using simple words or phrases. You will not be asked to define anything technical or complex. Your speaking will always be based on what you know about from your personal experience.

Look at the following speaking topics. Choose one topic and brainstorm the kind of information you could include, with particular focus on descriptions, definitions, and explanations.

- an important place in your life
- something that you fear
- important issue in your field of study
- an important national festival in your country

Brainstorm

Now organize the ideas so that they can be presented clearly. Don't forget to describe and define. To help organize your talk, make sure you:

1. Introduce what you are going to talk about

2. Explain what you are talking about and why you chose it

3. Say what it is like (describe it)

4. Give at least one example that explains more clearly what you are talking about

5. Summarize what you said

Now practice giving your response. If you have a study partner, or someone that can listen to your response, ask to work with him or her.

Next try these the following two TOEFL questions. Remember that you will not see the narrator's introduction on the test. If you have a study partner who can listen to your response, ask to work with him or her. You will find transcripts of these audio passages at the end of the chapter.

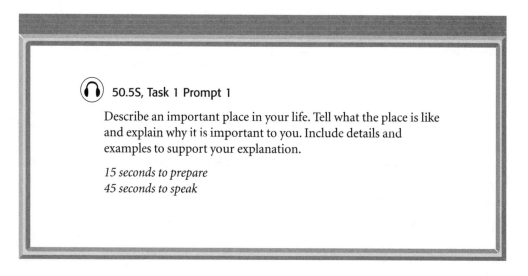

🎧 **50.5S, Task 1 Prompt 1**

Describe an important place in your life. Tell what the place is like and explain why it is important to you. Include details and examples to support your explanation.

15 seconds to prepare
45 seconds to speak

Notes

Evaluate yourself using the following criteria:

Criteria	Comments	Action to Improve
Clarity and pronunciation		
Organization		
Details and examples		
Grammar and vocabulary		

Now listen to the sample response. How was it different from yours? How was it similar? You will find a transcript of this audio passage (51. Lesson 5—Speaking, Task 1 Sample Response 1) at the end of the chapter.

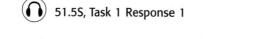 51.5S, Task 1 Response 1

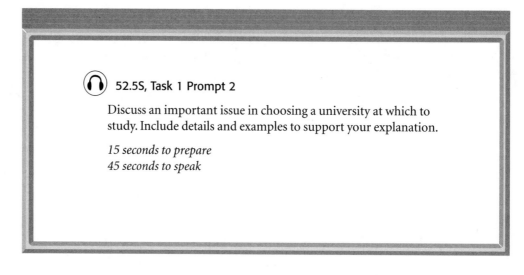

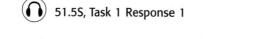 52.5S, Task 1 Prompt 2

Discuss an important issue in choosing a university at which to study. Include details and examples to support your explanation.

15 seconds to prepare
45 seconds to speak

Notes

Evaluate yourself using the following criteria:

Criteria	Comments	Action to Improve
Clarity and pronunciation		
Organization		
Details and examples		
Grammar and vocabulary		

Now listen to the sample response. How was it different from yours? How was it similar? You will find a transcript of this audio passage (53.5S, Task 1 Response 2) at the end of the chapter.

🎧 **53.5S, Task 1 Response 2**

Task 6 Revisited—Summarizing a Lecture

There are 6 tasks in the Speaking section of the TOEFL. The sixth requires a 60-second summary of an academic lecture.

The last question on the TOEFL Speaking section asks you to summarize information from a short lecture. You will listen to a short lecture and take notes. You will have 20 seconds to prepare your response. Then you will have 60 seconds to present a summary of the lecture.

When taking notes:
- Identify what kind of lecture it is: descriptive, cause and effect, informative, narrative, etc.
- Identify key parts by listening for stressed words and phrases
- Note key pieces of information such as names, dates, and places
- Identify how the lecture is organized, what the main points are, and what are examples

When summarizing:

- Present the main idea of the lecture
- Paraphrase some of the examples and details

Now practice the following TOEFL questions. Listen to the short lecture, take notes, and then summarize the main points using the strategies mentioned. Remember that you will not see the narrator's introduction on the test. If you have a study partner who can listen to your response, ask to work with him or her. You will find transcripts of these audio passages at the end of the chapter.

🎧 **54.5S, Task 6 Lecture 1**

Notes

🎧 **55.5S, Task 6 Prompt 1**

Using points and examples from the talk, describe the differences between men and women's writing styles and explain why these differences affect grant writing success rates.

20 seconds to prepare
60 seconds to speak

Evaluate yourself using the following criteria:

Criteria	Comments	Action to Improve
Clarity and pronunciation		
Organization		
Details and examples		
Grammar and vocabulary		

Now listen to the sample response. How was it different from yours? How was it similar? You will find a transcript of this audio passage (56.5S, Task 6 Response 1) at the end of the chapter.

🎧 **56.5S, Task 6 Response 1**

🎧 57.5S, Task 6 Lecture 2

Notes

🎧 58.5S, Task 6 Prompt 2

Using points and examples from the talk, summarize how schizophrenia has been regarded over the centuries and how treatments have reflected those perceptions.

20 seconds to prepare
60 seconds to speak

Evaluate yourself using the following criteria:

Criteria	Comments	Action to Improve
Clarity and pronunciation		
Organization		
Details and examples		
Grammar and vocabulary		

Now listen to the sample response. How was it different from yours? How was it similar? You will find a transcript of this audio passage (59.5S, Task 6 Response 2) at the end of the chapter.

🎧 59.5S, Task 6 Response 2

Great work! You have completed Lesson 5 in Reading, Writing, Listening, and Speaking. When you are ready, turn to Chapter 6 to review more TOEFL skills and strategies.

CHAPTER 5 AUDIO TRANSCRIPTS

46. Lesson 5—Listening, Note-Taking and Key Words Practice

Narrator: Listen to a lecture in a psychology class.

Professor: Picture a man walking into a restaurant. As soon as he enters the room, his heart starts beating rapidly, his palms start sweating, he, uh, feels a constriction in his throat, and when the host or hostess asks "how many" he can barely voice the words "two, non-smoking." And it becomes even harder if he's alone, because his condition is aggravated by the perception that he is the center of attention. He becomes intensely self-conscious; his movements heavy, unnatural, and forced. He believes everyone in the restaurant has suddenly stopped eating or talking to watch him. But more than watch him—pass judgment on him…everything from his dress, to his movements and the way he talks. His mind floods with the fear that he will "lose face" in the worst possible way. And the fear is a self-fulfilling prophecy…his own fear paralyzes him. It constricts the muscles in his body and throat that allow him to move and talk gracefully. It fogs his brain with confusion. His face turns red. Now he, uh, he probably knows that this is all in his mind, that he's being irrational, but he can't help it. He has what's known as Social Anxiety Disorder.

Social Anxiety is the third largest psychological problem in the U.S., affecting approximately thirty million people. But, even as big a problem as it's, uh, as it is…it's not even in the American Psychiatric Association's DSM (which stands for Diagnostic and Statistical Manual of Mental Disorders)…the bible, so to speak, for people in the psychiatry profession. The reason it's not listed is because it's not very well understood. It's estimated that ninety percent of people suffering from this, uh, condition are misdiagnosed. Now, this may be because the parts of the brain affected are also the same parts involved in disorders such as panic attacks, obsessive compulsive disorder, and depression—disorders, which in many cases, actually follow Social Anxiety. In other words, if you experience Social Anxiety, there's a good chance that later down the road it will escalate into one of these more serious, uh, disorders, if left untreated.

So, what are the causes? Who gets it and why? Well, unfortunately, if you have it you were probably born with it—a biological imbalance of a chemical called serotonin that transports signals between nerve cells in the brain. Although, it could also stem from an embarrassing social event in the past. Or it could be a combination of the two. The people who have it usually have a childhood history of shyness, and there's a good chance that a close relative also has it. But the symptoms—rapid heartbeat…uh, sweating…blushing…uh, breathlessness, confusion—usually appear sometime in the mid-teens. People who live with this condition, and do not seek help, end up with serious problems down the road…anything from dropping out of school…or chronic unemployment, financial dependencies…alcohol abuse (incidentally, it's estimated that twenty-five percent of all sufferers abuse alcohol)…uh, what else? Not getting married or having children, and worst of all—suicidal thoughts. As you can see, this can be a very debilitating disorder, to say the least. It can steal your happiness, and leave you shrinking away from life in fear.

So, whadya do? How do you cure a disease that experts don't completely grasp, and misdiagnose ninety percent of the time? A combination of therapy and drugs usually works best. Talking with a therapist is essential for understanding the nature of the individual's problem. One individual may be suffering from an embarrassing past event, while another is suffering more from a wiring of the brain. The types of treatments and drugs will differ among individuals. Cognitive Therapy helps patients confront negative feelings, shows them how to react differently to the triggers of the symptoms, and desensitizes them to the stimuli. Some of this may, in addition to one-on-one therapy with a psychiatrist, involve going to social skills training, and groups where patients can role play different situations that trigger their symptoms. As for drugs, there are many different types of medication, but the most popular is selective serotonin reuptake inhibitors (or SSRIs), because they have the fewest side effects of all drugs. But, again, this depends on the individual. While SSRIs work for one person, the same doctor may prescribe beta-blockers for someone who needs help controlling a specific symptom, say…heart palpitations or…sweating.

Whatever the scenario, both medication therapy and behavior therapy have proven successful in treating social anxiety disorder.

47. Lesson 5—Listening, Outlining Practice

Narrator: Now listen to part of a lecture on sociolinguistics. Students ask questions during the lecture.

Professor: Today we will be looking at some new findings concerning so-called feminine speech patterns and styles of interaction. From the readings, can somebody sum up the speech patterns that have been characterized as feminine? Ah…Jo?

Jo: Sure. Sociolinguists have observed that women's voices tend to rise at the end of a statement, rather than fall, which is the, uh, the more standard pattern. Also, women's speech patterns tend to include more questions, specifically tag questions, like "aren't you" or "don't you" at the end of a sentence. Um, they think this might be because women are seeking agreement or reinforcement of what they are saying.

Professor: Good. Those are some of the better-known observations. Any more? Yes, Nobu?

Nobu: I have a quote here from the readings that I don't really understand. Nancy Bonvillain notes that, "women typically use more polite speech than do men, characterized by a high frequency of honorific and softening devices." Can you explain what "honorific" and "softening" devices are?

Professor: Certainly. Honorific devices are formal stylistic markers; they are used to show respect for the person who is being addressed. Examples of honorific devices include um…well; a simple example is the use of a person's name or title, like calling me Professor Green rather than saying, "Hey Ann." Softening devices include the kind of things that Jo just mentioned— rising intonation and tag questions. They remove the assertiveness of statements and soften the impact. What softening devices do is give a sense of "fuzziness" to what is being said. … *[Realizes that there is still a lack of comprehension]* Ok, let's look at an example: "Pat's a mean person." That's an assertive, definitive statement. Note the downward inflection. "I think Pat's kinda mean, don't you?" is much softer. Softening devices include indicators of opinion *(I think)*, hedges *(kind of, sort of, a bit—phrases like that)* and tag questions *(don't you?)*. Does that make sense?

Nobu: Yes, thanks very much.

Professor: Now, you might have noticed that in our discussions, I have referred to these characteristics as "so-called" feminine speech patterns. Current sociolinguistic research indicates that they may not be so much a factor of gender as a factor of status. In other words, the linguistic devices observed in women's speech may reflect their real and perceived social status with respect to men.

Man 2: You mean it shouldn't really be called "feminine speech" but "status speech" or something? What would be a better name for it?

Professor: Good question, I haven't gotten that far myself yet. Let me tell you a bit more about what has been observed. In order to test how "feminine" so-called feminine speech really is, an experiment was devised to observe the frequency of the occurrence of particular characteristics. Seventy gender homogenous, three person task groups (thirty-five male, and thirty-five female groups) were given the NASA "Lost on the Moon" exercise to solve. All groups were videotaped and two independent coders analyzed their interactions. The coders identified statements with the following properties as "feminine": Number 1—a declarative content, but ending with a tag question *"I think we should put the rope next, don't you?"* Number 2—statements that are declarative in content, but ending with a rising inflection *"I think the gun goes next"* [note: rise in tone of voice]. Number 3—a response to a question that contains a suggestion, but is phrased as a question. [Pause…] Confused? So was I! Here's an example: the question might be *"What should we put next?"* A so-called "feminine" response would be: *"What about the rope?"* as opposed to a more assertive "male" response such as *"The rope goes next."* And finally number 4—a directly stated question that offers a solution to a task problem, for example: *"Should we put the rope next?"*

So, do you suppose the women's groups demonstrated a higher frequency of these verbal tags? Surprise! The results show that in gender homogenous groups such language patterns were initiated with equal frequency by men and by women. Um…now when I say equal, I mean statistically there was no significant difference; a goodness of fit test would suggest no difference between males and females on this behavioral measure.

Woman 2: So when women are with women and men are with men there is no difference to the way they speak? Women just use those polite devices when they are around men?

Professor: Hmm…that is too strong a statement to make at this point. There is a lot more research that needs to be done, and we are still far from being able to explain these results. A good next step would be to conduct the same experiment with gender heterogeneous groups.

48. Lesson 5—Speaking, Practice Sample One

Parliamentary democracy is a democratic political system in which the party with the greatest number of representatives forms the government and its leader becomes prime minister. Parliamentary democracy originated in Britain in the seventeenth century and is the oldest form of democratic government widely in use today, for example in Australia, Canada, India and over thirty other countries.

On the surface, the predecessor of parliamentary democracy, i.e. direct democracy, may seem more democratic. In a direct democracy, such as ancient Athens, all citizens participate in all decisions, whereas in a parliamentary democracy decisions are made by representatives on behalf of their electorate. In reality, Athenian democracy was not as participatory as modern day parliamentary systems because the definition of "citizen" was very exclusive. All forms of democratic government are distinct from governments controlled by an absolute monarch or a minority class.

49. Lesson 5—Speaking, Practice Sample Two

The literal translation of the Greek roots of the word *claustrophobia* is "fear of closed spaces." A more accurate definition might be "fear of not being able to escape." A person with claustrophobia may panic inside an enclosed space such as an elevator, airplane or crowded room. Some sufferers say it feels as if the walls are closing in. For people with claustrophobia, air travel can become impossible, car travel, difficult and even social situations can be so uncomfortable that they are avoided. As a result, claustrophobia can be a highly debilitating affliction.

Like many phobias, claustrophobia often results from some long forgotten childhood experience. One of my patients had an elder brother who used to smother him in a sleeping bag while play wresting. Because it is a learned phobia, it can be unlearned.

50. Lesson 5—Speaking, Task 1 Prompt 1

Narrator: In this question, you will be asked to talk about a familiar topic. After you hear the question, you will have 15 seconds to prepare your response and 45 seconds to speak.

Describe an important place in your life. Tell what the place is like and explain why it is important to you. Include details and examples to support your explanation.

51. Lesson 5—Speaking, Task 1 Sample Response 1

One of the most important places in my life has to be my father's kitchen. I am majoring in food science now, and I have a job at one of the best restaurants in town, and my dream is to one day open a restaurant of my own. I love everything about food and I know that passion comes from the hundreds of hours I spent in my father's kitchen when I was growing up.

As a kid, the kitchen was always just the best place to be: it was warm, busy, full of smells. There were always little treats, and best of all, my dad. For as long as I can remember, my dad has been a great cook, someone who just loves food. Because he enjoys cooking so much, he really appreciates people who enjoy eating.

My brother and sisters liked to eat too, but none of them spent as much time in the kitchen as I did. As soon as I could walk, I started hanging out in the kitchen. At first my dad used to tell me to keep out of the way, but finally he realized that I really wanted to be there and then he would let me sit up on the counter and watch closely while he worked. He would allow me to taste sauces and ask my opinion about the flavoring. "Maybe a little more salt," I might suggest. As the years went by he gave me more and more little jobs to do.

Whatever kitchen I end up working in, even if it is with a famous chef or in some fancy restaurant, nothing will compare to my father's kitchen.

52. Lesson 5—Speaking, Task 1 Prompt 2

Narrator: In this question, you will be asked to talk about a familiar topic. After you hear the question, you will have 15 seconds to prepare your response and 45 seconds to speak.

Discuss a current issue in your field of expertise or in a field with which you are familiar.

53. Lesson 5—Speaking, Task 1 Sample Response 2

In my field of graphic design a current hot issue is something called "emotional branding." This basically means promoting a brand by creating emotional associations with it, and therefore making it stand out. People are prepared to pay more for a product that makes them feel a certain way just by buying it. For more and more Americans it is no longer enough for a product to simply perform well; they are looking for brands that are actively involved in making the world a better place.

Designers come in to help companies convey that message to potential consumers. Take the oil company BP for example. BP actually stands for British Petroleum, but their business strategy aims to offer alternative forms of energy, so they have re-crafted the tag line into: "Beyond Petroleum." The logo is a dynamic burst of energy that is bright white at the core with radiant beams of yellow and green light projecting from the center.

The reason that emotional branding is somewhat controversial is that it is considered exploitative. Good design can certainly affect consumer behavior and a lot of people feel that it is immoral to take advantage of people's good intentions and efforts to make responsible choices. So, designers need to make personal decisions about how to use their skills and whether or not they feel emotional branding and marketing is ok.

54. Lesson 5—Speaking, Task 6 Lecture 1

Narrator: In this question, you will listen to a short lecture about men's and women's writing styles. You will then answer a question that asks you to summarize the lecture. After you hear the question, you will have 20 seconds to prepare your response and 60 seconds to speak.

Professor: Although it has long been acknowledged that a there are consistent linguistic differences between male and female oral communication it was long believed that these differences were greatly reduced when it came to writing styles. Some authors have even asserted that there is no difference between male and female writing styles in formal contexts. As part of a research project which attempts to identify reasons for the discrepancy in the numbers of men and women in science, we analyzed the writing styles in a number of grant proposals. We found significant differences in writing styles even in this highly formalized format.

First of all, we found that female writing exhibits greater usage of features identified as "involved" while male writing uses more featured defined as "informational." A so-called "involved" text shows interaction between the writer and the reader, whereas the so-called "informational" style creates greater distance between writer and reader. Put simply, male authors tend to give very specific information about the subject, whereas female authors create more intricate informational linkages between subjects. So readers of a female text need to be alert to those linkages.

And our second significant finding was a distinct correlation between the characteristics of male writing with non-fiction styles and female writing with fiction styles. Characteristics of non-fiction (and also male) writing include extensive use of determiners and prepositions, while pronouns are more prevalent in fiction (and female) writing. To paraphrase: men write about what is happening, and where. Women write about who is doing it. This finding supports our other observation concerning the informational style of men versus the involved style of women.

So, do these findings help us understand the variation in success rates when it comes to getting science grant proposals funded? I believe so. Selection committees want to be informed, as efficiently as possible. The male tendency to be explicit likely facilitates the efficient transfer of information. On the other hand, the so-called "involved" style of female writing may frustrate a board member who needs to read many similar documents in a very short space of time. Also, the frequent use of pronouns common to female writing might be considered irrelevant in a science research proposal. Selection committees don't care *who* will doing it, they care about *what* will be done.

55. Lesson 5—Speaking, Task 6 Prompt 1

Using points and examples from the talk, describe the differences between men and women's writing styles and explain why these differences affect grant writing success rates.

56. Lesson 5—Speaking, Task 6 Sample Response 1

The lecture describes two important differences between male and female writing styles. Women write in a more involved style and men write in a more informational style. Also, male writing is more like non-fiction whereas female writing is more like fiction. In other words, men write about the thing, or the action and the details about that, but women write about who is doing what. Umm . . . the professor thinks that umm, that the people who decide about grants . . . umm . . . that they might get frustrated by the female writing style, because it is less efficient. They just want to know *what,* they don't care about *who.* So that is why male and female writing styles might affect umm, might affect the success rates of grant proposals from men and women scientists.

57. Lesson 5—Speaking, Task 6 Lecture 2

Narrator: In this question, you will listen to a short lecture about a mental disorder. You will then answer a question that asks you to summarize the lecture. After you hear the question, you will have 20 seconds to prepare your response and 60 seconds to speak.

Professor: What is now known as schizophrenia is a mental disorder that has been witnessed in human societies for many centuries. One of the symptoms of schizophrenia—hearing voices—has not always been perceived as a curse. On the contrary, in some ancient civilizations it was believed that such voices came from the gods. Research partnerships between neuroscientists and classical historians are finding indications that the ancient Greek oracle speakers of several centuries BCE might have been schizophrenic. People who heard voices were revered as priests, as mouthpieces of the gods. Other types of mental disease were considered to be the invasion of other, more often evil than good, spirits.

In western civilization, "madness" was feared and most sufferers were left to wander the countryside or were committed to institutions. During the age of Enlightenment in the 18th and 19th century the public's awareness of such conditions grew, and improvements in care and treatment began to appear. Institutions became more humane, and treatments increasingly targeted. Doctors initially sought cures using herbal remedies. With the discovery of electricity came many treatments for psychosis including symptoms of schizophrenia. One doctor claimed that a certain type of shock treatment could cure schizophrenia. These claims were highly questionable even at the time and are now believed to have done more harm than good, in fact some 40% of patients undergoing this treatment ended up with fractured spines!

Nowadays schizophrenia is treated with an array of medications and psychotherapeutic interventions. The drugs can help control the symptoms of the disorder while education and psychotherapy can help patients and families learn to manage it more effectively. Virtually every rigorous comparison of medical approaches and social rehabilitation has shown that medication combined with social rehabilitation leads to a better outcome than either approach alone.

58. Lesson 5—Speaking, Task 6 Prompt 2

Using points and examples from the talk, summarize how schizophrenia has been regarded over the centuries and how treatments have reflected those perceptions.

59. Lesson 5—Speaking, Task 6 Sample Response 2

The professor talks about how the mental disorder schizophrenia was regarded by ancient Greeks, by nineteenth century medical workers and by modern psychiatry. The ancient Greeks didn't think it was a disease, they thought it was a way for the gods to talk to people. When modern medicine was developing, one or two hundred years ago, doctors tried to find cures for various types of "madness" including schizophrenia. They tried herbal medications and electrical treatments, and they locked people up in mental hospitals. Nowadays, doctors are finding successful ways of treating this mental illness. Usually treatment includes medication and psychotherapy.

Chapter 6: **Lesson Set 6**
Theme—Arts and Literature

Chapter 6 continues to review more reading, writing, listening, and speaking skills and strategies you will need to score high on the TOEFL. Make sure to complete all the practice exercises and sample questions so that you can get the most out of these lessons.

LESSON 6—READING: THE IMPORTANCE OF DETAILS

In this lesson, we will cover more reading skills and strategies that will help lead to success on test day. You will also have the opportunity to review some of the strategies you learned in previous lessons as well as to learn more about the question types found on the Reading section of the TOEFL. If you want to proceed with more reading strategies when you finish this lesson, turn to Lesson 7—Reading: Context Clues, Antonyms, and Cohesive Devices in Chapter 7.

The Importance of Details

Choosing details that build on each other to express an important point is an important writing technique. Transitional devices can help move the reader from sentence to sentence or paragraph to paragraph, but if details are not carefully chosen, the reader will not be able to identify a main idea in each paragraph and will therefore feel lost.

To understand the importance of details in a passage, complete the following practice exercise.

The Importance of Details Practice

Read the passage and follow the directions.

The "Art" of Christo and Jeanne-Claude

Known only by their first names and famous for wrapping large objects in giant swathes of material, Christo and Jeanne-Claude embody a debate within the art world over the essential nature of art. Their work could be seen, on the one hand, as the most avant-garde of contemporary art, or on the other as an enormous waste of money that has no relevance to art whatsoever. Examples of their work include wrapped buildings, islands surrounded with sheets of pink, and miles-long walls of rippling fabric. Each of their works, once constructed, might remain in place for as little as a day, or as long as several years before being systematically dismantled. Whether any individual viewer sees it as art, the work of Christo and Jeanne-Claude is noteworthy for its grand scope and unusually transient nature.

Born on the same day of the same year, the Bulgarian Christo and his French-born wife Jeanne-Claude met in Paris in 1958 and were married soon after. Their collaborative relationship began almost immediately. Their creations started small—at first they wrapped bottles, magazines, packages—but then rapidly escalated into the large outdoor works for which they have since become famous. While some people appreciate the work of Christo and Jeanne-Claude strictly as visual art, the artists themselves point out that they incorporate features of architecture, sculpture, and even urban planning into their creations. Christo and Jeanne-Claude finance all their work themselves even though each project can cost many millions of dollars. Funding comes from the sale of Christo's preliminary drawings and sketches.

Each project begins with an idea both Christo and Jeanne-Claude feel passionate about. First, they render their idea in sketches and collages, and then bring in consultants such as engineers, architects, and environmental specialists to help them turn the plans into reality. Once they have determined how to make their concept tangible, they embark on a long process of gaining the necessary permission from public officials or private landowners to build their vision. One cannot wrap the German Reichstag, blanket the Japanese countryside in blue umbrellas, or encase a Parisian bridge in sheets of golden fabric without encountering a certain bureaucratic resistance. In one case, Christo and Jeanne-Claude endured thirty-two years of refusals from officials before finally gaining permission to cover trees in a Swiss park with transparent sheeting.

Christo and Jeanne-Claude often describe themselves as environmental artists. An excellent example of the environmental nature of their work is the "Umbrellas" project, perhaps unsurpassed in scale within the art world. In 1990–1991, the artists and their assistants erected 3,100 giant umbrellas, nine meters in diameter and standing over six meters high. Half were erected in Japan, the other half in California. Hundreds of blue umbrellas were arranged over twelve miles of verdant Japanese river valley, tightly arranged among rice fields, some even standing in the river water itself. In California, golden yellow umbrellas were distributed loosely for fifteen miles across the brown hills and valleys of desert landscape. Each group of umbrellas commented on the contrasts in natural environment and patterns of human habitation between Japan and California. After only eighteen days, the exhibit was removed and all of its components recycled, the artwork's transience an observation about humanity's brief existence on earth.

Can a work with so brief a life be considered art? Perhaps the question is motivated as well by the sheer novelty of Jeanne-Claude and Christo's work. Certainly their medium is uniquely their own. Discussions about the nature of art often revolve around the point that art is essentially personal—a thing is art if its creator says that it is. Art is an expression of its maker's view of the world, his or her identity and personality. Whether the viewer sees it as art or not, the work of Christo and Jeanne-Claude is deeply personal, so personal that they accept no payment for their finished works and execute no one's designs but their own. The scale and public nature of their pieces and the fact that their work is often discussed for years before ever being constructed place them firmly in the center of debate over the nature of art.

1. Look at paragraph 2. Which of the following describe details that are included in the paragraph? Circle all that apply.

   (A) When Christo and Jeanne-Claude began to work together

   (B) Which types of art Christo and Jeanne-Claude incorporated in their work

   (C) Why Christo and Jeanne-Claude fell in love

   (D) How Christo and Jeanne-Claude pay for their work

   (E) What the wedding of Christo and Jeanne-Claude was like

   (F) Where Christo and Jeanne-Claude first studied art

   (G) How the art of Christo and Jeanne-Claude changed over time

   (H) Who Christo and Jeanne-Claude were most influenced by artistically

2. Of the details listed in question 1 that were not included in paragraph 2, are there any that you think might have been useful to add?

3. Which details listed in question 1 are not at all useful to include? Why?

4. Look at paragraphs 3 and 4. Write the details that are given in the chart that follows. Examples have been given to help you.

Paragraph 3	Paragraph 4
How Christo and Jeanne-Claude first choose an idea	How Christo and Jeanne-Claude characterize their art
What the first step in their artistic process is	

Answers

1. (A) When Christo and Jeanne-Claude began to work together

(B) Which types of art Christo and Jeanne-Claude incorporated in their work

(D) How Christo and Jeanne-Claude pay for their work

(G) How the art of Christo and Jeanne-Claude changed over time

2. It would be helpful to know what other artists have influenced their work, and where they studied art.

3. Information about their wedding or how they fell in love wouldn't contribute to the topic of the passage.

4.

Paragraph 3	Paragraph 4
How Christo and Jeanne-Claude first choose an idea	How Christo and Jeanne-Claude characterize their art
What the first step in their artistic process is	The 1990-91 "Umbrellas" project
Who they consult with to make their ideas real	3,100 9-meter diameter, 6 meter high umbrellas
How they deal with bureaucracies	Blue tightly packed over 12 miles in Japan
How persistent they need to be to accomplish some of their projects	Yellow spread out over 15 miles in California
	Represented population distribution in the two countries
	18 day exhibit, then everything recycled to comment on the non-permanence of humanity

Skimming

Skimming a passage is the best way to determine the main idea and important points, as well as what type of text it is. Remember that to skim a passage, you should pass your eyes quickly over the text (maybe in as few as 15–20 seconds), not really reading, but trying to notice the important parts. In this way, you get a general overview of the passage. When you skim just one paragraph, you should try to:

- Identify the topic sentence
- Recognize the basic organization
- Note repeated key words

Skimming Practice

Look at the following paragraph from today's reading and answer the questions that follow. Words that your eyes should pass over when skimming have been blacked out for you.

▮ project begins ▮ idea both Christo ▮ Jeanne-Claude feel passionate ▮ ▮ render ▮ idea ▮ sketches ▮ collages, ▮ then bring ▮ consultants such as engineers, architects, and environmental specialists to help them ▮ Once ▮ determined ▮ to make ▮ concept tangible, ▮ embark ▮ long process ▮ gaining ▮ necessary permission ▮ public officials or private landowners ▮ ▮. ▮ cannot wrap ▮ German Reichstag, blanket ▮ Japanese countryside ▮ blue umbrellas, ▮ encase ▮ Parisian bridge ▮ sheets ▮ golden fabric ▮ certain bureaucratic resistance. In one case, Christo and Jeanne-Claude endured thirty-two years ▮ refusals ▮ officials ▮ finally gaining permission to cover trees ▮. Swiss park ▮ transparent sheeting.

1. What do the boxed words tell you about the organization of the paragraph?

2. Which words are repeated in the paragraph? Why are they repeated?

3. What do the words highlighted in gray tell you about the type of text?

Next, using the information gathered from skimming, answer the following questions.

4. Which of the following best expresses the main idea of the paragraph?

   (A) Christo and Jeanne-Claude feel passionate about many ideas.
   (B) Christo and Jeanne-Claude have created art in Germany, Japan, and Switzerland.
   (C) Christo and Jeanne-Claude usually go through several steps before they complete a work of art.
   (D) Christo and Jeanne-Claude experienced a problem with gaining permission to create their art only once.

5. According to the passage, the first step in the artistic process of Christo and Jeanne-Claude is to

   (A) hire specialists to help them.
   (B) draw sketches and make collages of their idea.
   (C) gain permission of the government or landowners.
   (D) come up with an idea that they are both interested in.

6. Skim the paragraph one more time and choose one of the following text types that you think best describes it.

   (A) Descriptive
   (B) Compare/contrast
   (C) Historical narrative
   (D) Definition with examples

   _____

   _____

Answers

1. The paragraph describes a process that takes place over time.

2. "Permission" and "officials" are repeated to emphasize that they must work with governments in order to create art on a large scale.

3. The words are all descriptive, so something is being explained

4. (C) Christo and Jeanne-Claude usually go through several steps before they complete a work of art.

5. (D) come up with an idea that they are both interested in

6. (A) Descriptive

Note-Taking

As should be clear by now, you will be required to summarize quite a bit on the TOEFL. It's important to remember that before a good summary can be created, you must take good notes on the main idea and details of a reading passage or lecture. Let's practice this now.

Note-Taking Practice

Read the following short passage and take notes. Make sure to note the main idea and most important details.

Criticism of Hemingway

Every artist has critics; even Pulitzer Prize winning authors like Ernest Hemingway are no exception. A basic platform for the criticism of his works is the material he chose for his fiction and non-fiction. Some scholars feel that Hemingway tried to paint a falsely heroic picture of himself in his biographical works while in his fiction he relied too heavily on his own experiences. As a result, his fiction may be considered too personal and his non-fiction deemed unrealistic. The debate over how much a writer should use personal experience in his fiction is a long-standing one and Hemingway's stories are particularly well suited to fueling it further.

Hemingway's rhetorical style has been attacked as well, in essence branded as too simple. Critics claim that a lack of rhetorical devices makes Hemingway's works undeserving of the abundant praise they have received and that the author is equally undeserving of the title of literary genius. Without rhetorical sophistication, many assert, a writer is merely a writer, not a master.

Related to this simplicity in writing style is the simplicity with which Hemingway constructed his characters. His portrayal of women is especially odious to some, who say that his female characters were purposefully one-dimensional due to his inherent distrust of the fairer sex. Feminists instinctively find many of Hemingway's stories distasteful and complain that he had little understanding of the female mind.

Notes

Now listen to a short lecture. As you listen, take notes. Again, make sure to note the main idea and most important details. You will find a transcript of this audio passage (60.6R, Note-Taking Practice) at the end of the chapter.

🎧 **60.6R, Note-Taking Practice**

Notes

Paraphrasing

Look at part of a sentence from the reading passage. After it is an example of a paraphrase of the sentence.

- **Original Sentence**: Some scholars feel that Hemingway tried to paint a falsely heroic picture of himself in his biographical works.
- **Paraphrased Sentence**: When writing true stories about his own life, Hemingway tended to make himself out to be more courageous than he actually was.

To get more experience with paraphrasing, complete the Paraphrasing Practice that follows.

Paraphrasing Practice

Write paraphrases of the other three example sentences from the passage and lecture.

1. In his fiction he relied too heavily on his own experiences.

Paraphrased Sentence:

_____

_____

2. First and foremost, Hemingway's background as a journalist probably influenced his minimalist approach to writing.

Paraphrased Sentence:

_____

_____

3. It's amazing how just by describing situations or senses very specifically, Hemingway can get quite complex ideas across to his readers.

Paraphrased Sentence:

_____

_____

Answers

Answers will vary, but here are some sample paraphrased sentences.

1. Hemingway based too much of his writing on things that he had seen and done himself.

2. Likely because he originally wrote for magazines and newspapers, Hemingway's writing style was very minimalist.

3. One of Hemingway's strengths was his ability to convey complex ideas to his readers by carefully describing senses or conditions.

Summarizing Two Sources in Writing

Students in an American university will not only have to summarize what they have heard or read, but they will also need to synthesize, or combine, the information from two texts, or from a text and a lecture. In order to create a summary that synthesizes information, students need to understand the details that are similar and different between the two sources, and be able to paraphrase the information effectively.

Summarizing Two Sources in Writing Practice

Using your notes and paraphrased sentences, write one short summary that combines information from both the passage and the lecture to tell what you have learned about Ernest Hemingway's writing style. If you need to hear the passage again, listen to (60.6R, Note-Taking Practice)

In your summary, make sure to mention the main idea and to include the most important details from the text and lecture in paraphrased form. Remember to use some of the following expressions as you write:

To show similarities:

> *similarly, likewise, also, as well, like, both*

To show differences:

> *however, on the other hand, although, yet, whereas, unlike, in contrast*

Answers

Answers will vary, but here is one sample summary.

> Not everyone agrees that Ernest Hemingway was a great writer. Although he won a Pulitzer Prize, some critics think that his writing style, which often left a lot of inference to the reader, was too simple. Others point out that his material was perhaps too autobiographical, and that his portrayal of women was less than flattering. However, Hemingway's admirers claim that all of these criticisms are actually evidence of his literary genius—that the simple style of his writing was actually realism at its most effective.

Understanding the question types is important for knowing how and where you can apply your strategies. Keep reading to learn more.

Question Types

There are 13 question types on the Reading section of the TOEFL. These are:

- Identifying the Main Idea
- Summarizing the Most Important Points
- Understanding Rhetorical Function
- Understanding Details
- Understanding Details as They Relate to the Main Idea (Multiple-Choice)
- Understanding Details as They Relate to the Main Idea (Schematic Table)
- Inferring Word Meaning from Context
- Defining a Key Term
- Locating a Referent
- Understanding Coherence
- Drawing an Inference
- Inferring the Author's Opinion or Attitude
- Paraphrasing

This lesson will review the following question types in greater detail:

- Understanding Details
- Understanding Details as They Relate to the Main Idea (Multiple-Choice)
- Understanding Details as They Relate to the Main Idea (Schematic Table)

Question Type 4 Revisited—Understanding Details

There are 3 passages in the Reading section of the TOEFL, each of which is followed by 2–5 *detail* questions.

One type of question on the TOEFL test requires you to answer questions about details found in a reading passage. In order to answer this type of question correctly, you will need to use several of the strategies you have been practicing:

- Skimming the passage for main ideas and repeated key words
- Referring to the notes or drawings you have taken or created

You will also need to be able to identify the key words in a question and answer choices, and skim the passage for those same words or their synonyms. For example, from your skimming you might already remember that the key words *gain permission* are used several times in paragraph 3 of the Christo passage. If not, you can skim the passage (repeated here) quickly to find them.

The "Art" of Christo and Jeanne-Claude

Known only by their first names and famous for wrapping large objects in giant swathes of material, Christo and Jeanne-Claude embody a debate within the art world over the essential nature of art. Their work could be seen, on the one hand, as the most avant-garde of contemporary art, or on the other as an enormous waste of money that has no relevance to art whatsoever. Examples of their work include wrapped buildings, islands surrounded with sheets of pink, and miles-long walls of rippling fabric. Each of their works, once constructed, might remain in place for as little as a day, or as long as several years before being systematically dismantled. Whether any individual viewer sees it as art, the work of Christo and Jeanne-Claude is noteworthy for its grand scope and unusually transient nature.

Born on the same day of the same year, the Bulgarian Christo and his French-born wife Jeanne-Claude met in Paris in 1958 and were married soon after. Their collaborative relationship began almost immediately. Their creations started small—at first they wrapped bottles, magazines, packages—but then rapidly escalated into the large outdoor works for which they have since become famous. While some people appreciate the work of Christo and Jeanne-Claude strictly as visual art, the artists themselves point out that they incorporate features of architecture, sculpture, and even urban planning into their creations. Christo and Jeanne-Claude finance all their work themselves although each project can cost many millions of dollars. Funding comes from the sale of Christo's preliminary drawings and sketches.

Each project begins with an idea both Christo and Jeanne-Claude feel passionate about. First, they render their idea in sketches and collages, and then bring in consultants such as engineers, architects, and environmental specialists to help them turn the plans into reality. Once they have determined how to make their concept tangible, they embark on a long process of gaining the necessary permission from public officials or private landowners to build their vision. One cannot wrap the German Reichstag, blanket the Japanese countryside in blue umbrellas, or encase a Parisian bridge in sheets of golden fabric without encountering a certain bureaucratic resistance. In one case, Christo and Jeanne-Claude endured thirty-two years of refusals from officials before finally gaining permission to cover trees in a Swiss park with transparent sheeting.

Christo and Jeanne-Claude often describe themselves as environmental artists. An excellent example of the environmental nature of their work is the "Umbrellas" project, perhaps unsurpassed in scale within the art world. In 1990–1991, the artists and their assistants erected 3,100 giant umbrellas, nine meters in diameter and standing over six meters high. Half were erected in Japan, the other half in California. Hundreds of blue umbrellas were arranged over twelve miles of verdant Japanese river valley, tightly arranged among rice fields, some even standing in the river water itself. In California, golden yellow umbrellas were distributed loosely for fifteen miles across the brown hills and valleys of desert landscape. Each group of umbrellas commented on the contrasts in natural environment and patterns of human habitation between Japan and California. After only eighteen days, the exhibit was removed and all of its components recycled, the artwork's transience an observation about humanity's brief existence on earth.

Can a work with so brief a life be considered art? Perhaps the question is motivated as well by the sheer novelty of Jeanne-Claude and Christo's work. Certainly their medium is uniquely their own. Discussions about the nature of art often revolve around the point that art is essentially personal—a thing is art if its creator says that it is. Art is an expression of its maker's view of the world, his or her identity and personality. Whether the viewer sees it as art or not, the work of Christo and Jeanne-Claude is deeply personal, so personal that they accept no payment for their finished works and execute no one's designs but their own. The scale and public nature of their pieces and the fact that their work is often discussed for years before ever being constructed place them firmly in the center of debate over the nature of art.

The questions that follow are similar to TOEFL *detail* questions. Read and answer the questions, keeping in mind the strategies you have been practicing.

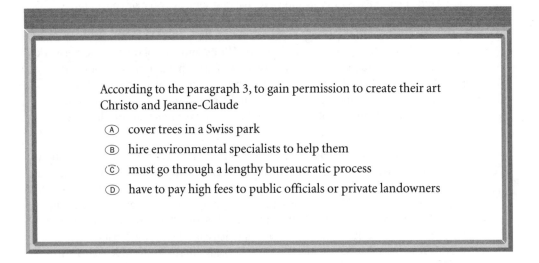

According to the paragraph 3, to gain permission to create their art Christo and Jeanne-Claude

(A) cover trees in a Swiss park

(B) hire environmental specialists to help them

(C) must go through a lengthy bureaucratic process

(D) have to pay high fees to public officials or private landowners

The correct answer is (C). According to the reading, the process of gaining permission to create their art in pubic spaces is long or lengthy. Choice (A) is not correct because it is an example of the result of gaining permission to create their art. Choice (B) is not correct because it is an earlier part of the process of creating their art. Choice (D) is not correct because the price of creating the art is not mentioned in this paragraph.

How do Christo and Jeanne-Claude finance their work?

(A) With their own money

(B) With the help of other famous architects and sculptors

(C) With millions of dollars they raise from famous corporations

(D) With money they earn from selling bottles, magazines, and packages

The correct answer is (A). Choice (B) is incorrect because it is not architects and sculptors, but architecture and sculpture that are mentioned. Choice (C) is incorrect because although they do raise millions of dollars, corporations are not mentioned. Choice (D) is not correct because bottles, magazines, and packages are examples of how Christo and Jeanne-Claude first started creating art.

All of the following are mentioned in paragraph 4 as characteristics of the "Umbrellas" project in California EXCEPT

(A) yellow umbrellas

(B) umbrellas standing in river water

(C) a fifteen mile distribution of umbrellas

(D) surroundings of brown hills and valleys

The correct answer is (B).

In deciding on the correct choice for detail questions, remember to be aware of distracters that:

- use key words, phrases, or information from the passage in a way unrelated to the question
- use key words or phrases from the passage but are untrue
- express ideas that are not mentioned in the passage

Now read and answer the following *detail* questions.

According to the passage, making sketches and collages of their ideas is

- (A) a process that takes place after Christo and Jeanne-Claude bring in consultants to help them
- (B) something both Christo and Jeanne-Claude feel passionate about
- (C) the most important part of Christo and Jeanne-Claude's projects
- (D) the second step in the Christo and Jeanne-Claude's artistic process

Choice (D) is correct because it is the next step after choosing an artistic idea. Choice (A) is incorrect because it occurs after making sketches and collages. The distracter used is the second type, the words *bring in consultants* are used in a way that is untrue. Choice (B) is incorrect because Christo and Jeanne-Claude feel passionate about an idea, not about making sketches and collages. It is also an example of the second type of distracter. The words *feel passionate about* are repeated to convey a meaning that is untrue. Choice (C) is incorrect because no part of Christo and Jeanne-Claude's projects is mentioned as more important than the other. Therefore this is an idea that is not mentioned in the passage, the third type of distracter.

Which of the following was a project that Christo and Jeanne-Claude worked on?

Ⓐ A German blanket

Ⓑ A park in Switzerland

Ⓒ A large blue umbrella in Japan

Ⓓ A set of golden sheets in Paris

The correct answer is (B).

Question Type 5 Revisited—Understanding Details as They Relate to the Main Idea (Multiple-Choice)

There are 3 passages in the Reading section of the TOEFL, one of which is followed by 1 *details-related-to-the-main-idea* question in multiple-choice format.

There are two questions in the Reading section of the TOEFL that test your understanding of how details relate to the main idea of the passage. One of these questions is in four-option multiple-choice format, and the other, which is covered later in this lesson, is in schematic table format. Both questions will appear on the same reading passage. To answer the multiple-choice format question, you must understand the main idea of the passage as well as how key details develop the main idea.

Looking back at the notes you have taken on the passage "The 'Art' of Christo and Jeanne-Claude," answer the following question.

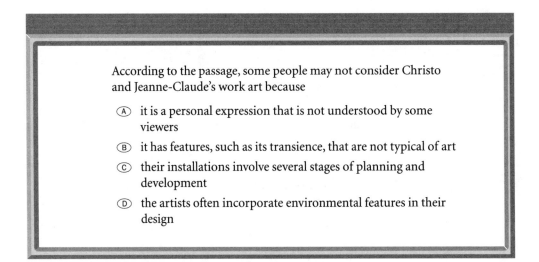

According to the passage, some people may not consider Christo and Jeanne-Claude's work art because

  (A) it is a personal expression that is not understood by some viewers

  (B) it has features, such as its transience, that are not typical of art

  (C) their installations involve several stages of planning and development

  (D) the artists often incorporate environmental features in their design

The passage discusses Christo and Jeanne-Claude's work by elaborating on various key features of their installations, at least some of which lead some people to question whether their work is art or not. The passage explains that all art is a personal expression, so choice (A) would not explain why some people would question their work as art. Choices (C) and (D) both explain features of the work of Christo and Jeanne-Claude, but the passage does not state or imply that either of these features is uncharacteristic of art. Features of their work which are not typical of art, such as its transience, are what make it controversial as art, so choice (B) is correct.

Question Type 6—Understanding Details as They Relate to the Main Idea (Schematic Table)

There are 3 passages in the Reading section of the TOEFL, one of which is followed by 1 *details-related-to-the-main-idea* question in schematic table format.

The schematic table format of a *details-related-to-the-main-idea* question asks you to select several appropriate phrases from a list and match them to the category to which they relate. To answer this question, you must understand how particular supporting details presented in the passage develop two or three important points in the passage. As with regular *detail* questions, in order to answer this type of question correctly, you will need to skim while using your notes to quickly find the answers in the passage.

Select the appropriate phrases from the answer choices and match them to the idea to which they relate. TWO of the answer choices will NOT be used. *This question is worth 4 points.*

Answer Choices	Features of all Christo and Jeanne-Claude's art
<ul><li>Made of 3,100 individual components</li><li>Covers a large scope</li><li>Incorporates designs from many artists</li><li>Addresses topics that are deeply personal to the artists</li><li>Taken apart after only eighteen days</li></ul>	
	Features of a specific piece of art by Christo and Jeanne-Claude
<ul><li>Seen as the most avant-garde of contemporary art</li><li>Environmental in nature</li><li>Includes ideas from various forms of art</li><li>Pieces were nine meters in diameter and over six meters high</li></ul>	

The following answer choices belong in the box under the heading "Features of all Christo and Jeanne-Claude's art":

- Covers a large scope
- Environmental in nature
- Includes ideas from various forms of art
- Addresses topics that are deeply personal to the artists

The following answer choices belong in the box under the heading "Features of a specific piece of art by Christo and Jeanne-Claude":

- Made of 3,100 individual components
- Taken apart after only eighteen days
- Pieces were nine meters in diameter and over six meters high

The answer choice "Incorporates designs from many artists" is incorrect because it uses key words or phrases from the passage, but it is untrue. Christo and Jeanne-Claude use only their own designs.

The answer choice "Seen as the most avant-garde of contemporary art" is incorrect because it uses key words from the passage in a way unrelated to the question. This is not a feature of art, but a reason for debating whether or not their work is art.

Now practice with distracters in *details-related-to-the-main-idea* questions. Two kinds of distracters to be aware of are distracters which:

- Use key words, phrases, or information from the passage in a way unrelated to the question
- Use key words or phrases from the passage but are untrue

When you are ready, turn to Lesson 6—Writing: More Practice with Descriptive Essays.

LESSON 6—WRITING: MORE PRACTICE WITH DESCRIPTIVE ESSAYS

In this lesson, we will cover more writing skills and strategies that will help lead to success on test day. You will also have the opportunity to learn more about the tasks required for the Writing section of the TOEFL. If you want to proceed with additional writing strategies when you finish this lesson, turn to Lesson 7—Writing: More Practice with Compare and Contrast Essays in Chapter 7.

Previous lessons covered the following essay types:

- Descriptive Essays
- Definition Essays
- Persuasive Essays
- Compare/Contrast Essays
- Essays in Response to a Reading Passage and a Lecture

This lesson continues to review descriptive essays.

Recognizing Descriptive Essay Prompts

There are two tasks in the Writing section of the TOEFL. In the first, you must read a passage, listen to a lecture, then write an essay about what you have read and heard. In the second, you must write an essay based only on a short prompt that asks you to describe or explain something or to express and support your opinion on an issue. For this second essay, you do not need any specialized knowledge. The prompt is based on topics that will be familiar to all test takers. You are given 30 minutes to plan, write, and revise this essay. Typically, an effective essay will contain a minimum of 300 words. Essays will be judged on the following:

- the quality of the writing, including idea development and organization
- the quality and accuracy of the language used to express these ideas

When you begin either writing task on the TOEFL, always read the prompt carefully to make sure that you know exactly which essay type you are being asked to write. You should be able to recognize that a descriptive essay is required for the second task if the prompt simply asks you to provide information.

Writing a Descriptive Essay

A common task facing academic writers is to prepare an essay that describes an idea, a process, a mechanism, or a concept. The essay form that is used in this situation is the descriptive essay. The goal of such an essay is to present and describe the features of a complex and perhaps unfamiliar subject so that the reader can easily understand them.

There are four main strategies a writer can use when writing a descriptive essay. These strategies are *description*, *definition*, *explanation*, and *exemplification*. Many descriptive essays use all four strategies. One way to employ the first three strategies—description, definition, and explanation—is to devote a body paragraph to each one (although it is also common to have body paragraphs that are a mix of two or three). Exemplification, or giving examples, is best used to support each of the other three.

Description

Use description when you want to answer the question, *What is it like?* The purpose of description is simply to provide essential information and details. Remember that when you are writing a description, you should choose your information carefully. It isn't necessary to provide every detail you can think of—doing so will only take more of your time and tire your reader. Instead, use only those details that will best convey an accurate impression of the thing or idea you are describing. Use specific terminology if possible; adjectives like *nice*, *good*, *bad*, and *great* are such common words that they have little specific meaning. One or two well-chosen examples will add strength to the descriptive paragraph. Here is an example of description:

> The painting consisted of an assemblage of geometric figures in contrasting red, green, and yellow.

Definition

Choose definition when you need to answer the questions *What is it?* or *What does it mean?* Sometimes you will need to introduce a term or idea that is unfamiliar to your reader, or to show exactly what you personally think that term or idea means. When that is the case, you should provide a definition to help your reader understand your discussion. A definition can take several forms, but most frequently it includes a description of the thing or idea and examples for the reader. Note that a defining paragraph may contain much of the same information as a description. However, the purpose of definition will always be to show the meaning of a term or idea. This is an example of definition:

> Calligraphy is a decorative style of handwriting often used for formal greetings, announcements, and invitations.

Explanation

Explanation is the best strategy to use when the question is *How does it work?* or *How does it happen?* An explanation will illustrate the steps in a process or the principles underlying a system. Use explanation when you think your reader may be unfamiliar with the process, system, or mechanism you are describing, or to show that you yourself understand it. Again, examples will always add strength to any explanation. Here is an example of explanation:

> Before beginning her novels, the author always prepared extensive notes, observations, and outlines to work from.

Exemplification

Examples are usually used to support each of the other three strategies. The best examples help the reader understand your point by providing a reference to something they already know or are familiar with. More examples are not necessarily better. Make sure that your examples actually demonstrate the point you are trying to illustrate; otherwise, you will confuse your reader instead of helping him.

> *Chance music*, developed in the mid-twentieth century, is a genre of music in which the composer's creative input is removed as much as possible from a piece. John Cage's work, *4'33"*, is a striking example of chance music, as the piece consists of four minutes and 33 seconds of silence.

Description, Definition, Explanation, Exemplification Practice

Read the three example paragraphs that follow. Decide whether the purpose of each is to describe, to define, or to explain. Then, reread each one carefully, and decide whether it contains the right amount, too much, or the wrong kind of information.

> 1. Stoneware is a kind of clay, distinguished from other clays by its lack of grog and high firing temperature, used for making pottery and other kinds of ceramics. It is usually gray or brown in color, and is commonly used for large bowls, mugs, and other utilitarian applications because of its durability. Stoneware is preferred by many potters because it works easily and accepts almost any kind of glaze.

Purpose: _____

Amount of Information: _____

2. Great authors like Hemingway, Dickens, and Tolstoy were successful because they had three things: a fertile subject matter, an interested audience, and a dedication to hard work. All three authors lived in places experiencing great social and cultural challenges—Dickens in the midst of the Industrial Revolution, and Tolstoy among the political, social, and economic upheavals of nineteenth-century Russia. The popularity of their work made all three writers into celebrities. But without the hours each writer spent daily on his work, none of them would have become the successful authors familiar to us today.

Purpose: _____

Amount of Information: _____

3. Van Gogh's works are impossible to overlook. Executed in strong, bold strokes of the brush, each of his paintings seems to flow with brilliant color. For most of his career, realism was not a feature of Van Gogh's style; instead, he represented his subjects in unnatural, exaggerated hues and disproportionate dimensions, his portraits almost caricatures, his landscapes scenes from a fairy tale or a febrile vision. Yet, despite the painter's departure from the naturalism of the Impressionists, his work is filled with a heartfelt sensitivity toward his subjects that no amount of realism could replace.

Purpose: _____

Amount of Information: _____

Answers

1. Purpose: Definition
Amount of Information: the right amount

2. Purpose: Exemplification
Amount of Information: too little—missing information about Hemingway

3. Purpose: Description
Amount of Information: wrong type—explanation of realism in his work does not address why it is impossible to overlook

Writing the Conclusion

The last part of the essay the reader sees is the concluding paragraph. This means that the conclusion needs to leave the reader with a positive impression of the strength and clarity of the essay as a whole. On the other hand, if this important component of the essay is written carelessly, the impression it gives to the reader may be just the opposite. To help you write a strong concluding paragraph, here are a couple of tips:

1. **The role of the concluding paragraph is to emphasize the important points made in the essay and to underline the essay's central message, lesson, or purpose.** The reader should not be left in doubt about your goal in writing the essay. However, try to avoid simply repeating the thesis statement and phrasing you used earlier in the essay; instead, show off your knowledge of English by summarizing the main points you made in the essay with new phrases and sentence structures.

2. **Be concise.** A long concluding paragraph is a disadvantage. It should not include new information or new arguments. Such information should be restricted to the essay's body paragraphs.

Clarity and Transitions

As you write an essay, it is important to help your reader keep the work of reading to a minimum. You also want to make it easy for the reader to see how all the ideas that you are discussing fit together. A good strategy for helping your reader navigate your essay is to use transition signals. Transition signals are adverb phrases or conjunctions that show how ideas connect or flow in a piece of writing. Usually, they are added at the beginning of sentences or clauses. Good use of transition signals is crucial to clear and successful writing.

Here is a list of those transitions that are commonly used in descriptive writing. The list has been divided into several subcategories, depending on the specific purpose each transition signal usually serves. Can you think of any to add to this list?

Transitions for listing or showing sequence

> *to summarize*
> *first/second/third*
> *once*
> *then*
> *next*

Transitions for adding information or examples

> *furthermore*
> *moreover*
> *in addition*
> *for example*
> *for instance*
> *to illustrate*

Transitions for showing results, consequences, or logical connections

as a result

consequently

as a consequence

thus

therefore

accordingly

Clarity and Transitions Practice

The following paragraph provides a complicated series of instructions. Without transition signals, these instructions may be difficult to follow. Read them carefully. Then, rewrite the paragraph, inserting appropriate transition signals from the list given to make the paragraph easier to understand. You may wish to join some sentences together into larger sentences. Try not to completely reword any sentences in the paragraph.

> Oh no! you think. The car shakes, and the steering wheel pulls strongly to one side. Your problem is clear: you've got a flat tire. What do you do? Slow down. Find a safe place to change your tire. Make sure you're not obstructing traffic. A well-lighted parking lot is a good choice at night. Remove the jack and spare tire from their storage places. Spares are rarely used. People usually don't maintain them. Checking the spare regularly is a good idea. Elevate the car on the jack. Remove the flat tire and replace it with the spare. Hand tighten the lug nuts. Lower the car. Tighten the nuts with the wrench. Stow the jack and tools. People may not see you clearly. You should reenter traffic carefully.

_____

_____

_____

_____

_____

_____

_____

_____

_____

_____

_____

_____

_____

_____

Answers

Answers will vary, but here is one example. Transition words are in bold.

> *Oh no! you think. The car shakes, and the steering wheel pulls strongly to one side. Your problem is clear: you've got a flat tire. What do you do?* **First**, *slow down.* **Then** *find a safe place to change your tire; make sure you're not obstructing traffic. A well-lighted parking lot is a good choice at night.* **Next** *remove the jack and spare tire from their storage places. Spares are rarely used,* **and** *people usually don't maintain them,* **consequently** *checking the spare regularly is a good idea. Elevate the car on the jack* **then** *remove the flat tire and replace it with the spare.* **Next** *hand tighten the lug nuts* **then** *lower the car. Tighten the nuts with the wrench* **and** *stow the jack and tools.* **Finally**, *you should reenter traffic carefully,* **because** *people may not see you clearly.*

Now that we have reviewed more about descriptive essays, it's time to practice writing.

Descriptive Essay Practice

Following is an example of the second task in the Writing section of the TOEFL. Once you have written your essay, spend at least 15 minutes evaluating it according to the principles outlined in this lesson.

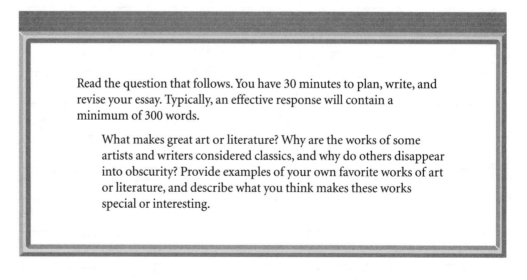

Read the question that follows. You have 30 minutes to plan, write, and revise your essay. Typically, an effective response will contain a minimum of 300 words.

What makes great art or literature? Why are the works of some artists and writers considered classics, and why do others disappear into obscurity? Provide examples of your own favorite works of art or literature, and describe what you think makes these works special or interesting.

Answer

Answers will vary, but here is one sample essay.

> It is difficult to predict what art will be seen as "classic" in the future. I think art gains permanence when it accomplishes one of two things: it either captures the identity of the time and place it was created, or it challenges some part of social structure in a way that causes reaction long after the work was created. Either way, the end result needs to be that the viewer, listener, or reader becomes involved in the art somehow.
>
> It seems unlikely that anyone who picked up a copy of a London newspaper to read the weekly installment of Charles Dickens' <u>A Tale of Two Cities</u> realized that they were reading literature that would be famous for centuries. The story is similar to many others in that it deals with the basic themes of love, family, and politics in the settings of France and England during the French Revolution. What makes it different, and great, is that Dickens used such vivid detail that even a person who reads <u>A Tale of Two Cities</u> today will still feel themselves drawn into life in the late 1700s.
>
> An example of art challenging social norms would be one of my favorite paintings, <u>Sunday on la Grande Jatte</u> by Georges Seurat. This painting has become a component of every Introduction to Art class because it represented entirely new concepts both to the act of painting and to how we view paintings. At the time it was created, many other famous painters were working in the Impressionist style, using broad, colorful strokes to give viewers an overall idea of the subject of their work. Seurat did something completely different by using thousands of tiny dots of color that fooled a viewer's eye into seeing trees, flowers, and even people.
>
> There is no question that there were other writers in Dickens' time, and certainly other painters painted while Seurat was alive. But both men are famous now because they were able to create art that stood out from the works of their contemporaries. In both cases, their work appealed to people as more than a story or picture, it encouraged the reader or viewer to think beyond the image or story, and to participate in the art.

Now that you have practiced writing, you are ready to begin Lesson 6—Listening: Details.

LESSON 6—LISTENING: DETAILS

In this lesson, we will cover more listening skills and strategies that will help lead to success on test day. You will also have the opportunity to review some of the strategies you learned in previous lessons as well as to learn more about the question types found on the Listening section of the TOEFL. If you want to proceed with more listening strategies when you finish this lesson, turn to Lesson 7—Listening: Note-Taking, Main Idea, and Combined Skills in Chapter 7.

Listening for Details

Perhaps you have noticed when listening to something spoken in English that it is fairly easy to understand generally what the speaker is trying to convey. However, for full comprehension, you will need to be able to listen to and understand the details of what you hear. Use the Listening for Details Practice that follows to improve this important skill.

Listening for Details Practice

Listen to a conversation between two people and answer questions about it. You will find a transcript of this audio passage (61.6L, Details Practice) at the end of the chapter.

🎧 **61.6L, Details Practice**

Now answer the following questions.

1. Which of the following books has the man read? (Circle all that apply.)

   (A) *Fahrenheit 451*
   (B) *The Great Gatsby*
   (C) *The Picture of Dorian Grey*
   (D) *The Fountainhead*
   (E) *The Brothers Karamazov*

2. After each author's name, write whether you think the speaker (a.) likes, (b.) dislikes, or (c.) is indifferent to the author.

   Ray Bradbury

   _____

   Fitzgerald

   _____

   Hemingway

   _____

   Shaw

   _____

   Oscar Wilde

   _____

   Ayn Rand

   _____

Dostoevsky

_____

3. Which novel does the man agree to read?

_____

4. Who wrote *Fahrenheit 451*?

_____

5. Where is Oscar Wilde from?

_____

Answers

1. (A) *Fahrenheit 451*

2. Ray Bradbury (a. likes)
Fitzgerald (b. dislikes)
Hemingway (a. likes)
Shaw (b. dislikes)

Oscar Wilde (b. dislikes)
Ayn Rand (c. is indifferent to)
Dostoevsky (a. likes)

3. *The Brothers Karamazov*

4. Ray Bradbury

5. England

Note-Taking

Remember, as you listen to passages on the TOEFL you should always take notes. Try to:
*   Write down key words, names, numbers, dates, or anything else you think is important
*   Listen for strong general statements by the speaker because they may be topic sentences or concluding sentences for paragraphs

Practice this now.

Note-Taking Practice

Listen to a lecture and take notes. You will use your notes to answer questions after you listen. You will find a transcript of this audio passage (62.6L, Note-Taking Practice) at the end of the chapter.

🎧 62.6L, Note-Taking Practice

Notes

Answers

Answers will vary.

Outlining

You know that an outline contains the main and supporting ideas in the order they are presented, but does not necessarily include any specific details. Here is an example of the beginning of an outline based on the lecture you just heard:

   I. Simplified texts in teaching—debate

      A. increased dramatically last 10 years

      B. opponents: "crime" to change, devalues work

      C. what makes great literature great?

         1. story?

         2. originality?

         3. prose?

         4. popularity?

      D. opinion: educational advantages > philosophical concerns

When you are ready, complete the Outlining Practice that follows.

Outlining Practice

Using your notes, write an outline of the lecture about simplified texts in the space that follows.

Now look at the table. The main ideas of the lecture are presented in the right-hand column, but they are not in the order they occurred in the lecture. Use your outline to put the information in the right-hand column of the table into the correct order by writing the main idea in the correct space on the left-hand side. The first one has been done for you.

Order of the Lecture	Summary of Topic/Main Idea
1 **(c) Simplified texts have increased in popularity, but purists don't believe in them**	(a) The professor recommends the use of simplified text to tell great stories to readers of all abilities
2	(b) Professor poses the question about what makes literature great, but does not believe in a simple definition of great literature
3	**(c) Simplified texts have increased in popularity, but purists don't believe in them**
4	(d) The professor gives examples of great literature: *David Copperfield, Pocahontas*
5	(e) There are many advantages to reading anything, whether it's diluted or not
6	(f) The Professor believes the advantages of graded reading outweigh the disadvantages and presents some ideas about what makes literature great
7	(g) Professor supports this claim by referring to research done by Steven Krashen
8	(h) The professor gives an example of a great non-fiction work: Benjamin Franklin's autobiography

Answers

I. Using graded readers in ESL classrooms

II. Debate over using diluted literature classics

    A. Author's original wording makes great

    B. Changing/simplifying bad = lost meaning

III. Using Simplified Readings

    A. Advantages

        1. Character and Plot more imp. than philosophical issues

        2. Good story = imagination = inspiration and motivation for learner

    B. Examples

        1. *David Copperfield* (fiction)—good story

        2. *Pocahontas* (nonfiction)—historical value

        3. Ben Franklin's autobiography—interesting but too difficult if not diluted

III. Advantages of reading

    A. Escapism

    B. Entertainment

    C. Exposure to different experiences/cultures

    D. Vocabulary

    E. Speaking skills

    F. Readers who read in English learn more English, more quickly

IV. Extensive Reading—Steven Krashen

    A. Definition

        1. Reading for meaning, not detail

        2. Not reading/understanding every word

        3. Competent readers are fast readers

    B. Conclusion

        1. Diluted literature = stimulating reading materials

Paragraph of the lecture
1 (c) Simplified texts have increased in popularity, but purists don't believe in them
2 (b) Professor poses the question about what makes literature great, but does not believe in a simple definition of great literature
3 (f) The Professor believes the advantages of graded reading outweigh the disadvantages and presents some ideas about what makes literature great
4 (d) The professor gives examples of great literature: *David Copperfield, Pocahontas*
5 (h) The professor gives an example of a great non-fiction work: Benjamin Franklin's autobiography
6 (e) There are many advantages to reading anything, whether it's diluted or not
7(g) Professor supports this claim by referring to research done by Steven Krashen
8 (a) The Professor recommends the use of simplified text to tell great stories to readers of all abilities

Understanding the question types is important for knowing how and where you can apply your strategies. Keep reading to learn more.

Question Types

There are 7 question types on the Listening section of the TOEFL. These are:

- Understanding Rhetorical Function
- Understanding an Idiomatic Expression in Context
- Drawing an Inference
- Understanding a Speaker's Implication
- Identifying the Main Idea
- Summarizing the Most Important Points
- Understanding Details

This lesson will review in greater detail the following question types:

- Drawing an Inference
- Understanding a Speaker's Implication

Question Type 3 Revisited—Drawing an Inference

There are 2 conversations and 4 lectures in the Listening section of the TOEFL. Each conversation is generally followed by 1 *inference* question, and each lecture is followed by 0 or 1 *inference* question.

Inference questions ask you to draw conclusions about specific details in the passage or to make comparisons between details. In order to answer these questions, you should:

- Listen carefully to the details of the lecture or conversation
- Try to understand unfamiliar words from context
- Listen for conditionals, intonation, and suggestions made by the speakers while the conversation is happening so that you can anticipate certain inference questions
- Use your knowledge about the situation to guess what sort of conclusion might be logical

The following are examples of inference questions:

- What probably happened to _____?
- What will _____ probably do next?
- What can be inferred about _____?

The following *inference* questions contain excerpts from the lecture. Remember that on the actual test, you will only hear the excerpt in such a question. If you want to get the most out of this listening practice, do NOT simply read the excerpt. Have a native speaker read the excerpt aloud to you, or have him or her record a reading of the excerpt on audiocassette.

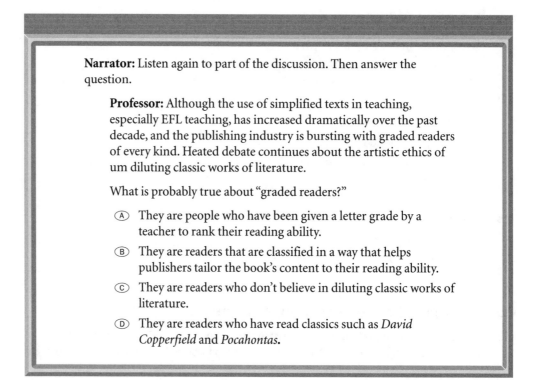

Narrator: Listen again to part of the discussion. Then answer the question.

Professor: Although the use of simplified texts in teaching, especially EFL teaching, has increased dramatically over the past decade, and the publishing industry is bursting with graded readers of every kind. Heated debate continues about the artistic ethics of um diluting classic works of literature.

What is probably true about "graded readers?"

(A) They are people who have been given a letter grade by a teacher to rank their reading ability.

(B) They are readers that are classified in a way that helps publishers tailor the book's content to their reading ability.

(C) They are readers who don't believe in diluting classic works of literature.

(D) They are readers who have read classics such as *David Copperfield* and *Pocahontas*.

This question is testing your ability to infer the meaning of the term "graded reader" from the ideas expressed in the introduction of the passage. The author sets up a contrast between the high volume of "graded readers" and the strong debate regarding the simplification of texts. A "heated debate" implies that, despite its popularity, there are an equal number of people who oppose graded reading. In the context of publishing, we should assume that a graded reader is a term that has meaning to publishers. Choice (A) is distracting you with a popular definition of grade (i.e. A, B, C, D, F). Choice (B) is the correct answer; it's a paraphrase of the other definition of grade (i.e. kindergarten, first grade, eighth grade, etc.). Choices (C) and (D) are incorrect answers that repeat familiar details from the lecture.

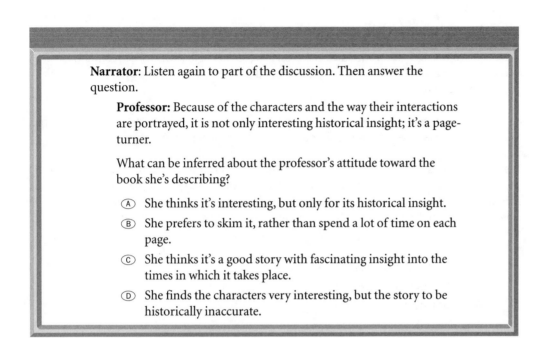

Narrator: Listen again to part of the discussion. Then answer the question.

Professor: Because of the characters and the way their interactions are portrayed, it is not only interesting historical insight; it's a page-turner.

What can be inferred about the professor's attitude toward the book she's describing?

Ⓐ She thinks it's interesting, but only for its historical insight.

Ⓑ She prefers to skim it, rather than spend a lot of time on each page.

Ⓒ She thinks it's a good story with fascinating insight into the times in which it takes place.

Ⓓ She finds the characters very interesting, but the story to be historically inaccurate.

This question can be answered without a larger context. *Page-turner* is an idiom for a fascinating or engaging book. If you know the meaning of this term, the correct answer, choice (C), is easy. Choice (A) attempts to distract you with the repetition of the word *only*. Choice (B) is written based on a potential misinterpretation of the term *page-turner* as a book one would read quickly. Choice (D) is incorrect because there is no evidence to support this inference.

Narrator: Listen again to part of the discussion. Then answer the question.

Professor: Now, Benjamin Franklin used grammar, vocabulary, and especially punctuation that would baffle even the most accomplished modern day reader!

According to the professor, what can be inferred about Benjamin Franklin?

Ⓐ His writing is very difficult to read, even for advanced readers.

Ⓑ He was a creative writer who rejected convention.

Ⓒ He didn't like following the rules of grammar.

Ⓓ His writing is very difficult to read, unless you're an accomplished reader.

Choice (A) is correct.

Question Type 4 Revisited—Understanding a Speaker's Implication

There are 2 conversations and 4 lectures in the Listening section of the TOEFL. Each conversation is followed by 1 or 2 *speaker's implication* questions, and each lecture is followed by 0 or 1 *speaker's implication* question.

Remember from previous lessons that something that is implied is not directly stated. An implication is the meaning of a statement that is not obvious in the literal meaning of the words.

The answer choices for *speaker's implication* questions will contain situations that will further confuse you because they were not discussed or did not occur. You will also see synonyms (two words with a similar meaning), homophones (two words that sound the same but have a different meaning), or other words repeated in the answer choices that are either out of context or not stated in the conversation.

The following are examples of implication questions:

- What does the man probably mean?
- What does the man suggest/imply?
- What does the woman want to know?
- What does the man say about _____?
- What does the woman advise the man to do?
- Why does _____ say _____?
- What does _____mean by _____?

For your convenience, the listening passage is reprinted here. You can also listen again to (62.6L, Note-Taking Practice).

Narrator: Now listen to part of a lecture in a teacher-training class on using graded readers.

Professor: Although the use of simplified texts in teaching, especially in EFL, or English as a Foreign Language, teaching, has increased dramatically over the past decade, and the publishing industry is bursting with graded readers of every kind. Heated debate continues about the artistic ethics of um diluting classic works of literature. There are those who argue that great literature is great because of the words, phrases, and structures chosen by the author. Therefore, they say, it is a crime to change those words, phrases, and structure in any way. By doing so, the very essence is removed and thus the work of art becomes entirely devalued.

Well, this debate brings up good questions regarding the definition of great literature. What makes a novel great? What makes it a classic? Is it the plot, the characters, the descriptions, the dialogues, the prose itself? Or does greatness lie in some kind of originality; does a work need to break barriers to be considered "art"? Or is it just a question of popularity? I don't believe there is a simple answer; in fact, I think…well anyway, I mustn't get sidetracked.

The question for us is, do we use simplified classics in teaching? In my opinion, the educational advantages of using simplified graded readers far outweigh the philosophical concerns about art. I believe great literature is great because of a combination of things. Characters and plot can be crucial; for me, it is these elements that take my imagination beyond the mundane, outside of ordinary life. Have you ever been asked: "if you were going to be stranded on a desert island and could only take three books, which three would you take?" I'll tell you one title that would be on my list: *David Copperfield*. There's a book that makes me laugh out loud, moves me to tears, and never fails to absorb me completely. The young hero experiences death and hardships, meets amazing characters, and he survives everything thrown his way. It is the events…the characters…the story that make this book so rich. Those can be very effectively conveyed in a simplified text.

Another example is *Pocahontas*. Unlike David Copperfield who is 100% fiction, we know that Pocahontas was a real person. However, as is the case with many legendary people, no one can be certain that all the stories written about her are completely true. She did indeed marry John Rolfe in 1614 and traveled with him to London in 1616. Regardless of any potential embellishments, this is a memorable story of Native American culture and the impact white settlers had when landing on the new continent. Because of the characters and the way their interactions are portrayed, it is not only interesting historical insight; it's a page-turner.

A non-fiction classic is Benjamin Franklin's autobiography. So much can be learned about the way the world worked in the late 1800s from this absorbing and intimately written book, even though it centers around one single life. Now, Benjamin Franklin used grammar, vocabulary, and especially punctuation that would baffle even the most accomplished modern day reader! Any version of his autobiography that is published today has been simplified to a certain extent. Why not simplify it far enough to enable EFL learners to access it?

I could go on. But aside from the fact that reading offers escapism, entertainment, and windows on unfamiliar or bygone worlds, there are many reasons from a pedagogical, i.e. instructive, point of view to encourage reading anything at all!

Steven Krashen demonstrated way back that extensive reading improves all aspects of language learning. This includes vocabulary, speaking skills, fluency, and writing skills. In other words, learners who read in English learn *more* English, *more* quickly than people who don't read. And, the more you read the better you read; the better you read, the more you enjoy it; the more you enjoy it the more you read…get my drift?

Extensive reading is the opposite of intensive reading (duh!). OK—but what does that mean? It means not reading for detail and not needing to understand or even read every single word. Competent readers are fast readers—stopping to use a dictionary all the time slows you down. OK, that's all very well, but if you don't understand any of what you are reading, it won't be a very positive experience. So, how to encourage extensive reading among English language learners? Provide stimulating materials at a level that is accessible. Many of the classics are great stories; great stories are stimulating. So, if simplified classics work for your learners, then for goodness sakes, use them! Don't let the purists put you off.

The following *speaker's implication* questions contain excerpts from the lecture. Remember that on the actual test, you will only hear the excerpt in such a question. If you want to get the most out of this listening practice, do NOT simply read the excerpt. Have a native speaker read the excerpt aloud to you, or have him or her record a reading of the excerpt on audiocassette.

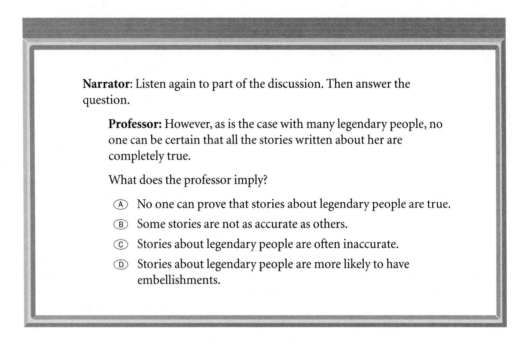

Narrator: Listen again to part of the discussion. Then answer the question.

Professor: However, as is the case with many legendary people, no one can be certain that all the stories written about her are completely true.

What does the professor imply?

  (A) No one can prove that stories about legendary people are true.

  (B) Some stories are not as accurate as others.

  (C) Stories about legendary people are often inaccurate.

  (D) Stories about legendary people are more likely to have embellishments.

Choice (A) is incorrect because it assumes that all stories about legendary people are doubtful and there's not even one that can be proven true. This is much too broad of an assumption and clearly not what the professor said, even though some of the same words are repeated. Choice (B) is too broad because it fails to recognize stories within the narrower context of stories about legends. Choice (C) implies that stories are more inaccurate than they are accurate, and exaggerates the professor's critique, which was that legendary stories are not "completely true" (translation: the stories are mostly true except for some inaccuracies). Therefore, choice (D) is correct.

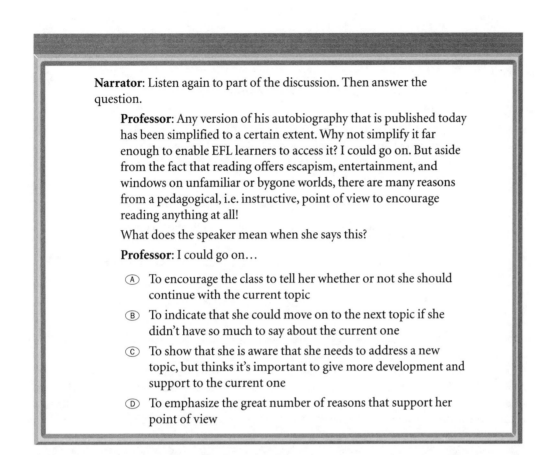

Narrator: Listen again to part of the discussion. Then answer the question.

> **Professor**: Any version of his autobiography that is published today has been simplified to a certain extent. Why not simplify it far enough to enable EFL learners to access it? I could go on. But aside from the fact that reading offers escapism, entertainment, and windows on unfamiliar or bygone worlds, there are many reasons from a pedagogical, i.e. instructive, point of view to encourage reading anything at all!

What does the speaker mean when she says this?

> **Professor**: I could go on...

- Ⓐ To encourage the class to tell her whether or not she should continue with the current topic
- Ⓑ To indicate that she could move on to the next topic if she didn't have so much to say about the current one
- Ⓒ To show that she is aware that she needs to address a new topic, but thinks it's important to give more development and support to the current one
- Ⓓ To emphasize the great number of reasons that support her point of view

Choice (A) is playing with the idea of "could" meaning possibility. If she were actually asking her students whether they wanted her to continue she would say, "Should I go on?" Choice (B) is trying to trap you with literal interpretations of clues: "could" meaning possibility, and "but" meaning contrast. However, it's obvious that she does not spend a lot of time talking about the benefits of reading, in general, even though she has a lot to say about it. Choice (C) is incorrect because she does not elaborate on the benefits of reading, in general. Therefore "I could go on" is a way to emphasize her opinion without elaborating, and the correct answer is (D).

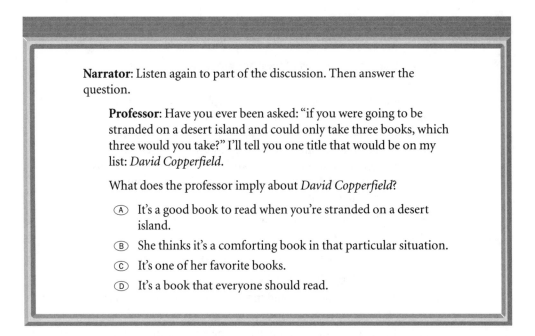

> **Narrator**: Listen again to part of the discussion. Then answer the question.
>
> **Professor**: Have you ever been asked: "if you were going to be stranded on a desert island and could only take three books, which three would you take?" I'll tell you one title that would be on my list: *David Copperfield*.
>
> What does the professor imply about *David Copperfield*?
>
> Ⓐ It's a good book to read when you're stranded on a desert island.
>
> Ⓑ She thinks it's a comforting book in that particular situation.
>
> Ⓒ It's one of her favorite books.
>
> Ⓓ It's a book that everyone should read.

Choice (A) is taking the question literally. Although the teacher mentions overcoming hardships as a theme in *David Copperfield*, and most people would consider being stranded on a desert island a hardship, choice (B) is also taking the question too literally. Choice (D) is taking the inference too far. The professor is telling her students, through a cliché, what her favorite book is. The correct answer is choice (C).

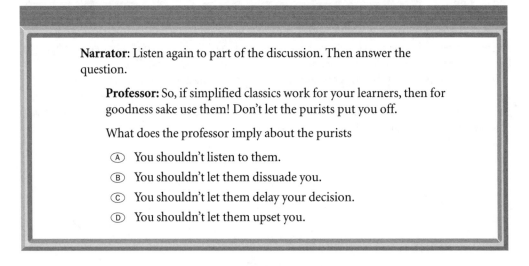

> **Narrator**: Listen again to part of the discussion. Then answer the question.
>
> **Professor:** So, if simplified classics work for your learners, then for goodness sake use them! Don't let the purists put you off.
>
> What does the professor imply about the purists
>
> Ⓐ You shouldn't listen to them.
>
> Ⓑ You shouldn't let them dissuade you.
>
> Ⓒ You shouldn't let them delay your decision.
>
> Ⓓ You shouldn't let them upset you.

The professor's attitude toward purists, or those who don't believe in changing an author's original language, is clearly expressed throughout the lecture. The professor concludes with a very strong statement that reinforces this view. Her attitude toward purists is obviously negative and so are all the answer choices, but only one correctly defines the meaning of the phrasal verb *put off*. Choice (B) is correct.

When you are ready, move on to Lesson 6—Speaking: Expressing an Opinion.

LESSON 6—SPEAKING: EXPRESSING AN OPINION

In this lesson, we will cover more speaking skills and strategies that will help lead to success on test day. You will also have the opportunity to learn more about the tasks required for the Speaking section of the TOEFL. If you want to proceed with additional speaking strategies when you finish this lesson, turn to Lesson 7—Speaking: Announcements and Notices in Chapter 7.

Remember that previous lessons covered the following speaking tasks:
- Describing Something from Your Own Experience
- Summarizing a Lecture
- Expressing and Supporting an Opinion Based on Personal Experience
- Summarizing a Conversation and Expressing an Opinion
- Synthesizing and Summarizing Information

This lesson will continue to review the following speaking tasks:
- Expressing and Supporting an Opinion Based on Personal Experience
- Summarizing a Conversation and Expressing an Opinion

First, let's review the basics of expressing and supporting an opinion.

Expressing an Opinion

It's a fact: everyone has opinions. However, not everyone is capable of expressing those opinions clearly and effectively. This is an important skill for the TOEFL, but it is also a critical skill to have in life. Try expressing your own opinions by completing the Expressing an Opinion Practice.

Expressing an Opinion Practice

Brainstorm ideas about when you might need to express your opinion. Try to recall situations in which you expressed your opinion recently—choosing a movie, deciding on an activity, having a political discussion.

Look at the following options for an evening's activity:
- going out to a theater to watch a movie with friends
- renting a movie and watching it at home with friends
- going out to eat at a restaurant
- cooking a meal and staying home to eat with friends

Discuss with a friend or study partner which option you prefer. Don't forget to support your opinion with examples. You can make notes in the space that follows.

_____

_____

_____

_____

_____

Here's a review of some phrases used when expressing an opinion. For extra practice, categorize these phrases in the table that follows.

> *As far as I'm concerned, I think we should …*
>
> *What I like about …is …*
>
> *The problem with …is that …*
>
> *The best thing about …is that …*
>
> *When you look at the big picture*
>
> *What about …?*
>
> *There's no doubt that*
>
> *The key point is*
>
> *The bottom line is*
>
> *Remember …?*
>
> *Overall,*
>
> *Let's take …(as an example)*
>
> *It's quite clear that*
>
> *It seems to me*
>
> *In a nutshell*
>
> *If you ask me*
>
> *Generally speaking*
>
> *From my point of view*
>
> *For one thing*
>
> *As far as I'm concerned*
>
> *And another thing is*
>
> *All in all*

To Express an Opinion	To Support an Opinion	To Give Examples	To Summarize

Answers

Answers will vary, but here is something one might say about choosing an activity for the evening.

I prefer staying at home and cooking a meal to eat with friends. If we go out to eat or watch a movie, we all have to worry about where we'll meet, and what time we're all supposed to be there. It always feels very rushed. I prefer to invite people to my home and cook a big pot of spaghetti—it's cheap, and we can all hang around the kitchen and talk while we make dinner.

To Express an Opinion	To Support an Opinion	To Give Examples	To Summarize
As far as I'm concerned, I think we should …	*There's no doubt that*	*Let's take … (as an example)*	*When you look at the big picture*
If you ask me	*It's quite clear that*	*For one thing*	*The bottom line is*
As far as I'm concerned	*The problem with …is that …*	*And another thing is*	*In a nutshell*
From my point of view	*The best thing about … is that …*	*What about …?*	*Generally speaking*
It seems to me		*Remember …?*	*Overall,*
What I like about …is …			*All in all*
			The key point is

Content of Your Response

Remember that it doesn't matter what your opinion is on the TOEFL. There is no right or wrong answer. What matters is that you express and support your opinion clearly. In the next activity you will practice expressing an opinion different from you own. This activity will show you that it doesn't matter what you think; what matters is how you express it.

Content of Your Response Practice

Look at the following statement:

> Reading is fun.

Think about this statement silently, and decide if you agree or disagree with it. Now brainstorm reasons for thinking that reading is fun AND reasons that reading is not fun. If you think reading is fun, pretend that you hate it. If you think reading is not fun (in fact you think reading is really boring!) pretend that you love it! Write those reasons down clearly, and categorize them.

Whatever your true opinion about reading is, make sure your presentation is clear:

- State your opinion (in this case, the opposite of your opinion)
- Give reasons that support your opinion
- Give at least one example that supports your opinion
- Summarize your opinion

Notes

Answers

Your reasons for agreeing and disagreeing that reading is fun will vary.

Reading Is Fun	Reading Isn't Fun
Always something to learn	Have to sit still and stay focused
Encourages imagination	Takes a long time
Allows escape from everyday life	Isn't visually interesting

Task 2 Revisited—Expressing and Supporting an Opinion Based on Personal Experience

There are 6 tasks in the Speaking section of the TOEFL. The second type requires a 45-second speech sample in which you give and support an opinion based on your personal experience.

You will hear a speaking prompt. You will then have 15 seconds to prepare a spoken response of 45 seconds to this prompt. Remember that you will not see the narrator's introduction to the question on the test.

Review the following example TOEFL questions. If you have a study partner, or someone that can listen to your responses, ask to work with him or her.

Think about the following questions: Does a question ask you if you agree or disagree with a statement or does the question ask you to choose one option over another?

Children should be required to participate in sports. Do you agree or disagree with this statement?

Some people think the government should spend money on exploring outer space. Others feel that there are more urgent issues that need to be addressed. What is your opinion?

Which is a better place for a child to grow up: the countryside or a big city?

Reading novels is better than watching movies. Do you agree or disagree?

When answering this kind of question either in writing or orally, the most important thing is that you *state your opinion* clearly and immediately. Your opinion is your thesis statement. You must follow your opinion with *reasons and examples* justifying that opinion.

Listen to an example of someone giving his opinion on the first topic. Note the phrases used to:

- express an opinion
- support an opinion
- give an example
- summarize the thesis

 **63.6S, Task 2 Sample Opinion**

Now practice the following TOEFL question. Remember that you will not see the narrator's introduction on the test. Afterward, evaluate yourself. You will find a transcript of this audio passage (64.6S, Task 2 Prompt) at the end of the chapter.

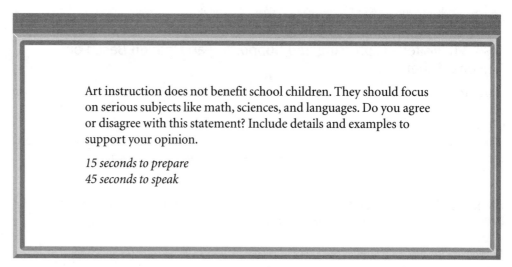 **64.6S, Task 2 Prompt**

> Art instruction does not benefit school children. They should focus on serious subjects like math, sciences, and languages. Do you agree or disagree with this statement? Include details and examples to support your opinion.
>
> *15 seconds to prepare*
> *45 seconds to speak*

Notes

Evaluate yourself using the following criteria:

Criteria	Comments	Action to Improve
Clarity and pronunciation		
Organization		
Details and examples		
Grammar and vocabulary		

Now listen to the sample response. How was it different from yours? How was it similar? You will find a transcript of this audio passage (65.6S, Task 2 Sample Response) at the end of the chapter.

🎧 **65.6S, Task 2 Sample Response**

Task 5 Revisited—Summarizing a Conversation and Expressing an Opinion

There are 6 tasks in the Speaking section of the TOEFL. The fifth requires that you summarize a conversation in which two people are discussing a problem then give your opinion on a solution.

In the fifth task in the Speaking section, you will listen to a conversation between two people. The two people generally discuss a topic related to life at a university. The topic is framed as a problem, and at least two solutions or attitudes to the problem are presented during the conversation.

While listening, you need to:
- Identify what the problem is
- Identify what advice is being suggested

After listening, you need to prepare a response that includes:
- a summary of the problem
- a summary of the advice given
- your opinion on that advice

KAPLAN
Test Prep and Admissions

Practice the following sample question and then listen to the sample response. As you listen to the sample, note how the speaker has organized the response. You will find transcripts of these audio passages at the end of the chapter.

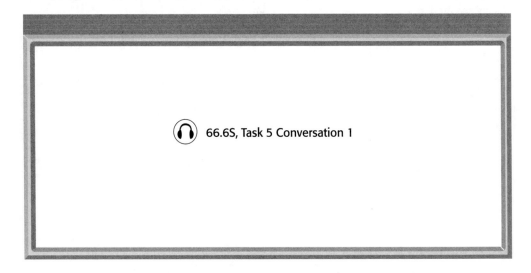

66.6S, Task 5 Conversation 1

Notes

🎧 67.6S, Task 5 Prompt 1

The students are talking about a problem faced by the man. Summarize his problem and the solutions being discussed. Then state which solution you prefer and why.

20 seconds to prepare
60 seconds to speak

Evaluate yourself using the following criteria:

Criteria	Comments	Action to Improve
Clarity and pronunciation		
Organization		
Details and examples		
Grammar and vocabulary		

Now listen to the sample response. How was it different from yours? How was it similar? You will find a transcript of this audio passage (68.6S, Task 5 Response 1) at the end of the chapter.

🎧 68.6S, Task 5 Response 1

Now practice the following TOEFL question. Remember that you will not see the narrator's introduction on the test. You may take notes while listening. Afterward, evaluate yourself. You will find transcripts of these audio passages at the end of the chapter.

🎧 69.6S, Task 5 Conversation 2

Notes

🎧 **70.6S, Task 5 Prompt 2**

The students are talking about a difficult choice. Summarize what the options are and what advice is being offered. Then state which option you prefer and why.

20 seconds to prepare
60 seconds to speak

Evaluate yourself using the following criteria:

Criteria	Comments	Action to Improve
Clarity and pronunciation		
Organization		
Details and examples		
Grammar and vocabulary		

Now listen to the sample response. How was it different from yours? How was it similar? You will find a transcript of this audio passage (71.6S, Task 5 Response 2) at the end of the chapter.

🎧 **71.6S, Task 5 Response 2**

Way to go! You only have two more lessons before you have completed the entire book. When you feel you are ready to review more reading, writing, listening, and speaking strategies, proceed to Chapter 7.

CHAPTER 6 AUDIO TRANSCRIPTS

60. Lesson 6—Reading, Note-Taking Practice

Narrator: Now listen to part of a lecture on the topic you just read about.

Professor: Now...I admit that I'm biased when it comes to Hemingway...I've been reading his short stories and, um, novels for years and years and I never get tired of them...but that's just praise based on my personal preference. So today I'd like to give you some more, shall I say...*scholarly* justification for Hemingway's greatness and how that greatness affected his works.

First and foremost, Hemingway's background as a journalist probably influenced his minimalist approach to writing which, ah, in turn influenced other great writers like, say, Raymond Carver. Though some critics say that Hemingway's rhetorical style was too simplistic, most literary pundits applaud his...well, his sheer genius. It's amazing how just by describing situations or senses very specifically, Hemingway can get quite complex ideas across to his readers. His dialogues are especially famous...they are simple, but so realistic. Reading them, you feel you are eavesdropping, spying on real conversations. It is because his rhetorical style is so direct that Hemingway is able to accomplish this.

Next, again...despite what many critics say, Hemingway was not incapable of using rhetorical "tricks." He tried double narration, when a story is told from several points of view...In fact, he loved to experiment with point of view and...oh, this brings up another point, he did try to write from a woman's perspective at times and, considering he was a man, did so quite well, I think. Many feminists might tell you differently and we can discuss this point further once you've all read more of his works.

Uhhh...anyway, getting back to my previous point...another rhetorical technique, the most frequently used, in fact, that...uh...Hemingway employed was inference. He didn't tell the reader everything, but left out some details so that the reader would have to infer, to work for the meaning. The result of this technique is that Hemingway's stories are extremely challenging for a reader, but also more satisfying because of the effort we must make to solve the puzzle.

61. Lesson 6—Listening, Listening for Details Practice

Man: Hey, I'm looking for a good novel to read, and I'm not really up on my classics. What do you recommend?

Woman: How about *Fahrenheit 451*?

Man (*dramatically*): "It was a pleasure to burn. It was a pleasure to see things eaten, to see things blackened and changed."

Woman: Okay. Okay. What about *The Great Gatsby*?

Man: Fitzgerald's writing is too pretentious for me.

Woman: Hemingway?

Man: I've read all of his novels.

Woman: Bernard Shaw?

Man: I don't like reading plays. I like seeing them.

Woman: Oscar Wilde?

Man: I said I don't like reading plays.

Woman: I was thinking of *The Picture of Dorian Grey*.

Man (*thinking, but leaning toward the negative*) : Uhhhh...I've read enough British Lit. What else you got?

Woman: Ayn Rand. *The Fountainhead*.

Man: She's more contemporary, isn't she?

Woman: So is Bradbury, but *Fahrenheit 451* is still a classic.

Man: Oh. I guess you're right.

Woman: How about Dostoevsky?

Man: I don't want to read any more stories about gamblers up to their eyeballs in debt, or poor peasants and their oppressive landlords. I've got enough of that in my own life.

Woman: Yeah, but Dostoevsky is a lot more optimistic than you are. I think you should try *The Brothers Karamazov*.

Man: That was his last novel, wasn't it?

Woman: And his greatest.

Man: All right. I'll give it a try.

62. Lesson 6—Listening, Note-Taking Practice

Narrator: Now listen to part of a lecture in a teacher-training class on using graded readers.

Professor: Although the use of simplified texts in teaching, especially in EFL, or English as a Foreign Language, teaching, has increased dramatically over the past decade, and the publishing industry is bursting with graded readers of every kind. Heated debate continues about the artistic ethics of um diluting classic works of literature. There are those who argue that great literature is great because of the words, phrases, and structures chosen by the author. Therefore, they say, it is a crime to change those words, phrases, and structure in any way. By doing so, the very essence is removed and thus the work of art becomes entirely devalued.

Well, this debate brings up good questions regarding the definition of great literature. What makes a novel great? What makes it a classic? Is it the plot, the characters, the descriptions, the dialogues, the prose itself? Or does greatness lie in some kind of originality; does a work need to break barriers to be considered "art"? Or is it just a question of popularity? I don't believe there is a simple answer; in fact, I think…well anyway, I mustn't get sidetracked.

The question for us is, do we use simplified classics in teaching? In my opinion, the educational advantages of using simplified graded readers far outweigh the philosophical concerns about art. I believe great literature is great because of a combination of things. Characters and plot can be crucial; for me, it is these elements that take my imagination beyond the mundane, outside of ordinary life. Have you ever been asked: "if you were going to be stranded on a desert island and could only take three books, which three would you take?" I'll tell you one title that would be on my list: *David Copperfield*. There's a book that makes me laugh out loud, moves me to tears, and never fails to absorb me completely. The young hero experiences death and hardships, meets amazing characters, and he survives everything thrown his way. It is the events…the characters…the story that make this book so rich. Those can be very effectively conveyed in a simplified text.

Another example is *Pocahontas*. Unlike David Copperfield who is 100% fiction, we know that Pocahontas was a real person. However, as is the case with many legendary people, no one can be certain that all the stories written about her are completely true. She did indeed marry John Rolfe in 1614 and traveled with him to London in 1616. Regardless of any potential embellishments, this is a memorable story of Native American culture and the impact white settlers had when landing on the new continent. Because of the characters and the way their interactions are portrayed, it is not only interesting historical insight; it's a page-turner.

A non-fiction classic is Benjamin Franklin's autobiography. So much can be learned about the way the world worked in the late 1800s from this absorbing and intimately written book, even though it centers around one single life. Now, Benjamin Franklin used grammar, vocabulary, and especially punctuation that would baffle even the most accomplished modern day reader! Any version of his autobiography that is published today has been simplified to a certain extent. Why not simplify it far enough to enable EFL learners to access it?

I could go on. But aside from the fact that reading offers escapism, entertainment, and windows on unfamiliar or bygone worlds, there are many reasons from a pedagogical, i.e. instructive, point of view to encourage reading anything at all!

Steven Krashen demonstrated way back that extensive reading improves all aspects of language learning. This includes vocabulary, speaking skills, fluency, and writing skills. In other words, learners who read in English learn *more* English, *more* quickly than people who don't read. And, the more you read the better you read; the better you read, the more you enjoy it; the more you enjoy it the more you read…get my drift?

Extensive reading is the opposite of intensive reading (duh!). OK—but what does that mean? It means not reading for detail and not needing to understand or even read every single word. Competent readers are fast readers—stopping to use a dictionary all the time slows you down. OK, that's all very well, but if you don't understand any of what you are reading, it won't be a very positive experience. So, how to encourage extensive reading among English language learners? Provide stimulating materials at a level that is accessible. Many of the classics are great stories; great stories are stimulating. So, if simplified classics work for your learners, then for goodness sakes, use them! Don't let the purists put you off.

63. Lesson 6—Speaking, Task 2 Sample Opinion

Well, I think it's essential that children participate in sports, so I feel that it should be required at school or wherever. It's good for their physical development, um, and they learn social skills because they, um, well, just by being part of a team and ah…I heard exercise actually helps people learn better. A lot of kids are overweight these days because they spend too much time in front of the TV or playing computer games instead of being active outdoors. So they should be encouraged to join a sports team and run about. Playing soccer, for example, really teaches kids about teamwork—they are literally all working together to score a goal. That is a great life lesson. And apparently, kids who get regular exercise learn better than couch potatoes. Something about getting oxygen to the brain, I don't know exactly. Anyway, um…I just think it is really important that kids get plenty of exercise, so physical education should be a compulsory subject.

64. Lesson 6—Speaking, Task 2 Prompt

Narrator: In this question, you will be asked to state and support your opinion on a certain topic. After you hear the question, you will have 15 seconds to prepare your response and 45 seconds to speak.

Art instruction does not benefit school children. They should focus on serious subjects like math, sciences, and languages. Do you agree or disagree with this statement? Include details and examples to support your opinion.

65. Lesson 6—Speaking, Task 2 Sample Response

Well, I think it is a waste of time to teach art to kids. The main reason I think that is because I believe children should work on getting into college or getting a good job. The world is really competitive nowadays, and children need to pass challenging tests in order to get to the next step, so they should focus all their energy into whatever will help them pass the tests. The other reason that I think art classes in school are a waste of time is that most students are not interested in art. There is plenty of time for them to learn about art when they are adults, if they become interested. They can go to museums and if they really enjoy learning about art, then maybe they will end up learning to paint or something. But you can't make money by doing art, so it is waste of time and resources teaching art to kids. In my opinion, art is just a luxury and young people should have other priorities.

66. Lesson 6—Speaking, Task 5 Conversation 1

Narrator: In this question, you will listen to a conversation. After you hear the question, you will have 20 seconds to prepare your response and 60 seconds to speak.

Student 1 (male): Oh, man, I just don't know what to do!

Student 2 (female): Hey relax, what are you working on?

Student 1: I can't decide if I should go to Italy or England for my semester abroad.

Student 2: What a great dilemma to have! I'm jealous!

Student 1: I suppose I shouldn't complain, but I am just really nervous about making the wrong decision.

Student 2: Well, sometimes it's useful to write things down. How about drawing up a table for each option? Write a list of advantages and disadvantages for each one.

Student 1: Actually, I've already done that. Here's my Italy list.

Student 2: Oh cool. Well, from this list it doesn't look like a difficult decision at all, you've written 28 advantages for Italy, and your disadvantage column is empty!

Student 1: I know, I really want to go to Italy, mainly because I want to work on my Italian, and I love the heat, and the food and—

Student 2 (interrupting): and the cappuccino, and the fashion, and the art and blah blah blah…you've got quite a list here. What does your England list look like?

Student 1: Well, in my mind, there would actually only be one advantage to going to England.

Student 2: And that is…?

Student 1: My parents want me to go there. Especially my mom. Her family emigrated to the US from England, and she still has a lot of relatives over there. But she doesn't know them. I think she kind of wants me to make connections with those relatives and build a bridge to her heritage or something.

Student 2: OK, well, I see why it's difficult, but I think you should follow your dream and go to Italy. Maybe you could do a quick trip to England either on your way there or on your way back.

Student 1: Yeah, I really don't want to upset my mom though.

67. Lesson 6—Speaking, Task 5 Prompt 1

The students are talking about a problem faced by the man. Summarize his problem and the solutions being discussed. Then state which solution you prefer and why.

68. Lesson 6—Speaking, Task 5 Sample Response 1

The students are talking about …umm…uh…one of the students is going to do a semester abroad. Umm…and he is trying to choose between England and Italy. It's pretty clear that he really wants to go to Italy, but his mom wants him to go to England. His friend advises him to follow his dream and go to Italy and I think that is good advice. He's a college student and needs to start making decisions for himself. If he follows his mother's wishes and goes to England even though he really wants to go to Italy, he might end up feeling resentful toward his mother. That would be bad for their relationship. I think he should explain to his mother why he wants to go to Italy, and I think she will understand. As his mother, she probably really wants her son to be happy, so if she knew what he really wanted, I think she would be supportive. The reason she wants him to go to England is that she has relatives there. She should go and visit those relatives herself, she shouldn't send her son like a kind of ambassador!

69. Lesson 6—Speaking, Task 5 Conversation 2

Narrator: In this question, you will listen to a conversation. After you hear the question, you will have 20 seconds to prepare your response and 60 seconds to speak.

Student 1 (female): Hi Tony, what's up?

Student 2 (male): Not much. What's going on with you?

Student 1: Not much. How's your media studies project going?

Student 2: Great, we are having so much fun in our group. Our presentation is going to be hilarious.

Student 1: You're lucky. My group is having a terrible time.

Student 2: Why is that? I thought all the assignments were interesting. What's the problem?

Student 1: Well, the assignment is fine. It's just that we're not working well as a group at all. In fact, Frank never even shows up when we schedule a planning session. Out of the four meetings that we've had, I think I've seen him once. And even then he was 10 minutes late.

Student 2: Well, that's no good. Doesn't he realize that this presentation is going to count toward 60% of his grade? You should remind him of that.

Student 1: He knows, but he doesn't care. He's here on a football scholarship so he doesn't need good grades. He just needs to scrape by. That's why he picked a "soft subject" like media studies. But the problem is that if he doesn't pull his weight, our presentation will be lousy and the rest of us will also get lower grades.

Student 2: You need to let him know he can't do that. Just tell him: "Frank, you are being a selfish little brat if you don't participate."

Student 1: That's easy enough for you to say. This guy plays line backer! He's bigger than my refrigerator.

Student 2: Hmm. Well, if you're nervous about confronting him then you need to let Professor King know that there's a problem. I know he told us that part of the challenge was to work well as a group, but this situation is unusual. Most students care about their grades, I don't know how you can persuade Frank to participate if he doesn't care about his grade.

Student 1: Yeah. That's what I am beginning to think too. I hate to be a snitch, but I don't know what else to do.

70. Lesson 6—Speaking, Task 5 Prompt 2

The students are talking about a difficult choice. Summarize what the options are and what advice is being offered. Then state which option you prefer and why.

71. Lesson 6—Speaking, Task 5 Sample Response 2

The man and the woman are discussing preparations for, umm, well…they are discussing progress on preparations for presentations that they will be making in a umm, in a media studies class. The woman has a problem because one of the members of her group (I think his name is Frank) is not participating in the preparation. So, umm, the woman is worried that their presentation won't be good and that her group will get a low grade. The man suggests that the woman talk about it, and tell him—Frank, that is—that he is being selfish. But the woman doesn't want to do that, I guess because that guy, Frank, the one who isn't participating…is a football player, so he is probably really big and strong. I think the man's suggestion is a good one. It doesn't matter how big and strong the guy is, he needs to know that he should contribute to the group. If Frank's behavior doesn't change, then I think the woman, umm, and…and other members of her group…should also talk to the professor about the problem.

Chapter 7: **Lesson Set 7**

Theme—Technology

Chapter 7 continues to review more reading, writing, listening, and speaking skills and strategies you will need to score high on the TOEFL. Make sure to complete all the practice exercises and sample questions so that you can get the most out of these lessons.

LESSON 7—READING: CONTEXT CLUES, ANTONYMS, AND COHESIVE DEVICES

In this lesson, we will cover more reading skills and strategies that will help lead to success on test day. You will also have the opportunity to review some of the strategies you learned in previous lessons as well as to learn more about the question types found on the Reading section of the TOEFL. If you want to proceed with more reading strategies when you finish this lesson, turn to Lesson 8—Reading: Synonyms, Inference, and Cause and Effect in Chapter 8.

Context Clues

If you don't know the meaning of a word, the best way to figure out its meaning is to use *context clues*. The following are types of context clues:

- examples
- contrasting words or ideas
- synonyms or further explanation through clauses

Context Clues Practice

Write a definition for each word or phrase in the table that follows by using information from the passage.

Passage 1

NASA, <u>though frequently thought to contain only</u> astronauts and shuttle engineers, is <u>actually</u> comprised of <u>many</u> departments, one of which is the Robotic Vehicles Group. Members of this department must research, develop, and test mobile robots, or robots <u>which move</u>, before they can be used <u>either</u> in terrestrial <u>or space</u> missions. NASA's robotic vehicles can have many functions, including planetary exploration and hazardous materials investigation. The former function necessitates robotic vehicles that can essentially be autonomous <u>since humans cannot accompany the robots</u> to many of the places they must venture outside Earth. Space-bound robotic vehicles should add immensely to the <u>small store of scientific knowledge humans currently have</u> regarding the surface of other planets.

Word/Phrase	Definition
be comprised of	
mobile	
terrestrial	
autonomous	
immensely	

Answers

Word/Phrase	Definition
be comprised of	made up of
mobile	able to move
terrestrial	on the ground
autonomous	independent
immensely	greatly, a lot

Antonyms

When learning new vocabulary, it is often useful to learn words with the opposite meaning, *antonyms*, at the same time. Look at the following words.

friendly

hostile

These two words are antonyms.

Antonyms Practice

Now look at the following list of words. Match the word in the list to its antonym. The first one has been done as an example.

    prompt
    impaired
    misery
    inattention
    devastating
    fragile
    segregated from
    ethical

1. hesitating ≠_____prompt_____

2. immoral ≠ _____

3. alertness ≠ _____

4. integrated with ≠ _____

5. resilient ≠ _____

6. beneficial ≠ _____

7. joy ≠ _____

8. enhanced ≠ _____

Answers

1. hesitating ≠_____prompt_____

2. immoral ≠ _____ethical_____

3. alertness ≠ _____inattention____

4. integrated with ≠ _segregated from_

5. resilient ≠ _____fragile_____

6. beneficial ≠ _____devastating____

7. joy ≠_____misery_____

8. enhanced ≠_____impaired_____

The Importance of Examples

It may seem obvious, but it is worth mentioning here: an effective essay or argument has to have examples to support the most important points. Complete the Importance of Examples Practice that follows.

The Importance of Examples Practice

Here is a reading that compares two methods of transportation. However, it is missing examples to support two of its body paragraphs. Read the text, paying special attention to the topic sentences of paragraphs 5 and 6, and then try to write supporting sentences.

Trains and Autos

Though trains saw widespread use over the course of the nineteenth century, the last hundred years have seen nothing but a decline in the use of railroads in the United States and a rapid growth in American car culture. While trains have begun recently to attract a little more interest from urban planners, there is no sign at all that the general public shares that interest. What accounts for this progressive loss of interest in train travel? What could possibly have made Americans so enamored of their cars?

Efficiency alone cannot be the answer we are looking for. Both automobiles and trains consume similar amounts of energy. The average car gets about thirteen passenger-kilometers per liter of fuel, no improvement at all over trains, though if trains are forced to run with few passengers, they can actually be much less efficient than cars. Consequently, if one's objective is to conserve energy, neither mode of transportation offers any real advantage, with one exception: interurban light rail and subways are about twenty-five percent more fuel efficient than cars.

Both rail and automobile transportation depend on expensive infrastructure; highway construction in the United States averages several million dollars per kilometer, and can easily go much higher. Railroads are almost as expensive to build, and railroad operators must also pay to maintain their locomotives and rolling stock. Therefore, there does not seem to be a particular advantage in either fuel efficiency or cost of construction and maintenance associated with either automobiles or trains.

On the other hand, trains hold very real advantages in safety. In the United States alone, more than 40,000 people die every year in car accidents, and hundreds of thousands more suffer personal and financial injury. By contrast, rail fatalities seldom number more than a few hundred per year worldwide. On a train, one needs never to worry whether the approaching driver is intoxicated or distracted by his cellular phone, nor does one need to worry about falling asleep at the wheel, striking a deer crossing the road, or any of the other myriad hazards that face automobile drivers on a daily basis. One would think such a safety record would attract more enthusiasm from potential passengers.

In addition to safety, riding a train generally offers far more peace of mind than relying on a car.

_____

_____

_____

_____

_____

_____

_____

Nevertheless, cars do offer a real advantage in versatility.

_____

_____

_____

_____

_____

_____

However, even versatility is probably not the best answer. The truth lies in the way Americans romanticize the car. For every teenager, getting his or her driver's license is a rite of passage. Teenagers often consider themselves to be adults once they can drive. In fact, we have a whole body of popular culture, from dating to work to weekend vacations, built around the car—and nowhere does the train put in an appearance. Americans find the tangible, versatile car to be a maker of self-identity the way trains could never be.

No matter how efficient they are, how safe, or how inexpensive, trains cannot offer the thrill and satisfaction inherent in the automobile. No teenager dreams about cruising to pick up his or her date on the train. No businessperson wants to spend money on train tickets—he or she wants the prestige of a showy new sports car. The parent with children doesn't want to take the train either. He or she must make frequent trips to soccer practice, ballet lessons, and scout meetings and a car is the most efficient way to do so. Until cars become so expensive to purchase and operate that they are out of reach of most people, trains and other forms of transportation will always take a back seat to the automobile.

Next, compare your paragraphs with the originals, and answer the questions that follow.

Paragraph 5: In addition to safety, riding a train generally offers far more peace of mind than relying on a car. Once on board the train, the passenger can read a newspaper, prepare for work, or simply relax and admire the scenery passing by. Driving, on the other hand, requires the patience to endure traffic jams and the rude person behind who drives with his horn. Then there is the maintenance, insurance, and perhaps a monthly bill the car owner has to pay.

Paragraph 6: Nevertheless, cars do offer a real advantage in versatility. It is never necessary to wait for the car—it's ready when its driver is, and is never behind schedule. Plus, there's plenty of room in the trunk for carrying groceries or skis. And a car can go all those places where no rail lines have been built. Additionally, cars can be customized and infinitely varied to suit any kind of need or taste.

1. Of the paragraphs you wrote, what supporting examples are the closest to those found in the original paragraphs? Are your examples more or less specific than the examples in the original paragraphs? Do you have more or fewer examples?

_____

_____

_____

_____

_____

2. In the original topic sentences, which words or phrases are used to help you understand what sort of examples you need to include? Do all of your examples relate to these key words?

_____

_____

_____

_____

_____

3. What type of text is this?

_____

_____

_____

_____

4. Restate the main idea of this passage in your own words.

_____

_____

_____

_____

5. What is the author's opinion about trains and autos? Look at the text again and underline examples of words or phrases that show this opinion.

_____

_____

_____

_____

Answers

1. *Answers will vary.*

2. *Answers will vary.*

3. This is a compare/contrast essay

4. Although the rail system in the United States offers an alternative to the car, the versatility of automobiles and American romanticism will keep people off the rails and on the road for a long time to come.

5. The author thinks that trains have some advantages over cars, but that cars are more popular because they are more versatile and are part of the American identity.

Example supporting sentences:

> …trains hold very real advantages in safety

> No businessperson wants to spend money on train tickets—he or she wants the prestige of a showy new sports car.

Cohesive Devices

You have already learned that many types of cohesive devices exist to help writers transition smoothly from one sentence or one paragraph to the next. Pronouns, demonstrative adjectives, articles, and transitional phrases can all be used for this purpose. Transitional phrases, in particular, can be grouped according to purpose. For example, the transitional phrase *for example* at the beginning of this sentence serves the purpose of transitioning into giving an example. Specific transitional phrases exist for the purposes of comparing, contrasting, adding new information, and showing cause and effect, among others.

Cohesive Devices Practice

Once again, look through the text (repeated here) and find as many examples as you can of transitional phrases that suit each of the following groups. Write them in the appropriate box in the table. Two have been given as examples.

Trains and Autos

Though trains saw widespread use over the course of the nineteenth century, the last hundred years have seen nothing but a decline in the use of railroads in the United States and a rapid growth in American car culture. While trains have begun recently to attract a little more interest from urban planners, there is no sign at all that the general public shares that interest. What accounts for this progressive loss of interest in train travel? What could possibly have made Americans so enamored of their cars?

Efficiency alone cannot be the answer we are looking for. Both automobiles and trains consume similar amounts of energy. The average car gets about thirteen passenger-kilometers per liter of fuel, no improvement at all over trains, though if trains are forced to run with few passengers, they can actually be much less efficient than cars. Consequently, if one's objective is to conserve energy, neither mode of transportation offers any real advantage, with one exception: interurban light rail and subways are about twenty-five percent more fuel efficient than cars.

Both rail and automobile transportation depend on expensive infrastructure; highway construction in the United States averages several million dollars per kilometer, and can easily go much higher. Railroads are almost as expensive to build, and railroad operators must also pay to maintain their locomotives and rolling stock. Therefore, there does not seem to be a particular advantage in either fuel efficiency or cost of construction and maintenance associated with either automobiles or trains.

On the other hand, trains hold very real advantages in safety. In the United States alone, more than 40,000 people die every year in car accidents, and hundreds of thousands more suffer personal and financial injury. By contrast, rail fatalities seldom number more than a few hundred per year worldwide. On a train, one needs never to worry whether the approaching driver is intoxicated or distracted by his cellular phone, nor does one need to worry about falling asleep at the wheel, striking a deer crossing the road, or any of the other myriad hazards that face automobile drivers on a daily basis. One would think such a safety record would attract more enthusiasm from potential passengers.

In addition to safety, riding a train generally offers far more peace of mind than relying on a car. Once on board the train, the passenger can read a newspaper, prepare for work, or simply relax and admire the scenery passing by. Driving, on the other hand, requires the patience to endure traffic jams and the rude person behind who drives with his horn. Then there is the maintenance, insurance, and perhaps a monthly bill the car owner has to pay.

Nevertheless, cars do offer a real advantage in versatility. It is never necessary to wait for the car—it's ready when its driver is, and is never behind schedule. Plus, there's plenty of room in the trunk for carrying groceries or skis. And a car can go all those places where no rail lines have been built. Additionally, cars can be customized and infinitely varied to suit any kind of need or taste.

However, even versatility is probably not the best answer. The truth lies in the way Americans romanticize the car. For every teenager, getting his or her driver's license is a rite of passage. Teenagers often consider themselves to be adults once they can drive. In fact, we have a whole body of popular culture, from dating to work to weekend vacations, built around the car—and nowhere does the train put in an appearance. Americans find the tangible, versatile car to be a maker of self-identity the way trains could never be.

No matter how efficient they are, how safe, or how inexpensive, trains cannot offer the thrill and satisfaction inherent in the automobile. No teenager dreams about cruising to pick up his or her date on the train. No businessperson wants to spend money on train tickets—he or she wants the prestige of a showy new sports car. The parent with children doesn't want to take the train either. He or she must make frequent trips to soccer practice, ballet lessons, and scout meetings and a car is the most efficient way to do so. Until cars become so expensive to purchase and operate that they are out of reach of most people, trains and other forms of transportation will always take a back seat to the automobile.

Comparison	Contrast	Addition	Cause or Effect
both . . . and	though		

Answers

Comparison	Contrast	Addition	Cause or Effect
both . . . and	though	in addition to	Consequently
	While	Then there is	Therefore
	On the other hand	Plus	
	By contract	In fact	

Understanding the question types is important for knowing how and where you can apply your strategies. Keep reading to learn more.

Question Types

There are 13 question types on the Reading section of the TOEFL. These are:

- Identifying the Main Idea
- Summarizing the Most Important Points
- Understanding Rhetorical Function
- Understanding Details
- Understanding Details as They Relate to the Main Idea (Multiple-Choice)
- Understanding Details as They Relate to the Main Idea (Schematic Table)
- Inferring Word Meaning from Context
- Defining a Key Term
- Locating a Referent
- Understanding Coherence
- Drawing an Inference
- Inferring the Author's Opinion or Attitude
- Paraphrasing

This lesson will continue to review four of these question types:

- Inferring Word Meaning from Context
- Defining a Key Term
- Locating a Referent
- Understanding Coherence

Question Type 7 Revisited—Inferring Word Meaning from Context

There are 3 passages in the Reading section of the TOEFL. Each passage is followed by 2 or 3 *word-meaning* questions.

Having an extensive vocabulary is extremely important in order to be able to understand the meaning of a text or lecture; however, sometimes the meaning of new words can be inferred or guessed from the context. Remember that some typical techniques for inferring the meaning of words are:

- looking for examples
- looking for contrasting words or ideas
- identifying synonyms, an explanation, or a definition in other parts of the passage

Look at the following three examples taken from the previous reading passage. Underline the words or phrases that relate to the inference technique, and then use this technique to guess the meaning of the word.

1. Underline the words that **give an explanation** of the word *infrastructure*.

   Both rail and automobile transportation depend on expensive **infrastructure**; highway construction in the United States averages several million dollars per kilometer and can easily go much higher. Railroads are almost as expensive to build and railroad operators must also pay to maintain their locomotives and rolling stock.

Meaning of *infrastructure*:

_____

2. Underline the **contrasting words** that help you infer the meaning of the word *endure*.

   Once on board the train, the passenger can read a newspaper, prepare for work, or simply relax and admire the scenery passing by. Driving, on the other hand, requires the patience to **endure** traffic jams and the rude person behind who drives with his horn.

Meaning of *endure*:

_____

3. Underline the **examples** that help you infer the meaning of the word *versatility*.

   Nevertheless, cars do offer a real advantage in **versatility**. It is never necessary to wait for the car—it's ready when its driver is, and is never behind schedule. Plus, there's plenty of room in the trunk for carrying groceries or skis. And a car can go all those places where no rail lines have been built. Additionally, cars can be customized and infinitely varied to suit any kind of need or taste.

Meaning of *versatility*:

_____

Answers

1. Both rail and automobile transportation depend on expensive **infrastructure**; highway construction in the United States averages several million dollars per kilometer and can easily go much higher. Railroads are almost as expensive to build and railroad operators must also pay to maintain their locomotives and rolling stock.

Meaning of *infrastructure*: large scale network

2. Once on board the train, the passenger can read a newspaper, prepare for work, or simply relax and admire the scenery passing by. Driving, on the other hand, requires the patience to **endure** traffic jams and the rude person behind who drives with his horn.

Meaning of *endure*: put up with

3. Nevertheless, cars do offer a real advantage in **versatility**. It is never necessary to wait for the car— it's ready when its driver is, and is never behind schedule. Plus, there's plenty of room in the trunk for carrying groceries or skis. And a car can go all those places where no rail lines have been built. Additionally, cars can be customized and infinitely varied to suit any kind of need or taste.

Meaning of *versatility*: flexibility, easy to make use of

Context

Remember that the meaning of some words cannot always be inferred from context. For example, if you do not know the meaning of the word *myriad*, you will probably not be able to guess its meaning from the context, especially if the answer choices include distracters to confuse you. Here's an example:

> On a train, one needs never to worry whether the approaching driver is intoxicated or distracted by his cellular phone, nor does one need to worry about falling asleep at the wheel, striking a deer crossing the road, or any of the other **myriad** hazards that face automobile drivers on a daily basis.
>
> (A) possible
> (B) horrible
> (C) countless
> (D) commonplace

Since all of the choices make sense within the context of the sentence, and there are no clues to help you infer the meaning of the word *myriad,* knowing this word's definition is the only way to answer the question correctly. It is important to keep this in mind as a motivating factor in continuing to learn as much vocabulary as you can.

Using the strategies you have just practiced, go back to the passage on trains and autos and answer the following questions.

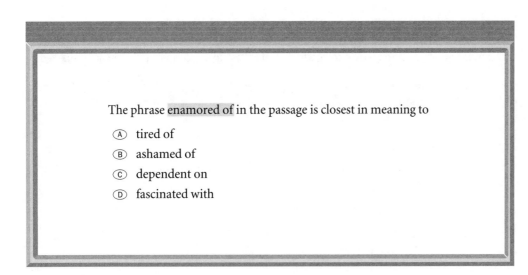

The phrase enamored of in the passage is closest in meaning to

(A) tired of

(B) ashamed of

(C) dependent on

(D) fascinated with

Choice (D) is correct. *Fascinated with* is the closest in meaning to *enamored of*. Choices (A) and (B) are both incorrect because they are negative and in this text it is not cars but trains that are mentioned in a negative light; Americans have lost interest in trains. In comparison, there has been a rapid growth in car culture. Choice (C) is also slightly negative, but it does make sense in the context. To eliminate this choice, you must know that the word *enamored of* does not mean *dependent on*.

Now answer the following TOEFL questions.

The word distracted in the passage is closest in meaning to

(A) confused

(B) annoyed

(C) entertained

(D) sidetracked

To be distracted means to lose focus on a task because something else ("a distraction") has attracted your attention. Choice (A) is incorrect. One is not ordinarily confused by a cell phone. Choice (B) is incorrect. It is slightly attractive, because being annoyed by something could possibly distract your attention. But one is not ordinarily "annoyed" by a cell phone. Choice (C) is incorrect. It is slightly attractive, because something that is entertaining you while you drive is arguably distracting you from driving. Choice (D) is correct. To be "sidetracked" by something means to have it occupy your attention; it implies a shift of focus to an object of lesser importance. That is clearly what is meant here: A driver should be focused on driving the car, not on talking on the phone. "Distraction" has a similar meaning: When your focus is shifted from a main task to a secondary task, you are distracted.

> The word inherent in the passage is closest in meaning to
>
> (A) intact
>
> (B) innate
>
> (C) lacking
>
> (D) identical

To be inherent is to be an essential and inseparable part or characteristic of. The passage describes the "satisfaction inherent in the automobile," meaning that satisfaction is an essential part of the experience that automobiles provide to drivers. Choice (A) is incorrect. Intact means whole or undivided. Choice (B) is correct. Innate means possessing from birth, or an essential part or characteristic of. Choice (C) is incorrect. Lacking means without. The passage makes clear that this is not what is meant. Choice (D) is incorrect. Identical means an exact copy of.

Question Type 8 Revisited—Defining a Key Term

There are 3 passages in the Reading section of the TOEFL. Each passage is followed by 0 or 1 *term-definition* question.

Typically, the best way of guessing the meaning of a new word or phrase that is important to the main idea of the passage is to identify its definition somewhere in the passage. However, if no definition exists, the same strategies used to infer the meaning of a word from context can be used to guess the meaning of the key term.

Look at the following sentences from the passage on trains and autos. Use inference techniques to find the meanings of the words in bold, and then write a definition for each.

> Consequently, if one's objective is to conserve energy, neither mode of transportation offers any real advantage, with one exception: interurban light rail and subways are about twenty-five percent more **fuel efficient** than cars.

Definition:

In addition to safety, riding a train generally offers far more **peace of mind** than relying on a car. Once on board the train, the passenger can read a newspaper, prepare for work, or simply relax and admire the scenery passing by.

Definition:

_____

For every teenager, getting his or her driver's license is a **rite of passage**. Teenagers often consider themselves to be adults once they can drive.

Definition:

_____

Answers

fuel efficient: uses energy economically

peace of mind: a state of calmness or relaxation

rite of passage: a task or event that is part of becoming an adult

Using the strategies you have been practicing in this lesson, answer the following questions.

Based on the information in paragraph 4, which of the following best explains the term rail fatalities?

- (A) Crashes involving trains
- (B) Passengers in trains
- (C) Deaths in train accidents
- (D) Problems with train operation

KAPLAN
Test Prep and Admissions

The correct answer is choice (C). The previous sentence mentions that more than 40,000 people die in car accidents every year. The phrase *by contrast* tells us that what follows must be statistics about people who die in train accidents. Choice (A) is close, but too general. Choices (B) and (D) are not related to accidents or death.

Now answer the following TOEFL question.

Based on the information in paragraph 7, which of the following best explains the term popular culture?

- Ⓐ People who have become famous
- Ⓑ Traditions and routines of modern life
- Ⓒ Habits that have become irritating
- Ⓓ Dating and work routines

Culture as used in the passage refers to the traditions and ways of everyday life. *Popular* reinforces the idea that what is being discussed are the traditions and ways of life of most people. *Popular culture*, often shortened to pop culture, therefore relates to "traditions and routines of modern life." Choice (B) is correct. Choice (A) is incorrect. Famous people, especially musicians, are often referred to as "pop stars," or "pop culture icons," but that is not the subject of the passage. Choice (C) is incorrect. The passage is not discussing whether people's habits are irritating or not. Choice (D) is incorrect. Dating and work routines are arguably a part of popular culture, but they are not the "whole body of popular culture" that the passage refers to.

Question Type 9 Revisited—Locating a Referent

There are 3 passages on the Reading section of the TOEFL. Each passage is generally followed by 1 *referent* question.

On the TOEFL, remember that it will not only be necessary for you to determine the meaning of words in a passage, but also to locate *referents*, other words or phrases used to refer to a word. Here's a review of some techniques that may help you to answer this type of question:

- Eliminating choices that do not correspond in number or gender
- Replacing the pronoun with the choices and checking for meaning or logical words or phrases
- Looking for words or phrases that have similar grammatical functions

One other important thing to remember about referent questions is that the noun to which a pronoun is referring does not necessarily have to precede the pronoun, or even be in the same sentence. Look at the following sentence from the passage as examples.

Until <u>cars</u> become so expensive to purchase and operate that they are out of reach of most people, trains and other forms of transportation will always take a back seat to the automobile.

This sentence shows a typical noun/pronoun relationship. The noun, *cars*, to which the pronoun *they* refers, precedes it. However, sometimes the pronoun can precede the noun, as in the following example:

No matter how efficient they are, how safe, or how inexpensive, <u>trains</u> cannot offer the thrill and satisfaction inherent in the automobile.

Moreover, sometimes the noun to which the pronoun refers is in a different sentence. For example:

The parent with children doesn't want to take the train either. <u>He or she</u> must make frequent trips to soccer practice, ballet lessons, and scout meetings and a car is the most efficient way to do so.

Now refer to the passage (repeated here) in order to answer the following questions. Use the identifying referents strategies you just reviewed.

Trains and Autos

Though trains saw widespread use over the course of the nineteenth century, the last hundred years have seen nothing but a decline in the use of railroads in the United States and a rapid growth in American car culture. While trains have begun recently to attract a little more interest from urban planners, there is no sign at all that the general public shares that interest. What accounts for this progressive loss of interest in train travel? What could possibly have made Americans so enamored of their cars? ☐ [A]

Efficiency alone cannot be the answer we are looking for. ☐ [B] Both automobiles and trains consume similar amounts of energy. ☐ [C] The average car gets about thirteen passenger-kilometers per liter of fuel, no improvement at all over trains, though if trains are forced to run with few passengers, they can actually be much less efficient than cars. ☐ [D] Consequently, if one's objective is to conserve energy, neither mode of transportation offers any real advantage, with one exception: interurban light rail and subways are about twenty-five percent more fuel efficient than cars.

Both rail and automobile transportation depend on expensive infrastructure; highway construction in the United States averages several million dollars per kilometer, and can easily go much higher. Railroads are almost as expensive to build, and railroad operators must also pay to maintain their locomotives and rolling stock. Therefore, there does not seem to be a particular advantage in either fuel efficiency or cost of construction and maintenance associated with either automobiles or trains.

On the other hand, trains hold very real advantages in safety. △ [A] In the United States alone, more than 40,000 people die every year in car accidents, and hundreds of thousands more suffer personal and financial injury. △ [B] By contrast, rail fatalities seldom number more than a few hundred per year worldwide. △ [C] On a train, one needs never to worry whether the approaching driver is intoxicated or distracted by his cellular phone, nor does one need to worry about falling asleep at the wheel, striking a deer crossing the road, or any of the other myriad hazards that face automobile drivers on a daily basis. △ [D] One would think such a safety record would attract more enthusiasm from potential passengers.

In addition to safety, riding a train generally offers far more peace of mind than relying on a car. Once on board the train, the passenger can read a newspaper, prepare for work, or simply relax and admire the scenery passing by. Driving, on the other hand, requires the patience to endure traffic jams and the rude person behind who drives with his horn. Then there is the maintenance, insurance, and perhaps a monthly bill the car owner has to pay.

Nevertheless, cars do offer a real advantage in versatility. It is never necessary to wait for the car—it's ready when its driver is, and is never behind schedule. Plus, there's plenty of room in the trunk for carrying groceries or skis. And a car can go all those places where no rail lines have been built. Additionally, cars can be customized and infinitely varied to suit any kind of need or taste.

However, even versatility is probably not the best answer. The truth lies in the way Americans romanticize the car. For every teenager, getting his or her driver's license is a rite of passage. Teenagers often consider themselves to be adults once they can drive. In fact, we have a whole body of popular culture, from dating to work to weekend vacations, built around the car—and nowhere does the train put in an appearance. Americans find the tangible, versatile car to be a maker of self-identity the way trains could never be.

No matter how efficient they are, how safe, or how inexpensive, trains cannot offer the thrill and satisfaction inherent in the automobile. No teenager dreams about cruising to pick up his or her date on the train. No businessperson wants to spend money on train tickets—he or she wants the prestige of a showy new sports car. The parent with children doesn't want to take the train either. He or she must make frequent trips to soccer practice, ballet lessons, and scout meetings and a car is the most efficient way to do so. Until cars become so expensive to purchase and operate that they are out of reach of most people, trains and other forms of transportation will always take a back seat to the automobile.

The word they in paragraph 2 of the passage refers to

- (A) cars
- (B) trains
- (C) kilometers
- (D) passengers

The correct answer is choice (B). The text compares trains and cars, so it makes sense that trains fit into the last part of the sentence, a comparative. Choice (A) is incorrect because *cars* cannot be compared to themselves. Choice (C) is incorrect because *kilometers*, a measurement, cannot be efficient. Choice (D) is incorrect because *passengers* are unlikely to be compared to cars.

Now answer the following TOEFL question.

The word it in paragraph 6 of the passage refers to

- (A) the car
- (B) schedule
- (C) versatility
- (D) a real advantage

Choice (A) is correct. *It* refers directly to the car. Choice (B) is incorrect. "Schedule" occurs after the pronoun *it*. In general, *it* refers to nouns already mentioned. Choice (C) is incorrect. "Versatility" is not something that is "ready," and it cannot be "behind schedule." Choice (D) is incorrect. "A real advantage" is not something that is "ready," and it cannot be "behind schedule."

Question Type 10 Revisited—Understanding Coherence

There are 3 passages on the Reading section of the TOEFL. Each passage is followed by 1 *coherence* question.

You have learned about cohesive devices such as pronouns, demonstrative adjectives, and transitional phrases. These devices are essential to questions on the TOEFL that require you to indicate where a sentence might best fit in the passage. For the following exercise, pay special attention to the transitional phrases.

Look at the three sentences that follow and write a sentence that would fit in the space marked by the asterisk (*). Make sure to use transitional phrases when you write your sentences. The first one has been done as an example,

1. In the United States alone, more than 40,000 people die every year in car accidents, and hundreds of thousands more suffer personal and financial injury. (*) By contrast, rail fatalities seldom number more than a few hundred per year worldwide.

    This is an alarming amount.

2. Teenagers often consider themselves to be adults once they can drive. (*) In fact, we have a whole body of popular culture, from dating to work to weekend vacations, built around the car—and nowhere does the train put in an appearance.

    _____

    _____

3. No matter how efficient they are, how safe, or how inexpensive, trains cannot offer the thrill and satisfaction inherent in the automobile. (*) In sum, no teenager dreams about cruising to pick up his or her date on the train.

    _____

    _____

Answers

Answers will vary, but here are some sample sentences in bold.

1. In the United States alone, more than 40,000 people die every year in car accidents, and hundreds of thousands more suffer personal and financial injury. (*) By contrast, rail fatalities seldom number more than a few hundred per year worldwide.

This is an alarming amount.

2. Teenagers often consider themselves to be adults once they can drive. **They're not wrong in thinking that way, either.** In fact, we have a whole body of popular culture, from dating to work to weekend vacations, built around the car—and nowhere does the train put in an appearance.

3. No matter how efficient they are, how safe, or how inexpensive, trains cannot offer the thrill and satisfaction inherent in the automobile. **Plus, they do not offer the freedom a car does.** In sum, no teenager dreams about cruising to pick up his or her date on the train.

Now answer the following questions.

Look at the four squares ☐ that indicate where the following sentence could be added to the passage.

If it were, automobiles would have to be more efficient than trains, but this is not true.

Where would the sentence best fit?

- Ⓐ [A]
- Ⓑ [B]
- Ⓒ [C]
- Ⓓ [D]

Choice (A) is incorrect. The sentence to be inserted does not address the question that has been asked in the passage. Choice (B) is correct. The pronoun *it* agrees in number and gender with *efficiency*, and the word *efficiency* is related to *efficient*. The sentence to be inserted lends support to the ideas expressed in the sentence before. Choice (C) is incorrect. The sentence to be inserted does not lend support to the ideas in the sentences around the insertion point. Choice (D) is incorrect. The sentence to be inserted does not lend support to the ideas in the sentences around the insertion point.

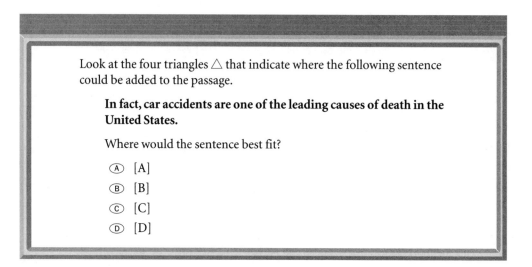

Look at the four triangles △ that indicate where the following sentence could be added to the passage.

In fact, car accidents are one of the leading causes of death in the United States.

Where would the sentence best fit?

Ⓐ [A]

Ⓑ [B]

Ⓒ [C]

Ⓓ [D]

Choice (A) is correct. The sentence to be inserted adds details and support to the ideas expressed in the sentence before the insertion point. Choice (B) is incorrect. The topic has changed, and the sentence to be inserted does not relate to the new topic. Choice (C) is incorrect. The topic is trains, and the sentence to be inserted is discussing cars. Choice (D) is incorrect. The sentence to be inserted does not lend support to the ideas expressed in the sentences before and after the insertion point.

When you are ready, move on to Lesson 7—Writing: More Practice with Compare and Contrast Essays.

LESSON 7—WRITING: MORE PRACTICE WITH COMPARE AND CONTRAST ESSAYS

In this lesson, we will cover more writing skills and strategies that will help lead to success on test day. You will also have the opportunity to learn more about the tasks required for the Writing section of the TOEFL. If you want to proceed with additional writing strategies when you finish this lesson, turn to Lesson 8—Writing: More Practice with the Response Essay in Chapter 8.

Previous lessons covered the following essay types:

- Descriptive Essays
- Definition Essays
- Persuasive Essays
- Compare/Contrast Essays
- Essays in Response to a Reading Passage and a Lecture

This lesson continues to review compare/contrast essays.

Recognizing Compare/Contrast Essay Prompts

There are two tasks in the Writing section of the TOEFL. In the first, you must read a passage, listen to a lecture, then write an essay about what you have read and heard. In the second, you must write an essay based only on a short prompt that asks you to describe or explain something or to express and support your opinion on an issue. You do not need any specialized knowledge to write this second essay. The prompt is based on topics that will be familiar to all test takers. You are given 30 minutes to plan, write, and revise this essay. Typically, an effective essay will contain a minimum of 300 words. Essays will be judged on the quality of the writing, including idea development, organization, and the quality and accuracy of the language used to express these ideas.

When you begin either writing task on the TOEFL, always read the prompt carefully to make sure that you know exactly which essay type you are being asked to write.

One common type of essay prompt found in the Writing section of the TOEFL is the compare/contrast essay. In the compare/contrast essay, you are required to compare two ideas, suggestions, or things, or discuss their similarities. You will also need to contrast them, or discuss their differences. Frequently, the prompt will also ask you which of the two alternatives you prefer and to use your discussion to support that preference.

Here are some tips to help you recognize a compare/contrast essay prompt as well as some sample prompts:

1. The prompt may include the words *compare* and *contrast*. Sometimes the prompt may use the word *compare* by itself, but remember, you will still need to discuss *both* similarities and differences in your essay.

   Some people say that learning from experience is better than learning from books. Do you agree? Compare and contrast learning from experience with learning from books. Use examples in your answer.

2. The prompt may ask you to discuss the *advantages* and *disadvantages* of two different things or ideas.

   An automobile manufacturer is considering your community and the neighboring community as possible sites for a new factory. Discuss the advantages and disadvantages of building the factory in each community. Use specific details and examples in your essay.

3. The prompt may present you with two alternatives, and ask you to identify your preference and to explain your choice.

   Do you think it is better for companies to hire less experienced employees for lower salaries or more experienced people for higher salaries? Explain your preference, using examples and details.

4. Comparative and superlative forms of adjectives and adverbs may be used in the prompt. *Better* is a common example.

> In some countries, university students study a variety of subjects as well as their chosen field. In other countries, students only take courses that are related to their major field. Which system is better? Be specific and provide examples in your response.

Recognizing Compare/Contrast Essay Prompts Practice

Read the following prompts carefully. Decide which require you to write a compare/contrast essay, and which do not. Underline the words or phrases that helped you make your decision.

1. Would you prefer to work for a higher salary but spend little time with friends and family or earn less money but have more time for your life outside of work? Use specific reasons and details in your response.

2. Television has taken the place of conversation in many families. Do you agree or disagree? Provide specific reasons and examples.

3. Do you think that the automobile has been a force for good or a force for bad? Why? Explain your opinion using specific reasons and examples.

4. While in most countries, children are sent to school for their education, some parents prefer to educate their children at home. Compare the advantages and disadvantages of each of these alternatives. Which do you prefer? Use specific reasons and examples in your answer.

Answers

1. <u>Would you prefer</u> to work for a higher salary but spend little time with friends and family <u>or</u> earn less money but have more time for your life outside of work? Use specific reasons and details in your response.
Compare and contrast essay.

2. Television has taken the place of conversation in many families. <u>Do you agree or disagree</u>? Provide specific reasons and examples.
This prompt requires an agree/disagree essay.

3. <u>Do you think</u> that the automobile has been a force for good or a force for bad? <u>Why</u>? Explain your opinion using specific reasons and examples.
This requires a choose and support an opinion essay.

4. While in most countries, children are sent to school for their education, some parents prefer to educate their children at home. <u>Compare the advantages and disadvantages</u> of each of these alternatives. Which do you prefer? Use specific reasons and examples in your answer.
Compare and contrast essay.

Planning a Compare/Contrast Essay

Once you have determined that the writing prompt requires you to write a compare/contrast essay, the next step is to begin planning your essay. Good planning should always precede actual writing. If your essay is well planned, the writing process itself will take less time and the result will be a clearly organized and well-thought out essay.

Prewriting planning should include the following steps:

1. Reading the prompt carefully, to be certain of the questions it asks and the essay type it requires.

2. Brainstorming—generating ideas through freewriting or similar technique.

3. Writing your thesis statement: a clear statement of your opinion or position that will direct the rest of your writing process.

4. Preparing an outline of the essay.

5. Writing the essay.

6. Editing and proofreading.

Generating Ideas for a Compare/Contrast Essay

Unless you have a very clear picture of the essay you will write in response to the prompt, the best way for you to begin is to generate a list of ideas. There are several ways to do this including freewriting (writing continuously for several minutes about the topic until you have thoroughly explored it), listing (noting down words or phrases related to the topic), and clustering (letting one word or idea about the topic lead you to another, until you have a page of notes connected by subtopic or theme). However, it is important to remember that in a compare/contrast essay you need to discuss features of both of the topics presented in the prompt and to make note of both similarities and differences between them. A good way to prepare for this is to employ a chart like this one:

		Item 1	Item 2
Similarities			
	Point A		
	Point B		
	Point C		
Differences			
	Point D		
	Point E		
	Point F		

Using such a chart allows you to think systematically about all the information and ideas you will need for your essay and to be sure that you have covered all the points the prompt requires you to discuss.

Outlining the Compare/Contrast Essay

A compare/contrast essay can be structured in two different ways. Which method you use depends on what you have to say about each of the two items you are comparing and contrasting. Here is a review of a topic previously covered in Lesson 4—Writing: Compare and Contrast Essays.

The first type of essay structure is called the *point-by-point format*. In the point-by-point format, each point of comparison and contrast gets its own paragraph. In the first body paragraph, you will begin by discussing the first important feature of Item 1, then discuss the same feature of Item 2. In the second body paragraph, you discuss the second important feature of each of the two items, and so on, in any subsequent paragraphs. The point-by-point format is best used if you want to discuss exactly the same features of each of the items you are comparing and contrasting.

By contrast, in the *block format*, the essay body is divided in half: the first half is devoted to a discussion of the first item, and the second half to a discussion of the second item. The block format is most useful when you will not be discussing exactly the same features of each item, or have a different amount of information to discuss about each item.

To illustrate these two formats let's consider the following compare/contrast topic.

Have you ever wondered what it might have been like to live centuries ago, when people enjoyed few of the technological amenities that we now use every day, like telephones? Life may have been much simpler back then. Do you think that our life now is better than the life of people centuries in the past?

Make notes in which you consider the relative advantages and disadvantages of living with and without advanced technology such as telephones.

Notes

Let's look at two sample outlines based on the topic of the advantages and disadvantages of newer, high-tech communication methods and older, traditional methods. Here are some notes one might make.

convenience (how fast? how easy? how expensive?)

volume/number (how many people can be reached? how much information can be communicated?)

personal/impersonal (how personal is the message? how individual is the communicator's voice? how well can non-textual information like emotion be communicated? what feedback can the communicator receive from the audience?)

Because these notes include three different subtopics, this is best suited to the point-by-point format. Here is a model outline written in point-by-point format.

Point-by-Point Format

Comparing and Contrasting High-tech and Low-tech Communication

I. Introduction

II. Point 1: Convenience

   A. Item 1: High tech

   B. Item 2: Low tech

III. Point 2: Volume/number of people

   A. Item 1: High tech

   B. Item 2: Low tech

IV. Third point: Personal/impersonal

   A. Item 1: High tech

   B. Item 2: Low tech

V. Conclusion

Now, let's consider different points for high-tech and low-tech communication methods. The notes on the same topic look like this:

High tech:

   convenient

   reaches many people

Low tech:

   personal, communicates emotion

Because different features for each of the two items being compared and contrasted are emphasized, this is suited to the block format.

A model outline made from these notes might look like this:

Block Format

The Relative Advantages of High-tech and Traditional Methods of Communication

I. Introduction

II. Item 1: High tech

    A. Point 1: Convenience

    B. Point 2: Efficient, large audience

    C. (Possible additional points)

III. Item 2: Low tech

    A. Point 1: Personal quality

    B. (Possible additional points)

IV. Conclusion

Outlining the Compare/Contrast Essay Practice

Now, using the notes you made on the topic of low-tech versus high-tech, prepare an outline for a compare/contrast essay. Choose the format, block or point-by-point, most appropriate for your ideas.

Answers

Answers will vary.

Introducing the Compare/Contrast Essay

The most important part of any essay is its introduction. This is especially true for a compare/contrast essay, because the material covered by this essay type is inherently more complex than in most other essays. A compare/contrast essay deals with not one, but two distinct topics, and it must discuss both the similarities and the differences between those two topics. Thus, without a good introduction, your essay may seem uninteresting or even confusing to the reader. However, with a little practice, you will soon be able to write effective introductions for compare/contrast essays.

A good introduction should accomplish four tasks:

1. It should grab the reader's attention immediately, and keep it. A strategy for accomplishing this task is called a hook. Hooks usually occur at the beginning of the introduction and can take several forms. Your hook can be an interesting fact, a question directed at the reader to make him or her realize that your topic is important, or a story told in a sentence or two. Other kinds of hooks are possible, too.

2. Your introduction should provide enough background information to let your reader understand your topic and why you have chosen it. However, it shouldn't provide a lot of detail or discussion— that is found in body paragraphs.

3. The introduction should clearly indicate your attitude or opinion toward your topic in a thesis statement.

4. It should indicate to the reader what points you intend to discuss in the body of the essay. This is called forecasting. Forecasting is especially important in longer, more complex essays.

Topic Sentences

Because compare/contrast essays are more complex than most other kinds of essays, you need to provide your reader with lots of help to show him or her the direction the essay is going. A good **topic sentence** is one of the best kinds of help you can offer your reader. Usually, your topic sentences will be the first sentences of each body paragraph in the essay. Topic sentences will clearly identify the topic and purpose of each paragraph, so that your reader can more easily follow your discussion. Subsequent sentences in each body paragraph will provide more specific information to support the topic sentences.

Transition Signals

An important component of the topic sentence is the transition signal. Transition signals are words or phrases used to tell the reader how the information following is related to the previous information or discussion: is it similar? does it contrast? is it unexpected? All these questions and more can—and should—be answered by well-chosen transition signals.

KAPLAN
Test Prep and Admissions

The following chart includes a number of transition signals commonly used in compare/contrast essays.

COMPARE	CONTRAST Direct Opposition Result	Unexpected
likewise	however	however
similar to	in, by contrast	nevertheless
like	in/by comparison	still
similarly	on the other hand	nonetheless
just as	on the contrary	although
both . . . and	while	even though
not only . . . but also	whereas	
neither . . . nor		

Compare/Contrast Essay Practice

Following is an example of the second task in the Writing section of the TOEFL. Once you have written your essay, spend about 15 minutes evaluating it according to the principles outlined in this lesson.

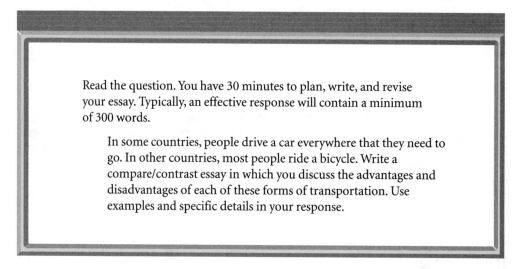

Read the question. You have 30 minutes to plan, write, and revise your essay. Typically, an effective response will contain a minimum of 300 words.

In some countries, people drive a car everywhere that they need to go. In other countries, most people ride a bicycle. Write a compare/contrast essay in which you discuss the advantages and disadvantages of each of these forms of transportation. Use examples and specific details in your response.

Answer

Answers will vary, but here is one sample essay.

> Both cars and bicycles are common forms of transportation in the world today. It seems that many countries have fallen in love with the automobile in much the same way as the United States has. Unfortunately, the growing price of oil and the increasing amounts of smog that are covering the world's cities are the sad effects of this love. In many cases, the bicycle offers a healthy, low cost alternative to cars.
>
> Riding a bicycle is an excellent way to get from here to there. Riders get exercise, they breathe more fresh air than people in a car would, and they get to be out of doors in the sunlight and warmth. However, being outside is not always an advantage. When the air is cold, or if it rains, a bicycle offers little protection from the elements, while people in a car are warm and dry.
>
> Cars have their disadvantages too, the least not being that they rely on an energy source to move. These days most cars still depend on petroleum to power their engines. This means exhaust fumes that contribute to smog and other forms of pollution. In contrast, the only exhaust a bicycle might have is the breath of its rider as he climbs a difficult hill. The environmental impact of cars is much greater than that of bikes.
>
> Finally, while there are some athletes who can ride a bicycle for a hundred miles a day, most people are not fit enough to use a bicycle to go everywhere they need to go. The effort and time involved in riding a bike thirty miles to work are much more than getting into a car and driving thirty miles. Most people simply live too far away from their jobs, stores, and families to be able to ride a bike there and back again regularly. Cars will get them there faster and in more comfort, but not without a plume of carbon monoxide right behind them.

Now that you have practiced writing, you are ready to begin Lesson 7—Listening: Note-Taking, Main Idea, and Combined Skills.

LESSON 7—LISTENING: NOTE-TAKING, MAIN IDEA, AND COMBINED SKILLS

In this lesson, we will cover more listening skills and strategies that will help lead to success on test day. You will also have the opportunity to review some of the strategies you learned in previous lessons as well as to learn more about the question types found on the Listening section of the TOEFL. If you want to proceed with more listening strategies when you finish this lesson, turn to Lesson 8—Listening: Taking Notes on a Conversation in Chapter 8.

Note-Taking

Note-taking is critical when you are listening to a lecture or conversation. Remember that as you listen you should:

- Write down key words, names, numbers, dates, or anything else you think is important
- Listen carefully whenever there is a change in speaker. Changes in speakers often result in changes in topic.
- Listen carefully to questions and answers from the professor to the students. They often contain transitions to new supporting points.

Note-Taking Practice

Listen to a discussion. Be sure to take notes on what you hear. Then, use your notes to answer the questions that follow. You will find a transcript of this audio passage (72.7L, Note-Taking Practice) at the end of the chapter.

🎧 **72.7L, Note-Taking Practice**

Notes

Now answer the following questions.

1. What is the main idea of the lecture?

   _____

   _____

   _____

2. What are some uses of robots? Think about examples from the lecture and also from your own knowledge and experience.

   _____

   _____

   _____

3. What is MRI? What does this acronym stand for?

   _____

   _____

   _____

4. What's the significance of the Kyoto lab?

   _____

   _____

   _____

Answers

1. A Japanese laboratory is developing robots that are designed to help model the functions of the human brain.

2. Brain and space research, building cars, cleaning

3. A Magnetic-Resonance Imaging machine creates images of the inside of something, similar to an X-ray machine.

4. It is a robotics lab that is focused on learning about the human brain.

Outlining

Unless you skipped Chapters 1–6, you know that an outline is a skeletal structure of a text. It contains the main and supporting ideas in the order they are presented, but does not necessarily include any specific details. Here is an example of the beginning of an outline based on the lecture you just heard:

I. Robotics—two schools of thought

    A. Create tools that are more efficient

    B. Learn about the human brain

II. How scientists learn about the human brain

    A. Simplified models of certain parts of brain

Outlining Practice

Using your notes, write an outline of the lecture (72.7L, Note-Taking Practice) in the space that follows.

Now look at the following table. The main ideas of the lecture are presented in the right-hand column, but they are not in the order they occurred in the lecture. Use your outline to put the information in the right-hand column of the table into the correct order by writing the main idea in the correct space on the left-hand side.

Order of the Lecture	Summary of Topic/Main Idea
Thesis/Main Idea of lecture:	(A) We could help patients with brain injuries and learn more about how we learn
Topic sentence of main supporting point 1:	(B) How can Robotics help us learn about the human brain?
Supporting point:	(C) One use of Robotics: help us learn about the human brain
Topic sentence of main supporting point 2:	(D) Ironically, using robots to understand humans could result in better robots
Supporting point:	(E) What are the benefits to using robots to understand the brain?
Topic sentence of main supporting point 3:	(F) Why is it controversial?
Supporting point:	(G) Controversial study of Robotics is counterintuitive to conventional studies which use robots to improve robots, not humans
Adding to supporting point:	(H) Scientists conduct experiments on humans using MRI and develop models

Answers

Outlines will vary, but here is one sample.

   I. Robotics—two schools of thought

      A. Create tools that are more efficient

      B. Learn about the human brain

  II. How scientists learn about the human brain

      A. Simplified models of certain parts of brain

      B. Observe humans performing specific tasks and track blood flow using MRI

      C. Decode magnetic/electric\MRI data into model

 III. How robots can teach about humans

      A. Motivation

         1. Help injured patients recover

         2. Learn about learning: "To teach is to learn"

      B. Method

         1. Program a robot to learn, and then observe how it processes new behavior

      C. Goal

         1. Understand the brain by creating the brain

         2. More autonomous robots

         3. Maybe closer to A.I. (robots now are "uniformly stupid")

Order of the Lecture
Thesis/Main Idea of lecture: (G) Controversial study of Robotics is counterintuitive to conventional studies which use robots to improve robots, not humans
Topic sentence of main supporting point 1: (F) Why is it controversial?
Supporting point: (H) Scientists conduct experiments on humans using MRI and develop models
Topic sentence of main supporting point 2: (B) How can Robotics help us learn about the human brain?
Supporting point: (C) One use of Robotics: help us learn about the human brain
Topic sentence of main supporting point 3: (E) What are the benefits to using robots to understand the brain?
Supporting point: (A) we could help patients with brain injuries and learn more about how we learn
Adding to supporting point: (D) Ironically, using robots to understand humans could result in better robots

Main Idea

At this point, you should understand the importance of recognizing and understanding the main idea of a passage. However, like any critical skill, it requires lots of practice. Complete the Main Idea Practice to reinforce this skill.

Main Idea Practice

Listen to a lecture. Take notes as you listen, and answer the questions that follow. You will find a transcript of this audio passage (73.7L, Main Idea Practice) at the end of the chapter.

 **73.7L, Main Idea Practice**

Notes

Use your notes to answer the following questions. You may need to listen to parts of the lecture (73.7L, Main Idea Practice) a second time.

1. What is the topic of the lecture?

    _____

    _____

2. What kind of hook does the professor use in the introduction?

    _____

    _____

3. The body of the lecture is broken into three main supporting points. What are they? Write them down in outline form, similar to the following outline.

      I. Introduction

      II. Body

          A. First supporting point

          B. Second supporting point

          C. Third supporting point

      III. Conclusion

4. Why does the professor mention the Code Red Worm?

_____

_____

5. What literary device does the professor use throughout the lecture to help the class understand the topic?

_____

_____

Answers

1. computer viruses, how they work, and how to prevent them

2. an anecdote

3.

  I. Introduction

  II. Body

    A. What viruses are

    B. How they work

    C. How to prevent them

  III. Conclusion

4. to provide an example of a specific subtype of virus

5. metaphors

Combined Skills

Comprehension is important both in reading and in listening. In addition to understanding what you read and hear, you will also have to be able to summarize and explain what you have just read or heard. Use the Combined Skills Practice to improve these skills.

Combined Skills Practice

Read a short passage, then listen to a lecture on the same topic. Take notes as you listen to the lecture, as you will need to refer to these notes to complete your response to the question.

Facial Recognition Software

In the field of Biometrics, or the use of biological information to verify identity, facial recognition software offers great promise in helping authorities locate criminals at large.

Facial recognition software works by synching up with video surveillance cameras to constantly scan a camera's field of vision for faces in a crowd that match faces in the software's database. Because video surveillance is virtually ubiquitous, there is great potential for using this technology in a wide range of public places. A good facial recognition program can account for variances in lighting, angles of a subject's face with respect to the camera, and changes in facial features such as facial hair and sunglasses.

When the software analyzes a subject's face, it considers many different frames to account for variations caused by facial expressions. Almost instantly, it processes the facial image and returns potential matches based on a certain probability threshold, which is input by a human. Obviously, at this point, human intervention is required to make a final judgment regarding potential matches.

Facial recognition software can also identify the relative locations of as many as eighty prominent facial characteristics, such as the distance between the eyes, length of the nose, and the shape of the cheekbones. So, if a fugitive has grown a beard and is wearing sunglasses as a disguise, the computer still has many features on which to base a match. In fact, facial recognition software can find a match with as few as twelve facial characteristics.

Notes

Now listen to the lecture. Remember to take notes as you listen. You will find a transcript of this audio passage (74.7L, Combined Skill Practice) at the end of the chapter.

 **74.7L, Combined Skill Practice**

Notes

Explain (in writing) how the information in the reading was similar to or different from the information in the listening.

_____

_____

_____

_____

_____

Now write a response to the following topic.

Summarize the points made in the lecture you just heard, explaining how they cast doubt on points made in the reading.

_____

_____

_____

_____

_____

_____

_____

_____

_____

_____

_____

_____

_____

_____

_____

_____

_____

_____

_____

_____

_____

_____

Answers

Answers will vary, but here is a sample explanation and sample response.

> The written passage stated that facial recognition was an available technology that can identify people by their facial characteristics, while the listening passage pointed out that the facial recognition is by no means accurate enough for use in a public setting.
>
> While it was hoped that facial recognition would serve as a powerful tool for law enforcement, it has not managed to meet expectations. Despite claims that facial recognition makes use of up to eighty different points on a face for identification, false positives and false negatives both occur with too much frequency to make the system effective. There are also major concerns about the constitutionality of the potential uses of the technology to track innocent people unawares.

Understanding the question types is important for knowing how and where you can apply your strategies. Keep reading to learn more.

Question Types

There are 7 question types on the Listening section of the TOEFL. These are:
- Understanding Rhetorical Function
- Understanding an Idiomatic Expression in Context
- Drawing an Inference
- Understanding a Speaker's Implication
- Identifying the Main Idea
- Summarizing the Most Important Points
- Understanding Details

This lesson will review the following question types in greater detail:
- Identifying the Main Idea
- Summarizing the Most Important Ideas
- Understanding Details

Question Type 5 Revisited—Identifying the Main Idea

There are 2 conversations and 4 lectures in the Listening section of the TOEFL. Each lecture is followed by 1 *main idea* question. The conversations do not have *main idea* questions.

Main idea questions test your ability to recognize a paraphrase of the main idea of the entire lecture, or a paragraph within the lecture.

Wrong answers relate to points in the lecture, but they do not summarize the lecture well. Distracters may either summarize one portion of the lecture but not the whole lecture, and thus are too narrow, or they may be too broad given the focus of the lecture.

While listening to the lecture, you should do the following in order to identify the main idea:

- Listen carefully to the short introductory statement at the beginning of each lecture for key information about the topic.
- Listen carefully to questions and comments from both the professor and the students. They guide the development of the topic and often contain the main ideas or main supporting points of the thesis.
- Try to understand how the speaker feels about the ideas he or she is presenting. The tone of the speaker can help you identify the purpose of the lecture. For example, informative lectures have a neutral tone. Persuasive lectures have a stronger tone, either positive or negative.

Common stems for *main idea* questions are as follows:

This talk is mainly about …

The professor is mainly discussing …

What is the main topic/idea of the discussion?

You may refer to your notes when answering all listening questions.

Here is a main idea question based on the robotics discussion you heard earlier in this lesson. The lecture is printed here. You can also listen to (72.7L, Note-Taking Practice) again.

Narrator: Now listen to part of a lecture in a cognitive science class.

Professor: In robotics there are, simply put, two schools of thought when it comes to the development of humanoid robots. The traditional justification for developing this technology is to create tools that are more economically efficient than ah…humans or to provide needy groups such as the elderly with ways of remaining more self-sufficient for longer. On the other hand, a team at the Computational Neuroscience Laboratories in Kyoto, Japan sees robotics as a means of learning about the human brain.

Student: I thought it was fairly widely acknowledged that robots are nothing like humans. If that's the case, how can the team learn anything about the human brain from robots?

Professor: Indeed, you are quite right. Robots and people are very different. The human brain contains billions of neurons that are interconnected in extremely complex ways. How connections between those neurons are made and how those neurological interactions control movement and problem solving is still poorly understood. No computer has yet come close to simulating how a brain works. However, teams of neurologists and computer scientists are collaborating to test theories of how the brain works by building humanoid robots that incorporate simplified models of what certain groups of neurons in the brain are doing. First they conduct experiments on human subjects in magnetic-resonance imaging machines…you know about MRIs, right? Good. So, they get subjects to perform specific task and then they observe which parts of the brain light up, indicating increased blood flow. This, they believe, represents internal models of the interactions required to perform the task. Then they combine the magnetic imaging data with electrical and magnetic recording techniques to "decode" how the mind works. From that so-called "decoding", they attempt to build models.

Student: I heard this group recently received a large grant to expand their research. Could you explain how that can be justified? What are the benefits of using robots to understand the brain? I can appreciate the value of developing robots to increase efficiency, but isn't this a bit of a stretch?

Professor: Good question, one that is frequently raised by critics of the Kyoto lab. Their motivation lies in using robots to gain insights into how people move; think; make decisions and interact. If doctors had a more solid understanding of how the brain works, it would certainly enhance their ability to help patients with brain injuries. First they are trying to find out how healthy brains work. Later on, they'll be able to simulate damaged brains by switching off, or limiting certain areas of the robotic controls. Secondly, by creating something that resembles the human brain, we'll be able to learn more about how we learn. There is a Japanese proverb that says: "To teach is to learn." In this research, scientists can literally observe how a robot learns. They can watch what algorithms are running in the robot's computer control center while a scientist "teaches" it a new movement or type of interaction. Those are the two main benefits that are hoped to come out of this research. How does that sound?

Student: Fair enough.

Professor: Now, can someone explain why this is such a controversial approach to robotics?

Student: Well, um…I am not sure, but it seems kind of backward compared to the stuff we have been studying in this class. I mean, we've be reading about projects that are trying to figure out how to get robots to do certain things, like handle hazardous materials or explore other planets. Most robotics labs are working out ways to improve a robot's vision or navigational controls using digital technology and basic mechanics. Um, this research doesn't seem to be about making the robot do something, it's about understanding how humans do stuff.

Professor: Very well said. The focus is indeed on the human brain, rather than on the robot. The goal is to understand the brain by creating the brain. Now, that is not to say that this research won't also yield benefits in the field of robotics. In fact many believe that using robots to understand the human brain could eventually help produce more autonomous robots. As you will find out in next week's reading, we are still a long way from true A.I.—artificial intelligence, that is. Most robots still can't do anything that they are not specifically programmed to do. Professor Minsky describes today's robots as "uniformly stupid."

Please leave your papers on the desk at the front. When I read them I hope I won't be reminded too much of today's robots!

What is the lecture mainly about?

(A) Two schools of thought in robotics

(B) How a controversial use of robotics works and its implications

(C) The benefits of using robotics to help us understand the human brain

(D) A comparison between the brain of a human and the brain of a robot

Choice (A) is mentioned in the introduction, but the professor quickly narrows the focus to one school of thought, robotics as a means of learning about the human brain, and develops only this thought in the lecture. Choice (C) is too narrow. This is only one of three main supporting points of the thesis. Choice (D) is also too narrow. It was a detail used to support one of the main supporting points of the lecture: how robotics can be used to learn about the human brain. Choice (B) is the only answer that addresses the main topic of the lecture and all the supporting points.

Question Type 6 Revisited—Summarizing the Most Important Points

There are 2 conversations and 4 lectures in the Listening section of the TOEFL. Each lecture is followed by 0 or 1 *most-important-points* question, for a total of 2 *most-important-points* questions in the Listening section.

This type of TOEFL question asks you to identify the three most important points in the lecture—the ideas that combine to express the main idea.

You may be asked to identify the most important points of the entire lecture or the most important points of a supporting idea within the lecture.

The incorrect options either provide details that don't support the main idea or details that are inaccurate. This question can be presented in two distinct formats:

- Choose three out of five options
- Click on *yes* or *no* for each of five options

Here is an example of the *choose-three-out-of-five-options* format.

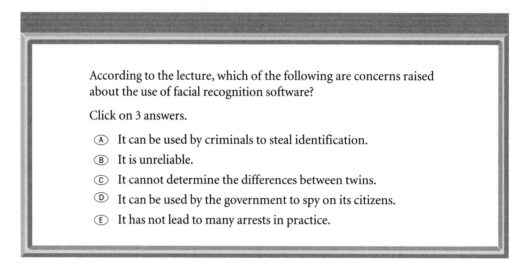

According to the lecture, which of the following are concerns raised about the use of facial recognition software?

Click on 3 answers.

Ⓐ It can be used by criminals to steal identification.

Ⓑ It is unreliable.

Ⓒ It cannot determine the differences between twins.

Ⓓ It can be used by the government to spy on its citizens.

Ⓔ It has not lead to many arrests in practice.

Choice (A) is incorrect. This is not mentioned in the lecture. Choice (B) is correct. The failure rate of the system is discussed, which is a measure of the system's reliability. Choice (C) is incorrect. This is not mentioned in the lecture. Choice (D) is correct. The possibility of the government using the technology to track ordinary people's movements is discussed. Choice (E) is correct. The point is made that arrests have been made as a result of the use of this technology.

Here is an example of the *click-on-yes-or-no-for-each-of-five-options* format.

In the lecture, the professor mentions several criticisms that have been made about the use of facial recognition software. Indicate whether each of the following criticisms are mentioned.

Click in the correct box for each phrase.		
	Yes	No
(A) It has failed to lead to arrests when put into practice.		
(B) It cannot accurately account for things like sunglasses or facial hair.		
(C) It is accurate only 39% of the time.		
(D) The government could use it to track the movements of innocent citizens.		
(E) It is a very expensive system to operate and maintain.		

Choice (A) is *yes*. The lecture mentions that few arrests have been made as a result of the use of this technology. Choice (B) is *yes*. The lecture mentions that sunglasses and hair can affect the software's ability to make measurements. Choice (C) is *no*. The lecture states that the software *failed* 39% of the time. Therefore, it was *accurate* 61% of the time. Choice (D) is *yes*. The lecture mentions that the government could use the technology to track people's movements. Choice (E) is *no*. The costs of operating and maintaining the system are not mentioned in the lecture.

Question Type 7 Revisited—Understanding Details

There are 2 conversations and 4 lectures in the Listening section of the TOEFL. Each conversation is followed by 2 or 3 *detail* questions, and each lecture is followed by 1 or 2 *detail* questions.

Detail questions require you to recall specific information from the spoken text. The choices will contain three incorrect statements and one correct one, or two incorrect statements and two correct statements.

When answering any question, always read the answer choices carefully, because the distracters contain familiar words that make the answer look attractive.

The incorrect statements are attributed to one of the following:
- false information
- a distortion of details from the lecture
- information that was not discussed

You will be able to use your notes when you answer detail questions. As you take notes pay special attention to numbers, proper nouns, and transition words.

The most common stem for this type of question is:

According to ___, who/what/when/where/why/how many/how much. . .?

Here is an example of a *detail* question based on the robotics lecture.

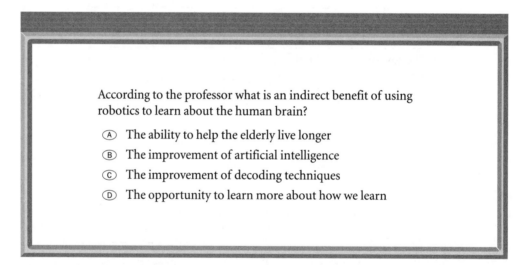

According to the professor what is an indirect benefit of using robotics to learn about the human brain?

- Ⓐ The ability to help the elderly live longer
- Ⓑ The improvement of artificial intelligence
- Ⓒ The improvement of decoding techniques
- Ⓓ The opportunity to learn more about how we learn

Choice (A) is a benefit of the traditional use of robotics. Choice (C) is neither a direct or indirect benefit; it's a technique. Choice (D) is a direct benefit. Choice (B) is the correct answer; the improvement of artificial intelligence is specifically cited as an example of an indirect benefit of using robotics to understand the human brain. Now, if you had not read this question carefully you might have missed the key word: *indirect*. The direct benefits are related to humans, not robots.

On some detail questions you will be instructed to click on more than one correct answer.

> With which of the following would the class probably agree were traditional uses of robotics?
>
> Click on 2 answers.
>
> (A) Simulating how a healthy human brain works
>
> (B) Improving the ability to teach and learn
>
> (C) Automobile parts transfer and assembly
>
> (D) Delicate operations on the eye

Choices (A) and (B) are details from the lecture related to using robotics to learn about the human brain; they are not traditional justifications for using robotics. That leaves choices (C) and (D), neither of which is related to understanding the brain, the controversial justification for robotics. Therefore, choices (C) and (D) are correct.

A variation of the detail question is one in which you are presented with three correct answers and one incorrect answer. You need to choose the answer that is incorrect, or NOT true. These questions take the following format:

> Which of the following is NOT...?
>
> All of the following . . . EXCEPT...

This question comes from the passage on facial recognition software.

> Which of the following is NOT mentioned as a problem associated with the use of facial recognition software?
>
> (A) It has not lead to the capture of many criminals.
>
> (B) It has a high failure rate.
>
> (C) It has the potential to be misused by governments.
>
> (D) It is expensive.

Choice (A) is mentioned; the lecture states that few arrests have been made as a result of using the technology. Choice (B) is mentioned; the system is described as having a 39% failure rate. Choice (C) is mentioned; the lecture describes the possibility of misuse by the government. Choice (D) is not mentioned in the lecture, therefore it is the correct answer.

When you are ready, turn to Lesson 7–Speaking: Announcements and Notices.

LESSON 7—SPEAKING: ANNOUNCEMENTS AND NOTICES

In this lesson, we will cover more speaking skills and strategies that will help lead to success on test day. You will also have the opportunity to learn more about the tasks required for the Speaking section of the TOEFL. If you want to proceed with additional speaking strategies when you finish this lesson, turn to Lesson 8–Speaking: Paraphrasing and Summarizing in Chapter 8.

Remember that previous lessons covered the following speaking tasks:

- Describing Something from Your Own Experience
- Summarizing a Lecture
- Expressing and Supporting an Opinion Based on Personal Experience
- Summarizing a Conversation and Expressing an Opinion
- Synthesizing and Summarizing Information

This lesson will continue to review the following speaking task:

- Synthesizing and Summarizing Information

First, let's review some helpful skills and strategies, starting with identifying the main points in an announcement.

Identifying the Main Points from an Announcement or Notice

You should recall from Chapter 3–Speaking: Informal vs. Informal that the third task in the TOEFL Speaking section requires you to read a short announcement on a topic related to academic life. Announcements and notices are items that you should generally be familiar with and be able to interpret. To ensure that you can identify and understand an announcement or notice, complete the following practice.

Identifying the Main Points from an Announcement or Notice Practice

Look at the following notices. Underline what you consider to be the key words.

CUTE!!!

Kittens for sale. Adorable playful balls of fluff looking for happy homes. These kitties are purebred, Persian long-hairs from a healthy bloodline. Several award winners in this family tree. This species sometimes requires intense care. They are not recommended as outdoor cats. Extremely friendly and loving, these valuable animals also make excellent pets, especially for older people. Call 555-4757 for more information.

Best Babysitter

Highly experienced babysitter looking for work. Do your tiny tots need a nanny? Please call me. I have been taking care of young kids since I was in high school and have always loved this job. I am currently completing the final year of my training as a kindergarten teacher and am seeking part-time work. Fully qualified, excellent references, trained in infant and child CPR. My rates are higher than the teenager next door, but the quality of care is incomparable. Cell: 555-2288.

HELP! I LOST MY LIFE!!!

Small, black weekly planner mislaid in library. Sometime over the weekend I lost my daily planner in the library. It contains everything I need: my time-table, all my phone numbers, my project deadlines, EVERYTHING. It is small, black, about 1/2" thick. There are a few loose sheets of paper folded inside. If you see it, please, please, please either call me in room 36A or leave it with someone from the cafeteria staff. If you like, I will buy you a big drink or a pizza in appreciation for saving my LIFE! Thanks,—Brian

Answers

CUTE!!!

<u>Kittens</u> for sale. Adorable playful balls of fluff <u>looking for happy homes</u>. These kitties are <u>purebred, Persian long-hairs</u> from a <u>healthy</u> bloodline. Several award winners in this family tree. This species <u>sometimes requires intense care</u>. They are <u>not</u> recommended as <u>outdoor cats</u>. Extremely <u>friendly and loving</u>, these v<u>aluable</u> animals also make excellent pets, <u>especially for older people</u>. Call <u>555-4757 </u> for more information.

Best Babysitter

<u>Highly experienced</u> babysitter looking for work. Do your tiny tots need a nanny? Please call me. <u>I have been taking care of young kids since I was in high school </u> and have always loved this job. I am currently completing the final year of my <u>training as a kindergarten teacher</u> and am seeking part-time work. <u>Fully qualified, excellent references, trained in infant and child CPR</u>. My <u>rates are higher</u> than the teenager next door, but the quality of care is incomparable. Cell: <u>555-2288</u>.

HELP! I LOST MY LIFE!!!

<u>Small, black weekly planner mislaid in library</u>. Sometime <u>over the weekend</u> I lost my daily planner in the library. It contains everything I need: my time-table, all my phone numbers, my project deadlines, EVERYTHING. It is <u>small, black, about 1/2" thick</u>. There are <u>a few loose sheets of paper folded inside</u>. If you see it, please, please, please either <u>call me in room 36A or leave it with someone from the cafeteria staff</u>. If you like, <u>I will buy you a big drink or a pizza in appreciation for saving my LIFE</u>! Thanks,—<u>Brian</u>

Expressing and Supporting an Opinion in Speech

You should recall from Chapter 3—Speaking: Informal vs. Formal that in the third task in the TOEFL Speaking section, after you have read the short announcement, you must listen to a conversation about the announcement. The speakers generally give their opinions about the topic of the announcement. Part of your job in this task is to then summarize the opinions of one or both of the speakers in your response to the question.

In Chapter 6, we reviewed certain conversational expressions used when giving and supporting opinions in speech. You should be able to recognize these as you listen to the conversation in the third task of the Speaking section, and you may use some of them as you summarize the speakers' opinions. Here are some more examples of these expressions:

To Express Strong Opinions	To Express Neutral Opinions	To Express Weak Opinions	To Add Supporting Reasons
Without a doubt...	*In most cases, I'd have to say that...*	*I suppose...*	*First of all...*
_____is/are /should definitely...	*Basically, I believe that...*	*_____ is/are/ should probably...*	*An even more important reason is...*
It's impossible to deny that...	*Generally speaking, I think that...*	*I'm not sure one way or the other, but I guess...*	*Most importantly...*

Practice these expressions while discussing the following questions. If you have a study partner, or someone that can listen to your responses, ask to work with him or her.

1. Do you prefer to give oral presentations or to write papers? Why?

2. Should governments spend money on robotics programs? Why or why not?

3. In your opinion, which technological advance has most influenced the world so far?

4. Do you agree or disagree with robots being used in the workforce? If so, should there be limits as to what they can do? If not, do you agree with the use of robots in any aspect of human life? Why or why not?

5. In your opinion, have humans come to rely too strongly on technology? Give examples to support your opinion.

Expressing and Supporting an Opinion in Speech Practice

Think about the following questions for a few minutes on your own. Make a few notes about your ideas.

What do you think has been the most significant technological development since your parents were your age? How has this development influenced people of different generations? Are there any downsides to this development? How do you predict this technology will continue to develop in the future?

Notes

You will need these notes later in the lesson.

Identifying Differences in Register

In the left-hand column of the chart that follows are excerpts (portions) of readings and lectures found in this chapter. The readings and lectures from which they were taken were all academic in nature. In the right-hand column, the same sentences have been paraphrased in a less formal style, or register.

Look at the differences between the formal and informal register, paying particular attention to the following questions:

- What words are different?
- What grammatical structures are different?
- How long is each type of sentence?
- How many sentences does it take to say the same thing?

Keep in mind that the register will differ between conversations and lectures on the TOEFL.

Formal Register	Informal Register
Though trains saw widespread use over the course of the nineteenth century, the last hundred years have seen nothing but a decline in the use of railroads in the United States and a rapid growth in American car culture.	Trains were popular in the nineteenth century, but they have been used less and less in the last hundred years. Car use has increased very quickly.
What accounts for this progressive loss of interest in train travel? What could possibly have made Americans so enamored of their cars?	Why have people continued to lose interest in train travel? Why do Americans love their cars so much?
The average car gets about thirteen passenger-kilometers per liter of fuel, no improvement at all over trains, though if trains are forced to run with few passengers, they can actually be much less efficient than cars	The average car gets about thirteen passenger-kilometers per liter of fuel. This is no better than trains. But if trains have to run with few passengers, they can be much less efficient than cars.
Consequently, if one's objective is to conserve energy, neither mode of transportation offers any real advantage.	So, if you want to conserve energy, neither mode of transport is better than the other.
On the other hand, trains hold very real advantages in safety.	On the other hand, trains are much safer.
It is never necessary to wait for the car.	You never have to wait for the car.
Cars can be customized and infinitely varied to suit any kind of need or taste.	You can customize your car however you want to.

Summarizing

In an academic setting you are often required to show that you have understood a lecture or a reading by summarizing the main points. The third task in the Speaking section of the TOEFL requires this of you as well. In order to summarize, you need to take notes on the main points. You should use pronunciation clues to identify key words and main points. Pronunciation clues include:

- stressed words or phrases
- contrasting stressed words or phrases
- pauses

Being Understood

When communicating in English, it is very important for you to make yourself easily understood. It is often better for you to use simple grammar constructions, short sentences, and familiar vocabulary than to try to sound too formal or sophisticated by using complex words and structures.

Try to speak simply and clearly. Keep your sentences short, use simple grammar constructions, and vocabulary that you are completely comfortable with. You will impress listeners much more if you can express ideas clearly than if you use fancy words.

Accentuating Important Points in Speech

Speakers can accentuate a particularly important point in several different ways. One way is to emphasize a word or phrase by stressing it. In the sentences below, the capital letters indicate an accentuated sound.

> In today's lesson, we'll continue our study of roBOtics.

Word stress is also used to emphasize two contrasting words or ideas:

> We should WELcome not FEAR the increase in the use of robots.

Another way is to pause before the word or between several important words that you want to emphasize:

> Yet the benefits of robots to humans are also plentiful and include (pause) precision, (pause) safety, (pause) and aid in the completion of otherwise impossible tasks.

Now let's move on to a review of the third speaking task.

Task 3 Revisited—Synthesizing and Summarizing Information

There are 6 tasks in the Speaking section of the TOEFL. The third requires you to read an announcement, listen to a conversation about the announcement, and synthesize and summarize information from both. You have 30 seconds to prepare your response, and your response should be about 60 seconds in length.

When reading the notice and listening to the conversation you should:

- Identify the main points
- Identify the main speaker's opinion and the reasons he or she holds that opinion

The topic usually relates to campus life at an American university. Topics might include:

- changes in timetables
- changes in fees
- new academic requirements
- availability of facilities
- other topics related to student life

The notice usually contains factual details, and the conversation usually contains student opinions regarding the notice. While reading the notice, you should identify the main points. One way of doing that is to underline key words and phrases. While listening to the conversation you should identify the main speaker's opinion and the reasons he or she holds that opinion. Take notes while listening.

Now practice the following TOEFL question. Remember that you will not see the narrator's introduction on the test. You may take notes as you listen. Transcripts of these audio passages are found at the end of the chapter.

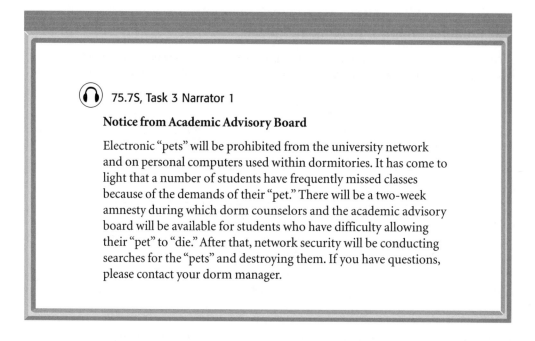

75.7S, Task 3 Narrator 1

Notice from Academic Advisory Board

Electronic "pets" will be prohibited from the university network and on personal computers used within dormitories. It has come to light that a number of students have frequently missed classes because of the demands of their "pet." There will be a two-week amnesty during which dorm counselors and the academic advisory board will be available for students who have difficulty allowing their "pet" to "die." After that, network security will be conducting searches for the "pets" and destroying them. If you have questions, please contact your dorm manager.

Notes

76.7S, Task 3 Conversation 1

Notes

 77.7S, Task 3 Prompt 1

Both students support the new rule prohibiting electronic pets. Explain why they support the new rule, using information from the conversation regarding a classmate's behavior.

30 seconds to prepare
60 seconds to speak

Evaluate yourself using the following criteria:

Criteria	Comments	Action to Improve
Clarity and pronunciation		
Organization		
Details and examples		
Grammar and vocabulary		

Now listen to the sample response. How was it different from yours? How was it similar? You will find a transcript of this audio passage (78.7S, Task 3 Response 1) at the end of the chapter.

🎧 **78.7S, Task 3 Response 1**

Practice the following TOEFL question. Remember that you will not see the narrator's introduction on the test.

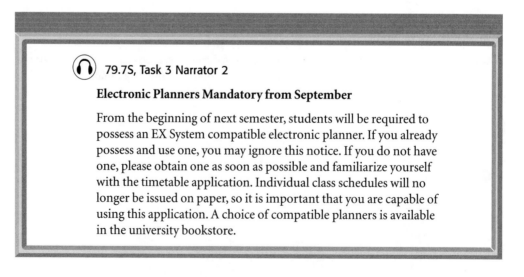

🎧 **79.7S, Task 3 Narrator 2**

Electronic Planners Mandatory from September

From the beginning of next semester, students will be required to possess an EX System compatible electronic planner. If you already possess and use one, you may ignore this notice. If you do not have one, please obtain one as soon as possible and familiarize yourself with the timetable application. Individual class schedules will no longer be issued on paper, so it is important that you are capable of using this application. A choice of compatible planners is available in the university bookstore.

Notes

80.7S, Task 3 Conversation 2

Notes

 81.7S, Task 3 Prompt 2

One of the students has a problem. Using information from the notice and from the conversation, describe what the student's problem is and how the other student will help.

30 seconds to prepare
60 seconds to speak

Now evaluate yourself using the following criteria:

Criteria	Comments	Action to Improve
Clarity and pronunciation		
Organization		
Details and examples		
Grammar and vocabulary		

Now listen to the sample response. How was it different from yours? How was it similar? You will find a transcript of this audio passage (82.7S, Task 3 Response 2) at the end of the chapter.

🎧 **82.7S, Task 3 Response 2**

You're almost there! You only have one more chapter to complete before you have reviewed all of Kaplan's *TOEFL iBT with CD-ROM*. When you are ready, turn to Chapter 8 to learn the last reading, writing, listening, and speaking skills and strategies.

CHAPTER 7 AUDIO TRANSCRIPTS

72. Lesson 7—Listening, Note-Taking Practice

Narrator: Now listen to part of a lecture in a cognitive science class.

Professor: In robotics there are, simply put, two schools of thought when it comes to the development of humanoid robots. The traditional justification for developing this technology is to create tools that are more economically efficient than ah…humans or to provide needy groups such as the elderly with ways of remaining more self-sufficient for longer. On the other hand, a team at the Computational Neuroscience Laboratories in Kyoto, Japan sees robotics as a means of learning about the human brain.

Student: I thought it was fairly widely acknowledged that robots are nothing like humans. If that's the case, how can that team learn anything about the human brain from robots?

Professor: Indeed, you are quite right. Robots and people are very different. The human brain contains billions of neurons that are interconnected in extremely complex ways. How connections between those neurons are made and how those neurological interactions control movement and problem solving is still poorly understood. No computer has yet come close to simulating how a brain works. However, teams of neurologists and computer scientists are collaborating to test theories of how the brain works by building humanoid robots that incorporate simplified models of what certain groups of neurons in the brain are doing. First they conduct experiments on human subjects in magnetic-resonance imaging machines…you know about MRIs, right? Good. So, they get subjects to perform specific task and then they observe which parts of the brain light up, indicating increased blood flow. This, they believe, represents internal models of the interactions required to perform the task. Then they combine the magnetic imaging data with electrical and magnetic recording techniques to "decode" how the mind works. From that so-called "decoding", they attempt to build models.

Student: I heard this group recently received a large grant to expand their research. Could you explain how that can be justified? What are the benefits of using robots to understand the brain? I can appreciate the value of developing robots to increase efficiency, but isn't this a bit of a stretch?

Professor: Good question, one that is frequently raised by critics of the Kyoto lab. Their motivation lies in using robots to gain insights into how people move; think; make decisions and interact. If doctors had a more solid understanding of how the brain works, it would certainly enhance their ability to help patients with brain injuries. First they are trying to find out how healthy brains work. Later on, they'll be able to simulate damaged brains by switching off, or limiting certain areas of the robotic controls. Secondly, by creating something that resembles the human brain, we'll be able to learn more about how we learn. There is a Japanese proverb that says: "To teach is to learn." In this research, scientists can literally observe how a robot learns. They can watch what algorithms are running in the robot's computer control center while a scientist "teaches" it a new movement or type of interaction. Those are the two main benefits that are hoped to come out of this research. How does that sound?

Student: Fair enough.

Professor: Now, can someone explain why this is such a controversial approach to robotics?

Student: Well, um…I am not sure, but it seems kind of backward compared to the stuff we have been studying in this class. I mean, we've been reading about projects that are trying to figure out how to get robots to do certain things, like handle hazardous materials or explore other planets. Most robotics labs are working out ways to improve a robot's vision or navigational controls using digital technology and basic mechanics. Um, this research doesn't seem to be about making the robot do something, it's about understanding how humans do stuff.

Professor: Very well said. The focus is indeed on the human brain, rather than on the robot. The goal is to understand the brain by creating the brain. Now, that is not to say that this research won't also yield benefits in the field of robotics. In fact many believe that using robots to understand the human brain could eventually help produce more autonomous robots. As you will find out in next week's reading, we are still a long way from true A.I.—artificial intelligence, that is. Most robots still can't do anything that they are not specifically programmed to do. Professor Minsky describes today's robots as "uniformly stupid."

Please leave your papers on the desk at the front. When I read them I hope I won't be reminded too much of today's robots!

73. Lesson 7—Listening, Main Idea Practice

Professor: A friend of mine called me recently; he was very distressed. He said, "Mike, what do you do about all those…well, I won't repeat all the same words he used…what do you do about all those pop-up ads?" Now, I could tell by the stress in his voice that pop-ups weren't the problem; I suspected he had a virus. And when I took a look at his computer, sure enough, his computer screen was littered with pop-ups, popping up faster than he was able to close them. It was like he was playing Space Invaders, and losing. We double-clicked on Internet Explorer and waited and waited and waited. In the meantime, Bill kept trying to kill the pop-ups. But then everything locked up. He hit control-alt-delete and waited some more. His programs were all in "not responding" status. All telltale symptoms of infection: lots of pop-ups, processing time slows to a crawl, uh…the computer locks up…well, fortunately, he had a back up of his critical files, so we used his system restore CDs to re-format the hard drive and restore his computer to its original condition. Now, the question is…what is a computer virus, how did Bill get it, and what can he do to protect his computer in the future?

A computer virus is code written for the express purpose of replicating itself on many different computers and hijacking the computers' functionality to some degree. Computer viruses work basically the same as biological viruses do. They don't really live until they take over the, uh, machinery of the thing they're invading…the cells in your body…the software in your computer. And like their biological counterparts, they also range in severity: anything from the common cold to Ebola. Some cause minor disruptions that can be fixed easily; others wipe out everything on your hard drive. Not only can they erase all your data, they can also steal it. So, I guess you could say Bill's computer had a bad case of the flu. It could've been a lot better, but…it could've been a lot worse too. But where biological and computer viruses differ is in how they cause you harm once they've spread.

You can get the flu by just breathing the same air as someone who has it; and when you do, the flu virus takes over your cells immediately to cause you harm. But, computer viruses need to be activated by a human, uh, action to make your computer "sick", so to speak. Well, most of them anyway. A subclass of viruses, called worms, can spread regardless of the user's actions, as was the case with the Code Red Worm that exploited a security hole in Microsoft's IIS server back in the summer of 2001. And that was a big deal because it affected 350,000 servers, and forced the White House to change its IP address temporarily to avoid an assault. But, anyway, most viruses need to be executed by a person. And most of them are spread through e-mail messages, as attachments. They can sit in your e-mail inbox, or on your hard drive (if you happen to save them there). But once you open it…once you double-click on it…the virus is launched. And once that happens, you can do nothing more than pray that it's the 24-hour flu and not Ebola.

Just like any doctor will tell you, the best medicine is preventive medicine. And this goes for your computer as well. This means having security software installed on your PC or Mac. First, make sure you have a firewall. As the name suggests, this is a software program that protects your computer from danger by screening out, uh…hackers, viruses, and worms. But the firewall is only the first line of defense. The second is uh, up-to-date anti-virus software. Since many viruses are attached in e-mails or masquerade as legitimate programs (which are called Trojan horses by the way) the firewall is not able to screen them out. The last line of defense is you. As I, uh, said before, it's the action of a person that launches the virus. So, be skeptical of any e-mails with attachments from people you don't know. Don't open them unless you trust the source.

Now, I've given you some broad strokes here. What I'd like to do now is go over some specific anti-virus software programs and other anti-viral strategies to keep your computer safe. But, before I do that, are there any questions so far?

74. Lesson 7—Listening, Combined Skills Practice

Professor: Unfortunately, the use of facial recognition in public video surveillance hasn't quite lived up to expectations. Remember all the hype surrounding the technology at the 2001 Super Bowl in Tampa? Well, two years later, Tampa police stopped using facial recognition software because it failed to lead to even one arrest. At Boston's Logan International Airport, two systems failed 39% of the time in a test with volunteers. Officials got a lot of flak from privacy and civil liberties groups who claimed the error rates are too high, given the imprecision of the software.

For example, the system assigns a value of comparison on a scale of one to ten. A match is declared if the score is above a predetermined threshold. So, let's say the administrator sets it at seven or eight. The probability of a match wouldn't have to meet such a high percentage. Also, the measurements of the face can also be distorted by changes in age and weight…not to mention obstructions caused by facial hair and sunglasses. All these variables open the door for falsely accused suspects, or false positives.

False negatives are also a drawback. Facecams have been touted as a way to prevent the recurrence of another 9/11. But only two of that day's nineteen hijackers were already known to authorities, which means that, even if all nineteen faces had been compared to those in the database, only two would have shown up as a match.

In addition to accuracy concerns, some worry about how this technology may be used for other things in the future…anything from an Orwellian government tracking our movements to, uh…businesses using information about our habits for direct mail advertising campaigns.

75. Lesson 7—Speaking, Task 3 Narrator 1

Narrator: In this question, you will read a notice and listen to a conversation about the content of the notice. After you hear the question, you will have 30 seconds to prepare your response and 60 seconds to speak.

Western University has put out the following notice on their website.

You have 45 seconds to read the announcement. Begin reading now.

76. Lesson 7—Speaking, Task 3 Conversation 1

Narrator: Listen to two students as they discuss this announcement.

Student A: What is this all about? People have to kill their electronic pets? What's an electronic pet?

Student B: Oh, it's a big deal. You know Sally? Well, she was totally crazy about some weird computer program that behaved like an animal. She had to feed it and stuff.

Student A: Are you serious? How can you feed a computer program?

Student B: I'm not sure how it worked exactly…I think she had to click on various things at regular intervals and then the animal got food and water and, I don't know, kind of cuddles and stuff.

Student A: Wow, sounds weird.

Student B: Yes, it was pretty strange. If she forgot to feed it or something, it would get sick, and then she would feel real bad. At one stage, she was working a lot in the library and her …"pet"…whatever it is, got really sick and she quit doing her assignments, she wouldn't show up for our study group.

Student A: Maybe it's just as well that they are going to be banned.

Student B: Definitely, but I imagine Sally will be pretty distraught! Good thing the counselors will be on hand.

77. Lesson 7—Speaking, Task 3 Prompt 1

Both students support the new rule prohibiting electronic pets. Explain why they support the new rule, using information from the conversation regarding a classmate's behavior.

78. Lesson 7—Speaking, Task 3 Sample Response 1

One of the students didn't know what electronic pets were, so she probably didn't have an opinion to start with. When the other student described the behavior or her friend who had an electronic pet, the first student agreed that they should be banned. The reason that both students support the ban is that the friend started doing poorly in her university work because she giving so much attention to her pet. She missed assignments and study group meetings. So by the end of the conversation, they both agreed that the electronic pet ban was a good thing.

79. Lesson 7—Speaking, Task 3 Narrator 2

Narrator: In this question, you will read a notice and listen to a conversation about the content of the notice. After you hear the question, you will have 30 seconds to prepare your response and 60 seconds to speak.

The University of the Arts posted this notice in preparation for the registration of the upcoming fall semester.

80. Lesson 7—Speaking, Task 3 Conversation 2

Narrator: Listen to two students as they discuss this announcement.

Student A: Oh no…I knew this was coming, but I really hoped I'd graduate before it happened.

Student B: What's the problem? Don't you like e-planners?

Student A: I guess that's just one of the challenges of being a so-called "mature" student. I just don't like technology. My fingers don't fit on those stupid little keys; I hate the screen; I can never remember what those symbols mean…

Student B: Wow, I thought everyone used e-planners. How have you managed without one?

Student A: I have an old-fashioned leather-bound notebook and pencil with an eraser on the end. It works just fine.

Student B: I'll give you a hand with the e-planner if you like. Once you get it set up, it's pretty user-friendly.

Student A: Well, that's very kind of you, I'd appreciate that. I never thought I'd have to learn so much high-tech stuff when I decided to go back to school.

Student B: You never know when it might come in handy! Let's go check out the selection in the bookstore. We'll find one you like and then I'll show you how the timetable function works.

Student A: Thanks, I feel better already.

81. Lesson 7—Speaking, Task 3 Prompt 2

One of the students has a problem. Using information from the notice and from the conversation describe what the student's problem is and how the other student will help.

82. Lesson 7—Speaking, Task 3 Sample Response 2

There is a new rule at this university that students will have to use something called an electronic planner. I guess this is a gadget for scheduling and things like that. One of the students is upset about the new rule, because he doesn't like technology and he has a difficult time with e-planners. He prefers to use a paper notebook. The other student is surprised that somebody doesn't know how to use the e-planner and offers to help out by showing how to set it up and how to use the timetable.

Chapter 8: **Lesson Set 8**
Theme—Sports and Entertainment

Chapter 8, the final chapter in this book, continues to review more reading, writing, listening, and speaking skills and strategies you will need to score high on the TOEFL. Make sure to complete all the practice exercises and sample questions so that you can get the most out of these lessons.

LESSON 8—READING: SYNONYMS, INFERENCE, AND CAUSE AND EFFECT

In this lesson, we will cover more reading skills and strategies that will help lead to success on test day. You will also have the opportunity to review some of the strategies you learned in previous lessons as well as to learn more about the question types found on the Reading section of the TOEFL. If you feel uncertain about any of the concepts or strategies you have learned so far, continue to review the lessons throughout this book.

Synonyms

Certain words that you may consider synonyms are actually not quite synonyms because one of them has a more specific meaning than the other. For example, the word *truck* is more specific than the word *vehicle*, just as the word *rose* is more specific than the word *flower*.

Synonyms Practice

Look at the list of words that follows the passage "A Guide to Acting." For each word, find a word with a more specific meaning in the passage. Some words may have more than one possible answer. The first has been done as an example.

A Guide to Acting

If America had ever had its own monarchy, it's possible that Hollywood stars would not have become as admired, and therefore as persecuted, as they are today. Tabloids and paparazzi now detail the events of these actors' lives just as society papers used to recount the goings-on of kings, queens, dukes, and duchesses in countries with a ruling noble class. Because they perform a service that is beneficial to all levels of society, the service of entertainment, actors may arguably merit greater respect than aristocrats. However, does the service they provide require enough skill to be deigned an art? Do they truly deserve their high salaries and status? What does an actor actually undergo in order to become "great"? There are many different methods an actor can follow, techniques he can learn, but some of the most interesting to the layman are those of emotional memory, improvisation, and physical exercise.

Method acting, an acting technique ascribed to Konstantin Stanislavski, prescribes emotional memory as the answer to any acting dilemma. Essentially, this means that an actor must recall a memory from his own past that is similar to the situation he must pretend to be experiencing. For instance, an actor is playing a grieving parent. His son has just died unexpectedly in a car accident. If the actor has lost a son in a similar way, he can remember his feelings at that time, transport himself back to that moment, and relive his emotions such that his character will clearly communicate them to the audience. Even if the actor has not had exactly the same experience, which is usually the case, he can draw on a memory which is similarly sorrowful. He can remember another family member or friend who passed away suddenly, or he can simply identify the emotion that needs to be transmitted, in this case grief, and go back to any memory that helps him recognize and feel it. A failure in school or the loss of a job might be enough to trigger this emotion. It may seem that actors who have had pasts which are emotionally turbulent might be best suited to the emotional memory technique, but those who are able to harness basic feelings from any past event can be equally successful.

Improvisation, more of a practice technique than a method, tends to impress audiences more than any other skill an actor can master. Picture an empty stage with an actor standing in the middle. He reaches into a paper bag and pulls out an object, a fork for example. Now he must create a skit based on or including that fork, with no script and no preparation. He could simply sit down on the stage and pretend he is eating, but show the act of eating so realistically that the audience forgets he has no food in front of him. He could pretend the fork is something else, a hair ornament, a tiny shovel, or a sword, and use it accordingly. He could likewise instantaneously develop a dialogue that repeats the word "fork" so frequently that the fork becomes a character in and of itself. The thrill of improvisation for the viewer is that it seems to necessitate such unbelievably quick creativity. The importance of improvisation for the actor is that practicing such rapid shifts of imagination allows him to move in and out of character with little effort.

Most people would agree that good acting requires mental effort, but most would not consider physical effort part of an actor's job description. After all, stunt doubles are typically employed to do any physically challenging or dangerous tasks such as jumping out of a burning building or swimming across a large expanse of water. Despite this reality, an actor who does not at least appear physically fit is much less likely to reach the heights of stardom in Hollywood. Also notable is the fact that many acting schools emphasize physical exercise as an important technique for relaxation. An aspiring actor often spends a significant amount of time raising his hands above his head, clenching his feet, swaying back and forth, and bobbing his head up and down just to point out a few examples. Ridiculous though it may sound, this ability to relax and to be limber is just another technique actors use to perfect their craft.

Watching a film or TV show, the average viewer has definite opinions about who is a good and who is a bad actor, yet these opinions rarely take into account the preparatory work that has gone into the final performance. Though amusing, acting is much harder than it looks, and the phrase "I could do that," should not be uttered lightly. In fact, had the monarchies of many countries labored as diligently to entertain and manipulate their subjects, perhaps there would be far fewer democracies in existence at present.

1.   reporters - ___paparazzi___ (paragraph 1)

2.   royalty - _____ (1)

3.   entertainer - _____ (1)

4.   problem - _____ (2)

5.   sad - _____ (2)

6.   use (verb) - _____ (2)

7.   learn - _____ (3)

8.   play (noun) - _____ (3)

9.   tool - _____ (3)

10. quickly - _____ (3)

11. moving - _____ (4)

12. said - _____ (5)

Answers

1. reporters - __paparazzi__ (paragraph 1)

2. royalty - __aristocrats__

3. entertainer - _actor_ (1)

4. problem - __dilemma__ (2)

5. sad - _grieving_ (2)

6. use (verb) - __draw on__ (2)

7. learn - __master__ (3)

8. play (noun) - _skit_ (3)

9. tool - __shovel__ (3)

10. quickly - __instantaneously__ (3)

11. moving - __physical effort__ (4)

12. said - __uttered__ (5)

Reading for Inferences and Paraphrasing

This book has continued to emphasize the importance of understanding inferences (what is not explicitly stated in a passage) and of paraphrasing (putting an author's words into your own words). To help you master these critical skills, complete the Reading for Inferences and Paraphrasing Practice.

Reading for Inferences and Paraphrasing Practice

This passage, also found in the Synonyms Practice, discusses the topic of acting in a fairly typical illustrative expository style. Read the passage and answer the questions that follow.

A Guide to Acting

If America had ever had its own monarchy, it's possible that Hollywood stars would not have become as admired, and therefore as persecuted, as they are today. Tabloids and paparazzi now detail the events of these actors' lives just as society papers used to recount the goings-on of kings, queens, dukes, and duchesses in countries with a ruling noble class. Because they perform a service that is beneficial to all levels of society, the service of entertainment, actors may arguably merit greater respect than aristocrats. However, does the service they provide require enough skill to be deigned an art? Do they truly deserve their high salaries and status? What does an actor actually undergo in order to become "great"? There are many different methods an actor can follow, techniques he can learn, but some of the most interesting to the layman are those of emotional memory, improvisation, and physical exercise.

Method acting, an acting technique ascribed to Konstantin Stanislavski, prescribes emotional memory as the answer to any acting dilemma. Essentially, this means that an actor must recall a memory from his own past that is similar to the situation he must pretend to be experiencing. For instance, an actor is playing a grieving parent. His son has just died unexpectedly in a car accident. If the actor has lost a son in a similar way, he can remember his feelings at that time, transport himself back to that moment, and relive his emotions such that his character will clearly communicate them to the audience. Even if the actor has not had exactly the same experience, which is usually the case, he can draw on a memory which is similarly sorrowful. He can remember another family member or friend who passed away suddenly, or he can simply identify the emotion that needs to be transmitted, in this case grief, and go back to any memory that helps him recognize and feel it. A failure in school or the loss of a job might be enough to trigger this emotion. It may seem that actors who have had pasts which are emotionally turbulent might be best suited to the emotional memory technique, but those who are able to harness basic feelings from any past event can be equally successful.

Improvisation, more of a practice technique than a method, tends to impress audiences more than any other skill an actor can master. Picture an empty stage with an actor standing in the middle. He reaches into a paper bag and pulls out an object, a fork for example. Now he must create a skit based on or including that fork, with no script and no preparation. He could simply sit down on the stage and pretend he is eating, but show the act of eating so realistically that the audience forgets he has no food in front of him. He could pretend the fork is something else, a hair ornament, a tiny shovel, or a sword, and use it accordingly. He could likewise instantaneously develop a dialogue that repeats the word "fork" so frequently that the fork becomes a character in and of itself. The thrill of improvisation for the viewer is that it seems to necessitate such unbelievably quick creativity. The importance of improvisation for the actor is that practicing such rapid shifts of imagination allows him to move in and out of character with little effort.

Most people would agree that good acting requires mental effort, but most would not consider physical effort part of an actor's job description. After all, stunt doubles are typically employed to do any physically challenging or dangerous tasks such as jumping out of a burning building or swimming across a large expanse of water. Despite this reality, an actor who does not at least appear physically fit is much less likely to reach the heights of stardom in Hollywood. Also notable is the fact that many acting schools emphasize physical exercise as an important technique for relaxation. An aspiring actor often spends a significant amount of time raising his hands above his head, clenching his feet, swaying back and forth, and bobbing his head up and down just to point out a few examples. Ridiculous though it may sound, this ability to relax and to be limber is just another technique actors use to perfect their craft.

Watching a film or TV show, the average viewer has definite opinions about who is a good and who is a bad actor, yet these opinions rarely take into account the preparatory work that has gone into the final performance. Though amusing, acting is much harder than it looks, and the phrase "I could do that," should not be uttered lightly. In fact, had the monarchies of many countries labored as diligently to entertain and manipulate their subjects, perhaps there would be far fewer democracies in existence at present.

1. Describe the main idea of the text in your own words.

   _____

   _____

2. Locate two of the topic sentences in the text, and then rewrite them using your own words.

   _____

   _____

3. Find the sentence in paragraph 4 that explains why acting schools require actors to do physical exercise, and then rewrite the sentence in your own words.

_____

_____

4. Look at the word *diligently* in paragraph 5. Using contextual clues to help you, try to guess a less specific synonym for this word.

_____

_____

5. Match the following examples with the techniques they would most probably fit under.

Using a blanket as a cape, a tablecloth, and then as a flag in a short play.

Technique: _____

Recalling a happy childhood memory to portray joy effectively.

Technique: _____

6. Based on information in the text, what can you guess might be true of an overweight person who wants to be an actor?

_____

_____

7. What is the author's opinion about the difficulty level of acting?

_____

_____

Answers

1. Actors are mistakenly perceived as having an easy life. They must work hard to succeed.

2. *However, does the service they provide require enough skill to be deigned an art?*
Are actors deserving of the acclaim and attention that they receive from the public?
Most people would agree that good acting requires mental effort, but most would not consider physical effort part of an actor's job description.
While many would agree that acting requires mental ability, it is also much more physically rigorous than people believe.

3. *Also notable is the fact that many acting schools emphasize physical exercise as an important technique for relaxation.*
Many acting schools encourage actors to exercise in order to promote relaxation.

4. thoroughly

5. Using a blanket as a cape, a tablecloth, and then as a flag in a short play.
Technique: _____ improvization _____

Recalling a happy childhood memory to portray joy effectively.
Technique: _____ method acting _____

6. It is less likely that an overweight actor will become a star.

7. Acting is much harder than the average person believes.

Cause and Effect

Cause and effect essays can be organized in several different ways. In some situations, there may be just one cause and one effect that need to be noted. In other cases, there may be several causes and only one effect or vice versa. In still other situations, there may be a causal chain. The following is an example of a causal chain.

A student forgets to turn on his alarm. → The student oversleeps. → The student misses his bus. → The student arrives late to class. → The student cannot finish his test in time. → The student fails his test.

Cause and Effect Practice

Now read this passage and answer the questions that follow it.

The Olympic Effect

Since their beginning in 1896, the Olympic Games have been the gold standard of athletic prowess: Olympic competitors are the best in the world, and no trophy compares with an Olympic gold medal. Increasingly, however, the athletic competitions have been matched, if not overshadowed, by the fierce competitions between cities and nations vying to host the Games. So much money and prestige is at stake in the Olympics that the phenomenon has been given a name: the Olympic Effect. Principally an economic force capable of affecting the business climate of the host community for years before, during, and after the Games, the Olympic Effect can also exert a powerful influence on the environment and society of the host community.

Economic impacts of the Olympic Games are complex. In the first place, preparations for the Games generally include vast investments not only in the stadiums, tracks, and other sports venues for the Games themselves, but also in local highways, hotels, and airports. Thousands of jobs are created and billions of dollars are spent: Australia spent $2.1 billion for the Sydney Games in 2000, and Greece at least $11 billion only four years later. Long-term effects are generally positive, as the Games tend to improve the international image of the host city. Tourism experiences the greatest benefit, though few thorough studies have quantified this effect. On the other hand, during the event, the region hosting the Games may actually experience a drop in tourism and retail income, as people try to avoid the crowds, traffic, and price hikes they expect to find in the host city. Some Utah ski resort operators experienced a twenty to thirty percent drop in visitors during the Salt Lake City Games.

The environmental repercussions of the Olympic Effect are also mixed. On the one hand, since the Sydney Games (the "Green Games"), participating communities have had active recycling programs, emphasized renewable energy sources, and built or extended mass transit systems, like Salt Lake City's 21-kilometer TRAX light rail system. Some, like Sydney and Beijing (2008) have made notable efforts to clean up their municipal environments. Sydney actually built most of its Olympic venue over a reclaimed toxic waste dump that had once blighted the city. To clear its polluted air, Beijing has converted much of its energy production from coal to natural gas, and implemented new smokestack and vehicle emissions guidelines. Medical researchers estimate that the benefit to Beijing residents' health will amount to many billions of dollars over the coming decades. On the other hand, the Games themselves result in great consumption of fossil fuels and strain on waste-disposal systems. The Winter Games in particular are often accompanied by accelerated human development of important wildlife habitat.

Social aspects of the Olympic Effect are varied, and include an improved global perception of the host city and a growth in civic pride. But the biggest social impact of the Olympic Effect is a predictable one: a sharp growth in public interest in those sports highlighted during recent Games. In the United States, this can best be seen in the ice sports. The figure-skating drama between Nancy Kerrigan and Tonya Harding in 1994 played a part in piquing this interest, and so did the gold medal of Tara Lipinski in 1998; American successes in speed skating and hockey can be added. The result has been a fifty-percent increase in the number of ice arenas in the United States in the last fifteen years. Dallas, Texas built eight between 2000 and 2002 alone. Related sports such as speed skating, hockey, and even curling have seen a tremendous growth in interest—even warm-winter Southern cities like Tampa Bay, Florida and Atlanta, Georgia now have hockey teams.

When the Olympic Games were first held in 1896, they were conceived as a celebration of the human body and of the human spirit. This has not changed. But now the Games are something more: they profoundly shape the lives of people who never set foot inside the arenas themselves. They are the paramount international pageant, turning the spotlight on cities, nations, and people, prompting them to find the best in themselves and hold it up for all to see. That is the true Olympic effect.

1. Are there more causes or more effects listed?

   _____

   _____

2. Which causal chains exist in the passage? Write them in the space that follows.

   _____

   _____

Certain transition words and phrases are typically found in a cause and effect essay as well. The chart lists some of them.

Cause	Effect
because	as a result
due to	consequently
one cause is	one result is
if...then	therefore
since	thus
leads to	results in

3. Are any of these words used in the passage? What other words help you recognize that this is a cause and effect essay?

Answers

1. There are more effects listed.

2. The Olympics are assigned to a city. Preparations begin, including new stadiums, tracks, highways, hotels and airports. Jobs are created and money is invested as the international image of the city improves. Once the event starts, tourism and retail business may increase.

3.

Cause	Effect
since	*results in*

Other words include: benefit, repercussions

Understanding the question types is important for knowing how and where you can apply your strategies. Keep reading to learn more.

Question Types

There are 13 question types on the Reading section of the TOEFL. These are:

- Identifying the Main Idea
- Summarizing the Most Important Points
- Understanding Rhetorical Function
- Understanding Details
- Understanding Details as They Relate to the Main Idea (Multiple-Choice)
- Understanding Details as They Relate to the Main Idea (Schematic Table)
- Inferring Word Meaning from Context
- Defining a Key Term
- Locating a Referent
- Understanding Coherence
- Drawing an Inference
- Inferring the Author's Opinion or Attitude
- Paraphrasing

This lesson will continue to review the following question types:

- Drawing an Inference
- Inferring the Author's Opinion or Attitude
- Paraphrasing

Question Type 11 Revisited—Drawing an Inference

There are 3 passages in the Reading section of the TOEFL. Each passage is followed by 0 to 2 *inference* questions.

One particularly difficult reading skill to master is the skill of drawing inferences. A good inference is one which is supported by information in the text but which is not directly stated. Look at the following sentences from the passage "The Olympic Effect."

> Since their beginning in 1896, the Olympic Games have been the gold standard of athletic prowess: Olympic competitors are the best in the world, and no trophy compares with an Olympic gold medal.

Based on these sentences, we can infer that:

> The Olympic Games did not exist in 1890.

This is a good inference because the sentences say that the Olympic Games began in 1896.

We can also infer that:

> Many athletes would be proud to win an Olympic gold medal.

This is a good inference because the sentences say that "no trophy compares" with an Olympic gold medal, meaning it is the highest honor. However, we cannot infer the following:

> The Olympic Games were created in 1896 to make Olympic competitors better athletes.

Though some key words, like *Olympic competitors*, *1896*, and the *Olympic Games*, are repeated from the original sentences, this is a bad inference because no reason for the creation of the Olympic Games is mentioned or implied in the sentences.

Using the inference strategies you have practiced, re-read the passage on "The Olympic Effect" (repeated here) and answer the questions that follow.

The Olympic Effect

> Since their beginning in 1896, the Olympic Games have been the gold standard of athletic prowess: Olympic competitors are the best in the world, and no trophy compares with an Olympic gold medal. Increasingly, however, the athletic competitions have been matched, if not overshadowed, by the fierce competitions between cities and nations vying to host the Games. So much money and prestige is at stake in the Olympics that the phenomenon has been given a name: the Olympic Effect. Principally, an economic force capable of affecting the business climate of the host community for years before, during, and after the Games, the Olympic Effect can also exert a powerful influence on the environment and society of the host community.
>
> Economic impacts of the Olympic Games are complex. In the first place, preparations for the Games generally include vast investments not only in the stadiums, tracks, and other sports venues for the Games themselves, but also in local highways, hotels, and

airports. Thousands of jobs are created and billions of dollars are spent: Australia spent $2.1 billion for the Sydney Games in 2000, and Greece at least $11 billion only four years later. Long-term effects are generally positive, as the Games tend to improve the international image of the host city. Tourism experiences the greatest benefit, though few thorough studies have quantified this effect. On the other hand, during the event, the region hosting the Games may actually experience a drop in tourism and retail income, as people try to avoid the crowds, traffic, and price hikes they expect to find in the host city. Some Utah ski resort operators experienced a twenty to thirty percent drop in visitors during the Salt Lake City Games.

The environmental repercussions of the Olympic Effect are also mixed. On the one hand, since the Sydney Games (the "Green Games"), participating communities have had active recycling programs, emphasized renewable energy sources, and built or extended mass transit systems, like Salt Lake City's 21-kilometer TRAX light rail system. Some, like Sydney and Beijing (2008) have made notable efforts to clean up their municipal environments. Sydney actually built most of its Olympic venue over a reclaimed toxic waste dump that had once blighted the city. To clear its polluted air, Beijing has converted much of its energy production from coal to natural gas, and implemented new smokestack and vehicle emissions guidelines. Medical researchers estimate that the benefit to Beijing residents' health will amount to many billions of dollars over the coming decades. On the other hand, the Games themselves result in great consumption of fossil fuels and strain on waste-disposal systems. The Winter Games in particular are often accompanied by accelerated human development of important wildlife habitat.

Social aspects of the Olympic Effect are varied, and include an improved global perception of the host city and a growth in civic pride. But the biggest social impact of the Olympic Effect is a predictable one: a sharp growth in public interest in those sports highlighted during recent Games. In the United States, this can best be seen in the ice sports. The figure-skating drama between Nancy Kerrigan and Tonya Harding in 1994 played a part in piquing this interest, and so did the gold medal of Tara Lipinski in 1998; American successes in speed skating and hockey can be added. The result has been a fifty-percent increase in the number of ice arenas in the United States in the last fifteen years. Dallas, Texas built eight between 2000 and 2002 alone. Related sports such as speed skating, hockey, and even curling have seen a tremendous growth in interest—even warm-winter Southern cities like Tampa Bay, Florida and Atlanta, Georgia now have hockey teams.

When the Olympic Games were first held in 1896, they were conceived as a celebration of the human body and of the human spirit. This has not changed. But now the Games are something more: they profoundly shape the lives of people who never set foot inside the arenas themselves. They are the paramount international pageant, turning the spotlight on cities, nations, and people, prompting them to find the best in themselves and hold it up for all to see. That is the true Olympic effect.

Based on the information in paragraph 2, what can be inferred about the economic benefits of the Olympic Games?

Ⓐ They largely affect sporting arenas.

Ⓑ They outlast the Games themselves.

Ⓒ They are not particularly widespread in a city.

Ⓓ They do not affect most people in the Olympic city.

Choice (B) is correct. Paragraph 2 states that "local highways, hotels, and airports" are built or improved during the Olympic Games. It is therefore a good inference to state that the economic benefits will outlast the Games since airports, hotels, and highways will still be used frequently afterward. Choice (A) is incorrect because highways, hotels, and airports are not sporting arenas. Choices (C) and (D) are both incorrect because many areas are affected, so the effects are widespread and affect most people in some way.

Now read and answer the following questions.

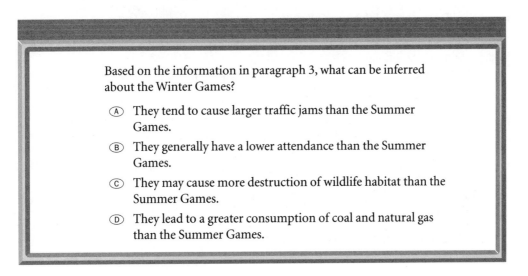

Based on the information in paragraph 3, what can be inferred about the Winter Games?

Ⓐ They tend to cause larger traffic jams than the Summer Games.

Ⓑ They generally have a lower attendance than the Summer Games.

Ⓒ They may cause more destruction of wildlife habitat than the Summer Games.

Ⓓ They lead to a greater consumption of coal and natural gas than the Summer Games.

Choice (A) is incorrect. The passage does not discuss the size of traffic jams. Choice (B) is incorrect. The passage does not mention attendance levels. Choice (C) is correct. The passage describes "accelerated human development of important wildlife habitat," which implies that it is altered or destroyed. Choice (D) is incorrect. The passage describes Beijing's transition from coal to natural gas, implying that the use of natural gas increased, and the use of coal decreased.

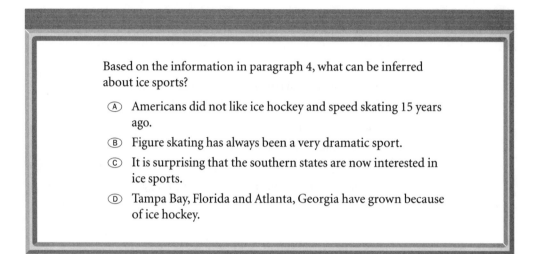

Based on the information in paragraph 4, what can be inferred about ice sports?

(A) Americans did not like ice hockey and speed skating 15 years ago.

(B) Figure skating has always been a very dramatic sport.

(C) It is surprising that the southern states are now interested in ice sports.

(D) Tampa Bay, Florida and Atlanta, Georgia have grown because of ice hockey.

Choice (A) is incorrect. It can be inferred that these sports were less popular 15 years ago, but we cannot infer that Americans "did not like them." The fact that there were *any* arenas 15 years ago is proof that at least some Americans did like these sports. Choice (B) is incorrect. The passage refers to a specific "drama" or incident related to figure skating, not to the drama of figure skating as a whole. Choice (C) is correct. The word *even* here is a cue that the author views this detail as surprising. Choice (D) is incorrect. *Growth* refers not to growth of the cities, but to the interest in ice sports in those cities.

Eliminating Distracters in Inference Questions

To answer inference questions correctly, you will also need to avoid distracters. The types of distracters for this type of question include:

- Answer choices that include words from the passage but that are untrue
- Answer choices that you might guess to be true based on previous knowledge or intuition, but which are unsupported by information in the passage

Now look at the following questions based on the passage. Each is followed by a correct answer choice. Write three incorrect answer choices for each, making sure to use distracters.

1. Based on information in paragraph 3, what can be inferred about the environmental effects of the Olympic Games?

(A) They can be both positive and negative.

(B)

(C)

(D)

2. Based on information in paragraph 5, what can be inferred about the purpose of the Olympic Games?

    Ⓐ It has changed over the years.

    Ⓑ

    Ⓒ

    Ⓓ

Question Type 12 Revisited—Inferring the Author's Opinion or Attitude

There are 3 passages in the Reading section of the TOEFL. One passage is generally followed by 1 *author's opinion* question.

A specific inference you will have to draw on one passage in the Reading section is the author's opinion or attitude regarding the topic of the passage. The passages in the Reading section are expository, so the author's opinion is not explicitly stated and may not be obvious. However, as you skim a passage to identify the main idea, most important points, and organizational structure, you can watch for clues that indicate author's opinion or attitude.

You may remember from Chapter 4 that positive or negative statements, as reflected in the meaning of adjectives and adjective phrases, can be indicators of author's opinion. The conclusion of a passage is also a good place to look for indicators of an author's opinion, since it is here that the author must summarize his or her ideas. Look at the conclusion to the passage "The Olympic Effect":

> When the Olympic Games were first held in 1896, they were conceived as a celebration of the human body and of the human spirit. This has not changed. But now the Games are something more: they profoundly shape the lives of people who never set foot inside the arenas themselves. They are the paramount international pageant, turning the spotlight on cities, nations, and people, prompting them to find the best in themselves and hold it up for all to see. That is the true Olympic effect.

The verb phrase "profoundly shape the lives of people" and the participle phrase "prompting them to find the best in themselves" both indicate that the author believes the Olympics have a powerfully positive effect on people generally. These two phrases in the conclusion provide key insight into the author's opinion.

To answer author's opinion questions correctly, you will also need to avoid distracters. The incorrect answer choices in an author's opinion question are generally plausible opinions on the given topic, but the passage does not provide sufficient evidence to conclude that the author holds these opinions.

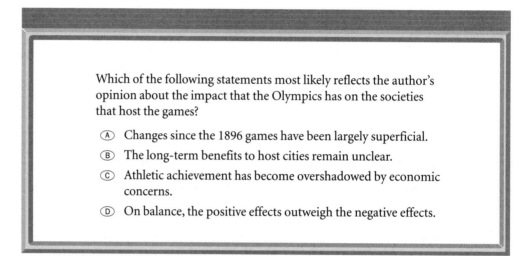

Which of the following statements most likely reflects the author's opinion about the impact that the Olympics has on the societies that host the games?

  Ⓐ Changes since the 1896 games have been largely superficial.

  Ⓑ The long-term benefits to host cities remain unclear.

  Ⓒ Athletic achievement has become overshadowed by economic concerns.

  Ⓓ On balance, the positive effects outweigh the negative effects.

The author discusses significant changes since the 1896 games in the ways that the Olympics affect people, so (A) cannot be correct. Although some questions about the long-term benefits to host cities may remain unanswered, the author discusses several evident effects, both positive and negative, so (B) is not a reasonable answer. The author discusses significant changes in the economic impact of the games, but nowhere is it stated that this overshadows athletic achievement. In fact, the first two sentences of the conclusion state that athletic achievement is still primary at the Olympics. As such, (C) is not an inference that can be drawn based on the information in the passage. Choice (D) is correct because, while the author outlines both positive and negative effects of the Olympics, the passage is generally weighted toward the positive effects.

Question Type 13 Revisited—Paraphrasing

There are 3 passages in the Reading section of the TOEFL. Each passage is followed by 0 or 1 *paraphrasing* question, for a total of 2 or 3 per test.

Rewriting sentences using your own words, also called paraphrasing, is extremely important both in university work and for the TOEFL. Paraphrasing is necessary to avoid plagiarism, stealing published authors' words. One question type in the Reading section of the TOEFL asks you to choose the correct paraphrase of a sentence from the reading passage. Incorrect answer choices are usually:

 • missing important information
 • different from the original meaning

For practice with this question type, read "The Olympic Effect" again and answer these questions.

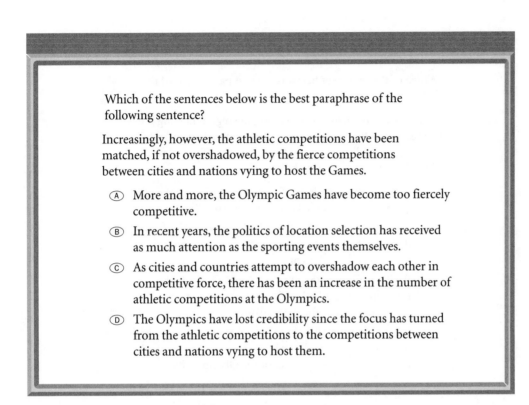

Which of the sentences below is the best paraphrase of the following sentence?

Increasingly, however, the athletic competitions have been matched, if not overshadowed, by the fierce competitions between cities and nations vying to host the Games.

(A) More and more, the Olympic Games have become too fiercely competitive.

(B) In recent years, the politics of location selection has received as much attention as the sporting events themselves.

(C) As cities and countries attempt to overshadow each other in competitive force, there has been an increase in the number of athletic competitions at the Olympics.

(D) The Olympics have lost credibility since the focus has turned from the athletic competitions to the competitions between cities and nations vying to host them.

The correct answer is choice (B). It correctly paraphrases the main idea of the original sentence that the focus of the Olympic Games has become divided between the games themselves and the choice of where the Games will be held. Choice (A) is incorrect because its meaning is different from the original meaning. The original sentence refers to competition for location selection becoming fierce, not to the games themselves. Choice (C) is also incorrect because its meaning is different from the original meaning. Choice (D) is incorrect for the same reason. There is no mention of the Games losing their credibility.

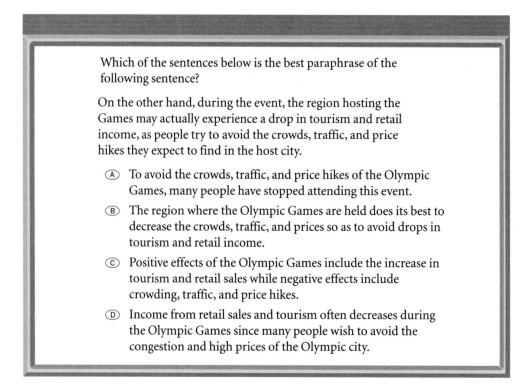

Which of the sentences below is the best paraphrase of the following sentence?

On the other hand, during the event, the region hosting the Games may actually experience a drop in tourism and retail income, as people try to avoid the crowds, traffic, and price hikes they expect to find in the host city.

(A) To avoid the crowds, traffic, and price hikes of the Olympic Games, many people have stopped attending this event.

(B) The region where the Olympic Games are held does its best to decrease the crowds, traffic, and prices so as to avoid drops in tourism and retail income.

(C) Positive effects of the Olympic Games include the increase in tourism and retail sales while negative effects include crowding, traffic, and price hikes.

(D) Income from retail sales and tourism often decreases during the Olympic Games since many people wish to avoid the congestion and high prices of the Olympic city.

Choice (A) is incorrect. This sentence explains why people have stopped attending a particular event, which is not what the original sentence describes. Choice (B) is incorrect. This sentence describes how cities try to reduce crowds and prices to attract tourists, which is not what the original sentence describes. Choice (C) is incorrect. This sentence describes an increase in tourism and sales, but the original sentence describes a decrease in both. Choice (D) is correct. This sentence describes a decrease in sales and tourism caused by people trying to avoid the crowds and high prices they expect during the games. This is a successful paraphrase of the original sentence.

When you are ready, move on to Lesson 8—Writing: More Practice with the Response Essay.

LESSON 8—WRITING: MORE PRACTICE WITH THE RESPONSE ESSAY

In this lesson, we will cover more writing skills and strategies that will help lead to success on test day. You will also have the opportunity to learn more about the tasks required for the Writing section of the TOEFL. If you feel uncertain about any of the concepts or strategies you have learned so far, continue to review the lessons throughout this book.

Previous lessons covered the following essay types:

- Descriptive Essays
- Definition Essays
- Persuasive Essays
- Compare/Contrast Essays
- Essays in Response to a Reading Passage and a Lecture

This lesson continues to review essays in response to a reading passage and a lecture.

Writing an Essay in Response to a Reading Passage and a Lecture

For the first essay in the TOEFL Writing section, you will have 3 minutes to read a passage about an academic topic. You may take notes as you read. Then you will listen to a lecture about the same topic and take notes while you listen. Information in the lecture will conflict somewhat with the information in the reading passage; that is, a different perspective on the topic will be presented.

After reading and listening, you will have 20 minutes to write a response to a question that asks you about the relationship between the reading and the lecture. The question will not ask you to express your opinion. You will be able to see the reading passage again when it is time for you to write, and you will be able to use the notes you took while reading and listening.

An effective response will be approximately 150–225 words long. It will be judged on the quality of your writing and on the completeness and accuracy of what you write.

Recall from Chapters 2 and 4 that we discussed the fact that the essay required for this task may have characteristics of a definition essay and of a compare/contrast essay. The reading passage and the lecture essentially define the topic in different ways, and you must synthesize and summarize those definitions.

Make sure to read the prompt carefully to determine exactly what it is asking you to do. In your response, be prepared to do the following:

- Summarize information provided in the reading passage and the lecture
- Define a specific term or idea
- Provide examples from the reading passage and lecture

Note-Taking

On the TOEFL, you will be able to take notes on reading and listening passages before writing about these passages. The most useful notes will contain all the key ideas from the passages and few unnecessary details. The following are tips to help you decide what is key information for your notes.

1. The written and spoken passages for the first writing task are often not in standard essay format. This means that there may not be a single sentence containing the thesis. You may have to read or listen to the entire passage to understand the main idea, or thesis.

2. Once you have identified the thesis of each passage, write it down in a single sentence. Your own summary must clearly identify the thesis of each passage.

3. What are the main arguments used in each passage to support its thesis? Write these down.

4. Examples, statistics, and other supporting details have been carefully chosen by the writer or speaker to prove a point and will help you to identify the main arguments.

5. Your notes should include the most important supporting details provided in the passage.

Note-Taking Practice

Read the following passage carefully. Take notes on what you read. Try to employ the note-taking strategies previously discussed.

Oprah's Book Club

One of the biggest phenomena to strike the publishing industry in the last decade was the advent of the Oprah Winfrey Book Club. Oprah Winfrey is the most-watched talk show host in American television, with 22 million viewers daily, or around eight percent of the American public. For several years, Oprah (as she's affectionately referred to) has been releasing a quarterly list of books that she thinks her fans ought to read.

While the critical response to her choices are somewhat mixed, the effect on sales of her chosen titles is unambiguous: they become instant bestsellers, sometimes propelling unknown authors to stardom, other times giving new life to established classics. John Steinbeck's *East of Eden*, Leo Tolstoy's *Anna Karenina*, and Gabriel Garcia Marquez's *One Hundred Years of Solitude* have all benefited from Oprah's golden touch, respected authors like Toni Morrison have been brought to a wider audience, and virtual unknowns like Wally Lamb have been brought squarely into the public eye. By mid-2004, Oprah had made forty-seven selections, and without fail, they flew from the bookstore shelves.

These numbers say something more significant than authorial fame and fortune, however. They tell us that a talk-show host can do something that the *New York Review of Books* cannot do: make reading interesting to millions of people who might otherwise have never picked up a book.

Notes

Now that you have practiced taking notes from a written passage, you will apply the same practice to taking notes from a short talk. You will find a transcript of this audio passage (83.8W, Note-Taking Practice) at the end of the chapter.

 83.8W, Note-Taking Practice

Notes

Summarizing

A *summary* is a condensed version of a written or spoken text. It contains the thesis and key ideas of the original text. A summary will contain only the most important supporting details from the original. Your summary should be about one-quarter of the length of the original. In the 20-minute timed TOEFL Writing section essay, your summary must reflect the logical relationship between the two passages—the reading and the listening. For example, does the listening contradict the reading? Or does the listening discuss a feature of the topic overlooked by the reading?

The structure of your response in the 20-minute timed writing task should be that of the conventional essay, with an introduction, body paragraphs, and conclusion. Your thesis should state your understanding of the relationship between the listening and the reading passages, and your body paragraphs should include the key ideas of each passage to support your thesis.

While your summary should accurately reflect information from the two passages, it should be written using your own words and not the language of the original. In other words, you must paraphrase. Simply repeating another person's words is considered plagiarism and is not only ethically wrong, but also prevents you from showing your skills as a writer. Paraphrasing allows you to demonstrate your understanding of the passages and your command of English at the same time.

Summarizing Practice

Write two summaries about Oprah's Book Club: one for the listening passage and one for the reading passage. Each should be ONE paragraph only. You should use the notes that you took while reading and listening.

Summary of Reading: Oprah's Book Club

Summary of Listening: Oprah's Book Club

Answers

Answers will vary, but here are two sample summaries.

Summary of Reading: Oprah's Book Club

Oprah Winfrey's Book Club has in part revitalized the publishing industry. The most watched talk-show host in America, her quarterly reading list has brought both old and new authors to the attention of the public, creating one commercial success after another. Despite a mixed critical response, her club is encouraging millions to read books they might never have considered.

Summary of Listening: Oprah's Book Club

While it has been good for the publishing industry, Oprah's Book Club has not achieved the same level of acclaim in the intellectual community because of a perceived "dumbing down" of the types of books selected in order to maximize profit. Famous authors have refused to have their books features on the show for this reason, despite the appearance of novels by literary greats such as Tolstoy, Steinbeck and Morrison.

Writing Conclusions

Your concluding paragraph is the last thing your reader sees of your essay. It is important that your conclusion leaves the reader with both a clear understanding of the message conveyed by your essay and a positive impression of your abilities as a writer. With a little practice, you will be able to write strong, effective conclusions that accomplish both of these goals.

Remember the two meanings of the English word *conclude*. The first, most common meaning is *to come to an end*: He *concluded* his speech with a flourish. This is not the meaning of *conclude* you should be focusing on as you write your concluding paragraph. Instead, you should be thinking of the second meaning, which is *to make a decision after a reasoned consideration of the facts*. In other words, you want your concluding paragraph to emphasize the message or lesson that logically proceeds from the facts and arguments you presented in the body of your essay. This means to remind your reader of your thesis and perhaps also to point out the broader implications or consequences of that thesis.

The following are tips to keep in mind as you write conclusions to your essays:

1. The conclusion's main job is to recall and emphasize the essay's thesis. It is best for you to do this in a fresh way, not simply by repeating the thesis statement.

2. The conclusion also benefits from a review of the essay's principal arguments or points of discussion. This is especially the case if the essay is particularly long or its topic difficult and complex.

3. Keep your conclusion concise. Do not include additional arguments or specific details. Instead, place these in the body paragraphs.

Essay Practice

Now you will read a passage, listen to part of a lecture, and write a response. This activity is similar to the first of two writing tasks that will be on the TOEFL.

You will have three minutes to read the following passage. You may take notes. After reading the passage, you will hear a short lecture on a related topic. Again, you may take notes while you listen.

The Super Bowl

The Super Bowl, the capstone of American football, is one of the greatest sports events in the world. With the possible exception of the Olympics, no other sports event in history has attracted as much interest from such a broad audience.

For those who want to see it in person, the face value for a Super Bowl ticket is $500 to $600. But the trading value is often much higher, $2,000 or $3,000. Not everyone can afford that price. And even the well-off may be limited by time and distance. That's why, according to the NFL in 2003, programming will be broadcast in more than 30 languages from 223 countries and territories throughout the world. Even in the United States, satellite radio is broadcasting the game in several languages for non-native speaking fans.

The Super Bowl also attracts staggering sums of money from advertisers, who consider the expense a good investment toward raising the profiles of their companies. During the dotcom boom in 2000, Internet companies were paying more than they made in revenue, pushing the average price for a thirty second slot to two million dollars. Companies that hadn't even made a dime were banking on the Super Bowl to vault their little, unknown dotcom to the realms of credibility and stature shared by traditional companies like Miller, Anheuser-Busch, Pepsi, and American Express. These companies realize that on Super Bowl Sunday many non-traditional fans tune in to see the clever ads or set the tone for their Super Bowl parties. The Super Bowl time slot is a target-rich environment for companies who want to increase their sales of beer, food, cars, credit, or any other product or service.

Why else would people go to all this trouble unless the Super Bowl was the greatest game of all time?

Notes

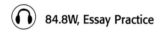 84.8W, Essay Practice

Notes

Directions: You have 20 minutes to plan and write your response. Your response will be judged on the basis of the quality of your writing and on how well your response presents the points in the lecture and their relationship to the reading passage. Typically, an effective response will be 150–225 words.

🎧 85.8W, Essay Prompt

Summarize the points made in the lecture you just heard, explaining how they cast doubt on the points made in the lecture.

_____

_____

_____

_____

_____

_____

_____

_____

_____

_____

_____

_____

_____

_____

_____

_____

_____

_____

_____

_____

Answer

Answers will vary, but here is one sample summary.

> The Superbowl is touted as the greatest game of all time, but the marketing and entertainment that surround the game is becoming at least as much of an event as the football game itself. The commercial spots wedged into timeouts and halftime cost upward of two million dollars for a mere thirty seconds of air time. The reviews of the commercials in popular media the next day make it seem like a short film festival instead of a series of ads.
>
> The game also seems overshadowed by the music and media industries. It seems that the question of which superstars are going to appear in the halftime show is almost as big a question as which team will win the game. In fact, the scandal that surrounded Janet Jackson's halftime performance a few years ago made it clear to some people that every second of the Super Bowl is just another planned marketing event.

Now that you have practiced writing, you are ready to begin Lesson 8—Listening: Taking Notes on a Conversation.

LESSON 8—LISTENING: TAKING NOTES ON A CONVERSATION

In this lesson, we will cover more listening skills and strategies that will help lead to success on test day. You will also have the opportunity to review some of the strategies you learned in previous lessons as well as to learn more about the question types found on the Listening section of the TOEFL. If you feel uncertain about any of the concepts or strategies you have learned so far, continue to review the lessons throughout this book.

Taking Notes on a Conversation

The structure of a conversation is different from that of a lecture. The speaker has organized the lecture before delivering it and has, therefore, predetermined its structure. In most cases, the lecturer has included transitions and rhetorical devices that guide a note-taker. However, the speakers in a conversation are involved in a turn-taking process where each responds to what the other has said. The structure of a conversation evolves as the speakers react to the information they hear. It may be more difficult to take notes on an unplanned conversation than on an organized lecture.

Here are some note-taking tips.

During the conversation:

- Make a column for each speaker
- Take notes for each speaker in the appropriate column

After the conversation, identify:
- The main characters involved in the conversation
- The central character (the one who has a particular need)
- The central character's need
- The central character's conflict (who or what is preventing him or her from satisfying the need)
- The resolution of the conflict (how his or her need is satisfied)

Now apply these tips to your note-taking as you complete the following practice.

Taking Notes on a Conversation Practice

Listen to a conversation. Take notes and then answer the questions that follow. You will find a transcript of this audio passage (86.8L, Note-Taking Practice) at the end of the chapter.

🎧 **86.8L, Note-Taking Practice**

Notes

1. What is the relationship between the man and woman? Explain your answer.

   _____

   _____

   _____

2. What is the conversation mainly about?

   _____

   _____

   _____

3. What are the man and woman probably watching while they're having this conversation?

   _____

   _____

   _____

4. What does the man imply about golf?

   _____

   _____

   _____

5. What does the woman suggest that the man do?

   _____

   _____

   _____

Answers

1. They are a couple. The man refers to the woman as "hon."

2. What is a sport?

3. They are probably watching a baseball game.

4. Golf is not a sport.

5. Watch the end of the game upstairs.

Understanding the question types is important for knowing how and where you can apply your strategies. Keep reading to learn more.

Question Types

There are seven question types on the Listening section of the TOEFL. These are:

- Understanding Rhetorical Function
- Understanding an Idiomatic Expression in Context
- Drawing an Inference
- Understanding a Speaker's Implication
- Identifying the Main Idea
- Summarizing the Most Important Points
- Understanding Details

This lesson will review three of these question types, focusing on how they apply to conversations:

- Drawing an Inference
- Understanding a Speaker's Implication
- Understanding Details

Question Type 3 Revisited—Drawing an Inference

There are 2 conversations and 4 lectures in the Listening section of the TOEFL. Each conversation or lecture is followed by 0 or 1 *inference* question.

An inference is a conclusion you draw based on details that have not been explicitly stated. *Inference* questions ask you to draw conclusions about specific details in the passage or to make comparisons between details. In order to answer these types of questions, you should:

- Listen carefully to the details of the lecture or conversation
- Try to understand unfamiliar words from context
- Listen for conditionals, intonation, and suggestions made by the speakers while the conversation is happening so that you can anticipate certain inference questions
- Use your knowledge about the situation to guess what sort of conclusion might be logical

The following are examples of inference questions:

"What probably happened to _____?"

"What will _____ probably do next?"

"What can be inferred about _____?"

Here is an example of an *inference* question. Listen to the conversation and answer the question. Be sure to take notes. You will find a transcript of this audio passage (87.8L, Question Type 3) at the end of the chapter.

🎧 **87.8L, Question Type 3**

Notes

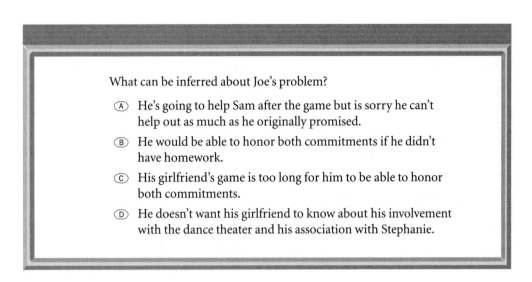

What can be inferred about Joe's problem?

- (A) He's going to help Sam after the game but is sorry he can't help out as much as he originally promised.
- (B) He would be able to honor both commitments if he didn't have homework.
- (C) His girlfriend's game is too long for him to be able to honor both commitments.
- (D) He doesn't want his girlfriend to know about his involvement with the dance theater and his association with Stephanie.

Choice (B) is the correct answer. Choice (A) is incorrect because it is untrue; Joe is not going to help Sam after the game. There is nothing in the conversation to lead one to infer either (C) or (D).

Question Type 4 Revisited—Understanding a Speaker's Implication

There are 2 conversations and 4 lectures in the Listening section of the TOEFL. Each conversation has 1 or 2 *speaker's implication* questions, and each lecture has 0 or 1 *speaker's implication* question.

Something that is implied is not directly stated. An implication is the meaning of a statement that is not obvious in the literal meaning of the words.

The distracters for implication questions may refer to something that was not discussed or did not occur. You may also see synonyms, homophones, or other words repeated in the answer choices that are either out of context or not stated in the conversation.

The following are examples of implication questions:

What does the man probably mean?

What does the man suggest/imply?

What does the woman want to know?

What does the man say about _____?

What does the woman advise the man to do?

Why does _____ say _____?

What does _____ mean by _____?

In the *speaker's implication* questions that follow conversations, you will often hear an excerpt from the conversation in which one of the speakers makes an implication. Remember that you will not be able to read the excerpt on the actual test.

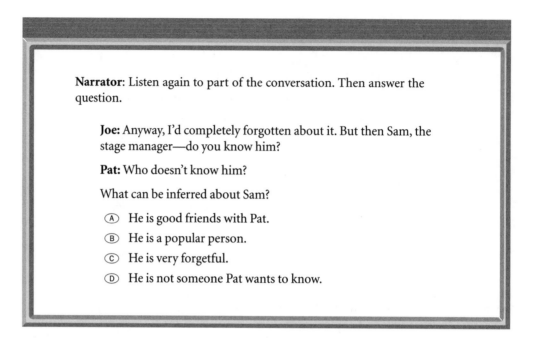

Narrator: Listen again to part of the conversation. Then answer the question.

Joe: Anyway, I'd completely forgotten about it. But then Sam, the stage manager—do you know him?

Pat: Who doesn't know him?

What can be inferred about Sam?

- Ⓐ He is good friends with Pat.
- Ⓑ He is a popular person.
- Ⓒ He is very forgetful.
- Ⓓ He is not someone Pat wants to know.

Choice (B) is the correct answer. There is nothing to indicate how close Sam and Pat are so (A) is incorrect. Choices (C) and (D) are not implied either.

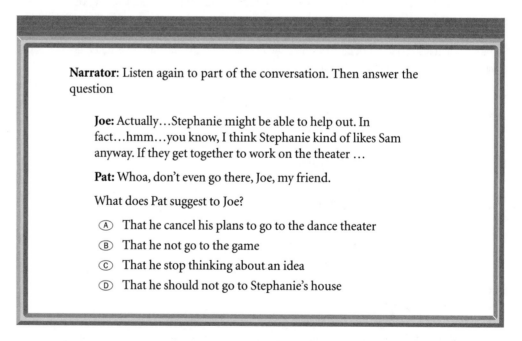

Narrator: Listen again to part of the conversation. Then answer the question

Joe: Actually…Stephanie might be able to help out. In fact…hmm…you know, I think Stephanie kind of likes Sam anyway. If they get together to work on the theater …

Pat: Whoa, don't even go there, Joe, my friend.

What does Pat suggest to Joe?

- Ⓐ That he cancel his plans to go to the dance theater
- Ⓑ That he not go to the game
- Ⓒ That he stop thinking about an idea
- Ⓓ That he should not go to Stephanie's house

Choice (A) is incorrect. Pat does not suggest that Joe cancel his plans. Choice (B) is incorrect. Pat does not suggest anything about a game. Choice (C) is correct. This is testing understanding of the idiom *don't go there*, which means "stop thinking about that," or "don't think that way." Choice (D) is incorrect. Pat does not suggest anything about going to Stephanie's house.

Question Type 7 Revisited—Understanding Details

There are 2 conversations and 4 lectures in the Listening section of the TOEFL. Each conversation is followed by 2 or 3 *detail* questions, and each lecture is followed by 1 or 2 *detail* questions.

Detail questions require you to recall specific information from the spoken text. The answer choices will contain three incorrect statements and one correct one. Read the answer choices carefully, because the distracters contain familiar words that make the answer look attractive, though it is not correct.

The distracters in detail questions are incorrect because they present:

- false information
- a distortion of details from the lecture
- information that was not discussed

The most common stem for this type of question is:

According to ___, who/what/when/where/why/how many/how much. . .?

Now answer the detail questions that follows based on the conversation, which is printed here. You can also listen to (87.8L, Question Type 3) again.

Narrator: Now listen to a conversation between two students.

Joe: Hey Pat, could I ask your advice about something?

Pat: Shoot.

Joe: Well the thing is, my girlfriend is playing in the finals of the intramural volleyball tournament tomorrow, and she really wants me to be there.

Pat (*filling in the rest of Joe's thoughts*): But…you have something else going on at the same time…

Joe: Well, yeah. Ages ago, I don't know, maybe three months ago…I signed up to help clean the dance-theater…you know, scrape gum off the bottom of seats and stuff.

Pat (*sarcastically*): Oh that sounds like fun.

Joe: Anyway, I'd completely forgotten about it. But then Sam, the stage manager—do you know him?

Pat: Who doesn't know him?

Joe: Okay. So, anyway, I bumped into him at the gym and he reminded me about it. I didn't know what to say, so I just pretended that I hadn't forgotten…

Pat: Just tell him your girlfriend's in this tournament.

Joe: Just tell him, huh? I feel bad though. I don't like *not* following through on a commitment. Especially with Sam…you'll never hear the end of it.

Pat (*surprised*): Really?

Joe: Well, he doesn't get angry. He just jokes about it. But, you know, he's sensitive about things like that.

Pat: Just offer to help out another time. I'm sure he'll understand.

Joe: Hmm, maybe…That might work. But, oh, well, sheesh…actually I think this is the end of the season. So…

Pat: Well, if he's going to be doing a major "end-of-season" cleaning job on that theater, he'll probably still be at it after the tournament ends. Why don't you go over and help him after watching your girlfriend's game?

Joe: No, that won't work. I'm late on that history assignment. You know…the one that was due last Thursday? I was able to extend the deadline. But I'm sure he'll penalize me if I don't get it in tomorrow.

Pat: Well, the only other alternative is to tell your girlfriend that you can't be at her game.

Joe: Oh man, no way. I value this relationship.

Pat: Well in that case, it seems pretty clear to me. If I were you, I would let Sam know as soon as possible, so he has time to find someone else.

Joe: Yeah, that's a good point. Actually…Stephanie might be able to help out. In fact…hmm…you know, I think Stephanie kind of likes Sam anyway. If they get together to work on the theater…

Pat: Whoa, don't even go there, Joe, my friend. You just take care of you. Your life is complicated enough without trying to play matchmaker!

Who did Joe run into at the gym?

- (A) Sam
- (B) Pat
- (C) Stephanie
- (D) His girlfriend

Choice (A) is correct. Joe ran into Sam, the dance theater manager, at the gym. All other characters were mentioned in the conversation, but Joe did not run into them at the gym.

Who plays volleyball?

- (A) Sam
- (B) Pat
- (C) Pat's girlfriend
- (D) Joe's girlfriend

Choice (D) is correct. Joe's problem stems from his girlfriend's volleyball tournament. Sam and Pat, choices (A) and (B), play a part in the conversation, but neither one of them is associated with playing volleyball. Choice (C) is never mentioned in the conversation.

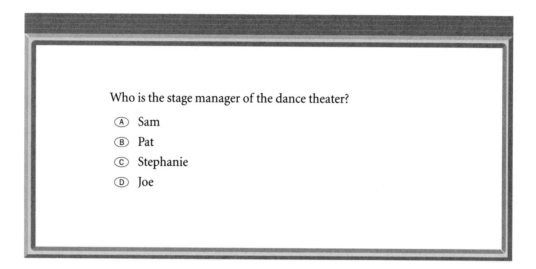

Who is the stage manager of the dance theater?

(A) Sam

(B) Pat

(C) Stephanie

(D) Joe

Choice (A) is correct. Sam is the stage manager of the dance theater. Pat and Joe are the two speakers. Stephanie is a person whom Joe refers to as a possible replacement for his volunteer work at the theater.

Which class does Joe say he has an assignment due in?

(A) Theater

(B) Math

(C) History

(D) English

Joe clearly states that he has to turn in a History assignment, choice (C). Choice (A) is mentioned in the conversation, but not as a class Joe takes. Choices (B) and (D) are not mentioned in the conversation at all.

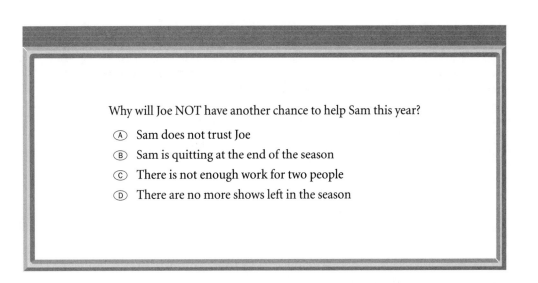

Why will Joe NOT have another chance to help Sam this year?

- Ⓐ Sam does not trust Joe
- Ⓑ Sam is quitting at the end of the season
- Ⓒ There is not enough work for two people
- Ⓓ There are no more shows left in the season

Choices (A), (B), and (C) are incorrect because they are not mentioned. Choice (D) is correct. The speakers say that it is the end of the season.

When you are ready, turn to Lesson 8—Speaking: Paraphrasing and Summarizing.

LESSON 8—SPEAKING: PARAPHRASING AND SUMMARIZING

In this lesson, we will cover more speaking skills and strategies that will help lead to success on test day. You will also have the opportunity to learn more about the tasks required for the Speaking section of the TOEFL. If you feel uncertain about any of the concepts or strategies you have learned so far, continue to review the lessons throughout this book.

Remember that in Lessons 1–7 we covered the following speaking tasks:

- Describing Something from Your Own Experience
- Summarizing a Lecture
- Expressing and Supporting an Opinion Based on Personal Experience
- Summarizing a Conversation and Expressing an Opinion
- Synthesizing and Summarizing Information

This lesson will continue to review the following speaking task:

Synthesizing and Summarizing Information

First, let's review some helpful skills and strategies, starting with paraphrasing.

Paraphrasing

Paraphrasing is a very important academic skill. You are often asked to report on something that you read or have heard "in your own words." This means you should not quote directly from the original. You need to demonstrate that you understand the main points of what you read or heard by stating those points in words that you choose. In order to paraphrase successfully, you must use synonyms of words in the original passage and different grammatical constructions.

When you are asked to paraphrase:

- Do not repeat phrases or sentences in their exact form
- Do not change the meaning of the original message
- Do not include your opinion

Paraphrasing Practice

Look at the following passages. Following each passage are sample paraphrases. Identify which are appropriate paraphrases and which are not.

1. The worldwide gaming industry is booming. In the United States, 67% of households with children own a video game system, and for several years annual sales of video games have exceeded $20 billion.

> Games are popular all over the world and this is good business. Just in America, the majority of families have some kind of video game system and every year for the past few years, that business has had a sales income of over $20 billion.

> The global gaming industry is very successful. Over two-thirds of U.S. households own video games. Annual sales have been greater than 20 billion dollars.

> The global gaming industry is very successful because children enjoy playing video games in American families. As a result annual sales income for that business has exceeded 20 billion dollars.

2. This growth is indicative of rapid improvements in computer technology games and offers even technophobes an entertaining introduction to that world.

> This success is due to the fast development in computing and an advantage is that even people who don't like technology can get into it.

> This success shows the fast development in computing and one advantage of it is that everyone can get into it.

> The rapid improvement in computer technology is demonstrated in this growth and one of the good things about that is that people who are afraid of it are being introduced to that technology in an entertaining way.

3. On the negative side, the violence that is prevalent in many video games has been linked to aggressive behavior. This is especially true of games in which the protagonist needs to be violent in order to win.

> A disadvantage is that there seems to be a connection between the aggressive behavior and violent video games, especially when the main character acts violently in order to be successful.

> There is also a downside. And that is that there is often a lot of violence in video games and that violence can lead to aggression in real life. That is most likely to happen if the proponent of the game needs to beat or shoot or whatever to win.

> The bad thing about video games is that they inspire violence in people who play them. There was a story in the news recently about a young boy who dropped his younger sister off a bridge. Later he said that his character had done something like that in a video game. It seemed like he didn't know the difference between the character he played and real life.

4. Moreover, the content often portrays negative sexual stereotypes and includes plots that are based on gender bias.

> Besides that, the stories are often sexist and the plots are all about strong men and weak women. I think we shouldn't reinforce those old-fashioned ideas.

> Besides that, the men and women are often presented in a way that doesn't respect them and the storylines are often based on prejudiced ideas about the sexes.

> Another thing is that video games portray negative sexual stereotypes and have gender-biased plots.

Answers

1. The global gaming industry is very successful. Over two-thirds of U.S. households own video games. Annual sales have been greater than 20 billion dollars.

2. The rapid improvement in computer technology is demonstrated in this growth and one of the good things about that is that people who are afraid of it are being introduced to that technology in an entertaining way.

3. A disadvantage is that there seems to be a connection between the aggressive behavior and violent video games, especially when the main character acts violently in order to be successful.

4. Another thing is that video games portray negative sexual stereotypes and have gender-biased plots.

Summarizing

On the TOEFL and in real academic settings, you will often be required to summarize information from a reading or listening passage. Summarizing is similar to paraphrasing in that you should not add information to what is given, and you should not give your opinion or try to explain any of the information contained in the passage. Summarizing is different from paraphrasing in that you need to identify essential information and present only that.

Task 4 Revisited—Synthesizing and Summarizing Information

There are 6 tasks in the Speaking section of the TOEFL. The fourth task asks you to read and listen to material on related topics. After reading and listening, you must give a 60-second response to a question about what you read and heard.

The fourth task in the Speaking section of the TOEFL is similar to the third task, in that you must read a passage, listen to someone speak on the same topic, and then synthesize and summarize what you have read and heard. However, the third task includes a short announcement followed by a conversation about the announcement, whereas the fourth task includes an academic text followed by a lecture on the academic topic.

As in the third task, you have 45 seconds to read the passage. You may take notes during the lecture. Then you have 30 seconds to prepare your response to a question that you will see and hear. You then have 60 seconds to respond. On the actual test, you will not see the narrator's introduction to the question.

When reading the passage and listening to the talk you should:

- Identify the main points
- Listen for examples and details that support the main ideas

When responding to the question you should:

- Paraphrase the main points that were mentioned in both the passage and the talk
- Summarize examples and details that support the main ideas
- Highlight any differences between the passage and the talk
- Highlight ways in which the talk reinforces information from the passage

Try answering the following sample TOEFL question. Read the short passage first and take notes.

Video Games: Pros and Cons

The worldwide video game industry is booming. In the United States, 67% of households with children own a video game system, and for several years annual sales of video games have exceeded $20 billion. This growth is indicative of rapid improvements in computer technology and on the positive side, games offer even technophobes an entertaining introduction to that world. From the player's point of view, gaming can give practice in following directions, problem solving, and using fine motor and spatial skills. Playing video games can also provide opportunities for adults and children to play together, in a spirit of friendly competition. When used with the ill or disabled, some games even have therapeutic applications with patients. On the negative side, the violence that is prevalent in many video games has been linked to aggressive behavior. This is especially true of games in which the protagonist needs to be violent in order to win. Moreover, the content often portrays negative sexual stereotypes and includes plots that are based on gender bias. Additionally, video games rarely require independent thought or creativity and some studies even indicate a negative correlation between academic achievement and overall time spent playing video games.

Notes

Now listen to the sample lecture and take notes. You will find transcripts of these audio passages at the end of the chapter.

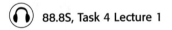 88.8S, Task 4 Lecture 1

Notes

🎧 **89.8S, Task 4 Prompt 1**

The professor outlines steps that parents can take to protect children from some of the negative aspects of video games. Summarize the professor's advice in relation to the passage you read.

30 seconds to prepare
60 seconds to speak

Evaluate yourself using the following criteria:

Criteria	Comments	Action to Improve
Clarity and pronunciation		
Organization		
Details and examples		
Grammar and vocabulary		

Now listen to the sample response. How was it different from yours? How was it similar? You will find a transcript of this audio passage (90.8S, Task 4 Response 1) at the end of the chapter.

🎧 **90.8S, Task 4 Response 1**

Now complete the following sample TOEFL question. Remember that you will not see the narrator's introduction to the question on the test.

As you read the passage, take notes of the main points. As you listen to the talk, take notes of the speaker's main points. Listen for details and/or examples that support or contradict the main points of the reading passage.

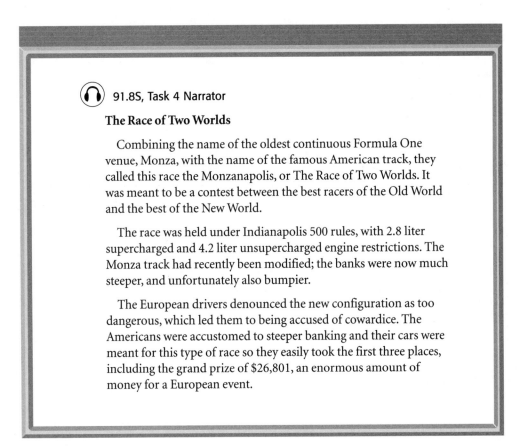

91.8S, Task 4 Narrator

The Race of Two Worlds

Combining the name of the oldest continuous Formula One venue, Monza, with the name of the famous American track, they called this race the Monzanapolis, or The Race of Two Worlds. It was meant to be a contest between the best racers of the Old World and the best of the New World.

The race was held under Indianapolis 500 rules, with 2.8 liter supercharged and 4.2 liter unsupercharged engine restrictions. The Monza track had recently been modified; the banks were now much steeper, and unfortunately also bumpier.

The European drivers denounced the new configuration as too dangerous, which led them to being accused of cowardice. The Americans were accustomed to steeper banking and their cars were meant for this type of race so they easily took the first three places, including the grand prize of $26,801, an enormous amount of money for a European event.

Notes

 92.8S, Task 4 Lecture 2

Notes

 93.8S, Task 4 Prompt 2

Summarize the similarities and differences between the two races and the reasons that the Americans won both.

30 seconds to prepare
60 seconds to speak

Evaluate yourself using the following criteria:

Criteria	Comments	Action to Improve
Clarity and pronunciation		
Organization		
Details and examples		
Grammar and vocabulary		

Now listen to the sample response. How was it different from yours? How was it similar? You will find a transcript of this audio passage (94.8S, Task 4 Response 2) at the end of the chapter.

🎧 **94.8S, Task 4 Response 2**

Congratulations on a job well done! You have now completed all eight chapters of Kaplan's *TOEFL iBT with CD-ROM*. If there is anything that you still find difficult, be sure to focus on those topics before you take the TOEFL. If you are feeling comfortable, you can take the TOEFL knowing you are prepared to succeed. Good luck!

CHAPTER 8 AUDIO TRANSCRIPTS

83. Lesson 8—Listening, Note-Taking Practice

Narrator: Listen to a professor in an American Studies class.

Professor: I think it's paradoxical that the success of Oprah's Book Club has itself generated substantial criticism. You see, taken on its own merits, the Book Club has been good for the publishing industry, for writers, and for readers, and there is no doubt that this success can be laid squarely at the feet of Oprah herself: when she speaks, her audience listens. But...as many people see it, that's just the problem.

Oprah's television audience is widely perceived as primarily thirty-something, non-career oriented, and, um, poorly educated. This is a segment of the population that Oprah's more intellectual critics do not identify with. These critics feared that their favorite authors would be ignored by publishers unless they wrote directly to Oprah's audience; in other words, "dumbing down" would be necessary for financial success.

This debate is embodied by the episode involving the respected author Jonathan Franzen. Franzen's book *The Corrections* was to have been an Oprah's Book Club selection, but Franzen actually declined the honor, indicating that he didn't care for many of Oprah's previous choices, and hinting that he didn't want his own book to join that company! I have seen Franzen both criticized and praised for his decision—some people accusing him of arrogance while others applauding his independence.

The Franzen episode illustrates the paradox: popular appeal and intellectual quality are seen as mutually exclusive. Yet a single glance at Oprah's list will show that to be false: how could any author be disappointed to appear alongside Steinbeck, Morrison, or Tolstoy?

84. Lesson 8—Writing, Essay Practice

Narrator: Now listen to part of a lecture on the topic you have just read.

Professor: It's funny. The day after Super Bowl Thirty-Nine I saw more news about the commercials that were on T.V. than the game itself.

Nowadays, the football game, and even the football stars, seems to be overshadowed by bigger stars in music, film, and television. It's all about which commercial was funniest, ah, which one was the most clever, and who wowed us or shocked us during the halftime show. Many people can tell you who performed in the 2004 Super Bowl, but far fewer remember who played the game. Even people who didn't watch the game that year knew who performed during halftime…because people are still talking about it—about Janet Jackson's "wardrobe malfunction," a phrase that became a, uh, household expression in the aftermath of Super Bowl Thirty-Eight…and led to a crackdown by the FCC. Notice how tame Paul McCartney's 2005 half-time show was compared to the tawdry antics of Justin and Janet. Some say the FCC response was to placate angry parents. Others say it was a, uh…correction long overdue in a culture run amok. But one thing's for sure…the Super Bowl is more of a big music video, or a "Sundance" for commercials, than it is an athletic match.

Consider the hefty price tag for a coveted 30 second commercial. In 2005, it was 2.4 million dollars. And if Brad Pitt was in it, add another 3 million or more. I mean, come on. You don't even see most of those commercials again. And what does Brad Pitt have to do with football? I don't think guys even like him, at least not ones that follow football. But my point is this: people should be talking about football on Monday morning and not a thirty second movie star cameo. When did pop culture hijack the greatest sports event ever?

85. Lesson 8—Writing, Essay Prompt

Summarize the points made in the lecture you just heard, explaining how they cast doubt on the points made in the lecture.

86. Lesson 8—Listening, Taking Notes on a Conversation Practice

Man: Who do you think's the best athlete of all time?

Woman: Hmmm…that's a tough one.

Man: Well, you can rule out women.

Woman: Uh, excuse me, male chauvinist, but Michelle Wie may be the next golfing champion in the world. She's only 15 and she's already qualified for the—

Man (*cutting the woman off*): Alright, hold it right there. Does golf really count?

Woman: Why doesn't it? It's a sport.

Man: Is it?

Woman: Okay, Mr. Jock. By that logic, baseball really isn't a sport either.

Man: Of course it is.

Woman: Let's look at the similarities. Both sports feature players who swing at a ball, have long breaks in between swings, and can still have a gut and be world-class performers.

Man: Yeah, but you overlooked one important thing: baseball players run!

Woman: For all of about 12 seconds, and that's if they run all around the bases.

Man: Well, I'd agree with you that the greatest athlete isn't to be found in baseball. I'd say basketball or football.

Woman (*defensively*): Or softball? Why does the best player have to be from a popular sport? What about tennis or volleyball or racquetball?

Man: Do you know any racquetball players?

Woman: No. But you get the point.

Man: Why don't we talk about this later? Let's finish watching the game.

Woman: But *Desperate Housewives* is coming on.

Man: Yeah…Can you watch it upstairs, hon?

Woman: Well, since men are the better athletes, why don't you trudge up the stairs?

87. Lesson 8—Listening, Question Type 3

Narrator: Now listen to a conversation between two students.

Joe: Hey Pat, could I ask your advice about something?

Pat: Shoot.

Joe: Well the thing is, my girlfriend is playing in the finals of the intramural volleyball tournament tomorrow, and she really wants me to be there.

Pat (*filling in the rest of Joe's thoughts*): But…you have something else going on at the same time…

Joe: Well, yeah. Ages ago, I don't know, maybe three months ago…I signed up to help clean the dance-theater…you know, scrape gum off the bottom of seats and stuff.

Pat (*sarcastically*): Oh that sounds like fun.

Joe: Anyway, I'd completely forgotten about it. But then Sam, the stage manager—do you know him?

Pat: Who doesn't know him?

Joe: Okay. So, anyway, I bumped into him at the gym and he reminded me about it. I didn't know what to say, so I just pretended that I hadn't forgotten…

Pat: Just tell him your girlfriend's in this tournament.

Joe: Just tell him, huh? I feel bad though. I don't like *not* following through on a commitment. Especially with Sam…you'll never hear the end of it.

Pat (*surprised*): Really?

Joe: Well, he doesn't get angry. He just jokes about it. But, you know, he's sensitive about things like that.

Pat: Just offer to help out another time. I'm sure he'll understand.

Joe: Hmm, maybe…That might work. But, oh, well, sheesh…actually I think this is the end of the season. So…

Pat: Well, if he's going to be doing a major "end-of-season" cleaning job on that theater, he'll probably still be at it after the tournament ends. Why don't you go over and help him after watching your girlfriend's game?

Joe: No, that won't work. I'm late on that history assignment. You know…the one that was due last Thursday? I was able to extend the deadline. But I'm sure he'll penalize me if I don't get it in tomorrow.

Pat: Well, the only other alternative is to tell your girlfriend that you can't be at her game.

Joe: Oh man, no way. I value this relationship.

Pat: Well in that case, it seems pretty clear to me. If I were you, I would let Sam know as soon as possible, so he has time to find someone else.

Joe: Yeah, that's a good point. Actually…Stephanie might be able to help out. In fact…hmm…you know, I think Stephanie kind of likes Sam anyway. If they get together to work on the theater…

Pat: Whoa, don't even go there, Joe, my friend. You just take care of you. Your life is complicated enough without trying to play matchmaker!

88. Lesson 8—Speaking, Task 4 Lecture 1

Narrator: Listen to part of a lecture in a childhood development class.

Professor: There is nothing intrinsically evil about video games, despite what some special interest groups would have you believe. With appropriate cautions, there are ways of avoiding the pitfalls of this entertainment medium, and possibly even reaping some of the benefits. The first challenge is to make use of the ratings system. Although an effective ratings system has been in place for years, it is not rigorously implemented. A study by the Federal Trade Commission reported that unaccompanied children, ages 13 to 16, were able to buy "mature" rated video games 85% of the time. So, the first piece of advice to parents is to check out the ratings and put pressure on rental or sales stores not to give children access to "mature" games. Better than checking just the rating, is playing the game with the child. Become familiar with different types of games; in that way you will be able to encourage the use of games that require strategic thinking and problem solving in addition to fast reflexes.

89. Lesson 8—Speaking, Task 4 Prompt 1

The professor outlines steps that parents can take to protect children from some of the negative aspects of video games. Summarize the professor's advice in relation to the passage you read.

90. Lesson 8—Speaking, Task 4 Sample Response 1

The professor says that parents can avoid one of the negative aspects of video gaming by paying attention to game ratings, I mean, umm, how video games are rated…umm…He says that there is a good rating system, but people don't pay attention to it so sometimes kids end up playing "mature" games. He also encourages parents to play the games with the kids. He says that you should become familiar with uh, different kinds of game so that you can choose games that have a positive side and that are more educational. For example he says some games are good for developing problem solving skills and fast reflexes.

91. Lesson 8—Speaking, Task 4 Narrator

Narrator: In this question you will read a short passage and listen to a short talk on the same topic. After you hear the question, you will have 30 seconds to prepare your response and 60 seconds to speak.

Now read the following passage. You have 45 seconds to read the passage.

92. Lesson 8—Speaking, Task 4 Lecture 2

Narrator: Listen to a professor describe the second "Race of Two Worlds."

Professor: After their humiliation in their own back yard the previous year, the European teams were determined to stop the Americans from winning again. Ferrari had three cars while Maserati had designed a special Indy-500-type racer.

The event was divided into three heats. In the first Musso lead Americans Eddie Sachs and Jim Rathmann. Sachs' engine blew up and for a while it looked as though the Italians had a chance of regaining their honor. However, Musso was eventually forced to give up his leading position because he became overwhelmed by the methanol fumes. This fuel was a first in European racing and many of their drivers succumbed to the fumes. The Americans, on the other hand were accustomed to methanol because it had been commonly used in the United States for years. Musso's withdrawal meant that the first heat went to Jim Rathman, who also took the second heat as well as the third, and so the crown once again went to an American. His average speed was 166.73 mph for the 500 miles; no European event driver had even come close to that speed all year.

Acknowledging that the Americans were second to none when it came to banked speedways, the Monzanapolis was not repeated again.

93. Lesson 8—Speaking, Task 4 Prompt 2

Summarize the similarities and differences between the two races and the reasons that the Americans won both.

94. Lesson 8—Speaking, Task 4 Sample Response 2

Umm, well, in the second race the Europeans really wanted to win badly. At first the Italian team did well, but then the driver, umm, I think his name was Mooso or something, anyway, he lost his position because he got sick from some kind of fuel. Then the American drivers were used to that fuel, so they were OK. Uh…then an American driver won the second and third races also. I guess the Europeans realized that they couldn't beat the American's when driving on steeper banks, so they didn't repeat the race again.

NOTES

NOTES

NOTES

NOTES

NOTES

NOTES

NOTES

NOTES

NOTES

NOTES

NOTES

NOTES

How Did We Do? Grade Us.

Thank you for choosing a Kaplan book. Your comments and suggestions are very useful to us. Please answer the following questions to assist us in our continued development of high-quality resources to meet your needs.

The title of the Kaplan book I read was: _____

My name is: _____

My address is: _____

_____

My e-mail address is: _____

What overall grade would you give this book?	Ⓐ	Ⓑ	Ⓒ	Ⓓ	Ⓕ
How relevant was the information to your goals?	Ⓐ	Ⓑ	Ⓒ	Ⓓ	Ⓕ
How comprehensive was the information in this book?	Ⓐ	Ⓑ	Ⓒ	Ⓓ	Ⓕ
How accurate was the information in this book?	Ⓐ	Ⓑ	Ⓒ	Ⓓ	Ⓕ
How easy was the book to use?	Ⓐ	Ⓑ	Ⓒ	Ⓓ	Ⓕ
How appealing was the book's design?	Ⓐ	Ⓑ	Ⓒ	Ⓓ	Ⓕ

What were the book's strong points? _____ .

How could this book be improved? _____

Is there anything that we left out that you wanted to know more about?

Would you recommend this book to others? ☐ YES   ☐ NO

Other comments: _____

_____

_____

Do we have permission to quote you? ☐ YES   ☐ NO

Thank you for your help.
Please tear out this page and mail it to:

Content Manager
Kaplan Test Prep & Admissions
1440 Broadway, 8th floor
New York, NY 10018

KAPLAN®

Thanks!

Introducing a smarter way to learn.

- Focused, practice-based learning
- Concepts for everyday life
- Recognition and recall exercises
- Quizzes throughout